THE DOMESTIC SOURCES OF AMERICAN FOREIGN POLICY
Insights and Evidence

Second Edition

THE DOMESTIC SOURCES OF AMERICAN FOREIGN POLICY
Insights and Evidence

Second Edition

Edited by

Eugene R. Wittkopf
Louisiana State University

St. Martin's Press
New York

Executive editor: Don Reisman
Manager, publishing services: Emily Berleth
Publishing services associate: Kalea Chapman
Project management: Till & Till, Inc.
Art director: Sheree Goodman
Cover design: Marek Antoniak

For information, write:
St. Martin's Press, Inc.
175 Fifth Avenue
New York, NY 10010

ISBN: 0-312-10315-8

ACKNOWLEDGMENTS

It is a violation of the Law to reproduce these selections by any means whatsoever
without the written permission of the copyright holder.

"Why America Must Change Course: The Domestic Roots of Global Influence" by Sam
Nunn, Pete Domenici, and Debra L. Miller. From Sam Nunn and Pete Domenici, Cochairmen,
and Debra L. Miller, Director, *The CSIS Strengthening of America Commission,* 1992. Copyright
© 1992. Reprinted by permission of the Center for Strategic and International Studies.
"Public Opinion and Foreign Policy: Attitude Structures of Opinion Leaders after the Cold
War" by Ole R. Holsti. This article was written especially for this book.
"The Pretty Prudent Public: Post Post-Vietnam American Opinion on the Use of Military
Force" by Bruce W. Jentleson. From *International Studies Quarterly* 36 (March 1992): 49–74.
Reprinted with permission from Blackwell Publishers.
"The Influence of Ethnic Interest Groups on American Middle East Policy" by Mitchell
Geoffrey Bard. This article was written especially for this book.
"The Japanese Megaphone: Foreign Influences on Foreign Policymaking" by John B. Judis.
From *The New Republic* 202 (January 22, 1990): 20–25. Reprinted by permission of *The New
Republic,* © 1990, The New Republic, Inc.
"The New Politics of the Defense Budget" by Gordon Adams. From *The New Politics of the
Defense Budget* by Gordon Adams. Carlisle Barracks, Penn.: Strategic Studies Institute, U.S.
Army War College (June 30, 1992).
"Operation Pundit Storm: The Media, Political Commentary, and Foreign Policy" by Eric
Alterman. From *World Policy Journal* 9 (Fall/Winter 1992): 599–616. Reprinted with permission
of the World Policy Institute at the New School for Social Research.
"The Electoral Cycle and the Conduct of American Foreign Policy" by William B. Quandt.
Reprinted with permission from *Political Science Quarterly* 101 (5, 1986): 825–837.
"The Presidency and Foreign Policy" by Stephen E. Ambrose. This article was adapted by the
author especially for this book from an article that appeared in *Foreign* Affairs.

Acknowledgments and copyrights are continued at the back of the book on page 357,
which constitutes an extension of the copyright page.

CONTENTS

THE DOMESTIC SOURCES OF AMERICAN FOREIGN POLICY: AN INTRODUCTION

The world has changed dramatically in the past several years. Many inside the government and outside of it believe it is also time for American foreign policy to change. To some, the end of the Cold War, the demise of communism, and the disintegration of the Soviet Union permit the United States to turn inward and attend to its many long-neglected domestic needs. Advocates of this viewpoint would have the United States abandon its grand strategy based on the themes of globalism, anticommunism, containment, military might, and interventionism[1] put into place following World War II to stem the tide of Soviet and communist expansionism. To others, however, the "unipolar moment"[2] that finds the United States as the world's sole superpower is cause for it to use its unchallenged supremacy to promote democracy and liberalism throughout the world. Globalism from this perspective remains very much a part of American foreign policy and, as in the past, may have to be sustained by military force and intervention into the affairs of others.

The United States is more likely to pursue engagement in the post–Cold War world than to revert to its historic foreign policy posture of isolationism. The shape of its interests abroad and the growing involvement of the U.S. economy in the world political economy virtually assure that. Still, it is by no means clear what specific foreign policy goals will be pursued, how the United States will shape its relations with other nations and transnational entities now that the menace of Soviet communism has passed, and how persistent resource constraints at home will affect its foreign policy capabilities.[3] The persistence of the anarchical international system guarantees that challenges from abroad will stimulate some answers to these questions, but they also will be shaped by domestic contention. Indeed, the end of the Cold War is likely to encourage, not constrain, domestic debate over the future of American foreign policy. "Winning the Cold War meant that the driving sense of purpose that had pervaded American society and politics since the late 1940s was suddenly gone, leaving a vacuum and uncertainty in

1

its place," observes Norman Ornstein. "The departure of anticommunism as a serious force that has left Americans without either the negative bond of a common enemy of the positive momentum of a sense of common purpose to unite them."[4]

The importance of anticommunist sentiment in the United States underscores the often profound impact that domestic politics exert on American foreign policy. Thus domestic needs and political demands within the American political system, the structures within which American foreign policy is formulated, and the processes of policymaking and the characteristics of those who manage and direct them must be understood if we are to comprehend why the United States behaves as it does in international politics.

The Domestic Sources of American Foreign Policy addresses how American foreign policy is shaped by what happens at home. It focuses on the factors that endow the world's largest and oldest democracy with sometimes unique characteristics in the community of nations and how these give its foreign policy a particular cast.

DOMESTIC POLITICS AND FOREIGN POLICY

The proposition that domestic stimuli are a source of foreign policy is not novel. Thucydides observed how in ancient Greece the external behavior of the Greek city-states was often shaped less by what each was doing toward the others than by what was occurring within them. He added that the actions leaders directed toward other city-states often sought to affect the political climate within the leaders' own polities, not relations with the targets of the actions.

Centuries later, Immanuel Kant observed in his treatise *Perpetual Peace* that democracies are inherently less warlike than autocracies because democratic leaders are accountable to the public, which restrains them from waging war. Because ordinary citizens would have to supply the soldiers and bear the human and financial costs of imperial policies, he contended, liberal democracies are "natural" forces for peace. History has been kind to Kant's thesis: Democracies rarely fight one another. The reasons may be more complex than Kant suggested, but nothing argues more persuasively for understanding the nexus between domestic politics and foreign policy than this empirical regularity.

To acknowledge the linkage between domestic politics and international behavior is to challenge conventional explanations of the relations among nations. Many students of international politics see the international system as a billiard table and compare the units of the system—nation-states—to billiard balls whose trajectories are determined exclusively by the impact of each on the others as they collide in continuous action-reaction sequences. What occurs *inside* the balls, and how that might propel them to move in one direction or another, is beyond the purview of the "billiard-ball" model. To look at the domestic sources of foreign policy, then, is to look at the conditions and activities within the state, instead of only conditions outside it. That perspective requires that we abandon the assumption that all states are unitary actors, as suggested by the billiard-ball metaphor within which societal cleavages and the political disputes they engender presumably have no effect. Instead, the domestic-sources perspective conforms to the view that the "foreign policy of governments is more than simply a series of responses to international stimuli, that forces at work within a society can also contribute to the quality and contents of its external behavior."[5]

The billiard-ball metaphor describes key aspects of political realism, a perspective that enjoyed widespread acceptance among policymakers and scholars during the Cold War, and before. Realism continues to be compelling in some instances, but the domestic-sources perspective is especially applicable to an understanding of post–Cold War American foreign policy and the sources from which it will derive. American society is relentlessly pluralistic: Its democratic form of government encourages the active involvement of the American people in determining what the government does, and its institutional structures invite debate among the officials selected to govern. American "exceptionalism" and the unique American experiment in governance undeniably create a situation where domestic influences on foreign policy are especially strong.

Developments in world politics also demand attention, of course. Today the United States finds itself increasingly caught in a web of global interdependence. Ironically, however, the internationalization of America's role in the world political economy increases the prospects for domestic pressures on the formulation of the nation's foreign policies. As other nations have long known, internationalization compromises the sovereign autonomy of the state, blurs the distinction between foreign and domestic politics, and elevates the participation of domestically oriented government agencies in the foreign policymaking process.[6] Continuing national security concerns reinforce the veracity of the billiard-ball metaphor that underlies political realism: The proliferation of nuclear, conventional, and unconventional weapons of destruction perpetuate the security dilemma all states face in an anarchical international system. Still, we would be remiss to ignore the impact that domestic political considerations will exert on how to cope with the security dilemma in the post–Cold War world.

DOMESTIC POLITICS AND AMERICAN FOREIGN POLICY

Political commentators and analysts typically share similar views about the salient issues in current American foreign policy, but they often differ widely in their explanations of policymakers' choices for dealing with them. Disagreement exists because the sources of American foreign policy are difficult to identify and trace.

Clearly a multitude of factors explain American foreign policy. Analytically, we can group its domestic sources into three broad categories: (1) the *societal environment* of the nation; (2) its *institutional setting;* and (3) the individual characteristics of the nation's *decision makers* and the *policymak-*

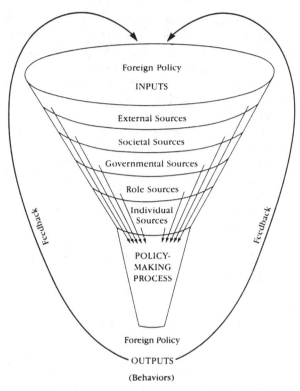

Figure I.1. The sources of American foreign policy. [Source: Charles W. Kegley, Jr., and Eugene R. Wittkopf, *American Foreign Policy: Pattern and Process*, 4th ed. (New York: St. Martin's Press, 1991), p. 529.]

ing positions they occupy. More discrete explanatory variables can be logically sorted and grouped into these three basic categories.

Figure I.1 illustrates the relationship between each of the domestic explanatory categories and American foreign policy and their interrelationships with one another.[7] The figure posits that domestic policy influences are *inputs* into the decision-making process that converts policy demands into foreign policy. (Foreign policy comprises the goals that the nation's officials seek to realize abroad, the values that give rise to them, and the means or instruments used to pursue them.) Conceptualized as the *outputs* of the process that converts policy demands into goals and means, foreign policy is typically multifaceted, ranging from discrete behaviors linked to specific issues to recurring patterns of behavior that define the continual efforts of the United States to cope with the environment beyond its borders. Noteworthy, however, is that neither discrete events nor broad policy patterns are likely to be explained adequately by reference to only one explanatory factor.

It is easy to identify many of the discrete variables that make up the domestic source categories, but the lines between the categories themselves are not always clear-cut. To help draw these larger distinctions as well as explicate the smaller ones, it is useful to think of the explanatory categories as layers of differing size and complexity.

The broadest layer is the *societal environment*. The political culture of the United States—the basic needs, values, beliefs, and self-images widely shared by Americans about their political system—stands out as a primary societal source of American foreign policy. Minimally, those beliefs find expression in the kinds of values and political institutions American policymakers have sought to export to others since World War II. Included is a preference not only for democracy over authoritarianism and totalitarianism, but also for capitalism over socialism. From the viewpoint of the American *liberal tradition*—captured in preferences for limited government, individual liberty, due process of the law, self-determination, free enterprise, inalienable (natural) rights, the equality of citizens before the law, majority rule, minority rights, federalism, and the separation of powers—fear of communism, a persistent pattern in American foreign policy during the Cold War, was clearly understandable. It inheres in Americans' views of themselves, their government, and their leaders.

In the post–Cold War world the domestic roots of American policy may be found increasingly in the structure and competitiveness of its economy. Democratic capitalism is, of course, a part of the liberal tradition, but now the ability of the United States to compete abroad is under stress. Unless the United States can hone its international competitiveness, it risks suffering the declining fate of the other global hegemons that also once enjoyed number one status in world politics.

Public opinion will help to determine whether the American people are happy with the choices their leaders make to improve U.S. economic competitiveness. Here, two traditions stand out. One, the *elitist* tradition, maintains that the only opinions that matter are those embraced by the small group of corporate, financial, legal, and university professionals who are in positions enabling them to "call the shots." Once known as "The Establishment," these influential Americans could seemingly shape public attitudes among the mass of the American people to support policies that fit the interests and values of the elites. The mass media are the key cog in the elitist machine, since it is the media that presumably enable the elite to manipulate the mass. Government decisions, from this viewpoint, are little more than expressions of elite preferences. Indeed, decision makers themselves, while sometimes members of the elite, are often little more than "proximate policymakers" who merely express elite preferences in formal acts of governance, such as laws passed by Congress.

The other tradition is *pluralism*. Here public policy flows upward rather than downward, as in the elitist model. Mass public opinion enjoys greater weight in this model, and it finds expression through interest groups, which seek to pressure the government for policies consonant with the preferences of "average" Americans. National security issues, especially during times of crisis, are normally thought to be beyond the purview of interest group activity, but there is some evidence that challenges that traditional view.[8] Beyond dispute is the increased ability of interest groups to pressure government in an environment that blurs the distinction between foreign and domestic policy as a result of global economic interdependence. From the perspective of pluralism, laws passed by Congress not only embody public policy, they also register the then-current balance of contending forces within American society.

The media appear less conspiratorial in the pluralist than in the elitist model, but their role is potent nonetheless. Indeed, to some the media *are* public opinion. Minimally, the media help to set the agenda for public discussion and often lay out for the American people the range of interpretations about foreign policy issues from which they might choose. Thus the media help to aggregate the interests of more discrete groups in American society.

Political parties also aggregate interests. In the two-party system of the United States, political parties are broad coalitions of ethnic, religious, economic, educational, professional, working-class, and other sociodemographic groups. One of the most important functions these broad coalitions serve is the selection of personnel to key policymaking positions. They can also serve as referenda on past policy performance. What role foreign policy beliefs and preferences play in shaping citizens' choices on these broad issues is difficult to determine. On the one hand, most citizens are motivated not by foreign policy issues, but by domestic ones. Their electoral choices typically reflect those preferences (as dramatically illustrated by George Bush's failed reelection bid). On the other hand, foreign and national security policy issues also often figure uppermost in some Americans' minds; for them foreign policy issues may be critical when they enter the voting booth. In an environment where a few thousands of votes in a few electoral precincts can mean the difference between a candidate's victory or defeat, foreign policy is not so easily dismissed.

The elitist and pluralist models are ideal types—caricatures, perhaps. Still, they help identify key elements of the societal environment as an explanation of American foreign policy: the state of the economy, political culture, the foreign policy beliefs and preferences of leaders and masses, and the role of the media, interest groups, and elections as expressions of (or of the absence of, as the case may be) political attitudes and preferences. The essays in Part I explore many of these ideas in greater depth.

As we peel away the societal environment as a source of American foreign policy, a second category is revealed: the *institutional setting*, consisting of the various branches of government and the departments and agencies assigned responsibility for decision making, management, and implementation. The category incorporates the diverse properties related to the structure of the U.S. government that limit or enhance the foreign policy choices made by decision makers and affect their implementation. The compelling assumption underlying the notion of institutional influences on foreign policy is that a relationship exists between the substance of foreign policy and the process of policymaking.

The structure of the American "foreign affairs government" encompasses a cluster of variables and organizational actors that influence what the United States does—or does not do—abroad. Most striking in this regard is the division of authority and responsibility for foreign policymaking between the

Congress and the president. The Constitution of the United States embraces the eighteenth-century belief that the abuse of political power is controlled best not through centralization but by fragmenting it in a system of checks and balances. Because of the division of authority and responsibility for the making and implementation of foreign policy, the separation of powers between the legislative and executive branches is an "invitation to struggle."[9]

The struggle for control over foreign policymaking is not confined to the executive and legislative branches. Many executive-branch departments and agencies that have grown in size and number as the United States embraced the trappings of a hegemonic power and pursued a globalist foreign policy also struggle to imprint American foreign policy. The growing interdependence of the United States with the world political economy reinforces these developments as several executive-branch departments oriented primarily toward domestic affairs now have bureaucratic stakes in the foreign policy game.

With growth has come fragmentation of authority over policymaking, a characterization that takes on a special meaning when we observe the often overlapping roles performed by the White House and National Security Council staffs, the State Department, the Defense Department, the Treasury Department, the Central Intelligence Agency, and other decision-making units with a role in the policymaking process. As more agencies have established a presence in the foreign affairs government, and as the political support enjoyed by these competing institutions has expanded, the management of policymaking by the president, whose role in the conduct of foreign affairs is preeminent, has become more difficult. To many, blame for the incoherence and inconsistency sometimes exhibited in American foreign policy lies here. Ironically, however, efforts to enhance presidential control of foreign policymaking by centralizing it in the White House have sometimes exacerbated rather than diminished incoherence and inconsistency by encouraging competition and conflict between the presidency, on the one hand, and the executives and institutions of the permanent foreign affairs government, on the other.[10]

If disagreements between the White House and the established departments responsible for foreign policy are a source of policy inconsistency and incoherence, the sheer size of the foreign affairs government and its bureaucratization promote policy persistence, not innovation. Thus the institutional setting of American foreign policymaking and the nature of democratic institutions generally inhibit the ability of the United States to alter its course in world affairs. The French sociologist Alexis de Tocqueville predicted as much over 150 years ago when he observed that "foreign politics demand scarcely any of those qualities which a democracy possesses; they require, on the contrary, the perfect use of almost all those faculties in which it is deficient."

In sum, understanding the institutional setting as a source of American foreign policy requires an examination of the responsibilities of numerous institutions and their relations with one another: the institutionalized presidency, the Congress, and the cabinet-level departments and the other agencies with foreign affairs responsibilities.

When we peel away the institutional setting as a domestic source of American foreign policy, the people who make the policies are illuminated. Here *decision makers* and their *policymaking positions* are the focus of attention. The underlying proposition is that the personalities, perceptions, psychological predispositions, and role responsibilities of the people recruited to positions of power and authority have a definable impact on American foreign policy. Indeed, the individual *decision maker* is the ultimate source of influence on policy, the final mediating force in the causal chain linking the other domestic sources to the ends and means of American foreign policy.

There are several ways personality and perceptual factors may impinge upon foreign policymaking. Ideas about communism and the Soviet Union instilled early in life, for example, may subsequently affect the attitudes and behaviors of those responsible for negotiating with the leaders of the post-Soviet states.[11] Similarly, policymakers' orientation toward decision making may profoundly affect the nation's foreign policy strategies. It has been suggested, for example, that twentieth-century American leaders can be characterized as either *crusaders* or *pragmatists*. The hallmark of a crusader is a "missionary zeal to make the world better. The crusader tends to make decisions based on a preconceived idea rather than on the basis of experience. Even though there are alternatives, he usually does not see them." The pragmatist, on the other hand, "is guided by the facts and his experience in a given situation, not by wishes or unexamined preconceptions. . . . Always flexible, he does not get locked into a losing policy. He can change direction and try again, without inflicting damage to his self-esteem."[12] Woodrow Wilson is the preeminent twentieth-century crusader, and Harry S Truman the personification of the pragmatist.

Personality factors also help to explain how presidents will choose to manage the conduct of foreign affairs. A president's approach to information processing, known as his cognitive style, his orientation toward political conflict, and his sense of political efficacy are all important in understanding how he will structure his policymaking system, and how he will deal with those around him.[13] In this case, personal predispositions form a bridge between the institutional setting of American foreign policymaking and the process of decision making itself.

Presidents sometimes engage in foreign policy actions not for their effect on the external environment but to influence domestic politics. Foreign policy can be used to mobilize popular support at home, to increase authority through appeals to patriotism, and to enhance prospects for reelection. Nothing better illustrates the connection between domestic politics and foreign policy.

Although policymakers doubtless use foreign policy for domestic purposes, it is unclear whether they do so because of *who* they are or because of the *positions* they occupy. Because of the frequency with which policymakers in the United States and other countries alike allegedly engage in this type of behavior, it seems that leaders' *role requirements,* not their personal predilections, explain this behavior. Policymakers' positions thus appear to stimulate certain predictable patterns of behavior. Conversely, the position an individual holds may constrain the impact of personality on policymaking behavior. Institutional roles thus reduce the influence of idiosyncratic factors on policy performance.

Individuals can, of course, interpret the roles they occupy differently. That fact blurs the distinction between decision makers and their policy positions as competing rather than complementary explanations of American foreign policy. Clearly, however, policymaking positions, or roles, severely circumscribe the freedom and autonomy of the particular individuals who occupy them, and thus diminish the range of politically feasible choices. Hence, we must understand the relationship between the person and the position and how each separately and in combination affects policy outcomes. Nowhere is that conclusion illustrated more clearly than with a simple aphorism drawn from bureaucratic politics: "Where you stand depends on where you sit."

In sum, a focus on decision makers and their policy positions as a category of domestic influences on American foreign policy draws attention to the capacity of individuals to place their personal imprints on the nation's conduct abroad, while simultaneously alerting us to the need to examine the forces that constrain individual initiative. Principal among these are the role-induced constraints that occur within bureaucratic settings. Because the making and execution of American foreign policy is fundamentally a group or organizational enterprise, we can surmise that these constraints are considerable. The essays in Part III will focus on these and on the capacity of individuals to transcend them.

THE DOMESTIC CONTEXT OF AMERICAN FOREIGN POLICY AND THE SOURCES OF AMERICAN FOREIGN POLICY

The categories described, which organize our examination of the domestic sources of American foreign policy, encourage a systematic examination of the linkages between what happens at home and what happens abroad. What happens abroad is also a function of the behavior of other nations and of extranational forces over which no nation, no matter how powerful, exerts control. A complete understanding of American foreign policy thus requires sensitivity to external as well as internal influences on American foreign policy.

A focus on the domestic sources of American foreign policy is warranted nonetheless. During the past two decades, American foreign policy has become highly politicized, to the point that the old aphorism "politics stops at the water's edge" now seems little more than a quaint historical cliché. Furthermore, the boundaries separating developments at home and abroad, whether in matters of national security, economic well-being, or social welfare, are often blurred or nonexistent—as the collapse of the Soviet Union dramatizes. As the internationalization of American politics proceeds, the nexus between domestic politics and foreign politics demands attention.

NOTES

1. For an analysis of these themes and the forces that sustained them, see Charles W. Kegley, Jr., and Eugene R. Wittkopf, *American Foreign Policy: Pattern and Process,* 4th ed. (New York: St. Martin's, 1991).

2. Charles Krauthammer, "The Unipolar Moment," *Foreign Affairs* 70 (No. 1, 1991): 23–33.

3. For examinations of the objectives, relationships, and capabilities that will shape American foreign policy in the post–Cold War world, see Charles W. Kegley, Jr., and Eugene R. Wittkopf, eds., *The Future of American Foreign Policy* (New York: St. Martin's, 1992); and Eugene R. Wittkopf, ed., *The Future of American Foreign Policy,* 2nd ed. (New York: St. Martin's, 1994).

4. Norman J. Ornstein, "Foreign Policy and the 1992 Election," *Foreign Affairs* 71 (Summer 1992): 2–3.

5. James N. Rosenau, "Introduction," in James N. Rosenau, ed., *The Domestic Sources of Foreign Policy* (New York: Free Press, 1967), p. 2.

6. Robert O. Keohane and Joseph S. Nye, *Power and Interdependence: World Politics in Transition,* 2nd ed. (Glenview, Ill.: Scott, Foresman/Little, Brown, 1989).

7. The figure properly notes that external as well as internal factors influence American foreign policy. For purposes of the analysis in this book, which focuses exclusively on domestic sources of American foreign policy, the external source category is not treated, and the four remaining categories are regrouped and renamed somewhat to refer to the societal environment, institutional setting, and decision makers and their policymaking positions. Combining the role and the individual categories into a single category effectively merges two competing explanations and asks not only about their separate effects but also about their potentially reinforcing interactions.

8. See, for example, Bernard C. Cohen, "The Influence of Special Interest Groups and Mass Media on Security Policy in the United States," pp. 222–241 in Charles W. Kegley, Jr., and Eugene R. Wittkopf, eds., *Perspectives on American Foreign Policy* (New York: St. Martin's, 1983); and Fen Osler Hampson, "The Divided Decision-Maker: American Domestic Politics and the Cuban Crisis," *International Security* 9 (Winter 1984–1985): 130–165.

9. Edwin S. Corwin, *The President: Office and Power* (New York: New York University Press, 1940), p. 200.

10. See I. M. Destler, Leslie H. Gelb, and Anthony Lake, *Our Own Worst Enemy: The Unmaking of American Foreign Policy* (New York: Simon & Schuster, 1984).

11. The classic study of this phenomenon is Ole R. Holsti's study of Secretary of State John Foster Dulles. See Ole R. Holsti, "The Belief System and National Images: A Case Study," *Journal of Conflict Resolution* 6 (September 1962): 244–252.

12. John G. Stoessinger, *Crusaders and Pragmatists: Movers of Modern American Foreign Policy* (New York: Norton, 1985), pp. xiii–xiv.

13. Alexander L. George, *Presidential Decisionmaking in Foreign Policy: The Effective Use of Information and Advise* (Boulder, Colo.: Westview Press, 1980).

Part I: THE SOCIETAL ENVIRONMENT

Consensus. Bipartisanship. Both terms relate to the belief that foreign policy is somehow "above politics." National interests override partisan and personal interests in the formulation and execution of American foreign policy, according to this viewpoint, which undergirds Americans' long-standing conviction that "politics stops at the water's edge."

That simple aphorism may once have been true, but it no longer is—as the fate of President Clinton's proposals to trim the federal deficit in part by cutting defense spending so vividly prove. It may always have been the case that the choices made by American policymakers are the result of internal considerations, not just international ones. The imperative need to maintain a power base, the pragmatic desire to preserve the freedom to maneuver in the future, and the political desire to remain popular with the voters are political motivations not confined to the present or the recent past. Still, the partisan and ideological character of foreign policymaking has been especially clear since the 1970s, when domestic divisions over the Vietnam War and how to deal with the Soviet Union increasingly pit Republicans against Democrats and conservatives against liberals.

The partisan and ideological character of the policy process contributes to disarray and discontinuities in American foreign policy, with the government seemingly unable to control the process or cope successfully. This proclivity led three well-known students of American foreign policy, including Anthony Lake, President Clinton's national security adviser, to write an assessment of American foreign policymaking whose conclusions are revealed by its title: *Our Own Worst Enemy: The Unmaking of American Foreign Policy:* "For two decades, the making of American foreign policy has been growing far more political—or more precisely, far more partisan and ideological. . . . We Americans—politicians and experts alike—have been spending more time, energy and passion in fighting ourselves than we have in trying, as a nation, to understand and deal with a rapidly changing world."[1]

Little has changed in the years since I. M. Destler and Leslie H. Gelb joined Lake to write their indictment. On virtually every foreign policy issue faced in the past decade—ranging from aid to the contras in Nicaragua to the reflagging of Kuwaiti oil tankers, from whether and how to aid the imploding Soviet Union and now the post-Soviet states to downsizing the Cold War military machine—partisanship and ideology, reinforced until recently by divided government, have shaped perceptions of the national interest.

As noted in the introduction to this book, the end of the Cold War is unlikely to end domestic divisions about American foreign policy. The congressional vote authorizing President Bush to use military force against Iraq pursuant to the authorization of the U.N. Security Council, which the Soviet Union as well as the United States backed, is perhaps illustrative. Bush carried the day by a vote of 250 to 183 in the House but only 52 to 47 in the Senate. Nearly all of his support came from a coalition of Republicans and conservative Southern Democrats, thus giving the vote an ideological as well as partisan cast. Congress had not been this divided on an issue of war and peace since the War of 1812.

The United States emerged triumphant in the Persian Gulf War, but it became a Pyrrhic victory for Bush. As the U.S. economy slipped into recession, the president increasingly found himself criticized for spending too much time on foreign policy and too little on domestic policy. Even as his popularity reached new heights with the defeat of Saddam Hussein, 43 percent of the American people disapproved of his handling of the economy. The number would skyrocket to 75 percent on the eve of the 1992 presidential election, by which time his overall approval rating would plummet to only 37 percent. As one analyst put it, "Most Americans supported the war and celebrated the outcome; then they turned to more pressing subjects."[2]

The Democrats took advantage of the inward-looking mood of the electorate in the first post–Cold War presidential election. A sign in Bill Clinton's campaign headquarters proclaiming "The Economy, Stupid!" reflected Democratic leaders' single-minded determination to make domestic policy the focus of attention. The end of the Cold War and, with it, the removal of virulent anticommunism from the domestic political agenda played to their strategy. Still, candidate Clinton was quick to tie the state of the economy to the continuing ability of the United States to play an active role in world affairs. "America must regain its economic strength to play a proper role as leader of the world," he declared. "And we must have a president who attends to prosperity at home if our people are to sustain their support for engagement abroad."

How to revitalize the economy is by no means clear. This, then, promises to be a contentious political issue. Many others will join it, ranging from deficit reduction to righting the nation's trade imbalance with Japan and others to coping with spiraling health costs driven in part by a demographically changing society. All of them promise to affect the ability of the United States to pursue a policy of constructive engagement in the post–Cold War world.

THE SOCIETAL ENVIRONMENT AS AN INFLUENCE ON AMERICAN FOREIGN POLICY

Our examination of the societal environment as a source of American foreign policy begins with a broad-ranging assessment of what's wrong with the American economy and how the ills that beset it constrain the ability of the United States to play a constructive leadership world in a changed and changing world. The chapter "Why America Must Change Course: The Domestic Roots of Global Influence" is drawn from a bipartisan report by the prestigious Center for Strategic and International Studies (CSIS), located in Washington, D.C. Co-chaired by Senators Sam Nunn (D-Georgia) and Pete Domenici (R-New Mexico), the commission that authored the report answers the question "why this report" this way: "For 30 years, the Center for Strategic and International Studies has surveyed developments around the globe that might affect the security of the United States. . . . We know every trouble spot from Azerbaijan to Pyongyang. With the fall of the Soviet Union, however, CSIS has come to the conclusion that some of America's biggest trouble spots are not abroad but here at home. They are in manufacturing, capital formation, education, the federal budget, science and technology." The selection that follows deals with each of these issues. Its conclusion is both ominous and hopeful: "Domestic issues . . . do not bode well for the long-term economic growth and social cohesion of our country or for the standard of living of most of our citizens. . . . Our current course will certainly not contribute to our economic strength and may ultimately cause its slow and steady erosion. . . . No international strategy can compensate for weaknesses at home. We have seen this illustrated all too vividly in the Soviet Union." Still, "America has the talent, resources, ingenuity, and staying power to turn the situation around. What we need is a broad-based understanding of the reality behind our problems, the civic determination and political will to address them, and a plan of action, built on a consensus among our citizens, to confront them."

Building a consensus on what to do at home and abroad will depend critically on the thinking and attitudes of the American people and policy influentials. The end of the Cold War raises interesting questions about the nature and structure of those attitudes. Anticommunism and anti-Sovietism figured prominently in domestic politics throughout the Cold War, where they served as rallying cries for conservatives and central planks in the Republican party's foreign policy platform. With their extirpation, it is conceivable that Americans' thinking about foreign policy issues will move in radically new directions and take on sharply different forms.

Ole R. Holsti examines these possibilities in "Public Opinion and Foreign Policy: Attitude Structures of Opinion Leaders after the Cold War." He begins by assessing the skepticism sometimes attributed to the relevance of public opinion in American foreign policymaking and then examines the post–Cold War foreign policy beliefs and preferences of American opinion leaders (elites), that stratum of American society most likely to be attentive to or to be able to shape the nation's foreign policy.

Drawing on a 1992 survey of opinion leaders, which continues a series begun in the immediate aftermath of the Vietnam War, Holsti demonstrates that the post-Vietnam divisions about the nation's world role continue even with the demise of Soviet communism. He identifies two distinct strands of "internationalist" thinking among American leaders—militant and cooperative internationalism—and shows how these relate systematically to differences among leaders about future threats to U.S. national security, the nation's interests and roles, specific international commitments and policies, and the means of American foreign policy. Holsti explains the persistence of leaders' attitude structures in the post–Cold War environment by noting the parallels between militant and cooperative internationalism and *realism* and *liberalism,* competing schools of thought about international politics that "predate the Cold War" and thus continue to "identify important elements in the structure of thinking about international affairs."

Among other conclusions, Holsti determines from the evidence about leaders' attitudes that "it may be easier to build domestic coalitions for interventions abroad or other international undertakings that have a tenor of cooperative rather than militant internationalism." Interventionism, both covert and overt, has, of course, figured prominently in post–World War II American foreign policy. Public opposition to military intervention in the wake of Vietnam among both elites and, perhaps even more, the mass of the American public contributed to what became the widely if amorphously described "Vietnam syndrome"—an expression symbolic of the introspective climate of opinion prevalent in the United States since the early 1970s that discouraged interventionist behavior generally and the prolonged use of military force abroad in particular. George Bush played on that theme in the aftermath of the Persian Gulf War, proclaiming proudly in March 1991, "By God, we've kicked the Vietnam syndrome once and for all."

But have we? Bill Clinton found that "Vietnam" still resonates ill in the American polity as he campaigned at home and abroad for limited U.S. intervention in Bosnia to forestall continued "ethnic cleansing" in the former Yugoslavia by Bosnian Serbs. "I see it as another Vietnam," said Vietnam veteran and Congressman John Murtha (D-Pennsylvania). Many Americans may have shared similar views, as public opinion polls in the spring and early summer of 1993 repeatedly showed the American people were uncertain and reluctant supporters of the Clinton administration's proposals to end the fighting in Bosnia. Later, they also became critical of continued U.S. involvement in Somalia.

Presidents typically can count on the American people to support their foreign policy initiatives. "My country, right or wrong" has a long heritage. Thus most Americans "rally 'round the flag"—and their president—in times of crisis and peril. Still, the division in Americans' foreign policy beliefs along militant and cooperative lines, which pertains to the mass public as well as elites,[3] suggests that some people are more supportive of an interventionist foreign policy than others. Partisanship and ideology figure prominently in these differences, but the nature of the issue at stake may also be relevant.

Bruce W. Jentleson's chapter, "The Pretty Prudent Public: Post Post-Vietnam American Opinion on the Use of Military Force," provides important insight in this respect. He argues, based on evidence of public support for the use of American military force during the 1980s and the Persian Gulf War, that the American people can distinguish "between force used to coerce *foreign policy restraint* by an adversary engaged in aggressive actions against the United States or its interests, and force used to engineer *internal political change* within another country." Furthermore, they are more likely to support U.S. efforts designed to promote restraint than those designed to promote internal political change. That finding should serve as a flag of caution for proponents of the "new interventionism" of the post–Cold War era, an outlook that sees domestic conflicts and prevention of human rights abuses by governments as legitimate causes for military intervention.[4]

Holsti's study of the foreign policy beliefs and preferences of American leaders is premised implicitly on the elitist model of foreign policymaking described in the introduction to this book. Jentleson's probe of mass attitudes, on the other hand, is more consistent with the pluralist model, which maintains that "average" Americans are able to express their views and to pressure the government, typically through interest groups, to heed them.

Despite the ubiquitous presence of interest groups, their ability to influence foreign policy is uncertain. If there is one interest group believed to be successful, it is the so-called Jewish lobby. Analysts often claim, for example, that the decision of the Truman administration to recognize the state of Israel within minutes of its declared independence in 1947 was largely a response to the influence of Jewish people in America. Similarly, many believe that continued U.S. support of the state of Israel in the face of often overwhelming international opprobrium is a consequence of the domestic influence of the Jewish lobby.

Mitchell Bard subjects these seemingly self-evident conclusions to scrutiny and finds them wanting. The Jewish lobby is more aptly described as an Israeli lobby, he cautions, and even on issues that pertain directly to Israel it is often not clear whether U.S. support for Israeli foreign policy positions is attributable to the Israeli lobby or to other factors. Noteworthy is his observation that the lobby typically frames its positions in terms of the national interest *of the United States*. Most important, he concludes that the mere existence of pressure does not demonstrate its success; where there is activity there is not necessarily influence.

Bard's analysis is consistent with the tenets of pluralism, according to which public policy is the expression of the balance of forces contending for influence in the policy process. In this case, "the balance of lobbying power [compared with pro-Arab forces] remains clearly in favor of the Israeli lobby." But what happens when the balance of power shifts in favor of the increasing number of agents who work for foreign governments? Then—as Ross Perot so frequently chided during the 1992 presidential campaign—policy choices may not reflect U.S. national interests but the interests of other nations.

In "The Japanese Megaphone: Foreign Influences on Foreign Policymaking," John B. Judis examines how Japan uses its financial resources to reinforce the Japanese viewpoint on key economic issues. Judis notes there is nothing illegal in Japan's funding of think tanks, academics, and lobbyists, but he worries that "the hundreds of millions that Japan is spending annually are tilting the debate about America's economic future without the public being aware of it. The Japanese are radically reinforcing opinions that mirror their own. 'It's like giving certain people a megaphone and forcing everybody else to shout.'" He concludes with the warning that "America's future . . . cannot be adequately debated as long as many of the leading participants have an undisclosed financial stake in one answer rather than another."

Debates about America's future will also shape the kind of military posture it devises to meet the still amorphous challenges of the post–Cold War world. What finally emerges, however, will not be the product of some rational calculation of the resources required to meet particular challenges but the result of an intensely political process involving large segments of American society—from South Carolina to California, from Texas to Minnesota—who benefitted from the Cold War military architecture and the budgets that sustained it—and who are now threatened by its unravelling. To many people, "downsizing" and "defense conversion" are euphemisms for joblessness and declining living standards.

Gordon Adams describes in "The New Politics of the Defense Budget" the radically new environment defense planners and budgeteers now face: "a dramatically changed world with a smaller immediate threat; severe fiscal constraints; a need to redefine military roles and missions, and the forces, hardware and budgets that go with them; all in the context of a congressional and public debate over the pace of defense reductions and the uses of savings from a smaller military budget." Gordon's essay examines each of these factors, with special attention given to "the domestic politics of defense." He argues that the defense budgets of the twenty-first century will emerge out of the complex interactions among the elements defining the new defense environment. Thus he rejects the notion that any single force will dominate, such as the "military-industrial complex," a once popular elitist conception of the domestic forces (in effect, a single, dominant interest group) often thought to have determined defense policymaking during the Cold War.

In addition to interest groups, we drew attention in the introduction to the mass media. Elites and pluralists alike believe the media play an important role in the process that enables societal forces to shape American foreign policy. How to view that role normatively (whether as a constructive or destructive force) is less certain. The media characteristically serve less as an independent critic of what the government is doing than as a supporter of government's activity. Thus, when the media tell us what to think about, and often what to think, the message frequently conforms to what the government has in mind—this despite the fact that presidents invariably come to view the media as their enemies.

"Pundits"—defined by *Webster's* as those who make comments or judgments "in a solemnly authoritative manner"—are a segment of the media establishment widely scrutinized by policymakers and critics in recent years. George Bush was especially critical of the "punditocracy" during his unsuccessful reelection bid. Curiously, however, the punditocracy, or some parts of it, were primary supporters of what may have been the defining foreign policy achievement of the Bush presidency—the eviction, by force, of Iraq from Kuwait. This, at least, is the argument of Eric Alterman in "Operation Pundit Storm: The Media, Political Commentary, and Foreign Policy," an account of how political commentators—pundits—played a role in generating and sustaining support for the Bush administration's decision to use force to expel Saddam Hussein from Kuwait following Iraq's invasion of the tiny sheikdom in August 1990. Alterman argues that "a tiny cadre of mostly neoconservative pundits" helped create a climate in "elite Washington opinion" supportive of the president's policies. They also helped to write off the critics, branding their views as "'pro-isolationism,' 'pro-appeasement,' or, in the case of Patrick Buchanan, pro-anti-Semitism." And once the war was over, the pundits helped to interpret the victory as proof that those who argued the United States was a declining power—"those nagging declinists"—"had everything wrong." Some readers may be dismayed by Alterman's sharp, often caustic edge, but his message about the role of political commentary in shaping the climate of foreign policy opinion is not easily dismissed.

Democratic theory promises that the voice of the people is ultimately expressed through the ballot box. If our political leaders do not perform to expectations, or if they pursue unpopular policies, elections provide the means to remove them from office. As noted earlier, however, it is difficult to determine how foreign policy issues and concerns motivate electoral behavior. Because most elections involve a variety of different and often overlapping issues, it is difficult to determine if voters cast their ballots for a candidate because of, or in spite of, his or her stand on a particular issue. Political leaders pay special attention to the effects of their behavior on the judgments of voters nonetheless—to a point that may have untoward effects on the nation's foreign policy.

William B. Quandt explores the connection between elections and foreign policy behavior in "The Electoral Cycle and the Conduct of American Foreign Policy." Noting the constitutional requirements that congressional elections be held every two years and presidential elections every four, Quandt concludes that "presidents have little time during their incumbency when they have both the experience and the power needed for sensible and effective conduct of foreign policy." His theme reinforces the judgment that the nature of American society and its political system sometimes have untoward policy consequences: "The price we pay [for the structure of the electoral cycle] is a foreign policy excessively geared to short-term calculations, in which narrow domestic political considerations often outweigh sound strategic thinking, and where turnover in high positions is so frequent that consistency and coherence are lost."

NOTES

1. I. M. Destler, Leslie H. Gelb, and Anthony Lake, *Our Own Worst Enemy: The Unmaking of American Foreign Policy* (New York: Simon & Schuster, 1984), p. 13.

2. Thomas Omestad, "Why Bush Lost," *Foreign Policy* 89 (Winter 1992–93), p. 72.

3. See Eugene R. Wittkopf, *Faces of Internationalism: Public Opinion and American Foreign Policy* (Durham, N.C.: Duke University Press, 1990); and Eugene R. Wittkopf, "Faces of Internationalism in a Transitional Environment," paper delivered at the annual convention of the International Studies Association, Acapulco, Mexico, March 1993.

4. See Stephen John Stedman, "The New Interventionists," *Foreign Affairs,* Vol. 72, No. 1, pp. 1–16. Portions of this article are reprinted in Eugene R. Wittkopf, ed., *The Future of American Foreign Policy,* 2nd ed. (New York: St. Martin's, 1994).

1. WHY AMERICA MUST CHANGE COURSE: THE DOMESTIC ROOTS OF GLOBAL INFLUENCE

Sam Nunn
Pete Domenici
Debra L. Miller

*T*he last [several] years have been an extraordinary time to be an American. We have seen rival governments and economic systems topple and unravel in virtually all of Eastern Europe and parts of Asia. Without its foes firing a shot, the Soviet Union, with the strongest army in the world, collapsed. No amount of military might could substitute for a government that did not work, an economy that could not produce, and a social policy that repressed the identities and aspirations of different nationalities and individual citizens. From these events, America has emerged as the sole superpower.

Our unchallenged preeminence in the world, however, has not left us altogether settled on our future course, nor free of internal problems. There is clear and increasing evidence that our own political and economic systems, though still resilient, must be strengthened. Our ability to continue to lead globally will be determined by our ability to put our own house in order.

We must change our course here at home in the 1990s. The facts are simple. We have the largest economy in the world, but we have vulnerabilities that run far deeper than the last recession. These weaknesses will continue to erode our economic strength and further burden future generations. Addressing these vulnerabilities will require reforms that will be painful at first.

If the United States is to strengthen its human resource base, educational standards must be tougher and children must study harder. If the country is to increase its level of saving, our political leaders must make some tough choices about how to balance the federal budget. If more U.S. businesses are to become globally competitive, they must develop new management practices and new production methods.

Note: Some figures have been deleted or renumbered.

If we make these reforms, we can turn the country around, regain momentum, and provide for long-term growth and prosperity. We will not only be more successful at home but we will continue to provide constructive leadership in the world. . . .

STAGNANT PRODUCTIVITY GROWTH AND OUR STANDARD OF LIVING

The economist Paul Krugman notes wryly that "productivity isn't everything, but in the long-run, it is almost everything." Our standard of living, the competitiveness of our goods and services, and even our national power are all affected by how productive we are.

America is still the most productive country in the world. Using output per worker as the yardstick, the United States is more productive than either Germany or Japan. That means that every year, the average American worker produces more than the average German or Japanese worker.

Despite that success, most economists believe that productivity is the number one economic problem facing the United States. First, American productivity growth has slowed down considerably during the past 20 years, while the productivity growth of other major countries has accelerated. Second, for productivity to have real payoffs, companies must be strong in a few other key areas: excellent product quality; responsiveness to consumer preferences; and being first to market. Too many U.S. companies have been weak in these areas, and that weakness is playing a large role in the actual economic performance of our nation.

The slowdown in productivity growth has had major consequences for our standard of living. During the 1950s and 1960s, American productivity growth rates in the business, nonfarm sector averaged 2.5 percent per year. As a consequence, real wages and living standards doubled every 28 years, or once a generation. Thus, in the 1950s and 1960s, most Americans could look forward to an ever-growing income stream for themselves and be optimistic about the earnings prospects of their children.

In 1973, however, productivity growth rates dropped abruptly; since 1979 they have averaged about 1 percent a year. As a consequence, the average American real income stagnated during the 1970s and 1980s. In fact, many families found that the only way to make ends meet was to have two wage earners rather than one. The numbers tell the painful story: In 1970, the typical family income (in 1990 dollars) was about $33,000. By 1990, this figure had grown by only $2,000. If productivity growth in the 1970s and 1980s had kept pace with its growth in the 1950s and 1960s, the typical 1990 family income would have been more than $47,000. . . .

Manufacturing Productivity and Service Sector Productivity

There is some recent good news in the productivity statistics, but it comes only from the manufacturing side of our economy. During the past decade,

U.S. manufacturing companies have rebounded from 1970s lows to a more healthy 3 percent productivity growth rate per year. Nevertheless, productivity growth in the manufacturing sectors of Japan, Germany, Sweden, France, Great Britain, and Italy is still higher than it is in the United States.

The productivity growth of our service sector, which employs more than three-quarters of our work force, has not kept pace with manufacturing. The service sector is extremely diverse and includes business, financial, and legal services; amusements and recreation; telecommunications; insurance; real estate; government; medical care; education; the police force; public interest advocacy groups; religious establishments; and retail trade.

The sheer diversity of the service sector makes it difficult to generalize about the causes of its slow productivity growth. One explanation is that parts of the sector are characterized by little or no competition. For example, many government agencies and many nonprofit organizations are not forced to become more efficient every year to remain viable—other institutions are not competing with them to provide similar services.

A second is that the service sector has been less able than the manufacturing sector to reap gains from new technology. For example, despite hefty investments in computers in the 1980s—at the rate of $9,000 per worker—the service sector showed very little productivity gains—less than two-tenths of a percentage point per year. Whether this is an intrinsic weakness of the sector or one that could be remedied by better management practices and greater investments in work force training is an open question.

There is, however, a growing body of opinion that productivity in the service sector is stronger than the statistics say it is. The data on service sector productivity just aren't very good. Statisticians and economists have yet to come up with good measures for the productivity of a government bureaucrat, a college professor, a telephone operator, a lawyer, or a doctor. A very common method of measuring productivity in the service sector is number of phone calls made per day. Clearly, this measure is inappropriate as a measure of productivity for many service subsectors.

Productivity Gains Translate into Greater Global Market Share

Despite the difficulties in measurement, it can safely be stated that our major competitors' productivity growth rates are increasing at a faster rate than ours (see Figure 1.1). In fact, in certain economic sectors, Japan is simply more productive than the United States. Japanese companies that produce automobiles, steel, electric machinery, and electronic equipment are generally more productive than American companies that produce these goods. U.S. companies retain the lead in, among other sectors, agriculture, petroleum and coal refining, paper, printing and publishing, machinery (except electrical machinery), utilities, and processed food. Usually, but not always, companies that are more productive can translate their efficiency into a greater share of the global market.

This brings us to the second reason why economists worry about U.S.

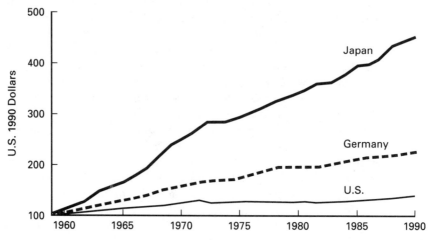

Figure 1.1. America's productivity growth rate is below that of our major competitors. The graph shows the index of GDP per employed person (1960 = 100; 1990 U.S. dollars). [Source: U.S. Department of Labor, Bureau of Labor Statistics, Office of Productivity and Technology (January 1992) unpublished data.]

productivity. Some foreign companies that are less productive than their U.S. counterparts are sometimes more successful in the global marketplace. Why? Because even some of our most productive companies are weak in the areas of quality, responsiveness to consumer preference, and being first to market. These factors have an enormous effect on a product's acceptance in global markets and ultimately our workers' standards of living. For example, U.S. automakers chose not to be the first to this market with smaller cars in the 1970s. That decision, coupled with fewer defects and lower costs of Japanese cars, played a key role in increasing Japanese market share in the U.S. auto market, even though U.S. productivity—output per worker—was higher.

What will it take to make the U.S. companies more productive? A variety of factors influence productivity growth, but the consensus is that one factor outweighs most others: investment. Specifically, investment in plant and equipment, research and development (R&D), infrastructure, and human resources through education and work force training all determine productivity. And, increased investment in human resources demands improvements in management practices, such as planning for the long term, use of the "quality approach," and encouragement of teamwork.

It's too easy to say we need more investment in machines, bricks, and mortar. We need to invest in people—the true source of ideas and solutions. Combining this with the more traditional forms of investment will increase our standard of living, increase the global competitiveness of U.S. products and services, and solidify America's position as a world leader. . . .

THE NEED TO ENCOURAGE SAVING

National Saving

National savings are the sum of all savings done by individuals, businesses, and governments (local, state, and federal) in the country. . . .

What are savings? They are funds that are taken out of current income for the purpose of financing the future. Said another way, savings are deferred spending—deferred so that greater consumption will be possible in the future.

Foreign investment aside, national savings equal national investment. A low level of savings results in reduced economic growth, low productivity growth, and fewer jobs. In contrast, a high savings rate permits more investment in plant and equipment, R&D, improvements in process technologies, education and training, and traditional and high-technology infrastructure—all of which are needed for accelerated productivity growth and a growing standard of living. However, the U.S. invests less as a percentage of its gross domestic product (GDP) in plants, equipment, and R&D than most other industrialized countries (see Figures 1.2 and 1.3).

The U.S. net national savings rate is at an all-time low: It plummeted from an average of 9.8 percent of GDP in the 1960s to an average of 3.6 percent in

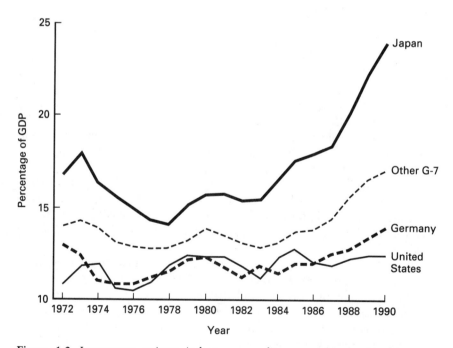

Figure 1.2. Investment: private industry expenditure on plant and equipment. [Source: Council on Competitiveness and OECD National Accounts. Taken from Council on Competitiveness, *Competitiveness Index 1991* (Washington, D.C.: Council on Competitiveness, July 1991), p. 8.]

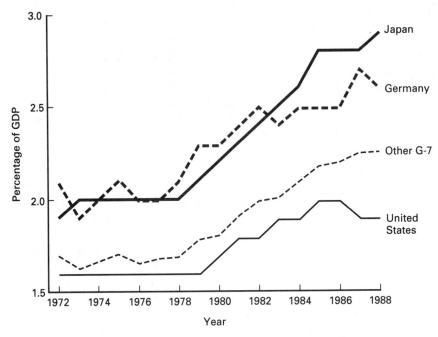

Figure 1.3. Investment: nondefense R&D expenditure (public and private). [Source: Council on Competitiveness and National Science Foundation (NSF). Taken from Council on Competitiveness, *Competitiveness Index 1991* (Washington, D.C.: Council on Competitiveness, July 1991), p. 9.]

the 1980s. In contrast, Japan and the EC countries save at a rate of well over 10 percent of their GDPs (see Figure 1.4).

A fall in personal savings rates explains part of the decline in our national savings rates. American families saved close to 10 percent of their incomes 20 years ago; now they save at roughly half that rate.

The primary reason for the decline in the national savings rate, however, is not private behavior; two-thirds of the decline in the national savings rate is due to the growing federal budget deficit. A low personal savings rate puts us at a disadvantage. But huge continuing government budget deficits threaten to turn disadvantage into disaster.

When the national savings rate is low, businesses must compete with the government to borrow saved money, and they are less able to make investments in plant and equipment, R&D, and worker training. Or, they must borrow from better savers—foreigners. In the 1980s, domestic investment was heavily fueled by foreign capital; that is why capital investment as a percentage of GDP decreased less rapidly than our national savings rate.

But reliance on foreign capital will be more difficult in the 1990s than it was in the 1980s. German unification and the dissolution of the former Soviet empire in Eastern Europe have focused many potential investors on investment

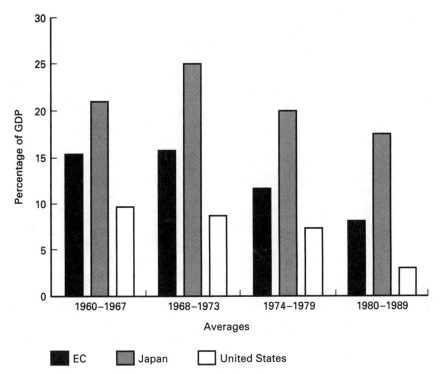

Figure 1.4. Net national saving as a percentage of GDP. [Source: Organization for Economic Cooperation and Development, *Economic Outlook, Historical Statistics, 1960–1989*, p. 78.]

opportunities in that part of the world. Developing nations such as Mexico are also becoming a magnet for foreign investment. Japan's internal economic difficulties have already had a dampening effect on Japanese investors' willingness and ability to invest in the United States. The Japanese stock exchange has lost 60 percent of its value, compared to its peak in 1988; Japanese investors have lost money in dollar-denominated equity investments because of fluctuations in the exchange rate; and Japanese investors who bought at the top of the American real estate market have taken losses. For all of these reasons, there may be less foreign capital available for investment in the United States in the 1990s.

How do we encourage more saving? Quite simply, we make changes in both U.S. tax and fiscal policies. Our current tax laws make it more attractive for companies to go into debt than to expand investors' equity; they encourage households to borrow and spend money and punish them for saving; they penalize U.S. companies in international trade, compared to our foreign competitors. Finally, the huge federal budget deficit diverts the little private savings there are away from productive investment in the future, principally to pay for public consumption in the present. . . .

Fiscal Responsibility

Federal budget deficits are sapping the strength of our country. When the Treasury spends money it doesn't have, it must borrow money from U.S. citizens, corporations and businesses, and foreign investors. These borrowings absorb private savings that otherwise would be available for private investment. Less money available for investment means less investment in modern equipment and factories, less productivity, and less economic growth. Everyone loses.

Deficits matter because they reduce net national savings. Deficits must be funded with borrowing, and this means the government must pay interest to those who have lent it money. Interest accounts for an ever-growing percentage of total federal outlays. Net interest on the national debt—the accumulation of past deficits—will be more than $200 billion [in 1992]. That makes interest the third largest "program" in the budget. Only defense and Social Security are larger—our net interest payments are roughly equal to total domestic discretionary spending. We may debate whether to spend more on infrastructure or education, but that money is already earmarked for servicing the debt.

The deficit results in a distortion of spending priorities. Just as the private sector has less money to invest, so too does the government have less money to invest in public programs and projects designed for long-term economic growth. As a consequence, resources are limited for highways and public infrastructure programs, education, and training programs, all important for increased private and public sector productivity. To take another example, the Social Security system supposedly was placed on a "sound financial basis" through program reform and payroll tax increases in 1983. The 1983 amendments were intended to build up a reserve in the Social Security Trust Fund so that when the time comes for the baby boom generation to retire, the nation would have the Trust Fund to pay the benefits. But now we've cracked into that bank, too, and we're spending the reserves for non-Social Security functions. Sure, that reduces our need to borrow money now, but we're mortgaging our future. When we have to pay back the Social Security Trust Fund—about 20 years from now—large tax increases or benefit cuts will likely be required.

Deficits matter because the costs and perils associated with being the world's largest debtor nation (which the United States has been since the mid-1980s) include a permanent loss of United States investment capital, and the risk of a weakened economy lessening the attractiveness of foreign capital investment. And, being indebted to other countries, we are subject to increased constraints on the independent conduct of our economic and foreign policies, and we are left more vulnerable to decisions made abroad.

Deficits matter because they are the most prominent example of our inability to come to grips with important public issues. Deficits and debt are concrete evidence of the gridlock and stalemate that afflict our public institutions. Philosophically, they feed into a societal attitude of being a nation unable to live within its means.

Both American voters and our trading partners are frustrated with our political system's seeming inability to deal with these issues. Solving the deficit problem would contribute to savings and productivity and help restore confidence in our political system.

DIMINISHED RETURNS FROM INVESTMENTS IN HUMAN RESOURCES AND MANAGEMENT

Education

America's elementary and secondary education system, once the envy of the world, is performing well below the best international levels. Too few schools and parents insist that their students meet high standards, too few colleges set rigorous entry requirements, and too few employers demand evidence of educational achievement from high school graduates seeking jobs.

Low educational achievement is a particularly acute problem in our urban centers, where the crises of poverty and family and community disintegration compound the woes. But the problem is not only urban, it is national: From rural communities to our most advantaged districts, American schools are failing to produce a sufficient percentage of students with the high-level knowledge, skills, and motivation necessary for informed citizenship and for a strong, globally competitive economy.

A well-educated and highly skilled population is key to a high standard of living. U.S. productivity growth declined during the past two decades in part because the skills of American workers failed to keep up with increasingly complex technology. During the past decade, manufacturing wages declined for the first time since World War II. Increasingly, we're becoming a nation that competes in the international marketplace because we're cheap—not skilled.

In contrast, our major competitors have made the necessary investments in education and in work force training and have experienced an increase in real wages. In these countries the workplace is organized very differently than ours. Workers' skills are constantly being developed, used, and upgraded. A greater percentage of workers in these countries can compete on the basis of high skills rather than low wages.

Despite its crucial relationship to productivity and competitiveness, our educational system is often neglected. The public bemoans the state of American schools, but few are willing to accept sacrifices in order to do something about it. Bearing the costs of achieving quality education is unattractive to the three-quarters of all taxpayers who do not have children in school. Even parents of schoolchildren are often unwilling to vote to raise their own taxes to improve their schools.

When school bond issues are defeated, when athletics win over academics, when television consumes 25 percent of the waking hours of students, and when many colleges and employers are indifferent to high school achievement, is it surprising that our educational system is performing so poorly?

As a nation, we have made substantial investments in education. The United States invests more in higher education than any other country. Among advanced industrialized countries, the United States ranks eleventh in public spending on elementary and secondary education as a percentage of GDP, and sixth in public spending on education per pupil. . . . In addition, our nation funds parochial and independent school systems, and those funds are not included in these international comparisons.

But these substantial investments are not paying off the way they should. Not all school districts are adequately funded. In many districts where funding has increased, people feel rightly that more spending does not equal better results. Education dollars that reach public schools are not always wisely or efficiently allocated. Our schools choke on bureaucracy and administrative inefficiency. There is a pervasive lack of standards and discipline. Consider the evidence:

- U.S. students are simply not learning what they need to know to compete and prosper in today's global economy. In comparison to students in other industrialized countries, our students, by many measures, rank at or near the bottom in math and science (see Figure 1.5).
- In the United States, teaching may as well be considered a second-rate profession in terms of educational preparation, licensing requirements, pay, status, or professional development. Few prospective elementary-school teachers are required to have even a rudimentary background in science and math and in how to teach those subjects. Only half of our math and science teachers are certified in their subjects, and only half of our high schools have physics teachers.
- More than one out of five U.S. students leave school before receiving a high school diploma. Only one-third of those who leave early will obtain a high school diploma or its equivalent by their mid-30s. In our inner cities, more than half of the students drop out before graduation.
- Our educational system virtually abandons the 50 percent of our young people who can not or will not go to college. Our high schools do little to prepare students for work or to guide them in making choices. Compared to many European countries, the American apprenticeship system is narrow in content and minuscule in coverage—it serves less than 1 percent of the work force. There is no widespread, formal system of education and training for service or manufacturing trades and technical professions. Our non-college-bound students are left to sink or swim on their own. Many sink.
- Many are given the same daunting choice when they report for work. Only 11 percent of all employees receive any formal training from their employers to prepare for their jobs, and fewer receive formal training to upgrade their skills once they are on the job. Although some employers do not believe they have a shortage of skilled workers, this is largely because they rely on production methods that do not require high skills. Our most successful companies have moved to high-productivity, "lean production" manufacturing processes that depend on high skills, innovation, and flexibility.

If our companies are to be competitive, more must adopt the high-skills approach. If our students are to prosper, they must obtain the skills needed by our most successful workplaces.

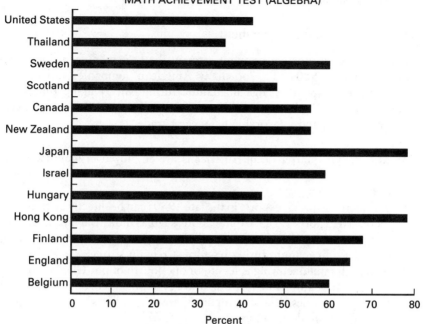

TWELFTH GRADE SCORES ON INTERNATIONAL
MATH ACHIEVEMENT TEST (ALGEBRA)

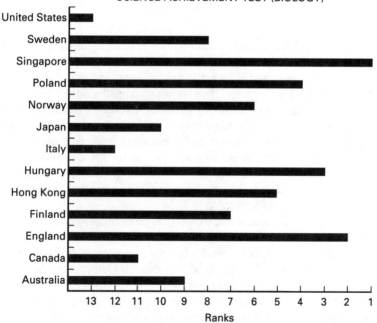

TWELFTH GRADE SCORES ON INTERNATIONAL
SCIENCE ACHIEVEMENT TEST (BIOLOGY)

Figure 1.5. U.S. students rank nearly last in math and science in international comparisons. [Source: International Association for Evaluation of Educational Achievement. Reprinted from *Changing America: The New Face of Science and Engineering,* Task Force on Women, Minorities, and the Handicapped in Science and Technology, 1988. Taken from Council on Competitiveness, *Picking Up the Pace: The Commercial Challenge to American Innovation* (Washington, D.C.: Council on Competitiveness, September 1988), p. 22.]

Manufacturing and Management

Although labor productivity growth rates in the U.S. manufacturing sector improved in the 1980s . . . , too many American companies still need to sharpen their competitive edge in manufacturing—in "making things." A strong manufacturing base is critical to our country's national defense, economic well-being, and a favorable balance of trade.

- Almost one-quarter of all Americans are employed in manufacturing. Traditionally, manufacturing has contributed many of the high-wage jobs in our economy.
- The increase in U.S. exports in the late 1980s can be directly attributed to increased exports of U.S. capital goods such as industrial machinery and computers as well as chemicals and aircraft. If we are to remain a strong exporter, our manufacturing base must remain strong.
- Although manufacturing is less than one-fourth of our GDP, more than 80 percent of all private research and development is done by manufacturing companies. These companies are thus agents of technological change and modernization.
- The health of the service sector is highly dependent on the health of the manufacturing sector, which is the major customer and supplier for service enterprises.

For example, as good as American companies have been at invention, they are not nearly as fast or as effective as their competitors in turning inventions into high-quality products and then getting those products into the hands of consumers. We run to discovery, and then we walk to production: U.S. companies spend twice as many resources on the development of new product ideas as they do on the process technologies to manufacture the products themselves. Foreign companies, especially in Japan and Germany, have been more successful in commercializing some American inventions than U.S. companies have: The color television, the VCR, and the fax machine were all invented in America, but U.S. companies do not make these products any longer. As a result, we have lost markets and jobs.

Beyond time-to-market problems, many U.S. companies—in both service and manufacturing sectors—face two additional management issues.

First, American companies were relatively slow to embrace the "total quality approach." Fascinated by the teachings of W. Edwards Deming, the American statistician, Japanese companies began using this approach in the 1950s and perfected it in the 1970s by concentrating on achieving customer satisfaction and driving out defects, waste, and rework to gain a competitive advantage in quality. . . .

Second, there is clear justification for concerns over U.S. corporate time horizons. American companies often have shorter time horizons than many of their foreign counterparts, especially in Japan and Germany. Certainly the lower cost of capital in Japan and Germany in the 1980s and the relationship between Japanese and German companies and their banks allowed them to plan long term. In addition, the Japanese and German advantage in commercializing technology helped; the National Academy of Engineering in a recent study noted that "companies with deep and genuine competence in commercial application of technology will have a distinct advantage in adopting longer time horizons . . . because they are able to reduce . . . risk."

Government tax policy also has an impact on corporate time horizons. Our tax code encourages debt and merges and acquisitions, providing incentives for companies to focus on short-term paper profits. We need only look at the record number of mergers, acquisitions, and leveraged buy-outs in the 1980s to understand how sensitive companies were to these incentives. In a survey of Japanese and American companies, American executives ranked return on investment "8" in importance (where "10" was the most important) and market share "2"; Japanese executives ranked return on investment "4" and market share "5." Unfortunately, the victims of American preoccupation with short-term return on investment have too often been core business health, long-term market development, and long-term profitability.

Finally, the commission notes with concern the problems of small and medium-sized businesses. Their vitality is of paramount importance to the nation. During the 1980s, most of the new jobs, especially in urban areas, have been created by small and medium-sized businesses. These firms account for almost one-half of U.S. exports, and they produce about one-third of the value added in all U.S. manufacturing.

Nevertheless, small and medium-sized businesses face real challenges. They have been hit hardest by U.S. fiscal policies and our savings and loan crisis: During the past five years and the recent credit crunch, small and medium-sized firms have been unable to borrow or otherwise attract enough capital to adequately modernize their plant and equipment or to fund research and development. Preoccupied with the day-to-day problems of meeting delivery schedules and payrolls, managers of small firms often have little time to devote to learning new management techniques or new production processes. Small firms in which each worker's effort counts are even more vulnerable to declining skill levels of the work force than are large firms. For all of these reasons, small and medium-sized manufacturing enterprises suffered a decline in productivity in the 1980s, while the productivity of larger companies was increasing.

Science and Technology

As a nation, the United States is very strong in science and technology. We produce world-class high-technology products in areas from computers and satellites to industrial controls. Our nation's research institutions—both public and private—are an invaluable resource, with facilities and scientists among the best in the world. American scientists have won two-and-one-half times more Nobel Prizes than scientists of any other country of the world.

These strengths feed on themselves. So do weaknesses.

| | JAPAN | | EUROPEAN COMMUNITY | |
	R & D	Product Information	R & D	Product Information
Advanced Materials	O↓	−↓	+↔	O↔
Advanced Semiconductor Devices	O↔	−↓	+↔	O↔
Artificial Intelligence	+↔	+↔	+↑	+↔
Biotechnology	+↓	+↓	+↑	+↔
Digital Imaging Technology	O↓	−↓	O↓	−↓
Flexible Computer-Integrated Manufacturing	+↔	O↔	+↓	−↓
High-Density Data Storage	O↔	−↓	+↔	O↔
High-Performance Computing	+↔	+↓	+↑	+↑
Medical Devices and Diagnostics	+↔	+↓	+↔	+↓
Optoelectronics	O↔	−↓	O↔	+↔
Sensor Technology	+↓	O↔	+↔	O↔
Superconductors	O↓	−↓	O↔	O↔

Current Status: Trend:
+ = U.S. Ahead   ↑ = U.S. Gaining
O = U.S. Even   ↔ = U.S. Holding   } as compared to Japan/EC
− = U.S. Behind   ↓ = U.S. Losing

Figure 1.6. Comparison of where the United States, EC, and Japan stand in twelve emerging technologies. [Source: Compiled from the knowledge residing within the Department of Commerce, mostly from contributions within the National Institute of Standards and Technology and the International Trade Administration. Taken from *Emerging Technologies: A Survey of Technical and Economic Opportunities* (Washington, D.C.: U.S. Department of Commerce, Technology Administration, Spring 1990), p. 13.]

New evidence shows that the United States is falling behind the European Community and Japan in the development and application of several important emerging technologies that are critical to national security and economic success in the future (see Figure 1.6). This is a looming failure for our country.

In 1991, the National Critical Technologies Panel identified 22 technologies as being critical to national security and economic well-being (see Figure 1.7). Some of the technologies are familiar—biotechnology, advanced manufacturing, microelectronics, and high-performance computing and networking. In the words of the National Critical Technologies Panel, "critical technologies in materials, manufacturing and information/communications are the 'building blocks' for virtually all sectors of the economy." Losing the lead in critical technologies can jeopardize not only our ability to produce competitive products in that sector but our ability to develop related technologies in other areas.

For example, because we have already forfeited large segments of our consumer electronics industry, our ability to get into the production of emerg-

MATERIALS
- Materials synthesis and processing
- Electronic and photonic materials
- Ceramics
- Composites
- High-performance metals and alloys

MANUFACTURING
- Flexible computer-integrated manufacturing
- Intelligent processing equipment
- Micro- and nanofabrication
- Systems management technologies

INFORMATION AND COMMUNICATIONS
- Software
- Microelectronics
- High-performance computing and networking

- Sensors and signal processing
- Data storage and peripherals
- Computer simulation and modeling

BIOTECHNOLOGY AND LIFE SCIENCES
- Applied molecular biology
- Medical technology

AERONAUTICS AND SURFACE TRANSPORTATION
- Aeronautics
- Surface transportation technologies

ENERGY AND ENVIRONMENT
- Energy technologies
- Pollution minimization, remediation, and waste management

Figure 1.7. National critical technologies. [Source: *Report of the National Critical Technologies Panel* (Washington, D.C.: National Critical Technologies Panel, March 1991), p. 3.]

ing new technologies, such as high-definition systems, flat screen displays, and other imaging products that have large market potentials, may be compromised because we now lack a consumer electronics manufacturing infrastructure in the United States.

The federal government's contribution to our R&D base has been of enormous importance to our national security, productivity, and economic growth during the past 50 years. Commercial spinoffs have often resulted from military R&D, and government-sponsored basic science research has had significant commercial returns, estimated at about 30 percent. Condensed-matter physics work led to the transistor; research on the microwave spectrum of ammonia led to the laser; the study of molecular biology—supported entirely by government basic research funds—led to the whole field of biotechnology.

Nevertheless, other governments approach science and technology with a more commercial focus than we do. Some carefully target key technologies. Ultimately, these strategies have paid off in the international marketplace. Most of our R&D budget goes to defense applications or to support basic science while, since the early 1980s, our federal R&D budget for civilian technology has stagnated. Unfortunately, U.S. companies overall have not picked up the slack; since 1990, their expenditures on R&D have remained flat, whereas those of Japanese companies have grown at a rate of 10 percent per year. We will continue to lose market share in high-technology sectors unless we invest not only in critical technologies development but also in the machinery, plant, and equipment to meet the market requirements for sophisticated volume products.

THE CRISIS IN FEDERAL INSTITUTIONS

There's something wrong in Washington. Our nation's federal institutions were once regarded as a vital source of strength. Today, a disenchanted electorate views Washington with increasing cynicism and mistrust. The growing gap between our public servants and the public itself signals a potential crisis of confidence that cannot be ignored.

The lack of confidence in our government institutions has at least three sources. First, the problems facing the country are extremely difficult to solve and require that politicians make hard choices. Unfortunately, politicians avoid taking these choices and voters don't hold them accountable. For example, regarding the budget deficit, . . . former Director of the Congressional Budget Office Rudy Penner writes:

> The basic problem is quite simple. It is fun to live on borrowed money. Deficit reduction brings nothing but pain in the short run, either in the form of higher taxes or less generous programs. No process can make painful options completely pain-less. Although process reforms may help at the margin, no such reforms can guaran-tee a solution to the deficit problem. It will take some courageous politicians to do that.

The second reason underlying the current malaise about government has to do with government's posture toward business and the economy. Despite rhetoric to the contrary, it is not clear that the federal government has accepted the notion that furthering the competitiveness of U.S. industries is one of its principal missions or that the coordination of economic policies and programs is desirable. Economic policymaking and program implementation [are] dis-persed among many federal agencies and many congressional committees. [They do] not always get the attention from the president that [they deserve], and no one agency has the lead on issues that could roughly be characterized as "competitiveness issues." For example, 12 different agencies distribute civilian R&D funds. Depending on the issue, up to 20 different federal agencies make policy on international trade, only loosely coordinated by the U.S. Trade Representative's office.

Critics of the current policymaking process argue that it does not reflect the economic priorities of the nation and has caused business to view government more as an adversary than an ally. . . . Hank Greenberg, CEO of American International Group, argues:

> It is clear that the problems the United States faces include burdensome regulation and, in many cases, mindless regulation ill-suited to a world-class market economy, a fiscal policy that has driven the country to the brink of financial weakness, a litigiousness matched nowhere else in the world, and an inconsistency in trade policy that confuses American companies while providing our foreign competitors with significant advantages in world markets.

A symptom of our society's current problems in making sound economic policy is its excessive reliance on expensive and ruinous litigation to solve everything from labor relations to environmental liability—more than 18,400,000 lawsuits were filed in 1990 alone. We need to rethink the policymaking process itself and the kinds of legislation and regulations that are created if we are to reverse that trend. One of the most horrendous examples is the Federal Superfund program, designed to clean up America's toxic waste sites. Superfund has been a gold mine for lawyers and consultants, but cleanup has been completed at fewer than 5 percent of the nation's 1,200 most dangerous waste sites. Why? Because an enormous amount of time and money has been spent in arguing over who should pay for the cleanup. While there is a legitimate role for regulation in society, well intentioned but badly conceived programs merely invite mass litigation, rather than accomplish their worthy goals.

Thus, in their relations with government, U.S. business faces formidable obstacles to productivity, profitability, and competitiveness. American companies have been hampered by the lack of a coordinated approach to economic policymaking and by late and inadequate consultations about proposed government policies and regulations. One of the tests for proposed regulations and legislation should be the impact they will have on the competitiveness of industry and on the vitality of the economy. But business is too seldom given a chance to ponder that test.

Finally, and for a variety of reasons, it has become increasingly difficult to attract good people to government. In the 1950s and 1960s, more people viewed government careers as meaningful public service. Public and private salaries for entry-level professionals were nearly the same. Since the late 1970s, however, every presidential candidate has run on a platform "against Washington." The notion of public service is scoffed at. Salaries reflect the changed attitude: Although pay reform legislation passed in 1990 acted as a corrective in some cases, the gap between public and private sector entry-level salaries for certain professions is still vast. The gap between public salaries for cabinet and subcabinet officials and their private sector counterparts is a yawning chasm, making it more and more difficult to attract excellent people to government.

Those of us on the commission who focus on domestic issues believe that the trends outlined on the preceding pages do not bode well for the long-term economic growth and social cohesion of our country or for the standard of living of most of our citizens. Those of us on the commission who are from the foreign policy community are also concerned: The global influence of the United States ultimately rests on the strength of the U.S. economy. Our current course will most certainly not contribute to our economic strength and may ultimately cause its slow and steady erosion during the next decade. No international strategy can compensate for weaknesses at home. We have seen this illustrated all too vividly in the Soviet Union.

. . . America has the talent, resources, ingenuity, and staying power to turn the situation around. What we need is a broad-based understanding of the reality behind our problems, the civic determination and political will to address them, and a plan of action, built on a consensus among our citizens, to confront them, full on.

2. PUBLIC OPINION AND FOREIGN POLICY: ATTITUDE STRUCTURES OF OPINION LEADERS AFTER THE COLD WAR

Ole R. Holsti

Many questions about the role of public opinion in foreign policy are at the center of persisting debates between the liberal and realist approaches to foreign affairs. Is public opinion a force for enlightenment—indeed, a necessary if not sufficient condition for sound foreign policy—as celebrated by the Wilsonians and other liberals? A long liberal tradition, dating back at least to Kant and Bentham, tends to emphasize that the foreign policies of democracies are more peaceful, at least in part because the public can play a constructive role in constraining policymakers; only accountability to the public can restrain the war-making proclivities of leaders.

Alternatively, are Alexis de Tocqueville, Hans Morgenthau, Walter Lippmann, George F. Kennan, and other realists correct in describing public opinion as a barrier to any thoughtful and coherent diplomacy, hindering efforts to promote national interests that transcend the moods and passions of the moment? The realist tradition is intensely skeptical of the public's contribution to effective foreign policy. At the very minimum, most realists would distinguish between foreign policy and other public policy issues; the public might be sufficiently informed to deal with local issues that impinge on their daily lives, but foreign affairs are too remote from their experiences, and in any case the public has little inclination to become more informed about such complex and remote issues. Finally, the effective conduct of diplomacy requires secrecy, flexibility, and other qualities which would be seriously jeopardized were the public to have a significant impact on foreign policy. Thus, to permit the public a strong voice in policy would be to place the democracies, if not stability of the international system itself, at a distinct disadvantage.

Moreover, it would permit the emotional to govern the rational. Hans Morgenthau summarized the case against an active role for public opinion in words that would gain the support of most if not all realists: "The rational requirements of good foreign policy cannot from the outset count upon the support of a public opinion whose preferences are emotional rather than rational" (Morgenthau 1978, 558).

Debates between liberals and realists have always gained intensity in times of profound turmoil and change. President Wilson's hopes for a new post–World War I international order depended significantly on democratizing foreign affairs and diplomacy. Elihu Root, a distinguished Republican and former secretary of state, effectively summarized the position of those who welcomed an increasing role for the public in the conduct of foreign affairs.

When foreign offices were ruled by autocracies or oligarchies the danger of war was in sinister purpose. When foreign affairs are ruled by democracies the danger of war will be in mistaken beliefs. The world will be gainer by the change, for, while there is no human way to prevent a king from having a bad heart, there is a human way to prevent a people from having an erroneous opinion (Root 1922, 5).

By more effective international education, "the people themselves will have the means to test information and appeals to prejudice and passion based on error" (Root 1922, 5).

World War II renewed that debate, but the events leading up to that conflict and the Cold War that emerged almost immediately after the guns had stopped firing in 1945 seemed to provide ample evidence to tip the balance in favor of the realist vision of international relations, including its highly skeptical view of public opinion. Realists who felt that an irresponsible American isolationism after 1919 had contributed to the outbreak of World War II worried that the public mood might trace out a pattern resembling the experience of the period after World War I: wartime idealism and internationalism, followed soon thereafter by cynicism and disenchantment with active American leadership in efforts to create a more stable international order.

The period encompassing World War II and its immediate aftermath coincided with the inception of scientific public opinion polling. The availability of survey date and the institution of systematic studies of voting behavior, combined with assumption of a leadership role in world affairs by the United States, served to stimulate a growth industry in analyses of public opinion. In part because the growing body of survey data yielded ample and consistent evidence of the public's limited factual knowledge about foreign affairs, the consensus that developed during this period of some fifteen or twenty years after the end of World War II and just prior to the Vietnam escalation centered on three major propositions:

- Public opinion is highly volatile and thus it provides very dubious foundations for a sound foreign policy.
- Public attitudes on foreign affairs are so lacking in structure and coherence that they might best be described as "nonattitudes."

- At the end of the day, however, public opinion has a very limited impact on the conduct of foreign policy.

However, just as World War II and the fears of postwar isolationism among the mass public gave rise to concern about public opinion and its impact on foreign policy, the war in Vietnam was a major catalyst in stimulating a reexamination of the consensus that had emerged during the two decades after World War II. The Vietnam War had at least two direct effects. Most *broadly*, many of those who had believed that a stronger executive hand on the tiller of public policy, relatively free from the whims and vagaries of public moods, best serves both national interests and global stability, came to reexamine their views in the light of the Vietnam War. At a *narrower* level, some critics of the war became increasingly persuaded that the Gallup, Harris, and other commercial polls distorted public attitudes toward the war by posing excessively restrictive and simplistic questions. For example, among the most widely asked questions was whether respondents supported or opposed current American policy in Vietnam; deeper probes that might have offered respondents an opportunity to express their views about other policy options were far less commonly employed by these polling organizations. Thus, in addition to secondary analyses of survey data relating to the war, the conflict in Southeast Asia also stimulated independent surveys designed specifically to assess foreign policy in greater depth and breadth than the typical survey conducted by the major polling organizations.

Armed with growing central archives of data generated by the major polling organizations as well as evidence produced by the independent surveys, during the past two decades analysts have begun to challenge important aspects of the consensus described above. Moreover, the scope of surveys has broadened to fill one of the glaring gaps in public opinion research—the neglect of opinion leaders. Virtually all approaches to government—from theories that view the United States as a pluralist democracy to those that depict it as a pseudodemocracy ruled by self-perpetuating elites who seek to use foreign policy as an instrument of narrow, class-based interests—recognize the disproportionate influence of some citizens. At least since Almond's seminal study of *The American People and Foreign Policy* (1950), it has been customary to distinguish between various strata of the public. Typically a distinction has been drawn between opinion leaders, the informed public, and the mass or uninformed public, although the precise terms and the shape of the distribution among strata may vary from study to study. But only rarely had systematic studies of respondents in the top strata been undertaken. Until the first of the Chicago Council on Foreign Relations surveys in 1974—followed by similar studies in 1978, 1982, 1986, and 1990 (Rielly 1975, 1979, 1983, 1987, 1991)—and the Foreign Policy Leadership Project (FPLP) surveys instituted two years later, there was relatively little systematic information about leadership views on foreign affairs.

In summary, the consensus of the mid-1960s on the nature, structure, and impact of public opinion has clearly come under vigorous challenge during the past quarter century. The Vietnam War, while not the sole causal factor in the reexamination of the conventional wisdom, was certainly a catalyst. However, because so much of our evidence on these questions has emerged from a four-decade-long period in which foreign affairs were dominated by the Cold War, we need to address questions about whether and how the end of that confrontation may affect or even render obsolete what we have learned about public opinion and foreign policy. At the most obvious level, there has been a sea change in public attitudes toward virtually all of the issues that dominated the Cold War era. Indeed, one could make a plausible case that in many respects changing public attitudes *preceded* rather than followed those at the pinnacles of government on such issues as the appropriate level of defense spending, the primary threats to American national security, assessments of Mikhail Gorbachev's goals, and the motivations underlying Soviet foreign policy (Americans Talk Security [ATS] surveys, 1988; Holsti 1991). For example, well before the demolition of the Berlin Wall or the final collapse of the U.S.S.R., the public ranked the danger to American national security from the "Soviet aggression around the world" in seventh place, just behind the greenhouse effect (ATS 9, 51–54).

The Foreign Policy Leadership Surveys, 1976–1992

There is also evidence that recent events have had an impact on the foreign policy view of opinion leaders, including those who participated in the FPLP surveys. These studies have been conducted by means of a mailed questionnaire every four years since 1976. The sample for each survey, representing leaders in a wide range of occupations—including politics, business, the military, the media, the State Department and Foreign Service, labor unions, churches, academia, law, and health care—was drawn in part from such standard sources as *Who's Who in America, Who's Who in American Women, Who's Who in American Politics,* and the *State Department Directory.* Others were included by virtue of their positions in specific institutions; for example, membership in the current class at the National War College, chief editorial writers of newspapers with a circulation of 100,000 or more, and labor union officers. The most recent survey, undertaken in March 1992, yielded responses to a sixteen-page questionnaire on domestic and foreign policy issues from 2,312 opinion leaders. This represents a return rate of 58 percent.

Each of the FPLP surveys has included a cluster of questions asking leaders to rate the importance of several foreign policy goals. The results, summarized in Table 2.1, indicate clearly that most respondents believe the Cold War to be over. Not even one leader in five accorded a "very important" rating to the two goals most closely related to the Cold War—matching Russian military power (Table 2.1, question P) and containment (2.1-Q)—and these received the lowest rating of the seventeen goals. Two other interesting points emerge from Table 2.1. There was a sharp increase in support for the United Nations (2.1-C); no doubt this response reflects, at least in part, the role that the U.N. Security Council played during the Persian Gulf War. The 1992 responses also revealed declining support for several economic goals, including two with

Table 2.1. The Importance of Foreign Policy Goals as Assessed by American Opinion Leaders, 1976–1992

	Percent Responding "Very important"				
Please indicate how much importance should be attached to each goal	1976 (N = 2,282)	1980 (N = 2,502)	1984 (N = 2,515)	1988 (N = 2,226)	1992 (N = 2,312)
World order security issues					
A. Preventing the spread of nuclear weapons	—	—	—	—	87
B. Worldwide arms control	66	55	70	68	73
C. Strengthening the United Nations	25	32	27	27	44
D. Protecting weaker nations against aggression	18	23	—	—	28
World order economic issues					
E. Fostering international cooperation to solve common problems, such as food, inflation, and energy	70	73	66	70	71
F. Protecting the global environment	—	47	53	69	66
G. Combatting world hunger	51	51	56	57	55
H. Helping to improve the standard of living in less developed countries	38	44	59	51	43

U.S. economic interests

I. Securing adequate supplies of energy	72	78	84	75	68
J. Reducing the U.S. trade deficit with other countries	—	—	—	63	49
K. Protecting the jobs of American workers	31	30	—	36	32
L. Protecting the interests of American business abroad	14	19	22	—	24

U.S. values and institutions issues

M. Promoting and defending human rights in other countries	—	27	33	39	38
N. Helping to bring a democratic form of government to other nations	7	10	18	25	23

Cold War/security issues

O. Defending our allies' security	37	44	47	51	34
P. Matching Soviet military power*	—	—	40	33	18
Q. Containing communism	39	41	38	37	13

* "Russian" instead of "Soviet" in 1992

strongly protectionist overtones—protecting American jobs (2.1-K) and business interests abroad (2.1-L). Protectionism is one of several foreign policy issues on which leaders—typically supporters of free trade—differ from the general public, which has become increasingly skeptical of free trade during the past two decades.

The Structure of Foreign Policy Beliefs

The end of the Cold War raises some questions not only about the *substance* of foreign policy concerns, as in Table 2.1, but also about the *structure* of foreign policy attitudes. A good deal of evidence indicates that assessments of the Soviet Union have played a key role in foreign policy belief structures (Hurwitz and Peffley 1990; Wittkopf, 1986, 1990). What, then, will be the effect of the disintegration of the Soviet Union? Will it result in a loss of coherence and consequent disorientation about foreign affairs for many Americans? Alternatively, are the key concepts that structure beliefs about foreign affairs sufficiently generic that they will survive the dramatic international changes of the past few years? The remainder of this chapter addresses these questions by examining some data from the 1992 FPLP surveys of American opinion leaders.

A series of studies of public opinion on foreign affairs by Wittkopf (1986, 1990) demonstrated that attitudes toward two dimensions—support or oppose *militant internationalism* (MI) and *cooperative internationalism* (CI)—provide an effective way of describing the belief structures of both elites and mass publics. Dichotomizing and crossing these dimensions yield four types, with the cells labeled as *hard-liners* (support MI, oppose CI), *accommodationists* (oppose MI, support CI), *internationalists* (support both MI and CI), and *isolationists* (oppose both MI and CI). Analyses of previous FPLP surveys supported Wittkopf's findings; the MI/CI scheme effectively describes core elements in leaders' beliefs about international affairs (Holsti and Rosenau, 1990). Knowing respondents' placement on the MI and CI dimensions provides a powerful predictor of attitudes toward a broad array of international issues. Seven questionnaire items focusing on military and strategic perspectives were used to develop an MI scale, and another seven questions dealing with such nonmilitary issues as Third World development, the United Nations, and economic cooperation served to define a CI scale. The 2,312 opinion leaders were then classified according to their responses to these fourteen questions, with the following results: *accommodationists* (53 percent), *internationalists* (33 percent), *hard-liners* (9 percent), and *isolationists* (6 percent).

We can now rephrase the questions posed above: Does the MI/CI scheme continue to provide a useful framework for describing and distinguishing among foreign policy beliefs, or has its effectiveness been eroded by the end of the Cold War? The answer will be sought in responses to four clusters of questions in the 1992 FPLP survey relating to perceived national security threats, U.S. international interests and roles, specific international commitments, and appropriate means for the pursuit of foreign policy goals.

FINDINGS

Future Threats to U.S. National Security

Evidence from a number of surveys has shown that even before the disintegration of the Soviet Union, much of the American public was inclined to focus on threats to national security other than those arising from the Soviet Union or traditional Cold War issues. The 1992 FPLP questionnaire asked respondents to assess the seriousness of thirteen potential threats to American national security during the remaining years of the century. The threats are not limited to traditional security concerns, as they include military, economic, social, environmental, demographic, and domestic issues (Table 2.2). Three of them were rated as "extremely serious" by more than half of the entire leadership sample: nuclear proliferation (2.2-A), an inability to deal with various domestic problems (2.2-B), and the federal budget deficit (2.2-C). The data also reveal a rather striking absence of a comparable concern about economic competition from Japan and Europe (2.2-K).

Responses of the four groups reveal that differences among them are significant on all threats. They also indicate that most of the intergroup differences sustain the potency of the MI/CI scheme. The two nuclear weapons issues (2.2-A, 2.2-I) and international drug trafficking (2.2-D) (defined by some as an issue for which there can be an effective military solution) elicited the highest concern from the *hard-liners* and *internationalists;* responses to another military issue, relating to unwise U.S. interventions abroad (2.2-L), fit the expected pattern less clearly.

Assessments of four economic–social issues that can only be resolved by international cooperation—the rich nation–poor nation gap (2.2-G), population growth (2.2-F), the environment (2.2-E), and the greenhouse effect (2.2-H)—also sustained the MI/CI scheme. Strongest concern in each case was expressed by the *accommodationists* and *internationalists.* Finally, as would be expected, except for nuclear proliferation, the *isolationists* focused largely on domestic threats, and they typically registered the lowest level of concern with the potential external threats, be they environmental, social, or military.

Thus, the group responses summarized in Table 2.2 generally support the MI/CI scheme. However, the perceived threats arising from trade competition (2.2-K) and the Middle East conflict (2.2-J) do not fit this pattern very well. Earlier studies have also shown that questions relating to trade/protectionism and the Israeli/Middle East conflicts typically yield reactions that are largely independent of partisan, ideological, or other classifications of respondents, including the MI/CI scheme.

U.S. International Interests and Roles

Much of the foreign policy debate of the past few years has focused on the proper role for the United States in a world transformed. When asked to assess American interests and roles in the post–Cold War international system, there is little evidence of support among opinion leaders for an indis-

Table 2.2. Predictions of Future National Security Threats by Opinion Leaders in 1992: Isolationists, Hard-Liners, Accommodationists, and Internationalists

This question asks you to evaluate the seriousness of the following issues as threats to American national security during the remaining years of this century. Please indicate how serious you regard each possible threat	Percent Responding "Extremely Serious"				
	All Leaders (N = 2,312)	Isolationists (N = 120)	Hard-Liners (N = 216)	Accommodationists (N = 1,222)	Internationalists (N = 754)
A. The possession of nuclear weapons by Third World countries and terrorists	62	51	68	54	75
B. An inability to solve such domestic problems as the decay of cities, homelessness, unemployment, racial conflict, and crime	60	47	31	68	57
C. The federal budget deficit	54	43	54	51	60
D. International drug trafficking	41	24	40	33	56
E. Environmental problems like air pollution and water contamination	40	14	15	47	37

F. Uncontrolled growth of the world's population	37	20	23	44	34
G. A growing gap between rich nations and poor nations	27	7	6	36	21
H. The greenhouse effect and other changes in the global climate induced by human activity	27	8	8	33	24
I. Nuclear weapons in republics that seceded from the former Soviet Union	25	15	30	19	34
J. Armed conflicts in the Middle East	16	11	13	15	19
K. Economic competition from Japan and Europe	14	17	22	10	19
L. American interventions in conflicts that are none of our business	13	10	8	16	9
M. Mass migrations	10	4	13	8	13

criminate retrenchment into isolationism. Over 90 percent of the opinion leaders agreed (2.3-A) that "the United States should be as ready to form economic and diplomatic coalitions to cope with the world's problems of hunger and poverty as it is to leading military coalitions against aggressors." Although a majority in all four groups favored such a role for the U.S., by far the strongest support came from the *internationalists* and *accommodationists*. Conversely, leaders in these two groups were least enthusiastic about Patrick Buchanan's dictum (2.3-I) that "What we need is a new foreign policy that puts America first, and second and third as well." Responses to both of these questions are highly consistent with the MI/CI scheme.

Four additional propositions in Table 2.3 that probe further for various aspects of isolationism received rather limited support. Only about a third of the respondents agreed that the U.S. should "concentrate more on our own national problems" (2.3-G), and an even smaller proportion supported the view that its vital interests are limited to the industrial democracies and nations in this hemisphere (2.3-H). Propositions indicating that U.S. international interests are limited to questions of international peace and stability (2.3-K) and that Third World conflicts cannot jeopardize those interests (2.3-L) gained the agreement of fewer than one respondent in six. Although the *isolationists* were generally most supportive of retrenchment, the differences across the four groups are rather muted, as they were on another item related to the Third World—that the U.S. can best promote democratic development by solving its own problems (2.3-D).

Several other questions focus on the *type* of international role that the U.S. should play. A slight majority stated that the U.S. should scale down its leadership role (2.3-C), but only about two-fifths of the leaders agreed that "the U.S. is no superpower" (2.3-F). Predictably, both propositions drew substantially greater support than the two groups defined by opposition to militant internationalism—the *isolationists* and *accommodationists*—and far less from the *internationalists* and *hard-liners*. Precisely the opposite pattern emerged in response to the proposition that the U.S. is "the dominant power" of the post–Cold War world (2.3-B), providing further support for the MI/CI scheme.

Finally, two questions with strong realpolitik overtones addressed the appropriate goals for the projection of American power abroad. The leadership sample divided almost evenly in its preferences if faced with a trade-off between supporting international stability and self-determination movements (2.3-E), but fewer than one leader in five favored intervention into the domestic affairs of other countries in support of a more democratic world order (2.3-J). (The latter finding is consistent with the data reported in Table 2.1: Few opinion leaders attach great importance to exporting American institutions.) As one would expect, the *hard-liners* and *internationalists* expressed significantly stronger support for both propositions than did leaders in the other two groups.

Specific International Commitments and Policies

As indicated above, few opinion leaders support a wholesale U.S. retrenchment from involvement in international affairs. Those taking part in the 1992 surveys were also asked to assess some specific U.S. commitments and actions (Table 2.4). Striking evidence of the impact of recent events is the fact that virtually all opinion leaders—96 percent—now support providing assistance to America's Cold War adversary (2.4-A). As predicted by the MI/CI scheme, *accommodationists* and *internationalists* were most supportive of an aid program to the former Soviet Union, but even the statistically significant difference among the four groups pales in comparison to the consensus supporting such assistance.

Five of the items in Table 2.4 focus on U.S. security commitments to Israel (2.4-B), South Korea (2.4-C), Taiwan (2.4-E), and Saudi Arabia (2.4-F), and the 1989 invasion of Panama to arrest Manuel Noriega (2.4-D). According to the MI/CI scheme, *hard-liners* and *internationalists*—supporters of militant internationalism—should provide significantly higher support for these undertakings than those in the other two groups. The data provide strong support for the MI/CI scheme with respect to South Korea, Taiwan, Saudi Arabia, and Panama, but the fit is less clear for the proposition that "the United States has a moral obligation to prevent the destruction of the state of Israel." Although the *isolationists* were predictably the least enthusiastic about this commitment, evidence from the previous four FPLP surveys also indicated that support for Israel cuts across partisan and ideological lines and did not fit the MI/CI scheme very well. Finally a proposal to withdraw all U.S. troops from Europe (2.4-G) should have the greatest appeal to opponents of militant internationalism—the *accommodationists* and *isolationists*. The pattern of responses confirms that expectation.

Foreign Policy Means

Table 2.5 summarizes responses to eleven questions about the means that the United States may use in pursuit of its international interests and goals. Five of them express support for military instruments of policy, four oppose such means for pursuing international goals, and two others favor cooperative strategies of statecraft.

Assessments of military means by opinion leaders generally yield a pattern consistent with the MI/CI scheme. As predicted, *hard-liners* and *internationalists* provided the strongest support for applying force in a short period of time rather than by a policy of graduated escalation (2.5-A), striking at "the heart of the opponent's power" (2.5-D), maintaining substantial military forces during the post–Cold War era (2.5-G), supporting friendly dictators (2.5-I), and letting military rather than political goals determine how force is to be used (2.5-K). It should be noted, however, that leaders in *all* groups opposed a policy of graduated escalation, a strategy which is often associated with the failures of the Vietnam War; moreover, only *accommodationists* expressed opposition to alignment with some friendly dictators.

With one exception, the four items expressing a critical view of military approaches to policy also conform to the expectations of the MI/CI scheme. *Accommodationists* and *isolationists* expressed the strongest support for propositions that the efficacy of military power is declining (2.5-E), U.S.

Table 2.3. Beliefs About American International Roles and Interests Among Opinion Leaders in 1992: Isolationists, Hard-Liners, Accommodationists, and Internationalists

Please indicate how strongly you agree or disagree with each statement	Percent Who Agree Strongly or Agree Somewhat				
	All Leaders (N = 2,312)	Isolationists (N = 120)	Hard-Liners (N = 216)	Accommodationists (N = 1,222)	Internationalists (N = 754)
A. The United States should be as ready to form economic and diplomatic coalitions to cope with the world's problems of hunger and poverty as it is to leading military coalitions against aggressors	92	74	65	96	92
B. The United States is the dominant power of the post–Cold War world and is capable of channeling the course of change toward a new world order	65	46	72	56	59
C. America's conception of its leadership role must be scaled down	57	57	30	73	38
D. The best way to encourage democratic development in the Third World is for the U.S. to solve its own problems	56	57	59	57	55
E. The U.S. should exercise its power in such a way as to assure continuing stability in world affairs even at the cost of denying self-determination to some groups	52	57	70	42	62

F. Although its power is greater relative to other countries, the U.S. is no superpower and it ought not act as if it is	38	36	18	49	26
G. We shouldn't think so much in international terms but concentrate more on our own national problems	35	48	42	32	34
H. Vital interests of the U.S. are largely confined to Western Europe, Japan, and the Americas	29	34	34	26	31
I. What we need is a new foreign policy that puts America first, and second and third as well	23	39	50	11	33
J. The U.S. should not hesitate to intrude upon the domestic affairs of other countries in order to establish and preserve a more democratic world order	19	16	28	12	28
K. The U.S. should only be involved in world affairs to the extent that its military power is needed to maintain international peace and stability	15	23	22	12	17
L. Third World conflicts cannot jeopardize vital American interests	14	15	17	14	14

Table 2.4. Assessments of Specific International Undertakings and Commitments by Opinion Leaders in 1992: Isolationists, Hard-Liners, Accommodationists, and Internationalists

Please indicate how strongly you agree or disagree with each policy or statement	Percent Who Agree Strongly or Agree Somewhat				
	All Leaders (N = 2,312)	Isolationists (N = 120)	Hard-Liners (N = 216)	Accommodationists (N = 1,222)	Internationalists (N = 754)
A. Providing food and other assistance to the former Soviet Union	96	91	87	98	95
B. The U.S. has a moral obligation to prevent the destruction of the state of Israel	66	48	61	66	69
C. The U.S. should maintain its military commitment to South Korea	61	54	72	51	76
D. Invading Panama to remove Manuel Noriega from power	49	53	79	30	71
E. The U.S. has a moral obligation to prevent the military conquest of Taiwan	48	36	54	39	62
F. The U.S. should maintain a permanent military presence in the Middle East in order to protect the oil fields of such friendly nations as Saudi Arabia	48	41	62	35	65
G. The U.S. should bring home all of its troops stationed in Europe	42	45	38	50	29

policy relies excessively on military advice (2.5-F), and military aid programs will draw the U.S. into unnecessary wars (2.5-J). The exception to this pattern emerges from the item that "stationing troops abroad encourages other countries to let us do their fighting for them" (2.5-C). As in most previous FPLP surveys, this proposition garnered considerable support from opinion leaders in all four groups, and the magnitude of differences in their responses is not statistically significant.

Finally, the two items that propose cooperative approaches—diplomacy and negotiation rather than military force (2.5-B), and strengthening the UN and other international organizations (2.5-H)—should draw the strongest support from *accommodationists* and *internationalists,* the two groups defined as supporters of CI. The data provide exceptionally strong support for the MI/CI scheme; not only are the group responses as predicted, but the magnitude of differences between them are very large, reaching a range of more than 50 percent on both questions.

CONCLUSION

The questions posed above hinged on the extent to which the end of the Cold War has altered the structure of beliefs about international affairs. The evidence presented in Tables 2.2 to 2.5 indicates, on balance, that positions on militant and cooperative internationalism, yielding four distinct types, continue to provide an effective way of organizing attitudes on a broad range of issues. From one perspective, this may seem an anomaly in the light of the unprecedented international changes of the past few years. From another viewpoint this finding is less surprising. The militant and cooperative internationalism dimensions correspond closely to the venerable theories of international relations cited at the beginning of this chapter: *realism* and *liberalism.* Realism views conflict between nations as a natural state of affairs, either because of human nature (e.g., Morgenthau 1978) or owing to the anarchic structure of the system (e.g., Waltz 1979), rather than as an aberration that is subject to permanent amelioration. Such realist concepts as security dilemma, relative capabilities, and a zero-sum view of conflict are also basic to the militant internationalism dimension. There are similar links between liberalism and the cooperative internationalism dimension. Liberalism denies that conflict is an immutable element of relations between nations. It defines security in terms that are broader than the geopolitical–military spheres, and it emphasizes the potential for cooperative relations among nations. Institution building to reduce uncertainty and fears of perfidy; improved international education and communication to ameliorate fears and antagonisms based on misinformation and misperceptions; and the positive-sum possibilities of such activities as trade are but a few of the ways, according to liberals, by which nations may jointly gain and thus mitigate, if not eliminate, the harshest features of international relations emphasized by the realists. Inasmuch as the debates between these schools of thought predate the Cold War, it is perhaps not so surprising that, in the main, the MI/CI scheme has

Table 2.5. Assessments of Foreign Policy Means by Opinion Leaders in 1992: Isolationists, Hard-Liners, Accommodationists, and Internationalists

Please indicate how strongly you agree or disagree with each statement	Percent Who Agree Strongly or Agree Somewhat				
	All Leaders (N = 2,312)	Isolationists (N = 120)	Hard-Liners (N = 216)	Accommodationists (N = 1,222)	Internationalists (N = 754)
A. If foreign interventions are undertaken, the necessary force should be applied in a short period of time rather than through a policy of graduated escalation	79	85	92	69	90
B. In dealing with major issues of the post–Cold War era, the United States should replace its reliance on military force with a commitment to diplomacy and negotiations	65	37	28	81	53
C. Stationing troops abroad encourages other countries to let us do their fighting for them	65	59	62	67	64
D. Rather than simply countering our opponent's thrusts, it is necessary to strike at the heart of the opponent's power	60	51	86	39	87

E. The efficacy of military power in foreign affairs is declining	59	53	38	70	49
F. The conduct of American foreign policy relies excessively on military advice	57	55	24	74	40
G. The U.S. needs to maintain substantial military force in order to cope with security threats of the post–Cold War era	54	52	82	37	76
H. The time is ripe for the United States and other countries to cede some of their sovereignty to strengthen the powers of the United Nations and other international organizations	50	17	10	65	43
I. The U.S. may have to support some dictators because they are friendly toward us	44	56	69	30	57
J. Military aid programs will eventually draw the United States into unnecessary wars	36	29	21	47	25
K. When force is used, military rather than political goals should determine its application	34	34	56	23	45

continued to identify important elements in the structure of thinking about international affairs.

It must also be acknowledged, however, that the MI/CI scheme is not sufficient to encompass all important aspects of foreign relations. The most notable example of this failure concerns trade and protectionism. Several questions not included in Tables 2.2 to 2.5 reveal that the pattern of responses is poorly predicted by placement in the four quadrants of the MI/CI scheme. Only one-fifth of the opinion leaders agreed with a proposal to erect "trade barriers against foreign goods to protect American industries and jobs," and only among those in one group, the *hard-liners,* did support reach as high as thirty percent. And when asked to choose between two economic growth scenarios—Japan grows at a 6.5 percent annual rate and the United States at 2.5 percent, or Japan grows at 1.1 percent per year and the U.S. at 1 percent— 57 percent of the entire sample preferred the former option even though the latter scenario would ensure that the Japanese could never catch up with the United States. For present purposes, the more important point is that leaders in all four groups favored the high-growth scenario and differences between them were rather narrow and not statistically significant. Although the MI/CI scheme does not adequately predict responses to trade and protectionism, this does *not* represent a post–Cold War change in the structure of foreign policy beliefs. Evidence from earlier FPLP surveys revealed that neither the MI/CI scheme nor such otherwise powerful variables as party and ideology effectively predicted positions on international trade (Holsti and Rosenau 1990).

A third point that emerges from the 1992 survey data is that the most contentious and divisive issues revolve around militant rather than cooperative internationalism. Several reasons come to mind. Recall that more than three-fourths of the entire leadership supports cooperative internationalism; that is, they are classified as either *accommodationists* or *internationalists.* On the other hand, the *hard-liners* and *internationalists*—those who support militant internationalism—constitute a minority. To the extent that one can draw broader conclusions from these figures, they suggest that it may be easier to build domestic coalitions for interventions abroad or other international undertakings that have a tenor of cooperative rather than militant internationalism. The probability of high casualties is also greater in the latter than the former case. This reasoning may offer at least a partial explanation for the (initially) broad support behind "Operation Restore Hope" in Somalia, in contrast to the decidedly more lukewarm enthusiasm for military intervention to restore peace in Bosnia.

The evidence also seems to support those who have portrayed American public opinion as rational and events-driven (e.g., Wittkopf 1990; Page and Shapiro 1992) rather than obsessed by nonrational factors such as the need for external enemies. Although space does not permit a full exploration of what constitutes support for the "rational and events-driven" thesis, the evidence on attitudes toward the former Soviet Union and communism may at least be cited as an illustration of the point. During the 1970s and 1980s, Cold War "axioms" were among the most divisive issues in the often-bitter debates about foreign affairs and America's proper role in the world. The most adamant supporters of Cold War reasoning and skepticism about Soviet intentions and foreign policy behavior were conservatives, Republicans, and *hard-liners*. It must certainly be counted as a sea change when in 1992 members of these overlapping groups supported a policy of U.S. assistance to the former Soviet Union by majorities of 95 percent, 95 percent, and 87 percent, respectively. There is, moreover, little evidence of tendency among opinion leaders to seek out other international adversaries. These findings are, of course, limited to opinion leaders and at best they are suggestive rather than exhaustive. But when combined with similar results from surveys of the mass public (Holsti 1991), they would seem to offer at least a bit of additional evidence for the "rational and events-driven" side in the continuing dialogue on the nature of American opinion on international affairs.

Finally, the evidence presented here may be of more than academic interest. Clearly the end of the Cold War has not brought peace to all parts of the world; it may even have increased the possibilities for the kinds of ethnic and self-determination conflicts that have broken out in the former Yugoslavia. Nevertheless, if we are also entering into a period of fewer major power confrontations and greater attention to such nonmilitary issues as trade, immigration, the environment, and the like—there is ample survey data that much of the American public believes this to be the case—it may also be an era in which public opinion plays a more autonomous role. Crises and confrontations abroad provide a setting in which opportunities and temptations for leaders to manipulate the public are far greater than on nonstrategic issues. Not only are the latter typically resolved over a longer time period, providing greater opportunities for the public, pressure groups, the media, and the Congress to play a significant role, but they also tend to be more resistant to White House claims that the needs for secrecy, flexibility, and speed of action make it both necessary and legitimate for the executive to have a relatively free hand. In short, we may be moving into a period in which the relationship between public opinion and foreign policy takes on added rather than diminished significance.

REFERENCES

Almond, Gabriel. 1950. *The American People and Foreign Policy.* New York: Praeger.
Americans Talk Security. 1988. *Surveys Concerning National Security Issues: Survey No. 9.* Winchester, Mass.: Americans Talk Security.
Holsti, Ole R. 1991. "American Reactions to the USSR: Public Opinion." In Robert Jervis and Seweryn Bialer, eds., *Soviet-American Relations After the Cold War.* Durham, N.C.: Duke University Press.
Holsti, Ole R., and James N. Rosenau. 1990. "The Structure of Foreign Policy Attitudes Among American Leaders." *Journal of Politics* 52 (February):94–125.
Hurwitz, Jon, and Mark Peffley. 1987. "How are Foreign Policy Attitudes Structured? A Hierarchical Model." *American Political Science Review* 81:1099–1120.
Hurwitz, Jon, and Mark Peffley. 1990. "Public Images of the Soviet Union: The Impact of Foreign Policy Attitudes." *Journal of Politics* 52: 3–28.
Morgenthau, Hans J. 1978. *Politics Among Nations.* 5th ed. New York: Knopf.

Page, Benjamin I., and Robert Y. Shapiro. 1992. *The Rational Public*. Chicago: University of Chicago Press.

Rielly, John E., ed. 1975. *American Public Opinion and U.S. Foreign Policy 1975*. Chicago: Chicago Council on Foreign Relations. Also in 1979, 1983, 1987, and 1991.

Root, Elihu. 1922. "A Requisite for the Success of Popular Diplomacy." *Foreign Affairs* 1:3–10.

Waltz, Kenneth. 1979. *Theory of International Politics*. Reading, Mass.: Addison-Wesley.

Wittkopf, Eugene R. 1986. "On the Foreign Policy Beliefs of the American People: A Critique and Some Evidence." *International Studies Quarterly* 30:425–445.

Wittkopf, Eugene R. 1990. *Faces of Internationalism: Public Opinion and American Foreign Policy*. Durham, N.C.: Duke University Press.

3. THE PRETTY PRUDENT PUBLIC: POST POST-VIETNAM AMERICAN OPINION ON THE USE OF MILITARY FORCE

Bruce W. Jentleson

A new "post post-Vietnam" pattern has emerged in which public support for military force is neither as generally strong as during the "Cold War consensus" nor as generally weak as during the "Vietnam trauma," but rather varies according to the *principal policy objective* for which force is used. The key distinction is between force used to coerce *foreign policy restraint* by an adversary engaged in aggressive actions against the United States or its interests, and force used to engineer *internal political change* within another country whether in support of an existing government considered an ally or seeking to overthrow a government considered an adversary. Within the limiting condition of the "halo effect" of quick-strike success,[1] I contend that the American public is much more likely to support the use of force for the restraint rather than the remaking of other governments. . . .

Three central variables can be identified and derived from the general literature on public opinion and foreign policy: (1) *Interests*—support for the use of military force varies according to the importance of the interests at stake; (2) *presidential cues*—support for the use of military force is a function of how effectively presidents evoke the public's inherent inclination to follow their lead; (3) *risk aversion*—public support is inversely correlated to the risks involved, in particular to casualties incurred. . . . Each of these theories helps identify basic patterns in public opinion on the use of military force. All, however, assume a certain nonpurposiveness in public opinion formulation which I question.

The public is said to respond to threats to vital interests, but the prior

Note: Some footnotes have been deleted or renumbered. Bibliographic references not cited in the edited text have been deleted.

question of how it defines which interests are "vital" is not addressed. The concept does have a degree of absoluteness; that is, both George McGovern and Ronald Reagan would consider the security of our own borders a vital interest. But much beyond that, McGovern and Reagan, or John Smith and Jane Doe, are likely to bring widely ranging perceptions to bear. We thus end up in the tautological circle of saying that force will be supported when a vital interest is at stake, and that we know that an interest is vital because force is supported to defend it.

As to presidential cues, to acknowledge elite manipulation must not be to eliminate the possibility of independent and even contrary opinions. In fact, a substantial amount of recent research has shown less strict and simple followership than in the past. The public has been shown to be less inattentive to foreign policy than traditionally portrayed (Aldrich, Sullivan, and Borgida 1989), as having policy preferences which are both stable over time (Shapiro and Page 1988) and internally coherent (Wittkopf 1986), and as being more measured in its reactions even to past Soviet threats than has often been asserted (Nincic 1988).

Nor can strict assumptions of risk aversion be made, not even with regard to casualties. Consider, for example, World War II, in which U.S. casualties were almost four times as high as in Vietnam but public support remained high. Moreover, even in the Korean and Vietnam cases, there may have been other forces at work. Public support for the Vietnam War stayed strong for the first two and a half years of the U.S. troop commitment and through almost 16,000 U.S. combat deaths. "It is difficult to fault the American people," writes Major Andrew F. Krepinevich, Jr. (1986, 270), "or their elected representatives when, after that long a period of active engagement, the Joint Chiefs of Staff only offer more of the same for an indefinite period with no assurance of eventual success."

. . . The alternative argument I propose posits the distinction between foreign policy restraint and internal political change as the principal policy objective for which military force is being used as the key independent variable. . . . Foreign policy restraint involves efforts to affect the external behavior of another state that aggressively threatens the United States, its citizens, or its allies. By "aggressively threatens" I mean more than just a deterrence situation in which an adversary poses an ongoing threat and a standing military posture is maintained. Rather, the threat is a more active one, involving actual and not just potential aggression. The aggression may be directly against the United States or, as has more often been the case, against U.S. allies, U.S. interests (including economic interests), or U.S. citizens (piracy in the past, terrorism in recent years).

The internal political change objective involves intervention in the classical sense, as defined by Oran Young (1968, 177–178) as efforts to influence the domestic "political authority structure" of another state. It may be either in support of an existing government considered an ally (counterinsurgency), or in support of a group that itself is considered an ally against a government considered an adversary (insurgency). It also may be direct through U.S. aid, advisers, and even troops, or it may be indirect through covert activities and/or through surrogates. . . .

. . . The distinction between foreign policy restraint and internal political change is akin to and consistent with William Schneider's (1983, 39) more general explanation of differences in foreign policy support between "valence" and "position" issues. Schneider defines valence issues as involving threats to shared basic values, and thus tending to evoke more consensual public responses, whereas position issues allow for legitimate alternative preferences in values and thus are inclined to a more divisive politics. The pursuit of foreign policy restraint by an aggressor state is more likely to be treated as a valence issue because the threat it poses tends to be more clear and present. Efforts to protect or depose other governments often involve threats based more on ideology promulgated than action taken. . . .

1980s LIMITED MILITARY FORCE CASES

Table 3.1 compares public support for the use of military force in the eight principal 1980s cases as measured by responses to basic support/opposition and approval/disapproval questions. The principal source for the polling data was the *American Public Opinion Index* . . . , supplemented by the *Gallup Opinion Index,* the Roper Organization, the *National Journal, The Washington Post, The New York Times,* and the Inter-University Consortium for Political and Social Research. Mean "support scores" were calculated based on the number of polls indicated in parentheses.

Two intracase distinctions are made in this initial analysis. First, in order to control for the halo effect, polls conducted after the fact (postpolls) were separated out in the Panama and Libya cases from those conducted when the

Table 3.1. Public Support for the Use of Force: 1980s

Case (number of polls)	Mean Public Support	Ranking
Panama		
Postinvasion (4)	82.5%	1
Preinvasion (2)	32	8
Libya		
Postbombing (8)	70.9	2
Prebombing (4)	65.2	3
Grenada postinvasion (13)	62.2	4
Persian Gulf reflagging (12)	55.5	5
Lebanon (37)	45	6
Afghanistan (5)	39	7
El Salvador		
Military aid, advisers (5)	30.5	9
U.S. troops (6)	26.2	11
Nicaragua		
Contra aid (43)	27.3	10
Invasion by U.S. troops (7)	19.7	12

outcome still was uncertain (prepolls). All the polls in the Grenada case were postpolls. Second, when the questions involved substantially different types or levels for using force, as in the El Salvador case with military aid and advisers as one option or U.S. troops as another, and in the Nicaragua case with contra aid or a U.S. invasion, separate intracase calculations were made. The last column gives rankings for each case or case subset by strength of public support as indicated by the mean scores.

Summary of Data

The most extensive public support for the use of military force (#1 ranking) was in the postinvasion polls for the December 1989 invasion of Panama. However, in two preinvasion polls asking about a possible U.S. military action against Noriega, public support averaged only 32 percent (#8 ranking). The April 14, 1986, bombing of Libya received the second highest level of support, again as measured after the fact. Yet in contrast to the Panama case, there was much less of a gap between pre- and postpolls. In four polls conducted between January 7, 1986, and April 13 (the day before the bombing,) the average response was 65.2 percent in support of U.S. military action. This was in fact an even higher level of support than the Grenada postpolls. As noted, there were no preinvasion polls for Grenada. The pollsters evidently were no less surprised than the general public.

The 55.5 percent mean support for the Persian Gulf reflagging policy is higher than often presumed. This was a much more extended and risky commitment than any of the quick-strike-and-out invasions. Yet its support score was almost as high as the halo-affected Grenada. The 45 percent support score for the deployment of the U.S. Marines to Lebanon falls close to the median for the overall set of cases.[2] It also was the most volatile case, with the balance between support and opposition shifting seven times. The Afghanistan case was the most difficult on which to find data. Afghanistan was mentioned in some general Reagan Doctrine questions, but only five Afghanistan-specific polls could be found.

The support scores in the El Salvador and Nicaragua cases drop off markedly. Only 30.5 percent supported the Reagan policy of providing military aid and advisers to the anticommunist government in El Salvador. Moreover, even though the six questions asked about the use of U.S. troops in El Salvador were all posed in worst-case-scenario terms of the government being in danger of falling, only slightly better than one in four respondents were prepared to support the use of U.S. troops even in such crisis circumstances.

The lowest levels of public support were in the Nicaragua case. The forty-three polls on contra aid covered almost six years, from May 1983 to March 1988. Yet the fluctuations were many fewer and much smaller than in other such (and shorter-running) cases like Lebanon. Not once was support greater than opposition. The overall mean was only 27.3 percent. And in the seven polls posing the option of a U.S. invasion, support came from fewer than one in five respondents. . . .

PRINCIPAL POLICY OBJECTIVES EXPLANATION

Panama

There is little question that the use of force in Panama, both as contemplated and as ultimately carried out, had internal political change (i.e., deposing Noriega) as its principal objective. . . . It wasn't until the invasion was a fait accompli that the public came around to supporting the use of force in Panama. This low preinvasion support surely didn't reflect any affinity for Noriega, who ranked up (down?) with the likes of Qaddafi and Khomeini in the American public's rogues' gallery (and against whom force was supported). Nor did the public doubt that important American interests were at stake (the security of the Canal, the war on drugs). And although President Bush never called for the use of force until he had actually done it, a position of not supporting but not ruling something out is surely an ambiguous cue. Thus, if the American public was ever to support the use of force for internal political change, here were rather conducive conditions. But support came only after the fact, and when it did, it clearly was the work of the halo effect.

Libya

While both objectives were present in the Libyan bombing case, the principal one was foreign policy restraint—more specifically, antiterrorism. To be sure, had the bombing played upon existing internal tensions within the Libyan military and spurred a coup, or had Qaddafi himself been a casualty, it would have been less than happenstance. But the context at the time was a dire sense of crisis over terrorism, which even the rather sober, London-based International Institute for Strategic Studies (IISS) characterized as "a growth industry" (IISS 1986, 19). The number of terrorist incidents had gone up dramatically, Americans were increasingly being targeted, and evidence of Qaddafi's hand was repeatedly there, most especially in the April 5, 1986, bombing of a West Berlin discotheque. There also were unconfirmed reports of plans by Qaddafi to launch a major terrorist campaign within the United States proper, including a plot to assassinate President Reagan (Oakley 1986, 617; Woodward 1987, 166–167, 181–187).

As indicated by the high prepoll support score in Table 3.1, the public did not need the halo effect to be supportive of force intended to restrain a terrorist state. Four of the eight prebombing polls phrased their questions in terms of U.S. military action as a response to Libyan terrorism. Their 65.2 percent mean score was not all that much less than the 70.9 percent postbombing support.

As a further indicator, Table 3.2 presents support score data disaggregated by policy objectives. Six questions specifically asked about support for using force to overthrow or assassinate Qaddafi (i.e., for internal political change). A 1981 poll showed only 25 percent supportive of a CIA plot, and only 10 percent of a U.S. invasion. A March 25, 1986, poll, in the wake of the Gulf of Sidra military skirmishes, found only 15 percent support for a U.S. invasion

Table 3.2. Libya: Support Scores by Policy Objectives

Question	Percent Who Support
Internal Political Change	
(a) CIA covert action to overthrow Qaddafi (12/81)	25
(b) U.S. invasion to overthrow Qaddafi (12/81)	10
(c) Assassinate Qaddafi (3/86)	20
(d) U.S. invasion to overthrow Qaddafi (3/86)	15
(e) Assassinate Qaddafi (4/86)	38
(f) U.S. invasion to overthrow Qaddafi (4/86)	46
Foreign Policy Restraint	
(g) Military actions for reasons of antiterrorism (Table 3.1, prepolls)	65.2
(h) April 14, 1986, bombing (Table 3.1, postpolls)	70.9
(i) Bomb again, if Libya continues (4/22/86)	80
(j) Bomb Syria or Iran, if they are proven to sponsor terrorism (4/22/86)	64
(k) Launch military attacks against other countries sponsoring terrorism (5/86)	52
(l) Bomb Libya's suspected chemical weapons factory (1/89)	67

Sources: (a), (b) Harris; (c), (d) ABC News; (e), (f), (k), (l) *Wall Street Journal*–NBC News; (i), (j) Gallup–*Newsweek*.

and only 20 percent support for an assassination attempt. Support did go up in the immediate wake of the April 1986 bombing, but only to 38 percent for an assassination attempt and 46 percent for a U.S. invasion. The latter figure was not insignificant, but was still less than the 48 percent who opposed an invasion and well less than the 72 percent who in the same poll approved the bombing.

In addition to the polls already reported in Table 3.1 (entries (g) and (h) in Table 3.2), the much higher levels of support linked to foreign policy restraint objectives can also be seen in other questions. When asked, "If Libya continues to sponsor terrorism against the United States, should we bomb again?", 80 percent said yes. When asked whether such military action should also be taken against Syria or Iran if the allegations of state-sponsored terrorism were proved against either, 64 percent said yes. When asked more generally about states (unspecified) sponsoring terrorism, 52 percent said yes. And later, when Qaddafi was discovered building a chemical weapons plant, raising another foreign policy restraint issue, 67 percent supported a military attack to destroy it.

Grenada

Grenada is a difficult case in two respects. First, since all the data are from postpolls, it is impossible to separate the effects of any other factors from the halo effect. Second, there is both complexity and ambiguity in the policy objectives. The Reagan administration stressed foreign policy restraint objectives: rescue the American medical students, respond to the Organization of East Caribbean States (OECS) security request, limit Soviet and Cuban influence. Administration critics, however, stressed the internal political change objective: invading a Latin American country, in the long tradition of the Monroe Doctrine and Cold War containment, to overthrow an unfriendly government. But the position reasoning of the public appears from the available survey data to have largely accepted the foreign policy restraint argument. For example, a *Newsweek* poll (11/7/83) found 69 percent agreeing that protecting the lives of Americans justified the invasion, but only 48 percent accepting overthrowing the "Marxist revolutionaries" as justification. A CBS–*New York Times* poll (10/27/83) found 67 percent believing Cuba was building a base there, and 54 percent that Grenada posed a security threat to other Caribbean nations. A Harris poll (11/3/83) found 75 percent citing Cuban plans to build a base as justification for the invasion, and 61 percent citing the security threat to other Caribbean nations. Two ABC polls (10/28/83, 11/7/83) found only 15–17 percent believing the administration was overstating Soviet influence, and only 10 percent believing that it was overstating Cuban influence.

One might be tempted to argue on this basis that to the extent that an administration can manipulate public perceptions to focus on foreign policy restraint objectives, even when its own principal objective might be internal political change, it can gain public support. But before the possibilities of opinion manipulation are generalized too far, we will need to consider Nicaragua.

Persian Gulf Reflagging

This was the clearest case among the 1980s cases of foreign policy restraint as the principal objective. The earlier Reagan–North–McFarlane gambit of arms for hostages, and birthday cakes to ostensible moderates, had been an effort of a different sort to meddle in internal Iranian politics. But the principal objective of the policy of reflagging Kuwaiti oil tankers and the accompanying increased naval deployment in the Persian Gulf was to restrain Iranian foreign policy aggression. Everything else—keeping the sea-lanes open and the oil flowing; preempting gains the Soviet Union could have made if it had been the only protector available to Kuwait and other Gulf states against Iran; restoring U.S. credibility in the region after Lebanon and the Iran–contra affair; and ending the Iran–Iraq war—flowed from and back to the need to contain Iran.

The fact that public support was as high as it was is all the more significant for the policy objectives argument because of two highly unconducive conditions. First, as already noted, this support ran counter to risk averse calculations. The public was well aware of the ample risk in being involved in ongoing hostilities with such a certifiably unpredictable enemy. Second, the support was in spite of the president's extremely low personal credibility at the time on matters relating to Iran. As also noted, association of the reflagging policy with the president actually lowered the level of public support. In nevertheless supporting reflagging, the American public showed itself to be able to separate out its outrage over Iran–contra from its belief that the same administration that had gone courting moderates now needed to send the U.S. Navy on a mission to contain Iran.

The data on position reasoning, although limited, do provide some evidence of public perceptions of foreign policy restraint as the principal policy objective. In a *Los Angeles Times* poll (6/3/87) asking "the most important objective" of the Reagan policy, 33 percent answered "to protect free access to international waters," 28 percent "to guard sea-lanes for the shipment of oil," and 14 percent "to halt Russian expansion southward into the gulf." All involved restraining aggression. In contrast, only 6 percent cited such internal political change objectives as "promoting friendlier relations with moderate elements" within Iran. A *Washington Post*–ABC News poll (6/3/87), which registered 75 percent support for the Reagan policy, explicitly stated its objective as "to protect our interests in the free flow of oil."

El Salvador

The dominant issue in El Salvador always was internal political change—in this case, the role of American military force indirectly (aid, advisers) or directly (troops) in preventing such change from happening. The polls showed remarkable consistency of public opposition. In only one of fifteen surveys asking about support for military aid and/or military advisers was there a plurality of support (ABC News, 5/15/83). In all the others the margin of opposition was no less than 6 percent (Harris, 5/5/83), and as great as 59 percent (Harris, 1/19/84). This was despite the worst-case-scenario wording of the questions on the use of U.S. troops: e.g., "What if sending U.S. troops seemed to be the only way of saving the current government in El Salvador from being defeated?" (ABC News–*Washington Post*, 3/82); "leftist guerrillas about to defeat the government of El Salvador" (Rielly 1983). Even when the option was kept limited to "hundreds more advisers" or "increased aid" as responses to the government being in danger of falling (CBS, 6/83, 1/84, 2/85), the public still rejected more advisers and was split evenly over increased aid.

Nor can this be understood simply as a post-Vietnam risk aversion calculus. There were, as noted, other cases (e.g., Persian Gulf reflagging) in which fears of escalation did not lead to lack of public support. While the "another Vietnam" cry went up more in this case than others, it was not as if the public had any informed idea of who the *Frente Martí Liberación Nacional* (FMLN) was, or how intelligence reports assessed their military capabilities, or what their strengths and weaknesses were in comparison to the Vietcong. Opposition even to military aid and even to U.S. troops as a last resort was not a fear built on knowledge of the particulars of the problems posed by El Salvador. Rather it was a manifestation of a more generalized disinclination to getting involved militarily in the internal politics of other countries.

Nicaragua

The purpose of contra aid, as we by now well know, was never a straightforward matter. But there is ample reason (Jentleson 1991a, 1991c) for concluding that the principal objective was internal political change—to make the Sandinistas "say uncle," in Ronald Reagan's own words. The original claim that the contras were an arms interdiction force "became a joke," one State Department official observed, "as the contras grew without interdicting so much as a helmet liner" (McNeil 1988, 153). Similarly, had regional security been the dominant objective, there were ample opportunities—in particular, the Contadora process and the Arias Plan—for serious negotiations which the Reagan administration did not, however, seriously pursue (LeoGrande 1986; Pastor 1987; Gutman 1988). Only Iran–contra revealed just how far the Reagan administration was prepared to go to bring down the Sandinistas.

What is especially important about the lack of public support for contra aid is that . . . Nicaragua provides a strong test of the policy objectives–public support argument. Here was a country which, as noted, the public viewed as a threat to American interests. Here was an opportunity to have someone else, namely, the contras, do the fighting for us. And here were clear cues coming from an enormously popular president on a policy he had made one of his highest priorities. Yet the American public could not be convinced, cajoled, coaxed, or cowed. This point is reinforced by the additional data and further disaggregation in Table 3.3.

The forty-three polls on contra aid are separated into those that explicitly mention "overthrowing" the Sandinistas as the purpose of the aid (18), and those that ask merely for general approval or opposition to contra aid (25). When the mention of the internal political change objective is explicit (the "overthrow" question), support is lower than when it is not. The lowest level of support remains the 19.7 percent average for the seven polls explicitly proposing an invasion by U.S. troops to overthrow the Sandinistas. To these are added eight polls that measured support for U.S. military maneuvers and training exercises in the region. Whereas these all involved a more direct use of force than contra aid, they had the least to do with overthrowing the

Table 3.3. Nicaragua: Support Scores by Policy Objectives

Question (number of polls)	Percent Who Support
Internal Political Change	
(in order of decreasing explicitness and directness)	
(a) Invasion by U.S. troops (7)	19.7
(b) Contra aid to overthrow Sandinistas (18)	23.7
(c) Contra aid (25)	29.8
Foreign Policy Restraint	
(d) Regional military exercises (8)	35.2
(e) Invade Nicaragua if it allows Soviet missile base (1)	45

Sandinistas, and came the closest to being geared to a foreign policy restraint objective. Public support in these eight polls averaged 35.2 percent. Still not particularly high in absolute terms, this was relatively higher than for any of the other uses of force related to Nicaragua.

This point is further strengthened by additional data from the 1986 [Chicago Council on Foreign Relations (CCFR)] survey. One question asked about support for sending U.S. troops "if Nicaragua invades Honduras to destroy contra bases." Only 24 percent expressed support and 60 percent were opposed. But when asked "if Nicaragua allows the Soviets to set up a missile base," support was 45 percent and opposition only 42 percent (Rielly 1987, 32). This ranked the Soviet missile base scenario third of eleven on the CCFR list, behind only Soviet invasions of Western Europe or Japan, and ahead of such other scenarios as sending troops to El Salvador if the government were falling and sending troops to overthrow Noriega. Cast in these terms, the issue was not just the pro-Soviet coloration of the Nicaraguan government; the prospect of Soviet missile bases on the American mainland was very directly about foreign policy restraint. The American public was far more supportive of the use of force for this objective than for any other objective related to Nicaragua.

Lebanon

This was the most difficult case in which to sort out policy complexity or overcome policy ambiguity (Jentleson 1986). Lebanon suffered from both occupation by foreign powers (Israel, Syria, and the Palestine Liberation Organization) and its own bitter civil war between Christians and Moslems (and increasingly among intracommunal factions as well). The "peacekeeping" mission on which the Marines were sent involved both getting the foreign occupiers out (i.e., foreign policy restraint) and remaking the warring internal factions into a viable government. Unfortunately, unlike the Libya and Nicaragua cases, there are no survey data on Lebanon that disaggregates public support by perceptions of discrete objectives.[3] My explanatory claim here is thus a more limited one, interpreting the midrange 45 percent score as mixed support for a mixed-objectives policy.

Afghanistan

As noted, very limited data are available on aid to the Afghan mujaheddin. There are many polls asking opinions of the Soviet invasion, which of course show strong condemnation. This is not the same, though, as supporting the president's policy of waging surrogate war. Moreover, in something of a sequential manner, this also was a mixed-objectives case. The primary and prior objective was to make it impossible for the Soviets to stanch their "bleeding wound" (Gorbachev's term) and to force them to withdraw. But especially as the Soviets began to withdraw, it became increasingly evident that the U.S. policy also had the objective of bringing the Najibullah regime down and the mujaheddin to power—i.e., internal political change.

It is interesting that this set of goals was much more consensual among elites than with the general public. Congress and the Reagan administration worked closely together and with minimal rancor; in fact, on a number of occasions, Congress actually pushed the Reagan administration to increase the amounts of aid as well as the sophistication of the weaponry, as in 1986 with the Stinger antiaircraft missiles. Elites may have been more reassured by the logic and abstractions of deterrence theory and thus less worried about direct military confrontation with the Soviets than was the general public.

Although the data are limited, the mixed-objectives nature of the policy appears also to have been a factor. For example, the lowest level of public support for aid to the mujaheddin was in an October/November 1988 poll, taken eight months after the Geneva agreement had been signed and when the Soviet troop withdrawal was almost complete; i.e., at a point when foreign policy restraint had been pretty much accomplished, and only the internal political change objective was left.

SUMMARY

Table 3.4 summarizes the analysis. It excludes the three halo-effect cases and disaggregates the Libya and Nicaragua cases consistent with the data added in Tables 3.2 and 3.3. The principal policy objective is listed for each case and subcase. The "mixed" assessment of Lebanon and Afghanistan reflects not just the presence of both types of objectives, which also was true of other cases, but the limits of the data available for disaggregating opinion within these two cases. The public support scores are reranked for this revised case set. This reranking shows that when the principal objective was to restrain an adversary, when that adversary had gone beyond simply posing a standing threat and initiated aggressive actions against American interests or citizens, the public was prepared to support military action. But when the principal

Table 3.4. Policy Objectives and Public Support

Case	Principal Policy Objective	Public Support Score (Reranking)*
Libya: antiterrorism	FPR	1
Persian Gulf reflagging	FPR	2
Lebanon	Mixed	3
Afghanistan	Mixed	4
Nicaragua: military exercises	FPR	5
Panama (pre-invasion)	IPC	6
El Salvador	IPC	7
Libya: get Qaddafi	IPC	8
Nicaragua: overthrow Sandinistas	IPC	9

*Reranking excludes halo-effect cases
FPR = foreign policy restraint
IPC = internal political change

objective was to remake the government of another country, the American public was disinclined to support the use of limited military force, either directly or indirectly.

THE PERSIAN GULF WAR, 1990–1991

The 1990–1991 Persian Gulf War provides a further test of the principal policy objectives argument. My analysis follows the three phases of U.S. policy: prewar (Operation Desert Shield), war (Operation Desert Storm), and the postwar Kurdish uprising.

Operation Desert Shield

Figure 3.1 shows the extraordinarily high levels of public support for Operation Desert Shield. The mean support score for the seven polls plotted on this graph is 67.6 percent. Other polls with comparable questions showed very similar results.[4] This was higher than for any of the non–halo-effect 1980s cases (Table 3.1). Even the lowest approval rating, at 59 percent, was relatively

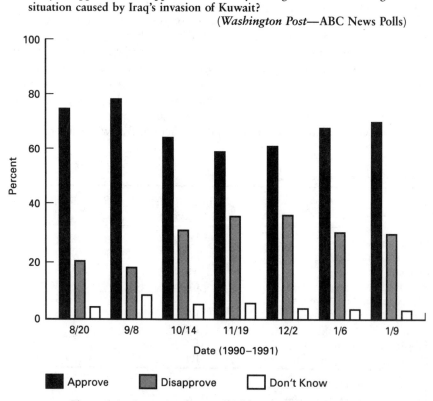

Do you approve or disapprove of the way George Bush is handling the situation caused by Iraq's invasion of Kuwait?

(*Washington Post*—ABC News Polls)

Figure 3.1. Operation Desert Shield: overall support level.

high. The highest rating of 78 percent was higher than at any point during Vietnam.

The low-cost, relatively easy military victory which eventually was achieved should not retrospectively obscure the real fears that were there, among both senior military officers and the American public. This was the largest foreign troop commitment since the Vietnam War, and the most rapid buildup since World War II. The troops were not yet engaged in hostilities, but there was little solace in that. Here were over 400,000 American troops being sent halfway around the world on an emergency basis as a "desert shield" against an aggressor the president was comparing to Adolf Hitler. In training and exercises alone, the American forces suffered substantial casualties.

It is difficult to explain the high level of public support strictly in interests-based terms. The public did consider the Persian Gulf a vital region. In the 1990 CCFR survey, 83 percent of the public designated Saudi Arabia as a vital interest (Rielly 1991, 19). But we have seen such expressions of vitalness before unaccompanied by support for military force. Similarly, although concern over oil was a factor, the "blood for oil" assertions pushed by the left did not reflect the prevalent public view. In one poll (*The Wall Street Journal*–NBC News, 8/21/90), for example, only 39 percent cited "a major shortage of oil that threatens an economic recession" as justification for military action.

As for presidential cues, George Bush was frequently criticized during Desert Shield for the weaknesses of his bully pulpiting. A *New York Times*–CBS poll taken November 13–15 found 51 percent who said that President Bush had not explained clearly enough why American troops were in the Gulf. Yet the American public nevertheless considered itself to have "a clear idea of what the United States military involvement in the Iraqi situation is all about—that is, why our troops are in Saudi Arabia." Yes responses to this question as asked by Gallup the week after the troops were first sent were 74 percent. In four succeeding polls through the middle of November, the range remained consistent at 69 percent to 76 percent.

Some risk aversion is evident in the dip in the curve in Figure 3.1 during October–November (see also Jentleson 1991b). The initial decline in mid-October actually had less to do with Desert Shield than with the domestic budget crisis at that time gripping the nation. But then came Bush's November 8 announcement of a doubling of U.S. forces to nearly 400,000 and a shift in strategy to ensuring "an adequate offensive military option." This made the reality of war much more imminent. Public support dropped to 53 percent. Yet public support for Desert Shield started going back up in December. The breakpoint appears to have been the diplomatic initiatives taken by the Bush administration beginning in late November. The administration succeeded in gaining passage of United Nations Security Council Resolution 678 setting a January 15, 1991, deadline for Iraq's withdrawal from Kuwait and authorizing the use of military force if Iraq failed to comply. The Bush administration also proposed bilateral diplomatic talks, including an offer for Secretary of State James Baker to go to Baghdad to meet with Saddam Hussein. Baker did meet on January 9 with Iraqi Foreign Minister Tariq Aziz in Geneva. When these negotiations collapsed because of Iraqi intransigence—a "total stiff arm," Bush called it—the claim that military force had become a last resort gained substantial credence. In a *Washington Post*–ABC News poll taken the evening the Baker–Aziz talks broke down, approval of Bush's handling of the crisis went up to 69 percent, the highest it had been since back in September. This was despite 80 percent of the public now believing that the policy which they approved was leading to war.

Polls also showed a declining willingness to rely on sanctions. There still was a desire to avoid war if possible, as evident in the close to even split on the question of whether to go to war immediately after the January 15 deadline or "wait longer" to see if sanctions work (e.g., a 49 percent/47 percent split in a *Washington Post*–ABC News poll, January 9–12). But the issue for the public was mostly one of timing. In the same *Washington Post* poll, when the question was posed as "to go to war *sometime* after January 15" (emphasis added) or "do not go to war," the split was 62 percent to 32 percent. Similarly, the *Los Angeles Times* reported (1/14/91) a drop from the almost 60 percent to only 39 percent of respondents who in November and December concurred that the United States could rely solely on sanctions. Thus, although there was some anticipatory risk aversion, the pattern was uneven. This is all the more remarkable because the stakes here were war and not just limited military action. A Harris poll (January 10–14) showed 78 percent of respondents believing that U.S. forces would suffer heavy or moderate casualties, but 72 percent said they would support the president anyway if he decided to go to war.

The main reason for these high levels of support, despite fears of the risks involved, was, in my view, the nature of the objectives in this case as virtually an ideal-type of foreign policy restraint. The post–World War II era has witnessed few instances of aggression as naked as the Iraq invasion of Kuwait. This wasn't a matter of searching the jungles of the Ho Chi Minh trail for black-pajama-clad guerillas, or interdicting arms-runners in the mountains of Central America. On August 2, 1990, Iraqi tanks had rolled, and Iraqi soldiers had marched openly and massively to conquer Kuwait. They stood poised to extend their aggression southward into Saudi Arabia. And they had seized thousands of hostages, including many Americans. All of this was made all the more ominous by Saddam Hussein's track record of past aggression, and his lethal arsenal of chemical (and potentially nuclear and biological) weapons.

This is not to say either that foreign policy restraint was the only objective, or that the definition and parameters of what foreign policy restraint entailed were constant or totally consensual. In fact, though, as Table 3.5 shows (and as did Tables 3.3 and 3.4 in previous cases), the variations in public support for the differentiated objectives further strengthen the policy objectives argument. Foreign policy restraint encompassed four principal objectives: defending Saudi Arabia, forcing Iraq out of Kuwait, protecting American hostages, and destroying Iraq's capabilities for weapons of mass destruction (nuclear, chemical, biological). Every one of these objectives had a high mean support score: 71.6, 61.6, 66.6, and 54.0 percent, respectively. In contrast, the two

Table 3.5. Operation Desert Shield: Support Scores by Policy Objectives

Question (number of polls)	Percent Who Support
Internal Political Change	
(1) Assassinate Saddam Hussein (3)	38
(2) Invade Iraq to overthrow Saddam (2)	33.5
Foreign Policy Restraint	
Use military force to:	
(1) Defend Saudi Arabia (16)	71.6
(2) Force Iraq out of Kuwait (20)	61.6
(3) Retaliate for mistreatment or killing of American hostages (5)	66.6
(4) Eliminate nuclear, chemical, or biological weapons (3)	54

internal political change objectives, assassinating Saddam Hussein or invading Iraq to overthrow him, had support scores of only 38.0 percent and 33.5 percent. This was despite the comparison to Hitler and other demonizations of Saddam. Saddam registered only a 9° on the 1990 CCFR [thermometer] scale, but there still was very limited public support for using force to get him. Thus, even in Desert Shield, with its extraordinarily high approval ratings, the public again showed a differentiation by policy objectives.

Operation Desert Storm (War)

Table 3.6 shows the surge in public approval from the already high levels for Desert Shield to the stratospheric levels for Operation Desert Storm. However, this has to be qualified as another example of the halo effect. From the very first night of the war, when all of America could see live on CNN American bombers lighting up Baghdad, and from the first superconfident briefings given the next morning by Secretary of Defense Richard Cheney and Joint Chiefs of Staff Chairman General Colin Powell, Americans had a sense of victory in the making. The surge in public approval thus was more than just the standard rally-round-the-flag effect; it was an incipient victory rally.

Since American casualties were so low, the Mueller thesis [that public support for war will decrease as casualties mount (Mueller 1973)] never got fully tested. However, there are some data indicating that public support was not strictly dependent on expectations of low casualties (Table 3.7). Among

Table 3.6. Operation Desert Storm and the Halo Effect

	Percent Approval of Bush Persian Gulf Policy	
	Immediate Prewar	Early Days of the War
New York Times–CBS News	66	82
Gallup	62	82
Washington Post–ABC News	69	76

Table 3.7. Operation Desert Storm: Delinking Public Support and Battle Deaths?

	Percent Who Support the War Overall	Percent Who Would Support Ground Attack If Ordered by Bush
Among all Americans	81	78
Among those who expect U.S. deaths of . . .		
. . . 500 or fewer	85	82
. . . close to 1,000	83	75
. . . close to 2,500	90	89
. . . close to 5,000	80	81
. . . 10,000 or more	60	60

Source: *Los Angeles Times*, February 19, 1991, p. A12.

those who expected minimal U.S. deaths (500 or fewer), 85 percent supported the war overall, and 82 percent stated they would support a ground war. Among those who expected close to 5,000 deaths, support was still 80 percent and 81 percent, respectively. Only at the level of 10,000 or more deaths did support fall significantly—but even then at 60 percent this was still something less than an antiwar movement.[5]

Of course, anticipatory combat deaths are not the same thing as actually having them happen to real people. Here, too, we should not forget how real the fear of substantial casualties was. In January, just before the launching of the air war, General Powell estimated U.S. casualties "in the several thousand" range (*New York Times*, 3/23/91, p. 4). Nor was the Potemkin village-like resistance of Iraqi ground forces anticipated. As in World War II, the logic of the principal policy objectives argument postulates a higher tolerance for casualties to be a function of the objective of restraining aggression.

Where the data do vary, though, is in the increased support for using military force to overthrow Saddam Hussein. As seen in Table 3.5, public support for using military force for such internal political change objectives was quite limited prior to the outbreak of war. But the shift on this issue was virtually immediate with the launching of Desert Storm. A *New York Times*–CBS poll (1/20/91) showed 81 percent support for overthrowing Saddam. In a *Wall Street Journal*–NBC News poll (1/25/91), 73 percent of respondents stated that the U.S. and its allies should continue the war until we "captured or killed Saddam." A *Newsweek* poll (2/15/91) found 84 percent support for continuation of the war "until Saddam's government is removed from power." The same poll found 60 percent support for assassinating Saddam. This was almost double the support in a prewar (January 3–4) poll.

Unlike Panama or Grenada, these responses cannot be accounted for by the halo effect. The questions were about something yet to be done, not faits accomplis. They also were not just responses to presidential cues. President Bush did compare Saddam to Hitler, and he did call on the Iraqi people to overthrow Saddam, but he never made the removal of Saddam an official U.S.

objective. Instead, what may have been manifested here is a transformation of the internal political change objective brought on by the shift from a limited use of military force to full-scale war. Once the nation is at war, a set of supreme ends is established—victory over an aggressor—and the range of actions acceptable to the public as means to those ends becomes much broader. In the Iraqi case, they had started the war, and then had rejected all efforts at diplomacy. Now that we were at war (read: now that he left us with no other choice) we needed to do whatever was necessary to defeat the aggressor pure and simple. If that meant overthrowing his government as a means to that end, then the public appears to have felt, so be it.

Further research and analysis would be necessary to assess the validity of this qualification to the central hypothesis. It does seem to point to another difference between limited uses of military force and wars. As such, and in the interim, it is a useful reminder of the differences between the eight 1980s cases and the 1990–1991 Persian Gulf War, and thus of the limits of generalizing from limited military force to wars (and vice versa).

Postwar Kurdish Uprising

On February 26 President Bush announced a ceasefire. Suddenly, though, there was the matter of the Kurds (and also the Shiites in southern Iraq), and the sense of finality was broken and the euphoria shattered. Thousands were slaughtered and literally millions fled as refugees into the mountains and toward the Turkish border. With the international media managing to get on location, it was an epic and graphic human drama played out on television screens across the United States.

The Bush administration immediately came under sharp criticism. Was this not like Hungary in 1956, with American leaders once again calling on oppressed people to rebel against their oppressors, but then leaving them without support at the mercy of a brutal regime? Could it have been as simple as having waited one more day before calling the ceasefire, and allowing General Schwarzkopf's forces to further decimate the Iraqi military? Or at least should not the threat to shoot down Iraqi aircraft also have included helicopter gunships?

Thus, in contrast to Desert Shield and Desert Storm, which were principally about foreign policy restraint, the issues raised by the Kurdish uprising were principally about the use of military force for internal political change. Public sentiment, as illustrated in Table 3.8, can best be characterized as prudent outrage. There still was a strong desire to get Saddam, and especially to end his brutality, but some caution and concern about how far to go in seeking to do so. The strongest support (78 percent) was for providing humanitarian assistance, food, and medical supplies to the rebels. Next highest (67 percent) was issuing an official warning; then came actual military actions to shoot down Iraqi helicopter gunships (57 percent), to destroy Iraqi tanks and artillery (51 percent), and to remove Saddam from power (50 percent). However, only 40 percent supported providing guns and military assistance to the rebels. And when the question was posed as "using U.S. ground forces to

Table 3.8. The Kurdish Uprising

Question	Percent Who Favor	Percent Who Oppose	Percent Who Don't Know
Would you favor or oppose the United States . . .			
Issuing an official warning to Iraq that further military action against the rebels will not be tolerated	67	25	8
Providing food and medical supplies to the rebels	78	17	5
Providing guns and military assistance to the rebels	40	52	8
Using U.S. aircraft to shoot down Iraqi helicopters and other aircraft being used against the rebels	57	36	7
Using U.S. aircraft to destroy Iraqi tanks and artillery being used against the rebels	51	41	8
Using U.S. ground forces to fight Iraqi military forces being used against the rebels	29	63	8
Using U.S. aircraft and ground forces to remove Saddam Hussein from power	50	43	7

Source: Gallup–*Newsweek,* April 4–5, 1991.

fight Iraqi military forces being used against the rebels," there was only 29 percent support—quite similar to support levels seen for similar potential involvements in Nicaragua and El Salvador.

Other polls showed similar results. While the Bush administration was sharply criticized for its initial inaction once it had started Operation Provide Comfort, its approval rating went back up to 69 percent (*Washington Post–ABC News,* 4/3/91). In the same poll, only 45 percent said yes and 51 percent no to whether "the United States should try to help the rebels overthrow Saddam or not." Another poll (*Newsweek–Gallup,* 4/4/91) showed 53 percent saying "stay out of the situation" and 37 percent "intervene for the rebels."

Thus, even amidst the triumph of Desert Storm and a renewed faith in American military power, the American public was wary about getting militarily involved in an internal political conflict. It showed a willingness to support some involvement and a desire still to get Saddam Hussein himself. But it apparently did see the difference between marching into Kuwait to restrain Iraqi foreign aggression and sinking into the quagmire of Iraqi internal political conflict.

CONCLUSIONS AND IMPLICATIONS

My principal intent, as noted earlier, has been to establish the plausibility in both empirical and theoretical terms of explaining the pattern of post post-Vietnam American public opinion on the use of military force in terms of the distinction between the policy objectives of foreign policy restraint and internal political change. These are postulated as strong tendencies, not behavioral laws. One limiting condition stressed throughout has been the halo effect of force used quickly and successfully for imposing internal political change, and then embraced by the American public. On the other side is the qualification of nonautomaticity of public support for the foreign policy restraint objective. Public support will not necessarily just be there; it must be cultivated and evoked through effective presidential leadership. But this evoking is far more likely to succeed when the principal objective is foreign policy restraint, even in the face of significant risks.

I do not at all propose this argument as a definitive refutation of the theories previously [cited]. All have a degree of validity, and for any one particular case one or more can provide a strong ideographic explanation. In a number of respects, though, the policy objectives differentiation provides the most powerful and parsimonious explanation.

First, it better accounts for the gap between delineations of interests and willingness to support the use of force. Its assertion of a particular and consistent preference for when force is to be used conveys a more purposive sense of strategy than do more static delineations of interests, be they military or economic.

Second, it allows for a greater degree of independent formulation of foreign policy opinion than do assumptions of elite manipulation. Without denying that the public remains tuned in to presidential cues, it seeks to explain why the public nevertheless at times goes its own way.

Third, the policy objectives variable partially absorbs but also overrides risk aversion. It absorbs it in that one of the reasons for the tendency toward low public support for using force for internal political change is Vietnam-taught risk aversion. But it overrides it in contending that the public is predisposed to oppose the use of force for internal political change, irrespective of case-specific risk calculations, yet open to supporting the use of force for foreign policy restraint even if there is a certain level of risk. The key exception, of course, is the halo effect of faits accomplis like in Panama and Grenada, although, as noted earlier, this is a self-evident one for which little theorizing is necessary.

The main normative implication is to call into question the traditional view of the public as boorish, overreactive, and generally the bane of those who would pursue an effective foreign policy. I do not dispute findings about the low levels of information with which the public arrives at its foreign policy views. Nor do I suggest sophisticated calculations or fine analytical distinctions in their thought processes. But however they arrive at it, and however they might attempt to articulate it, Americans do appear to have a much more pragmatic sense of strategy than they are given credit for—an approach to the world that is actually "pretty prudent" when it comes to the use of military force. A continued susceptibility to being whipped up into a flag-waving furor and overrelishing of big little victories do make the modifier necessary. But in its basic disposition as to when to use force and when not to, the American public has been showing "good judgment in the use of resources," and "caution and circumspection as to danger or risk"—i.e., "prudence," as defined by *Webster's*. This is, of course, a very different portrait than the "knownothingist" portrayal found in much of the literature on public opinion and foreign policy. Along with other recent research (Nincic 1988; Shapiro and Page 1988; Aldrich et al. 1989), it reinforces the need for rethinking and revision of this traditional conception.

Finally, with regard to post–Cold War U.S. policy, and in particular strategies for managing regional conflicts and other Third World threats and instability, there are the makings here of a "broad agreement on some basic principles that define the nation's proper orientation toward the world"—i.e, a consensus, as the term is defined by Holsti and Rosenau (1984, 218). It is a consensus important for both its scope and its limits. Short of a direct attack on the United States, force is not likely ever to be the first choice of the American public. But the key point is that military force is a more acceptable option to the public in some instances than others. The American public is less gun-shy than during the Vietnam trauma period of the 1970s, but more cautious than during the Cold War consensus of the 1950s and 1960s. Rather than simply recoil from force *qua* force, it takes a differentiated view based on the principal policy objective which the use of force is to serve.

Thus, in one sense the post post-Vietnam American public agrees that the world is a dangerous place. Threats do exist out there. There are countries, movements, and leaders that hold antipathies toward the United States. We cannot always count on the self-restraint of others. So when an adversary actually takes aggressive actions against us—poses a clear and present danger, if you will—the American public is prepared to support the use of force to restrain that aggressor. But where the American public draws its limits is in the further assertions that (a) it isn't just what governments do, but who they are, that threatens the United States, and (b) we both need to and can effectively use military force to remake governments in our chosen image.

The American public is thus more prepared than in the 1970s to support the use of military force to restrain aggressors. To the extent that this is recognized by adversaries, it will strengthen our standing deterrence posture. However, presidents who contemplate getting militarily involved in internal political conflicts—of which there may well be even more in the post–Cold War world than when bipolarity had its constraining effects—had better get in and out quickly and successfully. Otherwise the public is strongly disposed to oppose the policy. It is not infinitely manipulable (as even the Great Communicator found out). It can be more readily convinced that important interests are at stake in internal conflicts than that military force is the optimal way to defend those interests, not even indirectly.

All of this may be disappointing both to those on the left wing of the Democratic party who tend toward a view that the United States should never use force other than in strict self-defense, and to those on the nonisolationist right wing of the Republican party who may still aspire to omni-interventionism. It will be reassuring, however, to those who do not believe that the United States should use force to try to remake governments around the globe, but who do believe that instances will continue to arise in which it will be necessary to use force against aggressor states.

NOTES

1. [The "halo effect" refers to the fact that fewer people oppose a policy once it has proved to be successful than either prior to its inception or while its outcome remains uncertain.—Ed.]

2. The Lebanon case also had the greatest variation in question wording. Questions that were too biased or suggestive were discarded. Even so, we identified six different versions of the support/opposition question. We first analyzed each separately, but did not find any pattern of variation that could be linked to the question wording. We then aggregated them and calculated the mean based on all 37.

3. The usual question phrasing cast the objective as "keeping the peace," or "preventing further fighting," which are open to interpretation and perception as applied to either or both the foreign occupation and civil war.

4. The mean support score in nine *New York Times*–CBS polls asking approval of "President Bush's handling of Iraq's invasion of Kuwait" was 62.7%. In seventeen Gallup polls ("the way George Bush is handling the current situation in the Middle East involving Iraq and Kuwait") support was 67.7%.

5. Other polls showed similar results. An ABC poll (2/21/91) reported 76% of those who expected high casualties if a ground war were launched still approved of doing so. A *Time* poll (2/7/91) showed 83% who believed that a ground war would cause high numbers of U.S. casualties, but 58% still supportive.

REFERENCES

Aldrich, J. H., Sullivan, J. L., and Borgida, E. (1989). Foreign Affairs and Issue Voting: Do Presidential Candidates "Waltz Before a Blind Audience"? *American Political Science Review* 83:123–142.

Gutman, R. (1988). *Banana Diplomacy: The Making of American Policy in Nicaragua, 1981–1987*. New York: Simon & Schuster.

Holsti, O. R., and Rosenau, J. N. (1984). *American Leadership in World Affairs: Vietnam and the Breakdown of Consensus*. Boston: Allen & Unwin.

International Institute for Strategic Studies. 1986. *Strategic Survey, 1985–86*. London: IISS.

Jentleson, B. W. (1991a). The Reagan Administration and Coercive Diplomacy: Restraining More Than Remaking Governments. *Political Science Quarterly* 106 (Spring):57–82.

Jentleson, B. W. (1991b). The Domestic Politics of Desert Shield: Should We Go to War? Who Should Decide? *Brookings Review* 9 (Winter): 22–28.

Jentleson, B. W. (1991c). The Reagan Administration vs. Nicaragua: The Limits of "Type C" Coercive Diplomacy. In *The Limits of Coercive Diplomacy*, revised edition, edited by A. L. George, forthcoming.

Jentleson, B. W. (1986). The Lebanon War and Soviet–American Competition: Scope and Limits of Superpower Influence. In *The Soviet–American Competition in the Middle East*, edited by S. L. Spiegel, M. A. Heller, and J. Goldberg, pp. 321–339. Lexington, Mass.: Lexington Books.

Krepinevich, A. F., Jr. (1986). *The Army and Vietnam.* Baltimore, Md.: Johns Hopkins University Press.

LeoGrande, W. (1986). Rollback or Containment? The United States, Nicaragua and the Search for Peace in Central America. *International Security* 11:89–120.

McNeil, F. (1988). *War and Peace in Central America.* New York: Charles Scribner's Sons.

Mueller, J. F. (1973). *War, Presidents and Public Opinion.* New York: John Wiley & Sons.

Nincic, M. (1988). The United States, the Soviet Union and the Politics of Opposites. *World Politics* 40 (July):452–475.

Oakley, R. (1986). International Terrorism. *Foreign Affairs* 65:611–629.

Pastor, R. A. (1987). *Condemned to Repetition: The United States and Nicaragua.* Princeton, N.J.: Princeton University Press.

Rielly, J., ed. (1991). *American Public Opinion and U.S. Foreign Policy 1991.* Chicago: Chicago Council on Foreign Relations.

Rielly, J., ed. (1987). *American Public Opinion and U.S. Foreign Policy 1987.* Chicago: Chicago Council on Foreign Relations.

Rielly, J., ed. (1983). *American Public Opinion and U.S. Foreign Policy 1983.* Chicago: Chicago Council on Foreign Relations.

Schneider, W. (1983). Conservatism, not Interventionism: Trends in Foreign Policy Opinion, 1974–1982. In *Eagle Defiant: United States Foreign Policy in the 1980s,* edited by K. A. Oye, R. J. Lieber, and D. Rothchild, pp. 33–64. Boston: Little, Brown.

Shapiro, R. Y., and Page B. I. (1988). Foreign Policy and the Rational Public. *Journal of Conflict Resolution* 32:211–247.

Wittkopf, E. R. (1986). On the Foreign Policy Beliefs of the American People: A Critique. *International Studies Quarterly* 30:425–446.

Woodward, B. (1987). *Veil: The Secret Wars of the CIA, 1981–1987.* New York: Simon & Schuster.

Young, O. R. (1968). Intervention and International Systems. *Journal of International Affairs* XXII, No. 2.

4. THE INFLUENCE OF ETHNIC INTEREST GROUPS ON AMERICAN MIDDLE EAST POLICY

Mitchell Geoffrey Bard

*I*n the three most commonly used models of foreign policy decision making, the rational-actor, organizational-process, and bureaucratic-politics models, there is little or no consideration given to the role played by interest groups in influencing policy outcomes. The only decision-making model that places domestic politics at the center of its analysis is the pluralist model, and that model has been only tangentially applied to foreign policymaking.

If the bureaucratic-politics model is best described by the aphorism "Where you stand depends on where you sit," then the pluralist model might be summarized as "Which way you lean depends on who's pushing you."[1] Pluralism refers to the existence of a variety of relatively independent organizations competing in the political marketplace.

The critics of the pluralist model tend to define it in laissez-faire economic terms, arguing that public policy can best be understood as the product of the free play of group pressures and that an "invisible hand" working through competing interests yields an outcome that is beneficial to society. The model is defined this way to level the same type of critique against the concept of a free market of political ideas that is used against notions of the free economic market; that is, no real competition exists because of monopolies, oligopolies, and iron triangles, so political outcomes are inefficient, create inequalities, and undermine the national interest. These critics have done little more than construct a straw man to knock down, however, since the model never claimed that a "free market" exists in politics. Pluralism does not require that interest groups be equal or that political power be evenly distributed. On the contrary, it is far more likely that one or more interest groups will dominate a particular policy debate.

A good example of the application of the pluralist model is the competition between the Arab and Israeli lobbies in the making of foreign policy. In this case, there is no presumption of equality; the Israeli lobby is clearly dominant. Nevertheless, it does not necessarily follow that this advantage in the balance of lobbying power enables the Israeli lobby to influence policy.

DEFINING THE LOBBIES

One of the most commonly held notions in American politics is that Jews have a great deal of influence on U.S. foreign policy. In the view of some people "Jewish-Americans" control U.S. policy in the Middle East to the detriment of the national interest. This attitude is typified by former Senator James Abourezk, who has called the Israeli lobby "the most powerful and pervasive foreign influence in American politics today."[2]

Such critics persistently charge that American Jews have pervasive influence. The truth, however, is that the Israeli lobby is unable to affect major foreign policy decisions and is actually capable of influencing only a narrow range of policies that benefit Israel.

Most people are familiar with business and professional lobbies that try to influence policy. These lobbies usually hire one or more people, lobbyists, to try to persuade government officials to support their interests. American Jews are represented by such lobbyists, who use direct efforts to influence policymakers. But other, less-formal efforts are also used to influence policy.

The organization that is registered as a lobby is the American Israel Public Affairs Committee (AIPAC). This organization and others that attempt to directly influence policymakers may be designated the *formal lobby*. There are also organizations that do not engage in direct lobbying (e.g., B'nai B'rith and Hadassah), but who do disseminate information and encourage their members to become involved in the political process. In addition, there is a large component of Jewish political influence that is unorganized—Jewish voting behavior and public opinion. These indirect means of influence may be designated the *informal lobby*.

All of the above are generally referred to as the "Jewish lobby"; however, this label is inaccurate because a large proportion of the Israeli lobby is composed of non-Jews. The "Israeli lobby" can be defined as *those individuals and organizations that directly and indirectly influence American policy to support Israel.*

The Israeli lobby does not have the field to itself; there is a competing interest group—the "Arab lobby." The National Association of Arab-Americans (NAAA), like AIPAC, is a registered domestic lobby that forms the core of the formal lobby. There is also an informal lobby that exerts indirect influence. Just as the Israeli lobby is not exclusively composed of Jews, the Arab lobby is not composed entirely of Arabs; nevertheless the label is appropriate in this case because it refers to those *formal and informal actors that attempt to influence U.S. foreign policy to support the interests of the Arab states in the Middle East.*

THE INFORMAL LOBBY

American Jews recognize the importance of support for Israel because of the dire consequences that could follow from the alternative. The perceived threat to Israel is not military defeat; it is annihilation. At the same time, American Jews are frightened of what might happen in this country if they do not have political power. As a consequence, Jews have devoted themselves to politics with almost religious fervor. This is reflected in the fact that Jews have one of the highest percentage voter turnouts of any ethnic group. The Jewish population in the United States is under six million, roughly 3 percent of the total population, but 89 percent live in twelve key electoral college states. These states alone have enough electoral votes to elect the president. If you add the non-Jews shown by opinion polls to be as pro-Israel as Jews, it is clear that Israel has the support of one of the largest veto groups in the country.

The disproportionate influence of the American Jewish population is in direct contrast with the electoral involvement of Arab-Americans. There are less than three million Arabs in the United States, and roughly 80 percent of them are Lebanese Christians who tend to be unsympathetic to the Arab lobby's goals. This reflects another major problem for the Arab lobby—inter-Arab disunity. This disunity is reinforced by the general discord of the Arab world, which has twenty states with competing interests. The Arab lobby is thus precluded from representing "the Arabs."

The political activism of Jews forces representatives with presidential ambitions to consider what a mixed voting record on Israel-related issues may mean in the political future. There are no benefits to candidates taking an openly anti-Israel stance, and considerable costs in both loss of campaign contributions and votes from Jews and non-Jews alike. Potential candidates, therefore, have an incentive to be pro-Israel; this reinforces support for Israel in Congress. Actual candidates must be particularly sensitive to the concerns of Jewish voters; it follows that the successful candidate's foreign policy will be influenced, though not bound, by the promises that had to be made during the campaign.

Political campaign contributions are also considered an important means of influence; typically, Jews have been major benefactors. It is difficult to assess the influence of campaign contributions on legislative outcomes, particularly with regard to Israel-related issues where support or opposition may be a consequence of nonmonetary factors. In addition, one does not know if a candidate is pro-Israel because of receiving a contribution or receives a donation as a result of taking a position in support of Israel.

In the past, Jewish contributions were less structured and targeted than those of other interest groups, but this changed dramatically with the proliferation of Israel-related political action committees (PACs).

The first pro-Israel PAC was formed in 1978, but there was little activity until 1982, when thirty-three pro-Israel PACs contributed $1.87 million to congressional candidates. Like donations from other PACs, most of this money was given to incumbents, and because of the long association of Jews with the Democratic party, nearly 80 percent went to Democrats. The number of PACs more than doubled in 1984, as did their contributions. By 1991, however, the number of PACs had actually declined from a high of more than 70 to 54, and gave only $2.68 million to candidates.[3] On the Arab lobby side, only two PACs were active in the most recent campaign, and they spent a total of $30,000.

PUBLIC OPINION

The absence of a large voting bloc requires the Arab lobby to develop sympathies among the general public if it is to use public opinion or the electoral process as a means of influencing U.S. policy. The lobby has tried to support sympathetic American groups such as Third World organizations and to cultivate friendships in the academic and business realms, but, as opinion polls have consistently shown, there is relatively little popular support for the Arab cause. Going back to 1967, sympathy for the Arab states has averaged only 11 percent in Gallup polls. Since the late 1970s, support for Israel has generally been three to four times that for the Arab states. In the poll taken during the Gulf War, sympathy for the Arabs had dropped to 8 percent, and the margin was a record 56 points.

THE FORMAL ISRAELI LOBBY

The organization that directly lobbies Congress on behalf of the Israeli lobby is AIPAC. The lobby was founded by I. L. Kenen in 1954, when Israel's supporters decided to appeal directly to Congress for legislation to provide aid to Israel to circumvent State Department opposition. Up until 1973, Kenen was AIPAC's only lobbyist. Today, there are seven lobbyists, a staff of approximately 150, 12 regional offices, and a budget of $15 million. The current director is Tom Dine, a former legislative aide to Senators Church and Muskie. The director of AIPAC is generally considered one of the most influential men in Washington, and Dine is no exception.

AIPAC was not the first domestic lobby to concern itself with foreign affairs, but it is regarded as the most powerful. The lobby strives to remain nonpartisan and thereby keep friends in both parties. By framing the issues in terms of the national interest, AIPAC is able to attract broader support than could ever be possible if it were perceived to represent only the interests of Israel. This does not mean AIPAC does not have a close relationship with Israeli officials: It does, albeit unofficially. Even so, there are times when the lobby comes into conflict with the Israeli government. Despite such disagreements, the Israeli lobby tends to reflect Israeli government policy fairly closely.

Lobbyists usually roam the halls of Congress trying to get the attention of legislators so they can explain their positions. AIPAC has the luxury of being able to call its allies in Congress to pass along information and then leaving much of the work of writing bills and gathering cosponsors to the legislative staffs. The lobbyists themselves are mostly Capitol Hill veterans who know how to operate the levers of power.

Since it does not use stereotypical lobbying tactics, the Israeli lobby depends on the network it has developed to galvanize the Jewish community to take some form of political action. The network comprises at least seventy-five different organizations that in one way or another support Israel. Most cannot legally engage in lobbying but are represented on the board of directors of AIPAC so that they are able to provide input into the lobby's decision-making process. Equally important is the bureaucratic machinery of these organizations, which enables them to disseminate information to their members and facilitate a rapid response to legislative activity.

A second coordinating body is the Conference of Presidents of Major American Jewish Organizations. It is composed of leaders of forty-eight different organizations and is responsible for formulating and articulating the "Jewish position" on most foreign policy matters. The conference allows the lobby to speak with one voice in a way its opponents cannot. The conference is the main contact between the Jewish community and the executive branch, while AIPAC tends to be the conduit to the legislative branch.

Even with the Jewish population concentrated in key states, there are still only a total of six million Jews; therefore, the Israeli lobby is dependent on the support of non-Jewish groups and actively works to form coalitions with broad segments of American society. The lobby has successfully built coalitions comprising unions, entertainers, clergymen, scholars, and black leaders. These coalitions allow the lobby to demonstrate a broad public consensus for a pro-Israel policy.

THE FORMAL ARAB LOBBY

There had always been an Arab lobby in the United States, composed of what I. L. Kenen called the petro-diplomatic complex and consisting of the oil industry, missionaries, diplomats, and CIA agents. According to Kenen, there was no need for an "Arab" lobby because the petro-diplomatic complex did the Arabs' work for them.[4]

The Arab lobby became an official, active, and visible advocate of the Arab cause in the wake of the oil embargo. "The day of the Arab-American is here," boasted Richard Shadyac; "the reason is oil."[5] From the beginning, the Arab lobby has faced a disadvantage not only in electoral politics but also in organization. There are several politically oriented groups, but many of these are solo operations with little financial or popular support. Some of the larger, more representative groups include the Middle East Research and Information Project; the Middle East Affairs Council; Americans for Near East Refugee Aid; and the American Palestine Committee.

The National Association of Arab-Americans (NAAA) is a registered domestic lobby, patterned after AIPAC, that was founded in 1972 by Richard
Shadyac. He believed the power and wealth of the Arab countries stemming
from their oil reserves would allow the Arab lobby to take advantage of the
political process in the same way the Jews have been thought to.

Like AIPAC, the NAAA makes its case on the basis of U.S. national interests, arguing that a pro-Israel policy harms those interests. Aid to Israel is
criticized as a waste of taxpayer's money, and the potential benefits of a closer
relationship with the Arab states is emphasized. In 1977, after Anwar Sadat's
historic visit to Jerusalem, the Arab lobby made its displeasure over U.S.
support for the initiative known to President Carter, who wrote in his diary:
"They [Arab-Americans] have given all the staff, Brzezinski, Warren Christopher, and others, a hard time."[6]

The Arab lobby's concerns began to reach the highest levels of government,
gaining its best access during the Bush administration thanks to the support of
Chief of Staff John Sununu, who is of Lebanese descent. It was also during
Bush's term that the first perceptible changes in U.S. policy could be seen,
though the shifts were more tone than substance.

Most of the nation's major corporations have not supported the Arab
lobby; in fact, prior to the 1981 AWACS (Airborne Warning and Control
System aircraft) sale (discussed below), oil companies were about
the only corporations willing to openly identify with Arab interests. The
reason for this is that most corporations prefer to stay out of foreign policy
debates; moreover, corporations may feel constrained by the implicit threat
of some form of retaliation by the Israeli lobby. The major oil companies
feel no such constraints. According to Steven Emerson, the four companies
that comprise the Arabian American Oil Company (ARAMCO)—Exxon,
Standard Oil of California, Mobil, and Texaco—have "conducted a surrep-
titious multimillion-dollar campaign to manipulate public opinion and foreign
policy on the Middle East" for years.[7] Participation in the public-relations
campaign amounted to the price of doing business in the oil-producing nations.

The campaign began after the 1967 war when ARAMCO established a
fund to help present the Arab side of the conflict. That campaign took on
greater urgency in 1973 after the chairman of the board of ARAMCO met
with Saudi King Faisal and was pressured to take a more active role in creating
a sympathetic attitude toward the Arab nations. A month later Mobil
published its first advertisement/editorial in the *New York Times*. Since 1973,
ARAMCO has maintained its public-relations campaign and become involved in occasional legislative fights such as that over the AWACS sale,
but, on the whole, the campaign has had no observable impact on U.S. policy.

There are other nonoil companies that are involved in the Arab lobby, the
most well-known being Bechtel, and an increasing number can be expected to
be willing to participate as Arab investment in the United States grows. Estimates of current Arab investment range from $50 billion to $200 billion, and
Arab investors (nations and individuals) have bought shares and controlling

interests in a wide range of American companies, creating the potential for expanding Arab political influence.

CONTRASTS

There are at least two major differences between the Arab and Israeli lobbies. First, the Arab lobby almost always lobbies negatively, i.e., against pro-Israel legislation rather than for pro-Arab legislation. The NAAA's legislative initiatives, for example, rarely relate to the Arab world. Most of their time is spent trying to generate opposition to Israel's "occupation" of the West Bank, Golan Heights, and Gaza Strip as well as its alleged violations of human rights; attempting to cut U.S. aid to Israel and block its use for settlements on the West Bank; and pleading for the recognition of the PLO and the need for a Palestinian state. This agenda contrasts with that of the Israeli lobby, which, with the exception of opposing arms sales to Arab states hostile toward Israel, directs its activities toward promoting a pro-Israel rather than anti-Arab foreign policy.

The other major difference between the two lobbies is the use of paid foreign agents by the Arab lobby. Pro-Arab U.S. government officials can look forward to lucrative positions as lobbyists, spokesmen, and consultants for the Arab cause. For example, the outspoken critic of the Israeli lobby, former Senate Foreign Relations Committee Chair J. William Fulbright, was hired by the Saudis and the United Arab Emirates, and a former assistant secretary for legislative affairs and special assistant to President Kennedy, Fred Dutton, was hired as the agent for Saudi Arabia who spearheaded the AWACS campaign and reputedly conceived the "Reagan versus Begin" angle.

INFLUENCE

There is a kind of Cartesian mentality latent in the literature on interest groups that seems to suggest that interests groups exist and therefore must have influence. In the case of the groups under investigation here, this view is too simplistic. For example, if we examine the agenda of the NAAA, it is clear the Arab lobby has lost on every issue relating to Israel. In particular, U.S. aid to Israel has continued, with increasingly favorable terms being given regarding the balance of grants and loans, loan guarantees were provided, skepticism of the PLO has remained even in the wake of the Israeli–Palestinian declaration of principles on self-rule, and there is no support for the creation of a Palestinian state.

One example of the Arab lobby's relative weakness was seen in 1981, when AIPAC persuaded a majority of Congress to sign a letter opposing the AWACS sale. The NAAA tried to obtain support for a congressional resolution condemning violence in the Middle East and calling for a suspension of arms deliveries to Israel after its attack on Beirut. The NAAA recruited only seven sponsors in the House.

Similarly, the existence of an Israeli lobby does not prove that it influences

U.S. policy. Former Senator Charles Mathias, a man who was subject to lobby pressure, suggested that it does influence policy. He wrote that, "as a result of the activities of the [Israeli] lobby, Congressional conviction has been measurably reinforced by the knowledge that political sanctions will be applied to any who fail to deliver."[8]

This is actually a fairly recent phenomenon. Congress did not take an active role in Middle East policy until after the 1967 Six-Day War. Afterwards, in 1968, 1970, and 1971, Congress pushed the administration into selling fighter planes to Israel by appropriating arms-sales credits before the president had decided to sell the planes.

It is difficult to explain why the Israeli lobby was unable to get more support for Israel before 1967. One reason was the United States' perception that Israel was strong enough to defend itself without direct American assistance. Alternatively, Israel was not yet considered a strategic asset, and Iran was being groomed as the West's police force for the region. There was also the State Department's omnipresent fear that aid to Israel would antagonize the Arabs and threaten U.S. interests in the area. Finally, the Israeli lobby did not become organized to the extent it is now until after 1967. Before then, much of the lobbying activity was conducted by individual Jews who enjoyed access to decision makers as a result of personal relationships.

The situation changed dramatically after the October 1973 war began. In the first twelve days of the war, the United States airlifted $825 million worth of military supplies to Israel. President Nixon told Congress the resupply was necessary to offset the resupply of Syria and Egypt by the Russians. Congress then approved $2.2 billion in emergency assistance.

Between 1946 and 1971, Israel received a total of $1.5 billion in aid, but since 1974 total economic and military assistance has exceeded $40 billion. The shift in U.S. policy was a result of several factors, including a desire to ease Israel's economic burden, the belief that rearming Israel would convince the Arabs to abandon the war option, and the hope that the U.S.–Israel aid relationship could be used in negotiations with the Arabs as evidence of American leverage over the Israelis. Also, by demonstrating the military superiority of Israel, given U.S. arms, Secretary of State Henry Kissinger hoped to woo the Arabs into the American camp. What is significant about this policy is that it was consistent with Israeli lobby interests but was formulated independent of lobby input.

The Israeli lobby has successfully persuaded Congress to increase aid levels above administration requests several times. For example, in 1982, despite the U.S. recession, unhappiness over the Israeli operation in Lebanon, and administration opposition, Congress still voted to increase aid to Israel. Congressional increases may be influenced by direct lobbying, but administration requests and the general support for aid to Israel are more likely products of independent calculations of the national interest. It is unlikely, however, that similar aid levels would be proposed in the absence of an organized Israeli lobby. Nevertheless, it is difficult to assess influence when the administration, Congress, and the Israeli lobby all agree on a policy, as is usually the case with foreign aid. It is therefore necessary to look at legislation that is either opposed by some important interest or that would not be considered in the absence of an Israeli lobby.

LEGISLATIVE INNOVATION

There are several examples of legislation that would not have been introduced without Israeli lobby pressure: a resolution to reexamine U.S. membership in the United Nations if Israel were expelled; the prohibition of payments to UNESCO because of Arab-sponsored resolutions condemning Israel; the reduction of funding for the International Atomic Energy Agency because of the illegal rejection of Israel's credentials; the reduction of funding for the United Nations Relief and Works Agency because UNRWA camps were used, in violation of U.S. law, to train PLO terrorists; and a measure ending the automatic granting of visas to PLO members. These bills were relatively noncontroversial; the same cannot be said for legislation regarding the Arab boycott.

The antiboycott bill prohibits American firms from cooperating with the Arab boycott of Israel. *Candidate* Jimmy Carter had said, in an apparent appeal for Jewish votes during the foreign policy debate with President Ford, that the boycott was a disgrace and that he would do everything he could as president to stop it.

President Carter saw the situation a little differently, however, fearing that legislation that was too strong might endanger his Mideast peace efforts and cause OPEC to raise oil prices. American corporations, fearing a reduction in trade, vigorously opposed the bill. "Although American principles and ideals were at stake in the boycott controversy," *Congressional Quarterly* wrote, "the issue has been pursued almost exclusively by the nation's Jewish community."[9]

In 1976, both houses of Congress voted overwhelmingly for an antiboycott bill, but President Ford was able to defeat it through an end-of-session parliamentary maneuver. The business lobby recognized that some form of legislation would be adopted with the ascension of Jimmy Carter to power, so, in 1977, negotiations ensued between the Business Roundtable and representatives of the Israeli lobby that resulted in a compromise agreement that was adopted verbatim by the Congress.

The antiboycott bill demonstrated Israeli lobby influence. In this case, however, Congress was solidly behind the lobby's position. A more accurate test may be to look at cases where the lobby is at odds with not only the administration and "big business," but also with a large proportion of Congress. The proposed arms sales to Saudi Arabia in 1978 and 1981 offer two such cases.

THE SAUDIS GET F-15 JETS

Congressional review of arms sales has given the Israeli lobby access to the decision makers, and it has taken advantage of this access by trying to stop arms sales to hostile Arab states. The lobby's argument, in brief, is that arms sales to the Arabs endanger Israel, threaten the stability of the Middle East, and perpetuate the arms race. These arguments have generally been accepted by a majority of representatives and were used to force President Ford to modify his proposal to sell mobile HAWK antiaircraft missiles to Jordan in 1975. Ford eventually agreed to sell Jordan only immobile missile batteries. Similarly, in 1976, Ford wanted to sell air-to-ground missiles to Saudi Arabia; in order to head off a possible veto of the sale, he had to compromise by cutting the number of missiles to be sold from 1,500 to 650.

A far more difficult fight arose over the proposed sale of F-15 fighter planes to Saudi Arabia. The Israeli lobby mobilized its supporters to try to kill the sale; simultaneously, the largely dormant Arab lobby came to life.

The Arab lobby had been active from its inception, but it was not until the 1978 proposal to sell F-15s to Saudi Arabia that its presence was felt on Capitol Hill. There are several possible explanations for the lobby's sudden emergence. The best explanation is probably that this arms sale brought the first major congressional fight for something of vital interest to an Arab state. Previous arms sales had been for smaller quantities of less sophisticated weapons, which the Israeli lobby had tried to reduce in quantity rather than obstruct. The F-15 sale was the first all-out effort by the Israeli lobby to block a sale to the Arabs, and the Arab lobby knew it would have to fight to get the sale approved.

Proponents of the sale argued that Saudi Arabia is a moderate Arab state that needs support if a peace settlement is to be achieved in the Middle East. They also expressed a desire to maintain a "balanced" relationship in the region as well as to ensure U.S. oil interests. As in any arms sale, there was the threat the Arabs would go elsewhere to buy the weapons. There was also the omnipresent Soviet threat to the region. Israel's supporters had a different outlook, summed up by Senator Moynihan, who called the sale "a rationalization of American nervelessness in the area of international economic policy as well as political and military policy." [10]

The opponents of the sale forced a compromise: The F-15s were to be based beyond the range of Israel and would not be equipped with bomb racks or air-to-air missiles. These concessions won over some of the undecided but did not dampen the Israeli lobby's resolve to block the sale. In what was described as a "litmus test" for future support from Jews, the Senate voted to allow the sale.

The NAAA declared victory and celebrated the end of the Israeli lobby's "veto" over American Middle East policy. The Israeli lobby had taken on the administration, the petro-diplomatic complex, and much of the Senate, including some traditional supporters, and lost the battle. The F-15 vote illustrated the limits of the Israeli lobby's influence; but as subsequent events have ⌐¹   ⟍ it did not signal a change in U.S. policy, as witnessed by the fact that
included fifteen F-15s and seventy-five F-16s for Israel as well. This
⟍ a skirmish, however, compared to the lobbying war that would be
⟍r the proposed sale of AWACS to Saudi Arabia.

THE BATTLE OVER AWACS

The compromise on the F-15 sale—that the planes would not include bomb racks or carry missiles—was resented by the Saudis, who persistently asked for the additional equipment. In 1980, President Carter was forced to reject these requests after receiving a letter signed by sixty-eight senators (mobilized by AIPAC) opposing such a sale. In 1981, President Reagan decided to sell the Saudis not only the enhancement equipment, but also highly sophisticated AWACS radar planes.

The Israeli lobby immediately went to work collecting signatures on a letter opposing the sale, and by August AIPAC had lined up a majority of Congress against it. After the House disapproved the sale, the Arab lobby launched an intense campaign to persuade senators considered "vulnerable" to vote for it.

As one would expect, the oil and defense industries lobbied hard for the sale. By far the biggest lobbying effort, however, was orchestrated by Boeing—the main contractor for AWACS—and United Technologies, which alone had $100 million at stake. The presidents of Boeing and UT sent out more than 6,500 telegrams to subsidiaries, subcontractors, and distributors all over the country urging them to support the sale. Support from those directly involved should come as no surprise; what made this issue unique, however, was the involvement of many businesses and organizations, such as the Florist Insurance Company, which had no direct interest in the debate.

What was probably more important than the Arab lobby campaign, however, was the decision of the single most powerful foreign policy lobbyist to throw his full weight behind the sale. On October 1, President Reagan held a press conference in which his statements of support for the sale were seen as a direct challenge to the Israeli lobby. "While we must always take into account the vital interests of our allies," Reagan said, "American security interests must remain our internal responsibility." Then, in what was obviously a reference to Israel, he added: "It is not the business of other nations to make American foreign policy. . . . I suppose what really is the most important thing is a perception that other countries not get the perception that we are being unduly influenced one way or the other with regard to foreign policy." In the following three weeks, Reagan succeeded in changing the minds of eight senators who had cosponsored the resolution of disapproval, and the sale was allowed to proceed.

The turning point came when the president began to make his case personally to the senators. Several announced they were supporting the president after receiving "top secret" assurances regarding Israel's security. Others were given more tangible reasons to switch their votes, such as promises to support appropriations for projects in their home states. One of the best examples was Republican Roger Jepsen of Iowa, who was seen as the key senator needed for the sale's approval. According to one White House official, "We just beat his brains out." The White House generated calls and letters from Jepsen's constituents and threatened to stop cooperating with him in the future. As the official said, "We stood him up in front of an open grave and said he could jump in if he wanted to."[11] Jepsen chose not to jump and switched his vote to support the sale.

This time the Israeli lobby had been opposed by the president, big business, and many of the leaders of the Senate. The loss was a narrow one, however, and the lobby not only succeeded in forcing the administration to place a variety of restrictions on the sale but was also able to persuade the administration to compensate Israel with additional aid and weapons. Moreover, Congress did not approve any major weapons sale to an Arab state that was opposed by the Israeli lobby until the Gulf crisis in 1990. For example, when Reagan attempted to sell arms to Jordan in 1984, Congress stipulated that Jordan enter the peace process first; when King Hussein refused to do so, the sale was dropped. In 1986, the administration proposed the sale of Stinger missiles to Saudi Arabia and, for the first time in history, the sale was vetoed by the Congress.

ISRAEL GETS LOAN GUARANTEES

The influence of the Israeli lobby is sometimes more ambiguous, as in the case of Israel's efforts to obtain $10 billion in loan guarantees to help absorb Soviet and Ethiopian Jewish immigrants.

In 1989, the Soviet Union dramatically liberalized its emigration policy. This, combined with an upsurge in anti-Semitism, stimulated a massive exodus of Soviet Jews. In 1990, almost 150,000 Soviet Jews arrived, compared with 18,000 only two years earlier. Based on applications for exit permits, officials expected as many as one million Jews to immigrate to Israel within five years. The cost of absorbing this number was estimated at $50 billion.

Israel turned to the United States for help. In 1990, Congress approved $400 million in loan guarantees to help Israel build housing for the newcomers. The guarantees allowed Israel to obtain loans at lower rates, for longer periods than they could get on their own. The U.S. did not have to pay anything unless Israel defaulted, something it had never done.

In the summer of 1991, the Israeli lobby began an unprecedented effort to mobilize support for a $10-billion-loan-guarantee package to be spread over five years. The administration was not enthusiastic about the idea because of its general dissatisfaction with the Israeli government policies under Prime Minister Yitzhak Shamir. In particular, it was determined to freeze settlement activity on the West Bank, something Shamir refused to do. In addition, the administration was engaged in sensitive diplomacy with the Arabs to try to convince them to participate in peace talks with the Israelis.

Anticipating opposition, the Israeli lobby recruited more than 60 Senate cosponsors for the legislation. In addition, thousands of people planned to fly to Washington to lobby for support of the guarantees.

The day the citizen lobbyists arrived, September 12, President Bush unexpectedly called a news conference in which he threatened to veto the guarantee legislation and expressed anger with Israel's challenge to his Middle East policy and asked the American public to back his call to delay consideration of the guarantees for 120 days. He said he was "one lonely guy" facing "a thousand lobbyists" who had been mobilized by the pro-Israel community. The statement had anti-Semitic overtones that had a chilling effect on the Israeli lobby.

Bush also put Democrats in Congress in a bind. Though the Israeli lobby hoped Congress would overcome the president's opposition, it immediately became clear pro-Israel Democrats were unwilling to fight. One reason for their position was their belief they could not win the battle. A second, related reason was that the mood of the country had turned against foreign aid programs and the Democratic party planned to attack Bush in the 1992 campaign for devoting too much time, money, and energy abroad. Finally, the argument that the Arabs might not participate in peace talks if Israel received the guarantees (despite the fact the Arabs said no such thing) allowed the president to convince many members to "give peace a chance."

The administration's true purpose was to stop Israel from building settlements. It also became increasingly clear that Bush did not want to do anything to help the Shamir government. Thus, when the 120 days elapsed and Senator Patrick Leahy (D-VT) offered a compromise whereby Israel would get the guarantees, but with money deducted for the cost of any new settlements that Israel build, Bush rejected the idea.

Meanwhile, the Arab lobby had launched a counteroffensive against the guarantees, suggesting in newspaper ads and elsewhere that the money for Israel would be taken away from U.S. cities and exaggerating the program's cost.

In June 1992, a new Israeli government came to power with a dramatically different ideology that included a freeze on settlement activity. The Bush administration wanted to bolster Prime Minister Yitzhak Rabin and reward him for his flexibility. Consequently, when the two leaders met in August, Bush offered to provide the guarantees. Israel agreed to cover all fees and expenses, clearing the way for passage as part of the foreign aid bill that passed the Senate 87–12 and the House 312–105.

The Israeli lobby clearly put the loan guarantees on the policy agenda and marshaled the support to pass what was widely, though incorrectly, viewed as a huge foreign aid program at a time of widespread unease with such programs. But the lobby could not overcome the president's opposition. It was not until Bush reversed his position that it became possible to ensure the guarantees would be provided.

LIMITS TO LOBBY POWER

The inability of the Israeli lobby to stop the F-15 and AWACS sales demonstrates that the power of the lobby is limited. Support for the lobby's interests is by no means automatic, as critics would have us believe. In fact, one can find a number of policy decisions that were opposed by the Israeli lobby and others that were not made even under lobby pressure for them. This becomes even clearer when major diplomatic and military decisions are considered; for example, the Sinai disengagement agreements, the Syrian-Israeli agreement, and the Camp David peace treaty were made with little or no input from the Israeli lobby.

The most blatant example of the United States acting independent of Israeli lobby interests occurred in 1956, when the United States sided diplomatically with the Soviet Union against Israel, Great Britain, and France in the Suez War. Perhaps the lobby's biggest failure persists to this day: the United States' refusal to recognize Jerusalem as Israel's capital (though Clinton said during his campaign that he recognized it as such, and the Congress overwhelmingly voted to do so in 1990).

In 1983, the ambassador to Kuwait told the U.S.–Arab Chamber of Commerce in San Francisco bluntly: "American businessmen must understand that their success in the Mideast hinges on how the U.S. deals with Israel."[12] The Arab lobby has not been able to make such threats work. Overall, its influence is negligible, except in those rare instances where its interests coincide with those of the administration, key legislators, and a broad segment of the business community. The truth is U.S.–Arab ties have improved as U.S.–Israel relations have continued to grow closer. This became dramatically clear when the U.S. succeeded in forging a coalition with several Arab states in the war against Iraq at the same time it had forged a strategic partnership with Israel. The Gulf War also was a stimulus to the peace process, in which the United States is viewed as a key player by the Arabs precisely because of its close relationship with Israel.

At the moment, the balance of lobbying power remains clearly in favor of the Israeli lobby, but Arab economic power has allowed the Arab lobby to obtain greater access to the political process than ever before; nevertheless, unless a large number of Arabs immigrate to the United States and public opinion changes radically, the Israeli lobby should still prevail in the marketplace of political ideas.

CONCLUSION

In most of the interest group literature, there has been an emphasis placed on the description of group formation and maintenance, and relatively little investigation of influence. The main reason for this is that influence is frequently taken for granted. Reference to interests group influence on foreign policy tends to contradict this conventional wisdom, however, because there is said to be little or no interest group influence over foreign policy. This is sometimes explained in terms of the absence of any direct impact of most foreign policies on a segment of the public. The case of the Israeli lobby is frequently cited as an exception, but it really is only the most obvious example of an interest group that is concerned with foreign policy on the basis of nontangible, suprapersonal interests in a particular policy.

The Israeli lobby is generally considered to be the most powerful foreign policy interest group, so I would not expect other interest groups to enjoy the same degree of success in reaching their foreign policy objectives; nevertheless, the pluralist forces described in this chapter should apply to other groups concerned with different foreign policy areas. Thus, for example, an analysis of the balance of lobbying power between Americans of Greek and Turkish descent should help explain the direction of U.S. policy in the Mediterranean. The balance shifts according to the relative access, resources, cohesion, size, social status, and leadership of the competing groups. To these factors must be added the informal components of voting behavior and public opinion. The ability to build coalitions with other groups can shift the balance one way or the other.

The preceding analysis demonstrates that the Israeli lobby enjoys the balance of lobbying power; *ceteris paribus,* the lobby should achieve its objectives whenever the president supports it and will tip the balance in the direction of the legislature when the president opposes it. Whether the lobby will prevail in the latter case will largely depend on policy content and the locus of decision.

If the locus of decision is the executive branch, then the president's position will always prevail; however, decisions made in the legislative branch will be subject to far greater influence from nonexecutive actors, and the generally sympathetic Congress will *sometimes* support the Israeli lobby over presidential opposition, as it did in the antiboycott case. The lobby's ability to overcome presidential opposition also varies according to policy content, with the lobby enjoying far greater success on economic issues such as foreign aid than on security-related issues such as arms sales.[13]

Pluralism alone, as the other chapters in this book demonstrate, does not explain foreign policy decision making, but this chapter illustrates why interest group influence should not be excluded from any analysis of American foreign policy.

NOTES

1. Robert Pastor, *Congress and the Politics of U.S. Foreign Economic Policy* (Los Angeles and Berkeley: University of California Press, 1980), p. 49.

2. Peggy Strain, "Abourezk Rips Israel-Lobby Power as 'Dangerous,'" *Palestine Digest* (April 1977), p. 9.

3. John Fialka and Brooks Johnson, "Jewish PACs Emerge as a Powerful Force in U.S. Election Races," *Wall Street Journal* (February 26, 1985), p. 1; *Washington Report on Middle East Affairs* (November 1992).

4. I. L. Kenen, *Israel's Defense Line* (New York: Prometheus, 1981), p. 114.

5. Congressional Quarterly, *The Washington Lobby* (Washington, D.C.: Congressional Quarterly, 1974), p. 117.

6. Jimmy Carter, *Keeping Faith* (New York: Bantam Books, 1982), p. 299.

7. Steven Emerson, "The ARAMCO Connection," *The New Republic* (May 19, 1982, reprint), p. 3.

8. Charles Mathias, Jr., "Ethnic Groups and Foreign Policy," *Foreign Affairs* (Summer, 1981), p. 994.

9. Congressional Quarterly, "Carter Moves Cautiously on Anti-Boycott Proposals," *Weekly Report* (March 12, 1977), p. 437.

10. *Congressional Quarterly Almanac* (Washington, D.C.: Congressional Quarterly, 1978), pp. 410–411.

11. John Hyde, "How White House Won Jepsen's AWACS Vote," *Des Moines Register* (October 29, 1981), p. 1ff.

12. Harre W. Demoro, "Kuwait Envoy Talks Tough on U.S., Israel," *San Francisco Chronicle* (January 29, 1983), p. 7.

13. Mitchell G. Bard, *The Water's Edge and Beyond: Defining the Limits to Domestic Influence on U.S. Middle East Policy* (New Brunswick, N.J.: Transaction, 1991), pp. 267–287.

5. THE JAPANESE MEGAPHONE: FOREIGN INFLUENCES ON FOREIGN POLICYMAKING

John B. Judis

Kaoru Kusuda, a slight young woman who joined the Japanese foreign service after graduating from Keio University, arrived in Washington after tours of duty in Great Britain and Singapore. Kusuda, the first Japanese official especially assigned to monitor Washington think tanks, says, "The embassy and the foreign ministry think it is an important thing to follow their activities."

Kusuda's arrival was the latest move in Japan's massive effort to influence American opinion—an effort made more urgent by growing American resentment of Japan's $50 billion annual trade surpluses. According to Pat Choate, a vice president of TRW and Japan critic, . . . Japanese government agencies, corporations, and foundations spent $150 million in 1988 and $250 million in 1989 trying to win American "hearts and minds." This is far more than any other foreign country spends. Moreover, unlike the funds spent by Canada and Great Britain and their companies, the Japanese contribution is part of a concerted political and economic strategy.

Some of this money is directed toward what the Japanese call "good corporate citizenship," but much of it is aimed at reinforcing the viewpoint of the Japanese in the raging American debate over trade and foreign investment. Currently they are targeting their funds on scholars and think tanks that blame the trade deficit on American fiscal or corporate policies rather than on Japanese trade barriers or state-subsidized export strategies. Not surprisingly, the Japanese have avoided funding proponents of "managed trade" who believe that Japan must agree to specific increases in its imports. "What the Japanese are trying to do is maintain the status quo," says Donald Hellmann, professor at the University of Washington's Jackson School of International Relations.

According to Choate, the Japanese also spent a minimum of $100 million last year [1989] hiring Washington lawyers and public relations experts. Most of those hired have been what Washingtonians call "Guccis"—$350-an-hour former legislators or government officials like former Republican cabinet official Elliot Richardson or former Carter White House aide Stuart Eizenstat. Through these prestigious ex-officials, the Japanese expect to influence Congress and the White House policies on trade and investment. [In 1989], for instance, Japanese companies tried to keep semiconductors and telecommunications equipment off the administration's list of products that Japan was refusing to import and to block congressional efforts to fund American consortia in high technology.

There is nothing illegal about Japan's funding of think tanks and academics and hiring lobbyists. Nor is there any evidence that Japan's contributions have led scholars to reverse their positions. Without Japanese funding, policy experts would still be arguing about what causes American trade deficits and whether Japan's investments in the United States are a boon or a bane. But the hundreds of millions that Japan is spending annually are tilting the debate about America's economic future without the public being aware of it. The Japanese are radically reinforcing opinions that mirror their own. "It's like giving certain people a megaphone and forcing everybody else to shout," Choate says.

The money is also creating what the Japanese call "structural corruption"—a kind of systemic bias that does not require conscious acts of corruption but yields much the same results. Government officials in the U.S. Trade Representative's office and the Commerce Department are constantly tempted to allow their negotiating stance to be colored by lucrative future employment possibilities as Japan lobbyists. Two years ago [in 1988] Robert E. Watkins, deputy assistant secretary of commerce for automotive affairs and consumer goods, resigned after the Associated Press reported that he had sent about 500 letters and résumés to companies including Mazda, Toyota, and Nissan, describing himself as "uniquely qualified to establish and lead an automotive association committed to market principles."

Academics and think tanks are subject to similar temptations. The graduate student in Japan studies worries about who is going to fund his research, and the resident fellow at a think tank, who now has to raise his own salary, worries about how he is going to do so without substantial Japanese contributions. Hellmann says, "If you've got academic institutions and think tanks pandering to where the money is, then you become unable to generate new ideas and policies."

I

The Japanese are especially interested in think tanks because they play a critical role in Washington, translating academic research into policy recommendations. Think tankers like the Brookings Institution's Robert Lawrence frequently testify in congressional hearings on U.S.–Japan issues. Think tank reports also carry considerable weight in policy debates. Administration and congressional critics of the [1988] Omnibus Trade Bill relied heavily on an Institute for International Economics study of U.S.–Japan relations. The study, partially funded by the U.S.–Japan Foundation, claimed that a "complete elimination of Japanese trade barriers" would reduce the trade deficit only by $5 billion to $8 billion. "People were always citing the institute's research to show that the trade barriers were minor," says former Commerce Department official Clyde Prestowitz, a leading Japan critic.

The Japanese first approached Washington think tanks in 1972, after President Nixon slapped a 10 percent surcharge on imports, but they were initially rebuffed. According to a former Brookings fellow, when Sumitomo Bank offered the Brookings Institution a million-dollar grant that year, then Brookings President Kermit Gordon turned it down because the money came from "a foreign lobby."

In the intervening years, however, Washington's think tanks lost whatever qualms they had about accepting Japanese grants. With the rise of new conservative think tanks such as the American Enterprise Institute (AEI) and the Heritage Foundation and the decline in contributions from large American foundations such as Rockefeller and Ford, Washington's think tanks began to compete aggressively for funding. Most of the major think tanks in Washington, from the liberal Brookings to the conservative AEI and Center for Strategic and International Studies (CSIS), now gladly accept funding from Japanese firms and foundations. The exceptions are the liberal Economic Policy Institute and the new-right Free Congress Foundation, which favor aggressive trade policies: They have neither wooed nor been wooed by the Japanese.

The Japanese funders have sometimes sought immediate returns for their money. When Nomura Securities funded a Brookings-sponsored annual conference on Japan with other think tanks, Brookings officials became upset when Nomura tried to set the agenda. Brookings Senior Fellow Ed Lincoln explains, "The Japanese just don't have the same kind of eleemosynary background in their society, and the first thing they ask when they give money is what do we get."

In the face of this pressure, some think tanks have allowed the Japanese funders unusual kinds of influence. One of the first major Japanese grants after Ronald Reagan's election in 1980 went to CSIS. Housed on six floors of a K Street office cube, CSIS has been a major outlet of conservative foreign policy opinion. It is chaired by former NATO Ambassador David Abshire and still advertises a connection with former Secretary of State Henry Kissinger. It specializes in private briefings for political and business leaders.

In early 1981 CSIS accepted a million-dollar endowment from Toyota to found a chair of Japanese studies, the appointment to which would be for two-year nonrenewable terms. CSIS calls it their "Japan chair," but Japan specialists sometimes refer to it derisively as the "Toyota chair." Unlike universities, which customarily do not allow firms or individuals who endow chairs to have any say over who is appointed to them, CSIS consults Toyota officials about who is appointed. Appointees are also expected to give Toyota officials special briefings when they come to town. Former Treasury official C. Fred Bergsten, the director of the Institute for International Economics, thinks CSIS has gone too far. "To consult with any funder compromises the independence and integrity of an operation based on analytic research," he says.

Brookings, the oldest of the think tanks and traditionally a source of Democratic administration officials, began accepting Japanese grants in the early 1970s, but it insisted that Japanese firms donate their money to American foundations like the Japan Society, which then gave grants to Brookings's general fund, where Brookings's administrators parceled it out. [Later], however, Brookings accepted a major grant from Japanese business to endow a permanent chair in international economics, named after former treasury official Robert Roosa. According to Brookings officials, the three funding organizations, the Federation of Tokyo Bankers Association, the Life Insurance Association of Japan, and the Japan Securities Dealers Association, will not be consulted on who fills the chair or on the kind of work produced. But Ed Lincoln worries that accepting the gift was a "significant step" for Brookings. "The chair deals with international financial issues, but that is only one step removed from being directly involved with Japan." The pressures raised by such a gift are obvious. If Brookings were to appoint a critic of Japan's trade practices to the new chair, it might have trouble getting further gifts from Japanese companies.

The Committee for Economic Development (CED), a policy group based in Washington and New York, has played an important role in influencing government fiscal policy. But its ties to Japanese firms and lobbyists raise questions about its intellectual independence in addressing U.S.–Japan issues. Owen Butler, the chairman of CED and a former chairman of Procter & Gamble, now serves as a salaried senior adviser to Daiwa Securities America, the American subsidiary of the Tokyo financial firm. [In late 1989], Daiwa donated $1 million to CED for a program named after Butler.

CED produces biannual reports on "United States–Japan Trade Relations" with Keizai Doyukai, the Japan Association of Corporate Executives. The reports themselves are funded by the United States–Japan Foundation, whose money comes from the Japan Shipbuilding Association. The current report could be labeled the "Nissan report." CED chose former U.S. Special Trade Representative William Eberle, the president of a firm that lobbies for Nissan, to chair CED's committee. Keizai Doyukai's committee was chaired by Takashi Ishihara, the chairman of Nissan.

The 1989 report predictably reflected the view being promulgated by Japan and its Washington lobbyists. For instance, it blamed the trade deficit primarily on the U.S. budget deficit and warned that citing Japan for trade barriers under the bill "could trigger a protectionist spiral." It rejected a "managed trade" strategy favored by some of CED's business members. Such a view by itself is intellectually defensible, but it was not intellectually defensible to present this view, as CED did, as the result of the deliberations of independent American and independent Japanese businessmen.

II

The Japanese heavily fund Japan studies programs as well as think tanks. Chalmers Johnson, a Japan expert at the University of California, San Diego, estimates that Japan funds about three-quarters of university research about Japan. Like the think tanks, the Japan studies programs face the challenge of maintaining an environment of disinterested objectivity while seeking funds from donors very interested in the results of the research. Some of the programs have clearly failed to meet this challenge.

Washington's Reischauer Center for East Asian Studies, which is part of Johns Hopkins's Paul Nitze School for Advanced International Studies, doubles as a think tank and a graduate school. From its building down the street from Brookings, it not only teaches students but also publishes papers and holds conferences for legislators and business leaders. The Reischauer Center has always been unusually dependent on Japanese political and financial support, which has created concern among some academics. Johns Hopkins officials announced the formation of the center in Tokyo in June 1984 at the same time as it awarded Japanese Premier Yasuhiro Nakasone an honorary degree.

The center made Nakasone the honorary chairman of its advisory council, and in 1987 the Japan Shipbuilding Foundation endowed a chair at the center in Nakasone's name. In raising funds, one former faculty member says, the center has "peddled the Nakasone connection." For instance, in the center's promotional film, its director, George Packard, attributes the founding of the Reischauer Center to Nakasone's "extraordinary kindness and encouragement."

According to Packard, the center gets about 10 percent of its annual budget, or $300,000, from Japanese sources—a large amount, considering the contribution of student tuitions and the fact that the center also covers China and Southeast Asia. Donors include Japanese government agencies and major Japanese corporations, among them Toyota, Sony, All Nippon Airways, Nomura Securities, and NEC. The chairmen of these corporations and a representative from Japan's Ministry of International Trade and Industry (MITI) have sat on the center's advisory council.

The center's annual reports on U.S.–Japan relations mirror Japanese positions. In the center's 1988 report, which was funded by Equitable Japan and the Nissho Iwai Corporation, it denounced the Omnibus Trade bill, passed with wide Senate and House support and signed by the president, as "protectionist." The center's report also referred to the "alleged dumping" of Japanese semiconductors, even after an official Commerce Department finding that dumping had occurred. . . .

The Japanese themselves tend to think of the center as a lobby. The Japanese newspaper *Asahi Shimbun* included an account of the center's activities in a 1985 article titled "The Fifth Branch of the U.S. Government: Lobbyists." Robert Angel, a political scientist at the University of South Carolina, says: "Japanese government and business public relations types seem to interpret the center's appeals for funding as an opportunity to support a public relations platform in Washington."

Packard, a former aide to Ambassador to Japan Edwin O. Reischauer, is both director of the center and dean of the Nitze School. Packard is also a business consultant on salary to KRC Pacific Partners Limited, which advises American and Japanese firms. He writes advertorials for the Japanese Chamber of Commerce in New York. He has served on the board of Telejapan, a Japanese television company that produces what it claims to be independent shows for American television. Former *Newsweek* reporter Kim Willenson quit the board after learning that officials of MITI were supervising Telejapan. Willenson says that Packard told him he was "making a mountain out of a molehill."

Packard denies that either his own outside connections or the Japanese contributions to the center have any bearing on its teaching or publications. "We are uninfluenced by Japanese money," Packard says. Packard dismisses his academic critics: "In the academic world, there is a bitterness toward those who try to explain Japan's side."

But the center and Packard have what Chalmers Johnson calls a "truth in advertising problem." If the center were billed as a joint operation of Japanese and American businesses, and if Packard were presented on television or in op-ed pieces as a consultant and fund-raiser with links to Japanese companies rather than simply as an academic dean, then the public would not be misled. But when the center and Packard both present themselves solely under the guise of disinterested scholarship, the public is indeed being fooled, and the debate over U.S.–Japan relations is being corrupted.

III

To influence directly the White House and Congress, Japan has assembled a virtual who's who of lobbyists and advisers in Washington. The Japanese have hired more than 110 former government officials. Almost every important ex-trade official works for the Japanese in some capacity. These include three former U.S. trade representatives: Eberle; William Brock, who advises Toyota; and Robert Strauss, who is a senior partner in the law firm Akin, Gump, Strauss, Hauer, and Feld, which lobbies for the Japanese electronics giant Fujitsu, and who, according to a Toyota representative, advises that company.

Most of the top Democratic and Republican party officials work for the Japanese. Last December [1989], when the Democratic party was going to choose a chairman, three of its four leading candidates—Ron Brown and former Representatives Jim Jones and Michael Barnes—all represented Japanese firms. Former Democratic chair Charles Manatt represents Japanese firms, and when Hogan and Harston's Frank Fahrenkopf was Republican chair, he helped one of his law firm's Japanese clients gain entrée to the Department of Commerce.

Many lawyers and public relations men who enjoy or have enjoyed high White House connections work for the Japanese. These include former

Eisenhower White House aide Robert Gray, former Nixon aides Leonard Garment and Stanton Anderson, former Carter domestic policy chief Eizenstat, and former Reagan and Bush campaign aide James Lake.

Some government officials who become lobbyists reenter government as trade negotiators. The Bush administration's U.S. Trade Representative, Carla Hills, hired Julius Katz of the public relations firm Hill and Knowlton as her deputy. Hill and Knowlton represents more than 25 foreign firms and government agencies, including Toyota, Hitachi, and the Japan Trade Center. When Katz's appointment was announced, the general manager of Hill and Knowlton circulated a memo in which you could practically hear the spinning of the revolving door. "I thought you might want to write Jules a note of congratulations," the official prompted. "Obviously, he is with us until his confirmation and perhaps he will return after a stint with USTR."

Japan and America's other economic rivals do not condone these sorts of interlocking relationships between their own governments and foreign lobbyists, reasoning that they make it too hard for the government to distinguish between its interests and those of its competitors. In Japan no self-respecting lawyer, let alone former government official, is willing to lobby for an American company. "They would be seen as paid men," one Japanese official remarked. But what is culturally and morally forbidden in Japan is accepted procedure in contemporary Washington. "In Washington," Chalmers Johnson says, "the fix is always in."

This army of lobbyists and advisers furnishes Japanese companies with the troops necessary to win battles in Washington. The Japanese usually know what the administration plans to do before most administration members do. Through their lobby and their funding of think tanks, the Japanese have also acquired a virtual monopoly of economic expertise. When House or Senate members want to learn about a complex trade issue, they will almost inevitably fall back on someone who is an adviser to, a lobbyist for, or a recipient of funding from the Japanese. When the House Ways and Means Committee held a retreat in 1986 to discuss trade legislation, journalists Doug Frantz and Catherine Collins recently reported in *Selling Out,* they invited Strauss and Eberle to brief them.

When a policy organization names a distinguished group of experts to develop a position paper on trade, Japan's lobbyists invariably lead the list. The Council on Foreign Relations appointed a multinational working group [in 1989] to develop a paper on "Business and Government in an Interdependent World." The Americans included Eberle and former Deputy Trade Representative William Walker, who also lobbies for Japanese firms.

Through its lobbyists and advisers Japan also has unprecedented clout and access in the White House and Congress. In the Bush White House, Stanton Anderson [commanded] the attention due a friend and a key fund-raiser for the 1988 campaign. When congressional Democrats vote, they are likely to take seriously the recommendation of a former Democratic official who now commands party influence and fund-raising resources. "If you're a Democrat and a protectionist, you run up against Chuck Manatt, Bob Strauss, and Ron

Brown," says one lobbyist for a domestic manufacturer. "If you're interested in your career, why bump up against these powerhouses?"

Most of Japan's lobbying feats go unnoticed except by the businesses affected, but there have been some dramatic public successes. In a battle lasting two years, lobbyists got Congress to reduce drastically the sanctions against Toshiba for selling advanced submarine technology to the Soviet Union—a sale that cost the United States an estimated $30 billion to counter. When the Senate first learned of the sale in June 1987, it voted 92–5 to bar Toshiba sales for three years. A year later, after Toshiba had spent $10 million lobbying, the House and Senate finally reached a compromise, limiting the ban to government sales by Toshiba's subsidiary, Toshiba Machine. Instead of costing Toshiba $10 billion, Congress's action cost it several hundred million.

During the same years the lobby also defeated Representative John Bryant's bill that required foreign investors to disclose their holdings in American firms, even though most Western European countries and Japan require even closer scrutiny of foreign investments. After the House narrowly passed the measure, the Japan lobbyists, led by Eizenstat, Richardson, and former USTR General Counsel Richard Rivers from Strauss's law firm, secured its defeat in the Senate by 83–11.

The Japan lobby rarely wins battles on its own. Instead it throws its considerable weight behind one side in a debate. During Bush's first year the lobby mounted a major offensive to prevent the administration from citing Japan for blocking American sales of semiconductors under the "Super 301" legislation passed by Congress in 1988. Citing these products would have entailed raising a threat of sanctions against Japan if negotiations didn't remove trade barriers.

One lobbyist, who asked not to be identified, described the battle to keep semiconductors off the list as "a war." The Japanese may have spent as much as $5 million lobbying on this issue alone. Stanton Anderson's law firm received $167,000 between April and June alone from the Electronics Industry Association of Japan (EIAJ). William Walker's law firm, Mudge Rose Guthrie Alexander and Ferndon, received $181,000 from the EIAJ during the same period for lobbying White House aides Michael Boskin, Steve Ferrer, and Roger Porter. During the first six months of 1989, Strauss's firm collected $577,585 from Fujitsu. And these were only a few of the law firms and Japanese companies involved.

In the Bush administration debate over Super 301, the Japan lobby's massive effort tipped the scales in favor of Boskin, Porter, and budget director Richard Darman and against the Commerce Department. When the Bush administration announced the products that it was citing Japan for, semiconductors were not on the list. "I thought the decision reached by the President was masterful," lobbyist Anderson said. Four months later U.S. Trade Representative Hills announced the United States would no longer pursue the Reagan administration's demand that Japan import a targeted percentage of American semiconductors.

Recently the Japan lobby . . . also tried to frustrate attempts by the American electronics industry to develop an American high-definition television industry. As was the case with semiconductors, the lobby . . . reinforced efforts by a vocal faction within the administration. At the beginning of September [1990] Secretary of Commerce Robert Mosbacher, who had kicked lobbyists Anderson and Walker out of his office in March, threw in the towel. At Anderson's request, Mosbacher held a high-level meeting in Japan with the chairman of NHK, the Japan broadcasting company that is heavily committed to HDTV. During the same visit Mosbacher announced that he no longer favored American government support for HDTV.

The Japanese are also fighting congressional attempts to exclude foreign companies from government-funded industrial consortia that are meant to help the United States compete in high technology. Congress has been willing to include companies like Phillips or Thomson that do their research and development in the United States, but it wants to exclude companies that use the United States merely to assemble their products and refuse to allow American companies to join similar consortia. This applies to the Japanese companies. According to congressional sources, Mitsubishi Electronics, which employs Jim Lake's public relations firm, [lobbied] heavily against the proposals.

In waging these battles, Japan's lobbyists invariably appeal to American support for free markets and free trade, implying that the United States is violating international standards of good capitalist behavior. But in the battles over foreign investment disclosure, semiconductors, and government funding of high-technology consortia, the Japanese are using their lobby to block precisely the kind of trade and industrial strategy that they themselves used to win foreign markets for their consumer electronics industry. Like the proverbial bad parents, the Japanese are saying, "Don't do as we do, do as we tell you."

During the 1980s the Japanese developed an even more subtle strategy for influencing Congress and the White House. They got American businesses that depended upon Japanese companies to pressure Congress and the White House. They tried this first with imported car dealers and, during the mid-'80s, with computer and other high-technology companies that used Japanese components.

During the fierce debate over Toshiba sanctions, computer firms like NCR, Apple, and Hewlett-Packard that used Toshiba disk drives, printers, and other components lobbied Congress against sanctions. Some of the same firms protested the Reagan administration's semiconductor agreement with Japan and have sought the agreement's repeal. In fighting against government funding of American HDTV efforts, the Japanese have been able to rely on companies like Ampex that now get an important part of their profits from selling Japanese technology. "We've got to the point where we can say, 'We've met the enemy and he is us,'" says Bill Reinsch, an aide to [then] Pennsylvania Senator John Heinz.

The Japanese also use a traditional front group strategy to get their point across. Japanese subsidiaries now play a significant role in the Electronics Industry Association, but in debates with the American Electronics Association, the EIA presents itself as merely a rival American trade association. The EIA first opposed any government HDTV funding whatsoever and then, when that position appeared impolitic, insisted that foreign subsidiaries enjoy the fruits of any government intervention. The EIA's position was not without merit intellectually—its position paper was ably drafted by the Berkeley Roundtable on International Economics—but it lacked candor. What appeared to be a plea for free market principles was also part of a strategy for foreign domination of the American HDTV market.

IV

Japan's funding of think tanks and universities and its support for a powerful lobby in Washington have created an untenable situation in Washington. The most important questions facing Americans concern our economic future, and some of these revolve around our relationship with Japan and Japanese companies. Our trade with Japan is the single greatest cause of the U.S. trade deficit; and Japan has come to dominate precisely those areas of industry upon which our growth and prosperity will rest. The United States has to decide how to respond to what Akio Morita and Shintaro Ishihara in *The Japan That Can Say "No"* candidly call "economic warfare," but it's hard for Americans to have a meaningful debate when Japan and its lobbyists have acquired such extensive influence over the debate itself.

To put it as simply as possible: The United States must hold discussions among its own citizens before it can hold discussions with Japan. There have to be two separate debates or discussions. Americans first have to decide among themselves what is in their national interest. But the effect of Japan's influence campaign is to make the first debate impossible. When two prominent Americans rise to discuss U.S.–Japan trade relations, there's a good chance one or both is in the pay of the Japanese.

What can be done? The American public must at least be informed when a participant in the discussion of U.S. trade and investment has financial ties with the Japanese. The current means for such disclosure are, however, woefully inadequate.

Lobbyists for foreign companies are supposed to register with the Justice Department's Foreign Agents Registration Office. But the office is hopelessly understaffed . . . and the regulations themselves are extremely loose. Those who advise foreign companies but do not directly lobby public officials—like Brock or former chairman of the Council of Economic Advisors Martin Feldstein—do not have to register. Nor do lobbyists like Ron Brown who [represented] American subsidiaries of Japanese companies. This means that the public has no way of knowing that these people have a financial stake in holding certain views about trade and investment issues.

Senator Heinz . . . introduced a bill that [would have required] publicists or lawyers who represent the American subsidiaries of foreign companies or who represent foreign firms and their subsidiaries in administrative and judicial cases to register with the Justice Department. But Heinz's bill [was] fiercely fought by the lobby. Al Yamada, who lobbies for Toyota U.S.A., says,

"I think it is unfair. When you register as a foreign agent, you have all kinds of restraints."

. . . Heinz's bill [did] not cover the case of advisers, think tanks, policy groups, and universities. Here, part of the responsibility for disclosure must rest with the individuals and institutions themselves. When the Council on Foreign Relations publishes its . . . report on business–government relations, it should acknowledge that the authors included two prominent Japan lobbyists. And academics like Packard should identify their business interests when appearing in public forums. But when voluntary self-disclosure fails, the responsibility for revealing potential conflicts of interest reverts to the press.

So far the press had not lived up to this responsibility. The classic instance is an October 1986 *Washington Post* article on the debate over Reagan's semiconductor agreement. The story was headlined, "FORMER U.S. OFFICIAL ASSAILS JAPANESE PACT." It reported that "former Commerce Undersecretary Lionel Olmer" had criticized the agreement in a debate with Alan W. Wolff, "who represented the domestic semiconductor industry."

The story's headline and the identification of the principals gave the reader the impression that a disinterested former official had challenged the opinion of a paid industry lobbyist, but in fact, Olmer was employed at the time the piece appeared as an adviser to Nippon Telephone and Telegraph. Moreover, Wolff, besides representing the semiconductor industry, was himself a former trade official in the Carter administration. The argument was really between two former trade officials, both of whom had a financial stake in their own positions.

The practice continues unabated. In an October 1989 *Washington Post* story on Japan, Packard is identified merely as "dean of Johns Hopkins School of Advanced International Studies." In an October column attacking proponents of managed trade, *Washington Post* reporter Hobart Rowen cites as an authority "Washington attorney William N. Walker," who is in fact a New York attorney who lobbies for the Japanese electronics industry. Readers who assume that Packard or Walker are expressing disinterested opinions are being misled. And the *Post* is not alone. Of major national publications, only *Business Week* consistently ferrets out potential conflicts of interest.

Only when the participants are adequately identified can the great debate begin. Should the government try to break down Japanese trade barriers through demanding specific quotas? Should it scrutinize foreign investments? Should the U.S. government help develop its own HDTV industry? Should it help fund a consortium to develop the next generation of computer chips? Should it establish a new cabinet department that performs the same kind of functions that Japan's MITI does? America's future rests on the answers to these questions, but they cannot be adequately debated as long as many of the leading participants have an undisclosed financial stake in one answer rather than another.

6. THE NEW POLITICS OF THE DEFENSE BUDGET

Gordon Adams

Dramatic changes are taking place in U.S. defense resources and planning in the 1990s. . . . These . . . changes indicate that the United States is at a major turning point in its defense plans and budgets. They also suggest that the politics of defense budgets and spending are dramatically more complex than sometimes argued. For much of the Cold War period, defense budgets in peacetime remained relatively stable and successive generations of military hardware proceeded largely uninterrupted. Few bases were closed, while overall employment in the defense industry remained relatively stable.

The stability of policy and the apparent imperviousness of the defense structure to major changes encouraged the development of a school of thought which saw that structure as a "military–industrial complex" or "national security state." According to this analytical construct, defense decisions were made within relatively closed boundaries, among a constituency which linked the Department of Defense (DOD) and the military services to the defense industry and both to constituencies and elected representatives who benefitted from defense spending decisions.[1] This system was well-defended against major change or systematic reform; hardware programs advanced almost inexorably into production, and bases were carefully protected by the services, local supporters, and elected representatives in Washington, D.C.

The unraveling of the Cold War military architecture and the budgets that sustained it indicates that this theory of the politics of defense was, at best, inadequate and, at worst, inaccurate. The power of the military–industrial complex, if it was real, ought to have been sufficient to prevent severe budget decline, hardware cancellation, and base closings, the very events taking place in the 1990s.

This [chapter] argues that the politics of defense has always been more

Note: Some notes have been deleted or renumbered.

complex than this simple theory suggests. Briefly put, defense decisions and budgetary allocations have always been influenced by international forces and events, fiscal and economic requirements, bureaucratic behavior, and domestic politics. These factors tend to be discussed as if each were, by itself, a sufficient explanation of defense plans, programs, and budgets. In fact, each of these elements interacts with the others. Simply put, those who would separate politics and finance from policy in the defense policy arena cannot fully understand how and why defense decisions are made.

International forces and events clearly set a critical context for defense plans and budgets. U.S. national security documents are written in response to the international situation, laying out a national strategy that is sometimes asserted as the sole explanation for defense plans and budgets. By contrast, the international arena is said by some to play a secondary or even inconsequential role in shaping the programs and details in the annual DOD budgetary presentation.

Fiscal and economic considerations also play a role in defense plans. The defense budget began to decline in FY 86, well before the international upheavals of the late 1980s had begun. Even during the height of the Cold War, overall federal fiscal policy and the state of the economy played a role in the volume of resources available for defense and the rate at which those resources were obligated.

Global events and fiscal constraints are still insufficient to explain a wide number of defense decisions, including the persistence of duplicate roles and missions among the military services and the acquisition of some hardware programs whose relationship to overall national strategy is questionable or whose actual military value is doubtful. The logic of bureaucratic behavior is the third factor in the politics of defense. There is demonstrable evidence that the push and pull of bureaucratic lobbying and conflict have an impact on defense outcomes.[2]

Finally, defense planning, decision making, and budgeting are an integral part of the American political system, involving Congress, communities, industry, and the national electorate. Debates over the survival or demise of key weapons programs, over decisions to go to war, over base closings and contract awards, and even over the size of the defense budget itself are played out in a domestic political context. It is hard to doubt, for example, that the strong national defense stand taken by candidate Ronald Reagan in 1980 had an impact on his electoral fortunes, which, in turn, made possible the defense budget and program expansion of the early 1980s.

The interplay among these different factors is nothing new. Arguably, however, that interplay was somewhat less visible during much of the 1950s–1980s, since peacetime defense budgets remained relatively stable, as did the specific, major military threat to the United States. Periods of great change, however, tend to expose these complexities of the policy process.

As the United States enters the post–Cold War world, the defense policy process faces a difficult set of fundamental choices: a dramatically changed world with a smaller immediate threat; severe fiscal constraints; a need to redefine military roles and missions, and the forces, hardware, and budgets that go with them; all in the context of a congressional and public debate over the pace of defense reductions and the uses of savings from a smaller military budget. The defense plans, programs, and budgets of the twenty-first century will be shaped by the interaction of these forces.

Moreover, each of the factors which has an impact on defense is changing. The first observable change was fiscal, as the debate over defense budgets shifted from the turf of the threat to the turf of the deficit, with the passage of the Gramm-Rudman-Hollings Deficit Reduction Act in October 1985.[3] The second major change was global as the Soviet threat declined, and first the Warsaw Pact and then the Soviet Union itself disintegrated. The bureaucratic politics inside DoD also moved from an ethos of relative agreement to one of competition for scarce resources and a simultaneous necessity for greater joint cooperation in planning and operations. Congressional views of defense shifted from a policy to a fiscal perspective, while the congressional process underwent an explosion of staff, committees, subcommittees, and non-defense-related member and committee involvement in defense issues. Finally, the politics of the country shifted from a concern with global threats and competition to an inner-directed focus on domestic U.S. problems. Combined, these changes are putting the defense budget and planning system under the greatest stress they have faced since the buildup prior to World War II.

GLOBAL CHANGE AND NATIONAL STRATEGY

Since the Korean War, it has been relatively easy to argue the case for some significant level of U.S. defense spending. The large strategic and conventional military capabilities of the [former] Soviet Union, combined with an apparently aggressive Soviet strategy of involvement in conflicts in other regions of the world, set a baseline against which most U.S. defense budgets were justified by a succession of administrations.

The Soviet threat provided an understandable explanation for the size and distribution of technologies in U.S. strategic nuclear forces, especially with the clear Soviet attempt to "catch up" to U.S. strategic capabilities after the 1962 Cuban missile crisis. The United States, seeking to maintain some rough parity with Soviet strategic forces, needed a triad of capabilities some part of which would remain invulnerable to Soviet attack, needed bombers which could penetrate sophisticated and extensive Soviet air defenses, and needed, in the mid-1980s, to develop the kind of strategic defenses which could protect against at least a limited Soviet attack, if not complicate nuclear battle planning for the Soviet military.

So, too, Soviet and Warsaw Pact conventional military capabilities justified U.S. (and NATO) conventional forces and hardware, as well as tactical nuclear capabilities. As long as a massive Soviet military force was forward-positioned in the heart of Europe, along with Soviet-armed client states, a firm Western alliance was needed to defend its member countries and to provide the framework for a significant, forward-deployed U.S. military presence in Europe. U.S. conventional military hardware programs could be justified as necessary to compete technologically with a massive Soviet military investment, from helicopters to tanks to aircraft to air defenses.

U.S. forward-deployed tactical nuclear weapons could be justified by the need to confront overwhelming Warsaw Pact nuclear superiority with the risk that an attack would be met with a nuclear response. The need to rebuff a Warsaw Pact attack justified a sizable U.S.-based conventional force and significant airlift and mobilization planning. A growing Soviet naval capability clearly provided one important justification for a sizable U.S. navy, with up to fifteen carrier battle groups. By and large, moreover, the Soviet nuclear and conventional capabilities based in eastern Russia and Siberia, as well as the risk of a Soviet proxy attack from North Korea, provided a justification for forces deployed in Japan, South Korea, and the Pacific.

There were debates among U.S. military planners over the wider framework within which U.S. force structure could be explained, but even forces designed for and used between 1950 and 1990 in regions other than Europe and the northern Pacific were derivative of the forces developed for those theaters. Moreover, U.S. uses of force, whether in Latin America or Southeast Asia, were justified in terms of the global threat posed by Soviet military power and intervention. The Eurasian focus of a global conflict drove force planning and most acquisition choices, even if the forces never actually engaged in combat against the Soviet Union and its allies.

If one had to imagine a change which would significantly undermine Cold War force structure justifications, hardware choices, and strategic planning, it would be hard to find one more fundamental than the dissolution of the Warsaw Pact, the disintegration of the Soviet Union, and the withering away of the Soviet military and its research and production complex. Yet all of this took place between 1989 and 1992. The *weltanschaung* of the Cold War simply evaporated. While one could continue to argue that the military forces that remain behind in the successor states to the Soviet Union are sizable, with large nuclear capabilities and a significant number of personnel and equipment, their capabilities have declined rapidly, and it is virtually impossible to argue that these forces pose a direct and immediate threat to the United States. . . .

Smaller nuclear forces, with a divided command, could pose security problems for the United States, but these are clearly of a different nature than the problem of strategic deterrence in the face of a Soviet nuclear superpower. Strategic forces that are scarcely being modernized require dramatically different planning assumptions for U.S. strategic force acquisition. A dissolved conventional military and military alliance eliminate much of the justification for large, forward-deployed forces in Europe. Significantly longer warning times lead to basic changes in the planning assumptions for U.S.-based land and air forces, active and reserve. The complete disappearance of significant Soviet activity in other regions, from Asia to Africa to Latin America, means entirely different assumptions about the role of the U.S. military in those theaters.

In the 1990s, U.S. strategic policy and defense planners find themselves at a juncture much like that they faced in the late 1940s—previous assumptions about the U.S. role in the world and the place of military force were fundamentally outdated. A new strategic rationale for forces and budgets had yet to emerge. The size, composition, roles, and missions of the military had to be shaped and redefined. The 1990s constitute another such basic starting point.

The military situation of the United States in the 1990s is different, however, from the 1940s. In 1990, the nation had a 2-million-person military in place, with another 1.5 million in reserve; 28 army divisions, 14 carrier battle groups, more than 500 ships in the Navy and 36 Air Force wing equivalents. What justifies this size and structure? How will the debate over its downsizing and restructuring proceed? What should be the directions in which it should be reshaped?

A national debate has begun on these issues as part of a broader discussion of national strategy in the post–Cold War world. . . . What is striking about this debate over the future directions of U.S. national strategy is its fundamental nature and the seriousness with which alternative proposals are being treated. The definition of U.S. national security, the content of policy and strategy, and the size and structure of military forces are all at stake. It is also evident that this policy debate is providing only partial guidance, at best, for the reshaping of defense budgets and military forces.

In fact, this debate reflects similar disagreements which prevailed before the Cold War, when the rationale for U.S. national strategy and its forces was equally unclear. One could argue that the United States lacked an integrated strategy, while strong strains of neutrality and antimilitarism existed in the domestic political arena, until the early 1950s.[4] Due to the strength of isolationism in American politics prior to World War II, the scope of U.S. foreign policy was limited. The nation shunned entangling alliances and concentrated most of its efforts on hemispheric affairs. The restricted parameters of America's foreign policy made a large standing army unnecessary and the need for close integration between diplomacy and the armed forces unnecessary. It has been suggested that the U.S. victory in World War II was accomplished in large part without the guidance of an integrated national strategy.

Only in 1950, after a difficult process of national reassessment, was a coherent plan created to direct America's external relations and establish objectives which could form the basis of an integrated military force posture. The disappearance of the principal threat to the United States and its interests has thrown that apparently coherent plan into disarray. The weakness of the link between national strategy and specific defense decisions, in the environment of the 1990s, reveals more starkly the interplay of other factors in defense decision making.

RESOURCE PRESSURES

Defense planning, programs, and budgets have never been free from considerations of resource constraints, though policymakers have consistently argued that they should be. As already noted, defense budgets began to decline well before the disintegration of the Warsaw Pact and the Soviet Union, largely in response to resource constraints. Although the early years of the Reagan administration saw a rapid growth in defense funding, by mid-decade the rapid increase in the federal deficit had led to a congressional reaction. Defense budget reductions began in FY 86, as the result of a broader domestic fiscal decision: the passage of Gramm-Rudman-Hollings in October 1985. Given the broad political resistance to revenue increases and further reductions in discretionary domestic spending, the deficit reduction targets could only be met through reductions in the defense budget. . . .

Resource pressures on defense planning are not new, though they take on a stark relief in the 1990s in the absence of a clear national strategy. Since the ability to raise armies depends on the federal government's capacity to raise revenues, on the state of the economy, and on the public's perception of its ability to support military spending, resource availability has to be considered in the debate over the defense budget. Even in the era of clear statements of national strategy, resource considerations had an impact on defense spending. For example, the *Gaither Report* of 1960 stated:

> However, even large increases in defense spending would not have drastic consequences for our way of life. We could manage moderate increases in defense without any reduction of our present levels of consumption and investment. Even large increases might be possible without any reduction in the private sector of the economy.[5]

President Eisenhower refused to adopt the recommendations of the *Gaither Report,* however, almost entirely for economic reasons. This decision at the end of his term was consistent with the tone of defense policy throughout his administration. The "new look" was a means to escape the heavy expenditures which the strategy of containment required and rejected the premise of NSC-68, the 1950 strategic policy statement, that the United States could afford to devote 20 percent of its GNP to defense.

The early history of the Reagan administration is the exception that proves the resource constraint rule. One of the first defense decisions of the new administration was to request a $32.6 billion increase in the defense budget, the largest and fastest increase in peacetime history. While that fiscal buildup continued through FY 85, throughout the subsequent years, fiscal restraint has largely dominated the defense debate.

INTERSERVICE RIVALRIES AND JOINTNESS

With the end of the Cold War and the struggle to define defense budgets in a context of shrinking resources, the relationship among the military services has also begun to emerge as a major factor influencing defense policies, programs, and funding. It became clear during and after the Gulf War that each service was determined to ensure for itself a major role in that conflict, driven, in part, by the desire to demonstrate its utility for military missions beyond those considered part of the Cold War confrontation with the Soviet Union. . . .

Given the resource constraints of the 1990s, the services have also been struggling over the size of the wedges in the budgetary pie. The Navy and the Air Force, for example, have argued over the power projection mission, with an undertone that carriers and strategic bombers provide competing capabilities for that mission. Both the Army and the Marine Corps argue for an important role in providing early deployment of significant ground forces to combat zones. Vice Admiral Roger F. Bacon, Assistant Chief of Naval Operations for Undersea Warfare, noted in April 1992 that attack submarines could provide a wide range of important military capabilities, including missile land attack and covert insertion of special forces, missions not typically assigned to the submarine force.

At the same time that shrinking budgetary resources have exacerbated interservice tensions, they have also increased the pressures for "jointness," ranging from increased cooperative procurement to joint training and exercising. The Air Force and the Army have signed an agreement on joint doctrine; the Navy and the Air Force continue to explore possible cross-service applications of the Navy AX attack bomber technology. One crucial lesson of the Gulf War was clearly the growing need for joint exercises and training to enhance interservice combat operations.

The history of interservice tension in the U.S. military is a long one. . . . Military bureaucracies, like other bureaucracies, develop their own internal values and operating procedures and regularly promote their claim for fiscal resources against each other. Give the size of the U.S. military and the existence of three independent and one semi-independent services, it is hardly surprising that such tensions occur and that each service asserts its independent mission.

Without the Soviet threat to justify duplications and inefficiencies, the politics of interservice rivalry and negotiation is likely to become significantly more transparent as a source of force and budgetary planning for DOD. The absence of a clear threat or strategic design, combined with rapidly declining resources, is likely to exacerbate both inter- and intraservice tensions. At the same time, the need for a strategic design and for greater efficiency in the use of existing resources is also likely to intensify pressure for interservice agreement, jointness, and the elimination of inefficiencies in the administrative structures of the services. This paradox of conflicting pressures will require . . . a united military voice in the decision-making process. Not to do so risks opening an irreconcilable gap between resources and missions, and strains the already fragile credibility the Pentagon carries to Capitol Hill when defending its force structure proposals and cost predictions. . . .

THE DOMESTIC POLITICS OF DEFENSE

Strategy, resource constraints, and bureaucratic behavior among the armed services provide a partial, but still incomplete, explanation for defense plans, programs, and resources. U.S. defense debates take place in a political context which has its own impact on the policy and hardware outcomes. There can be no doubt, in the atmosphere of the early 1990s, that domestic politics has played and will continue to play a forceful role in the evolution of U.S. military forces and budgets. Debates over long-term strategy and force structure pit prominent spokespersons from Congress against the secretary of defense, the chairman of the Joint Chiefs of Staff, and the heads of the military services. Debates over the future of such hardware programs as the Marine Corps' V-22 Osprey, the Navy's F-14 fighter, the Air Force's strategic bomber, and the Navy's Seawolf submarine further reflect the impact of the wider domestic political context on defense.

More broadly, . . . the compelling political demand for some kind of "peace dividend," whether for deficit reduction or domestic needs, is putting inexorable downward pressure on defense resources. More, perhaps, than at any point in time in the post–Cold War era, domestic politics and political needs have intruded into the defense debate. As the Cold War rationale for defense budgets and program choices disappears, the domestic politics of defense becomes a more apparent and, at least in the short term, a more decisive factor in defense policy and budgeting.

Although some analysts are inclined to argue that domestic politics dominates defense decisions, political impact on the behavior of the services and other policymakers is actually relatively subtle. To some extent, the depth of information and resources needed for a detailed scrutiny of national strategy, force structure, and the defense budget, as well as the complex structure of the defense acquisition system, insulates a large number of defense decisions from outside political pressures. Nevertheless, congressional and electoral politics historically has intruded in significant ways into the defense policy process.

The defense budget clearly provides the principal context for the domestic politics of defense, while Congress and national elections provide the arena. The budget is the mechanism through which the executive branch sets defense priorities and reflects its policies. Hardware choices are only possible with funding; troops are trained and exercised, bases built and sustained, and ships sailed with budget resources. Moreover, the defense budget is the communications link between the executive branch and Congress. Through it, elected legislators fashion their own role in military policy and oversee the activities of the services and the Pentagon.

Congress is deeply involved in the process of defense decision making and funding through its scrutiny of the budget. By contrast with many other countries, Congress starts with a significant database on defense choices, policies, and programs, including the Office of Management and Budget's budget document, the secretary of defense's annual report, detailed descriptions and cost data on major weapons systems, research and development, military construction, and operations and maintenance programs, an itemization of military construction projects, detailed data on the composition of the military forces, volumes of financial data on DOD spending, historical data on DOD spending covering more than 40 years, as well as a variety of specialized briefing sheets and publications.

Moreover, Congress and its defense committees receive even more detailed classified data justifying DOD's budget requests, as well as unclassified and classified briefings and testimony from a stream of witnesses from DOD and the military services. From the start, Congress faces less of a problem ferreting out secrets from the Pentagon than it does sifting through the volume of data to separate the important from the insignificant.

Moreover, the congressional process for reviewing the defense budget request is complex. Congressional committees play the key role in this process. The Appropriations committees of the House and Senate have primary responsibility for approving expenditures. Since the 1960s the Armed Services committees of the two chambers, whose membership does not usually overlap with the appropriators, have also become major participants in the defense budget process, authorizing funding for specific programs. After 1974, a third layer of congressional review was created, the budget committees. The Budget Committee in each chamber considers the entire executive branch budget request and approves overall funding levels for thirteen "functions" of the federal budget, including "national defense." . . .

To support its complex process for defense decision making, moreover, Congress has considerable resources at its disposal. In and around the formal interactions between congressional committees and the services stand a number of less formal institutions which fill critical information needs for Congress or ensure constant interaction between Congress and DOD over the defense budget. Perhaps most important, Congress has developed an ample supply of staff expertise on defense matters, both for individual members and for the defense committees, as well as a variety of research institutions reporting to Congress on defense matters. Individual members each have at least one staff person with sole or partial responsibility for defense. Each of the committees reviewing the defense budget has staff—minimal for the Budget Committee, but numerous for the Armed Services and Defense Appropriations committees. These committee staff are often people with military or defense policy experience who sometimes move back and forth between the Pentagon and Congress. The possession of a skilled, experienced staff ensures that members of Congress, especially on the key committees, have their own capability to assess defense budgets independently of the Pentagon.

This independent capability has been substantially reenforced by the existence of a number of governmental research and auditing institutions which report to Congress on defense matters, including the budget. For years the General Accounting Office, an auditing arm of Congress, has conducted close scrutiny of defense budgets and spending through its National Security and International Affairs Division. The Congressional Research Service also maintains a staff capability to research defense budget issues for Congress. The 1974 Budget and Impoundment Act created still another organization, the Congressional Budget Office (CBO), which includes a significant National Security Division, researching budget proposals and options in the defense arena for Congress. Most recently, the Congressional Office of Technology Assessment (OTA) has begun to analyze defense policy issues for Congress. These different, even overlapping research capabilities significantly strengthen the ability of Congress to analyze and understand defense budget issues independently of DOD.

Still another important network, which intrudes into the political debate over defense, is the vast array of private and nonprofit think tanks, research and policy groups, trade associations, and contracting firms, which focus on the defense budget, defense policy, and defense acquisition, among other concerns.[6] While not all focus exclusively on the budget, many of them scrutinize the DOD budget request closely and provide Congress (and the Pentagon) with their views.

The military services themselves also maintain constant communication with legislators through congressional liaison offices within the Pentagon, which respond to congressional inquiries, and extensions of those offices on Capitol Hill, where the military can brief Congress on budget and policy issues and make themselves available to respond to congressional needs.

Finally, the media provide another important element in the domestic debate over defense, including a substantial "trade press" devoted to specialized coverage of defense matters. Well-informed, consistent coverage of the significant flow of defense information and of congressional debate informs that debate, translates arcane data into accessible language for policymakers, and serves as an informational beltway among Congress, the executive branch, and the defense analytical community.

Thus, there are multiple channels through which defense choices encounter domestic politics. That the debate becomes political is made all the more possible by the fact that *the budget is not delivered to Congress in the framework of a national strategy*. The "titles" in the budget are devoid of any strategic meaning or measure of military output: military personnel, operations and maintenance, procurement, research and development, family housing, etc. This structural characteristic tends to decouple resource allocation decisions from the strategic goals of national security policy.

As a consequence, the political debate over the defense budget tends to be dominated by line-items. The incentives for elected representatives, moreover, have not favored debate over strategy, since their primary concern is reelection. When it comes to defense matters, the priorities of constituents are typically focused on the level and location of spending, not its strategic rationale. Even with the end of the Cold War, members of Congress have little to gain by reducing or eliminating defense bases or projects, while the electoral rewards for promoting defense spending in the district are great.

While the retention of military bases is the common example of congressional promotion of district interests, there are also frequent congressional wrangles over hardware programs, motivated, in part, by pressures from constituents. In 1986, for example, the Air Force decided to terminate the T-46 trainer program due to cost overruns and delays. The Senate concurred with the Air Force's decision and voted no funds for the plane in its 1987 defense budget. The maker of the plane, Fairchild Republic Company, is headquartered in New York. After intense lobbying by the New York congressional delegation, the House voted to approve an earlier House Armed Services Committee provision that delayed cancellation and required the Air Force to complete additional testing before reducing or eliminating the T-46 program.

Even strong critics of the Pentagon are not immune from constituent pressures to protect programs and spending levels. Senator Alan Cranston of California campaigned for president in 1984 on a platform which called for deep cutbacks in defense spending and cancellation of several strategic weapons programs. His enthusiasm for reducing defense spending did not include the B-1B bomber, however, a strategic weapon produced in California. In the early 1990s, Senator Christopher Dodd of Connecticut, generally critical of defense budget requests, became a strong supporter of the Navy's Seawolf submarine, a program which DOD sought to cancel after one boat with its FY 93 defense budget request.

Defense contractors are often well aware of the importance of such political support. They work closely with committees and members of Congress to encourage support and, to some degree, activate the local networks of subcontractors and suppliers involved in such programs to provide "grass roots" encouragement for their programs.

The highly visible political interaction between the contractors and Congress, often with the active involvement of DOD, is what has given rise to the "military–industrial complex" school of analysis. One major problem with this school, however, is the reality that not all efforts to maintain a base or a hardware program succeed. In fact, . . . DOD, acting under congressionally sponsored legislation, . . . announced two successive rounds of base closings in 1988 and 1991. Moreover, with declining defense budgets in the late 1980s, DOD has been able to cancel a large number of weapons programs, involving significant employment in many congressional districts.

A close scrutiny of the politics of defense budgets and weapons systems contracting suggests that this "complex" has not been able to prevent such changes. There appears to have been little correlation between the location of a contract and the votes in Congress for or against that contract or between contractor campaign contributions to members of Congress and their votes on particular contractor's programs. Moreover, there is very little evidence that Congress has had a significant impact on the source selection process inside the military services or DOD.

In the post–Cold War world, the congressional politics of defense is likely to become more prominent. Combined with the absence of a perceived threat, bureaucratic infighting, and resource limitations, the struggle for survival in defense will be played out visibly in this political arena. Tensions between DOD and Congress had already begun to grow after 1989, focusing increasingly on disagreements over specific hardware decisions. Congressional decisions in 1990, 1991, and 1992 regularly returned to the budget funding the Pentagon had eliminated for such programs as the M-1 tank, the F-14 fighter, and the V-22 Osprey, while funding for other programs, such as the F-15 fighter, disappeared despite congressional opposition to the Pentagon's decision. The arguments over these programs tend to mix issues of politics, fiscal constraint, and policy.

With respect to the Marine Corps' V-22 Osprey, for example, the secretary of defense canceled the program in 1989, arguing that, though it was an attractive technology for future Marine Corps lift requirements, it was not affordable in declining budgets. Members of Congress have supported the program with a wide variety of arguments, including the importance of modernizing Marine Corps lift for missions it would undertake in the post–Cold War era, the significant improvement the V-22 represented over current helicopter lift, the cost-effectiveness of the V-22 option, and the potential of the technology for commercial applications, as well as the harmful consequences of termination for economic activity and employment in such states as Texas and Pennsylvania. Although this latter argument has been cited as a case of politics prevailing over policy choices, it is far from clear that the other defenses of the V-22 are irrelevant. In reality, as with many such arguments, the politics is difficult to separate from the policy issues involved.

Moreover, as the budget decline has continued, tension has increased in Congress between the rate of that decline overall and the pressures a rapid budget reduction would have on eliminating bases and hardware programs, leading to increased layoffs in congressional districts. This broader budget priorities issue, moreover, constitutes the link between the specifics of the defense debate and broader issues in national politics. National electoral politics and spending priorities have often had an influence over defense choices.

Since defense spending has been a vehicle for a display of presidential "toughness," the defense budget has been manipulated symbolically as a presidential campaign issue. At various times, national campaign promises have influenced changes in defense decisions. In 1980, for example, presidential candidate Ronald Reagan made the defense budget and the B-1 bomber major symbols of his commitment to restoring strong defenses. Once elected, he increased defense budgets dramatically and reversed the Carter administration's 1977 decision terminating production of the bomber. In 1988, commentators characterized President Reagan's veto of the 1989 Defense Authorization bill, which had broad bipartisan support, as an effort to make the Democratic party appear weak on defense and to boost the campaign of then-Vice President Bush.

Defense plans and decisions clearly take place in a political context, which has an influence on the outcome of those decisions. The interplay is complex, however, combining strategy, bureaucratic, and resource issues. In an era of declining major threats to U.S. security and rising demands for alternative uses of budget resources, political demands are likely to have a large and visible impact on defense decisions.

CONCLUSION

Like most areas of federal policy, the politics of defense decisions is not reducible to just one factor. Some would prefer to argue that national interests and national strategy guide defense planning and budgeting. While this has clearly been the case since the late 1940s, it constitutes an incomplete explanation for defense outcomes. Moreover, with the dramatic change in global events since 1989, the lines which connect defense plans and budgets to specific international threats have become significantly blurred.

The absence of a clear link between interests, strategies, forces, and budgets has brought into sharper relief the other factors which influence the defense debate. Resource limitations, which have always had some effect on defense decisions, loom large in the 1990s as a factor driving military forces and budgets downwards. To a large extent, the defense budgets from FY 86 through FY 93 could be said to have been driven as much, if not more, by fiscal limitations than by a clearly defined threat and strategy.

Bureaucratic behavior as a factor in defense decision making has also become clearer in the post–Cold War era. Without a clear justification for specific forces, infrastructure, or hardware, the services have been pressured into strategies that defend their size, program, and budget as much by the intrinsic need to slow the downsizing process itself as by a clear definition of military requirement. Contrarily, the services are also gradually being forced into greater "jointness" by the inexorable logic of constrained resources and the increasing inability of any one service to provide a full menu of military capabilities.

Finally, issues of strategy, resources, and bureaucratic behavior are being played out in increasingly visible ways in the political arena. The future of national goals and interests and global defense strategy is being debated at the presidential and even the congressional level. Parochialism and electoral self-protection combine with policy disagreements, leading members of Congress to walk a fine line between the desire for defense budgetary savings, the wish to define a different defense policy for the 1990s, and the need to protect district interests . . .

NOTES

1. For perspectives on this concept, see Richard F. Kaufman, *The War Profiteers* (New York: Doubleday, 1972); Paul A. C. Koistinen, *The Military-Industrial Complex: A Historical Perspective* (New York: Praeger, 1980); and Seymour Melman, *The Permanent War Economy* (New York: Simon & Schuster, 1964), among others. For the "national security state" perspective, see Marcus Raskin, *The Politics of National Security* (New Brunswick, N.J.: Transaction Books, 1979). Another view of this relationship describes it as a "subgovernment" or an "iron triangle," similar to other close relationships between the private sector, congressional actors, and executive branch agencies. See Gordon Adams, *The Politics of Defense Contracting: The Iron Triangle* (New Brunswick, N.J.: Transaction Books, 1981), especially Chapter 1, note 18. For a more critical view of this concept, see Kenneth R. Mayer, *The Political Economy of Defense Contracting* (Hartford, Conn.: Yale University Press, 1991).

2. There is a wealth of literature on the bureaucratic behavior of the Defense Department and the military services, including a number of significant case studies. See, among others, Robert Art, *The TFX Decision: McNamara and the Military* (Boston: Little, Brown Publishers, 1968); Harvey M. Sapolsky, *The Polaris System Development: Bureaucratic and Programmatic Success in Government* (Cambridge, Mass.: Harvard University Press, 1972); Ted Greenwood, *Making the MIRV: A Study*

of Defense Decision Making (Cambridge, Mass.: Ballinger Publishing Company, 1975); J. Ronald Fox, *Arming America: How the U.S. Buys Weapons* (Boston: Division of Research, Graduate School of Business Administration, Harvard University, 1974); and Merton J. Peck and Frederic M. Scherer, *The Weapons Acquisition Process* (Boston: Division of Research, Graduate School of Business Administration, Harvard University, 1962). See also the U.S. Senate Staff Report to the Committee on Armed Services, and the final report of the Packard Commission, President's Blue Ribbon Commission on Defense Management, *A Quest for Excellence: Final Report to the President* (Washington, D.C.: U.S. Government Printing Office, 1986).

3. The Gramm-Rudman-Hollings (GRH) act set specific legal targets, procedures, and a time line for federal deficit reduction. Although the GRH process has not resulted in the elimination of the deficit, it has put severe constraints on all areas of federal spending. See Glenn Gotz, "Notes on the Gramm-Rudman-Hollings Deficit Reduction Plan" (Santa Monica, Calif.: Rand Corporation, March 1986).

4. Barbara Tuchman has noted that "Americans have shown their dislike of organized war by a desperate attachment to three principles: unpreparedness until the eleventh hour; the quickest feasible strategy for victory regardless of political aims; and instant demobilization, no matter how inadvisable, the moment hostilities are over." Barbara Tuchman, "The American People and Military Power in an Historical Perspective," *America's Security in the 1980s*, Adelphi Paper #173 (London: International Institute of Strategic Studies, 1982), p. 5.

5. Joint Economic Committee, "Study Paper No. 18: National Security and the American Economy in the 1960's," *Study of Employment, Growth and Price Levels* (Washington, D.C.: U.S. Government Printing Office, January 30, 1960), p. 2.

6. Such groups include a wide number of institutes at the center of the political and policy spectrum: the American Enterprise Institute, Brookings Institution, Carnegie Endowment, Center for Strategic and International Studies, Council on Foreign Relations, and Defense Budget Project, among many others. There are also more advocacy-oriented defense policy groups.

7. OPERATION PUNDIT STORM: THE MEDIA, POLITICAL COMMENTARY, AND FOREIGN POLICY

Eric Alterman

I

Few events in recent American history demonstrate the destructive power of the punditocracy with greater clarity than America's decision to go to war with Iraq in January of 1991. Casting about for a replacement of its One Big Thing in the aftermath of the Cold War, the punditocracy found itself at sea in a world without clear enemies to condemn or a credible international crusade to plan. Dogged by increasing evidence of protracted decline and diminished international influence, the insider political dialogue manifested a kind of inchoate desperation—not altogether unlike that communicated by George Bush's syntax. "If only we knew who the bad guys were," the pundits seemed to be saying, "we'd know who we were again."

How it happened that the extrication of the Iraqi army from the kingdom of Kuwait came to be *the* most important priority of the American people in the winter of 1991 can only be understood in this context. George Bush's success in leading the American public into war might never have been possible without the energetic cooperation of the punditocracy who, for a brief shining moment, found a new Big Thing to demonstrate its self-worth. The punditocracy's role explains not only the delusion of omnipotence that seized the nation in the aftermath of the hundred hours' fighting, but also the presumably serious insistence on the part of almost everyone who appeared in the media at the time that the defeat of a nation with a gross domestic product the size of Kentucky's somehow represented America's "defining moment."

During the six months that George Bush, Dick Cheney, Colin Powell, and Norman Schwarzkopf laid the groundwork for their successful assault on Saddam Hussein's army, a tiny cadre of mostly neoconservative pundits performed a similarly delicate operation on elite Washington opinion. Although it was undoubtedly President Bush's actions on behalf of Operation Desert Storm that spoke loudest during this period, the punditocracy's battle plan proved, in many respects, no less effective. The pundits concentrated their fire on a few superficially simple issues in this Arabian drama and treated them in highly inflammatory fashion, thereby simultaneously constricting and distorting the war's public discourse. In the debate that led to Congress's decision to declare war, as well as during the fighting itself, the punditocracy shaped the political dialogue in a manner that substituted the Iraqi bogeyman for their fallen Stalinist icon and celebrated American military prowess with a degree of reverence that bordered on worship. Then, in the war's aftermath, they proceeded to ignore many of its considerable costs, as well as nearly all the fundamental questions it should have raised about America's future.

In the languid months that preceded the Iraqi invasion of Kuwait, Washington was having a difficult time convincing itself that it still mattered. David Broder helped get the year off to a depressing start by telling the city's powermongers —in a front-page article, no less—that they didn't matter any more. "Nation's Capital in Eclipse," explained Broder's headline, "As Pride and Power Slip Away."

In the White House, tempers were flaring over the reemergence of the dreaded "wimp issue" just in time for midterm elections. The exploding budget deficit forced the president to publicly repudiate his "no new taxes" pledge, infuriating conservatives who began, once again, to search for a potential challenger. One of their favorites, Patrick Buchanan, could be seen every day on television accusing the president of "refusing to stand up and lead our side in the great fight," and looking "like a wimp on the tax issue." Meanwhile, as Bush watched his approval ratings sink to new depths, his son Neil got himself embroiled in the ever-burgeoning S&L [savings and loan] debacle. . . .

Life was no prettier in the punditocracy. Robbed of its Big Thing, its ideological flailings had the character of Churchill's pudding: They lacked theme. Of course the pundits hated environmentalists, taxers and spenders, terrorists, and particularly, drug-smuggling dictators, but clearly passions were waning. One well-known Cold Warrior speculated about trying a second career as a novelist or jazz critic. The beat went on, but the thrill was gone.

Tax rises, oil spills, flag-burners, Jesse Helms, and Piss Christ: Every issue seemed more depressing than the last. Just days before the Iraqi invasion, "The McLaughlin Group" spent a good portion of the show discussing what should be done about Roseanne Barr's mangling of "The Star-Spangled Banner" at a baseball game. Morton Kondracke insisted that Americans boycott her sponsors because Ms. Barr was "unpatriotic" and "down on the country."

As if sent directly from Central Casting, Saddam Hussein rode in on his black horse, and rescued Washington from all this. The gratitude was almost palpable. Ben Wattenberg headlined his column: "Thanks Saddam, We Needed That." "In a way," observed the editors of *The New Republic*, "Saddam Hussein did the world a favor. . . ." Suddenly Washington was in the grip of what *New York Times* bigfoot R. W. Apple, Jr., called "the heavy speculation, the avid gossip, the gung-ho, here's where it's happening spirit that marks the city when it grapples with great events." "Hey, whaddya know," quipped Michael Kinsley, "we're not declining after all." America was "back" yet again.

Hussein, among others, had a right to be surprised by all this. Right up until the day he invaded Kuwait, the very same Mr. Hussein had been considered a valued commercial customer and regional balancing force by at least three American presidents. Both before and during his invasion of Iran, Hussein had enjoyed private screenings of U.S. satellite intelligence data. When the war with Iran ended and he turned his poison-gas pellets on his own Kurdish population, Hussein continued to receive sophisticated American technology and taxpayer-subsidized loans for his grain and technology purchases. President Bush himself had approved these loans earlier in the year. Assistant Secretary of State John Kelly, meanwhile, had testified before Congress in support of more loans to Hussein just three days before the invasion. Bush's State Department had gone so far as to frustrate official criminal inquiries into Hussein's U.S. loan network, in order to ensure that his cash-for-weapons pipeline continued unobstructed.

Though it could not compete with Hussein's regime in the cruelty and aggression departments, Kuwait, meanwhile, was not exactly the ideal place to mount a principled American defense of freedom and democracy. The ruling al-Sabah family ran a theocratic dictatorship in which Jews and Christians enjoyed virtually no rights. Its leader, the emir, made a regular practice of "marrying" young virgins on Thursday nights, the eve of the Islamic Sabbath, and "divorcing" them the next day. In the United Nations, the Kuwaiti regime attacked the United States with greater frequency and often stronger rhetorical violence than did the Soviet Union. And when one of our ships, the U.S.S. *Stark,* was torpedoed by Iraq while protecting Kuwaiti shipping in 1987, the Kuwaitis refused permission to allow America's dying sailors the right to use their hospital facilities.

President Bush's motivations in deciding to opt for war are not fully knowable. A late-afternoon meeting with Margaret Thatcher on August 2 was apparently quite influential, as were the parallels in the president's own mind drawn between Hussein and Hitler. Foreign policy crises, moreover, were not exactly unwelcome in the Bush White House, for the president's approval ratings took a nose dive whenever he was forced to deal with domestic matters. His chief of staff, John Sununu, called the prospect of a short, successful war "pure gold" for the president. The evidence is sketchy, but one can also postulate an important contribution by the punditocracy. James Fallows, for instance, discerns a powerful combination of Bush's own political and psychological weaknesses with hairy-chested pundit rhetoric to transform the president from wimp to war hero. "Following Bush's conversion," observes Fallows,

> instantly, all pundits who had been grumbling about Bush wimping out on "no new taxes" and insisting that he had no backbone were now talking about how he had been transformed into the man of greatness standing up to Iraq. Bush's turnaround

seemed to me to be a virtually—almost structurally—pundit-driven activity, and it confirmed his two worst tendencies: not wanting to get involved in domestic politics and thinking that this was the transcendent issue of all time.

Whether Bush himself was swayed by punditocracy intimations regarding his political manhood, the issue's transcendence is explicable only in terms of the particular ideological framework constructed for the invasion by Bush and his neoconservative allies in the punditocracy. The ability of both of these parties to manipulate the public dialogue—the pundits by word and Bush by deed—ensured that the truly essential questions about the war and U.S. national interest would never be asked. Instead, the debate was driven by the president's willingness to unilaterally ratchet up the size and scope of the American commitment and the pundits' ability to reinforce the prowar agenda at crucial moments in the debate. This latter contribution turned out to be crucial during the belated congressional debate in early January 1991, when a deeply divided Congress accepted the punditocracy's definition of the stakes of the conflict and acceded—reluctantly—to the president's war plans.

In the immediate aftermath of the Iraqi invasion of Kuwait, America's media discovered two facts about the U.S. political debate it apparently found surprising. First, the Reaganite coalition of Old Right conservatives and New Right neoconservatives was in the process of imploding; and second, the debate's center of gravity could now be found in the punditocracy.

In the latter case, editors and news reporters who had historically prided themselves on ignoring their own editorial pages suddenly found themselves interviewing columnists and talk-show regulars with the respect and attention they would normally reserve for congressmen and cabinet secretaries. When they asked one another why they were doing this, the answers came back, "Congress is out of town," or, "The Democrats are afraid to undercut the president." Both were true, but neither fully explained why the reporters had no choice but to rely on the punditocracy. The true reason was that there was no other debate to report; the punditocracy was it. Not only was the only coherent opposition to George Bush's initial decision to deploy 200,000 troops to the desert pundit-centered, but with the exception of Stephen Solarz and a few others, so, too, were the only coherent explanations as to why war was necessary. Not coincidentally, Solarz's most complete and cogent presentation of the "war is necessary" argument appeared in *The New Republic*.

The displacement in the public debate of Congress and the old-line political establishment by the punditocracy had been evident for more than a decade. Its widespread recognition in August 1990 became necessary only because the stakes were suddenly so high. On an issue as large and symbolically potent as taking the country to war—a war that had been unimaginable until just days before its planning began—most of the nation's hypercautious, poll-driven politicians were helpless to form independent judgments without first hearing the parameters of the debate communicated to them by the pundits.

Similarly, the Old Right/neocon coalition had been crumbling for quite a while as the glue of anticommunism grew increasingly less cohesive. With the

Soviets down for the count, the neoconservatives were eager to press for the establishment of a global *Pax Americana*—the "universal dominion" of the United States, in Charles Krauthammer's phrase, whereby America and its Western allies would undertake the liberalization of foreign nations across the globe by political, military, and economic means. Much of the Old Right, however, had reverted to its pre–World War II "America First" roots. Led by Buchanan, they were not interested in spreading democracy, but only in defending their vision of it at home. Buchanan accused the neoconservatives of practicing what he called "democratism," a form of "idolatry" that substituted "a false god for the real, a love of process for a love of country."

Between the neocons and isolationists lay a host of post-Reaganite positions that embraced neither one. The fervently anti-Soviet Zbigniew Brzezinski reconsidered his support for U.S. policy based on "earth control," and retreated into a more modest vision of global security via an American/ European/Japanese trilateral compact. Edward Luttwak, the strategic genius behind so many punditocracy war plans of the 1980s, had, by August 1990, come around to the view, originally enunciated by Sherle R. Schwenninger four years earlier, that traditional geopolitical conflicts such as that between Iraq and Iran no longer had much relevance to the overall security and prosperity of the United States. In the "main struggle for the main arena of international life," Luttwak explained, a nation's power and influence were determined not by its geopolitical assets but by its geoeconomic ones. "Disposable capital is increasingly displacing military innovation, and market penetration is displacing the possession of foreign garrisons and bases" as the coins of the strategic realm.

Clearly, ideological fault lines had shifted. While Ronald Reagan could count on a popular punditocracy front to support him in every foreign endeavor involving the U.S. military, the contingent working the field for George Bush was considerably smaller. Fortunately for the president's war plans, Washington's post–Cold War intellectual transformation remained for practical purposes largely rhetorical. Although the Soviet threat was gone, the minds shaped by the Cold War remained programmed for permanent crisis. Even while some of the most influential members of the punditocracy were evolving into neoisolationists and geoeconomists, the Cold War consensus they helped to create came back to haunt them. The idea of conservatives opposing a war thus produced a kind of cognitive dissonance in insider Washington that, however interesting, enjoyed little influence in the system itself. As "the unchallenged superpower . . . the center of world power" and "the apex of the Industrial West," in Charles Krauthammer's evocative phrasing, we simply had to do something. And given a mind-set shaped by the Cold War, that something had to be military. Daniel Patrick Moynihan dissected this phenomenon on the Senate floor:

> What we find is a kind of time warp in which we are acting in an old mode in response to a new situation. . . . It is in that mode of which we are in a bipolar, permanent crisis with the enemy. It used to be totalitarian, Leninist Communism. Without a moment's pause almost, we shifted the enemy to this person at the head

of this insignificant, flawed country whose boundaries were drawn in 1925 in a tent by an English colonial official, an artifact of the Treaty of Sèvres.

What is easy to forget in light of the obliteration of the Iraqi army is just how shocking was the idea of war in the first place. Indeed, when Washington first received word of the Iraqi campaign, few insiders seemed to be aware that any "defining moments" might be in the offing. On "The McLaughlin Group," Fred Barnes predicted that "it would be crazy to think that we're going to send troops over there and defend Kuwait." He was joined by fellow inside dopester Robert Novak, who promised, "We're not going to send troops in there. C'mon, there's no chance of that." These observations were consistent with the early readings of the president as well. Following an early-morning meeting of the National Security Council, President Bush told the press that intervention was "not being considered," and "we're not contemplating such action."

Outside of the Gulf itself, world reaction was hardly thunderous. In Germany and Japan, both of whom lack the internal oil resources enjoyed by the United States, the invasion was a ho-hum affair. As Japanese Consul General Msamichi Hanabusa explained, "Who will control oil . . . is not a very serious issue for Japan. It is of course better that oil is in friendly hands. But experience tells us that whoever controls oil will be disposed to sell it . . . oil is a fungible commodity." If awoken at all by news of the invasion, our economic competitors simply turned over and went back to sleep.

Virtually alone in Washington, William Safire and the neoconservative pundits called for immediate war. The groundwork for Operation Pundit Storm actually began three months earlier, shortly after Hussein threatened to "incinerate half of Israel" with a gas attack should he be attacked first. This alerted the powerfully pro-Israel neocons to the fact that they had an enemy in the Middle East to whom they had been paying insufficient attention. William Safire, much to the amusement of less principled commentators, had been raising hell about Hussein's gassing of the Kurds in 1988 and the United States' generally shameful history with respect to their unhappy struggle for autonomy. Safire, together with Jim Hoagland, also conducted a lonely campaign during the first two years of the Bush administration to expose Hussein's manipulation of U.S. banking and agricultural credits to feed his military appetite and intimidate his neighbors. Once the threat to Israel was made explicit, however, they were joined in this campaign by A. M. Rosenthal, Mortimer Zuckerman, Charles Krauthammer, and others. The latter holds the honor of first affixing the adjective "truly Hitlerian" to Hussein, almost a week before the invasion.

Once news of the invasion came through, so, too, did the neocon calls for Saddam's head. *The New Republic* editors recommended an immediate "massive bombing campaign" launched "at the slightest provocation" to destroy Hussein's military machine. "The United States must act," they insisted, "the sooner the better." Krauthammer predicted that if Saddam were not stopped by force, the United States would face "a nightmare not just of indiscriminate aggression, but of indiscriminate aggression with missiles, poison gas and soon nuclear weapons." He chastised the president for being unwilling to stop this "thug on the loose" because Bush was "not eager to get bogged down in a land war in a God-forsaken patch of desert," and anyway, had been "shamelessly propitiating [Hussein] since it helped him win the Iran–Iraq war in 1988." Safire took aim at the president's "past appeasement of Saddam Hussein" as well. He titled his first column "Now or Later?" Fewer than three weeks into the crisis he insisted, "The question is no longer 'Will there be a war' between the world and Iraq but 'What is the best strategy to win the war already begun?' "

A. M. Rosenthal, positively aflame with war fever, generously granted that "not every Iraqi is an evil dreamer of death," but nevertheless saw U.S. hostages in Iraq—soon to be released unharmed—as "tethered . . . sacrificial goats," at the mercy of "the one, true Muslim conqueror, crying destruction to the Jews, and death to all Arabs who question his vision, course and glory." Like Safire, he insisted that we were already "at war with Iraq." Perhaps the most ambitious of the hawks were Robert Bartley's crew at *The Wall Street Journal,* who recommended that American forces simply "take Baghdad and install a MacArthur regency." The prowar punditocracy's first team was rounded out by columnist Ben Wattenberg, Richard Perle, David Gergen, and Mortimer Zuckerman of *U.S. News;* Fred Barnes and Morton Kondracke in *The New Republic* and on "The McLaughlin Group"; the eloquent Johns Hopkins professor Fouad Ajami in both *The New Republic* and *U.S. News;* and James Hoagland in *The Washington Post.*

Whatever its motivations, the punditocracy drumbeat seemed to echo that of the Hearst newspapers' "Remember the Maine" campaign that preceded the Spanish-American War, albeit in far more sophisticated form. Its most potent weapon in this crusade was the same impatience with complexity and nuance that had helped make the growth of its power and influence possible in the first place. Those who questioned the wisdom of threatening war over Kuwait were constantly written off as "proisolationism," "proappeasement," or, in the case of Patrick Buchanan, pro-anti-Semitism. Those who did so with the added disadvantage of professional expertise were contemptuously branded "Arabists" and "fellow travelers" by "McLaughlin Group" panelist Morton Kondrake.

Guided by the twin influences of these pundits and the president's unilateral measures, the public debate proceeded on an uneven and often uneasy course to war. Bush's own role was paradoxical. On the one hand, by declaring that the invasion "would not stand," deploying 200,000 troops to Saudi Arabia, doubling that number four months later, and positioning those forces for an offensive war, Bush restricted the terms of the debate in such a fashion that a decision for peace would have necessitated a humiliating public retreat. He secured countless votes in Congress and percentage points in approval for the war option in U.S. opinion polls simply by successfully equating a diplomatically brokered solution with an ignominious defeat for the United States. But however valuable the president's willingness to stretch his constitutional prerogatives may have been, he never proved able to articulate a consistent rationale as to why this war was necessary. He could not seem to make up his mind about his reasoning and therefore frequently confused people by switching from economic to moral to political rationales from moment to moment. Bush attempted to demonize Hussein as "worse than Hitler," but he sounded small and petty doing so. As Charles Krauthammer complained in late November, "Bush has been so clumsy in advancing his case as to have nearly discredited it." Fortunately for the president, however, the pundits were more than willing to take over.

Throughout the fall, much of the subsequent public discussion inspired by the president took place on a rhetorical level so silly that many prowar pundits could not bring themselves to support it. Bush's alleged devotion to the idea of a "new world order" was explicitly disavowed by prowar pundits from Krauthammer to Kristol to Kissinger. Such talk was directed strictly at what Washington calls "the hustings," and taken seriously by almost no one, save perhaps A. M. Rosenthal and the soon-to-pay-for-it Kurds. Going to war "for good against evil," to "combat aggression," or to defend "national sovereignty" also did not enter into the punditocracy's reasoning in any serious fashion.

A cousin of the "new world order" argument that was taken seriously, however, was the insistence by many liberal pundits that the president was dedicated to the 1940s ideal of entrusting the United Nations to be the primary enforcer of peace in an otherwise anarchic world. This belief was encouraged, no doubt, by the Bush administration's newly minted enthusiasm for the approval of the Security Council for its actions, coupled with its success in convincing thirty-three nations to provide either token fighting forces, material, or medical teams to the war effort. These were no small achievements. But when Richard Cohen wrote that "maybe the most important consequence of the Gulf crisis has been the revival of the United Nations," he demonstrated nothing so much as how easy it had become to snow desperate liberals. It had been a point of pride within the Reagan administration for the entire decade of the 1980s to mock the self-righteous moralizing of that pathetically ineffective debating society on Manhattan's East River. If, after more than a decade of contempt, George Bush had truly gotten religion regarding the United Nation's potential, he could have secured a resolution under Article 43 of the body's Charter creating a true UN force with a UN military staff. Such a path would have helped spread international costs and contributions evenly among the world community and could have saved James Baker the humiliating spectacle of traveling the globe, tin cup in one hand, billy club in the other. But it would also have restricted the president's freedom of action in exactly the fashion envisioned by the UN founders. As such, it was never seriously considered.

The "war for oil" argument, though stronger than the "new world order" counterpart, was never sufficiently powerful to stand on its own. It is hardly prudent to fight a war to ensure one's oil supply, as the Japanese consul general pointed out, when one can simply pay for it. The key weapon in the warriors' political arsenal therefore was the fear inspired by the idea of a nuclear-armed Saddam Hussein. William Safire introduced this argument— by coincidence the only justification, according to the CBS–*New York Times* poll, acceptable to a majority of Americans to support an offensive war—just five days into the crisis. Initially, Safire predicted that the Iraqis would have a nuclear bomb ready to deliver to the United States by 1994. ("The first city he will take out is New York.") A few months into the crisis, in the midst of four consecutive columns on the subject, the *Times* man moved the deadline up a year, to 1993. Along with his compatriots in the prowar punditocracy, Safire argued that we were no longer talking simply about oil, peace, order, or democracy. We were "dealing with our own survival." Unfortunately, neither Safire nor anyone else in the West had any dependable information about the Iraqi nuclear program.

Throughout the autumn of 1990, the president and the punditocracy worked in tandem to create a heightened sense of crisis over the Iraqi occupation of Kuwait and thus an increased sense of inevitability about the war should Hussein refuse to capitulate. Liberals, in particular (along with those pundits unfairly perceived as liberals), were tremendously eager to be seen as supportive of the president during this period. David Broder found it "almost impossible to imagine a more serious, calm, cautious, rational, and prudent set of people than those this president has assembled" in his tiny coterie of advisers. Richard Cohen expressed awe over the president's "masterful assembling" of the crisis. Haynes Johnson congratulated Bush for his "skill and sureness of purpose." And Anthony Lewis applauded the president's "wisdom . . . professionalism and care for long-term interests" of the nation. This strategy of rallying round the commander-in-chief backfired, however, when it became clear that he had no intention of using his newly discovered "mastery, skill, wisdom," etc., for anything but an offensive war.

Had it been up to George Bush and a healthy proportion of the punditocracy, the decision to go war would have been left entirely to them. Richard Cheney noted in early December that, in the opinion of the administration, George Bush had all the authority he needed to go to war with or without congressional approval. Charles Krauthammer gratefully observed around the same time that Congress had been completely "irrelevant" to the decision-making process regarding the war. Fred Barnes argued that "Congress has no business getting involved. They would stew and whine and yap and they couldn't even pass a budget." Morton Kondrake seconded Barnes's analysis, adding "Congress is chicken."

By the time Congress finally did get around to exercising its constitutional prerogative to determine whether to commit the nation to war, it had almost ceased to matter. The punditocracy had succeeded in defining the debate so narrowly and perversely that the antiwar position would be considered the functional equivalent of national humiliation, retreat, denial, and general cowardice in the face of evil.

Here was the field upon which the congressional debate was finally conducted during the second weekend of 1991. Instead of addressing the difficult considerations about the American national interest the crisis posed, Congress simply asked itself the question Safire had raised more than six months earlier: War "Now or Later?" Senate Armed Services Committee Chairman Sam Nunn had single-handedly slowed the prowar juggernaut with his late

November committee hearings, but his argument for continued sanctions was nowhere near strong enough to stand up to the patriotic crescendo orchestrated by Bush and the pundits. . . .

David Broder saw fit to laud Congress for dealing with the question of war "in a manner befitting the gravity of the subject," with a debate that was "civil, somber, always serious, and often eloquent." Again, this was less a reflection of the subject of Broder's commentary than of the deterioration of his own standards. In fact, no debate worthy of the name even took place. Members read their own remarks to largely empty chambers, with little substantive intercourse, exchange of ideas, or engagement of their colleagues' positions.

II

As the U.S. Air Force lit up the late night Arabian sky with its eerily beautiful arsenal on the morning of January 17, 1991, George Bush went before the American people to explain why "the world could wait no longer," and the confusion level within the American political dialogue achieved a kind of perverse epiphany. False information, incomplete field reports, and raw Pentagon propaganda were transmitted across the American airwaves unfiltered by editors, producers, or any of the traditional gatekeepers of independent journalism. Retired colonels, admirals, and Pentagon consultants paraded through the punditocracy's third ring as the networks' impartial experts and pronounced every aspect of the effort to be an unqualified success—and a morally exemplary one at that. On the op-ed pages and weekend talk shows, the punditocracy discovered in victory not merely the vindication of Bush's war strategy but a reaffirmation of every dogma its members had ever wanted to believe: America's decline was a myth; military power remained the only important determination of national strength and international influence; and we lived in what would always be, as Ben Wattenberg put it, "the most powerful nation in the world."

From a strategic standpoint, the punditocracy saw the war as an almost unmitigated success. Even the faultlessly moderate Jim Hoagland, winner of the 1991 Pulitzer Prize for commentary, observed that "the United States has not been so dominant on the world stage since the brief period after World War II." David Broder saw the war as a victory for "peace and the rule of law" as well.

So it seemed in the thick of battle. But from the distance of just a few weeks' perspective, the gleam of war's strategic brilliance grew decidedly dimmer. The allies did succeed in briefly weakening Saddam Hussein, but they did not by any stretch of the imagination cripple him. CIA Director Robert Gates told a Senate committee in early 1992 that Hussein's military forces remained "a great challenge" to the United States, armed with "a cadre of scientists and engineers . . . able to reconstitute any dormant program rapidly." Following the ground war, Hussein retained at least 700 tanks, 1,400 armored personnel carriers, 340 artillery pieces, and 20 divisions, including Republican Guard divisions, who remained wholly untouched by the fighting and who could hardly be said to be at "peace" with the Kurds and Shi'ites. Most of the Iraqi Air Force sat out the war as well. Within a year of the triumph, hawkish columnists James Hoagland, A. M. Rosenthal, and William Safire were calling for yet another war against Hussein, this one to accomplish all the things the last one had failed to do. . . .

Initially, the war seemed to imperil the future of the two-party system. Richard Cohen gloated over the "party's isolationist chickens coming home to roost." David Broder insisted that the war "showed the nation once again that Democrats cannot define the destiny of America." *The Wall Street Journal* editors wondered how "so many elected members of a political party could end up on the opposite side from the American people? . . ."

In the longer term, the punditocracy employed the war to shape the overall direction of American strategic policy. Enough of doomsayers, conservationists, butter-before-guns types, and liberals who whined about bad schools and unmanageable debts. Everything was just fine. The war had proven us to be, in Ben Wattenberg's words, "the most influential nation in history." In the sands of Kuwait, the punditocracy decided it had finally found incontrovertible proof that those nagging declinists had everything wrong. Charles Krauthammer argued that the defeat of Iraq demonstrated that the very idea of American decline was "nonsense." He deployed as his sole piece of supporting evidence a comparison between the relative difficulty the United States had faced in defeating North Korea in 1950 with that of defeating Iraq forty years later. The war had proven, added Michael Novak, "the end of the decline . . . the decline of the declinists . . . the daughter of disaster for the declinists." . . .

Perhaps the most dangerous idea to emerge from the detritus of Baghdad's destruction was the notion that the Gulf War provided a worthwhile model for a future international security system. Despite the obvious costs involved, the idea of the United States serving as the gendarme of the Western world, putting our massive military might at the service of Western interests, swelled punditocracy breasts with pride. Anthony Cordesman, who won William Safire's award for the most impressive television pundit of the war, greeted *New York Times* readers on the morning after the cease-fire with a paean to "America's new combat culture" based, at least in Cordesman's hope, on what would be a further redistribution of money and resources to military means. Charles Krauthammer sketched out the contours of this culture's foreign policy in his plea for a new *Pax Americana* based on unilateral U.S. intervention on a worldwide basis. "Our best hope," argued Krauthammer, "is in American strength and will, unashamedly laying down the rules of world order and being prepared to enforce them." As always, Krauthammer's candor and eloquence were instructive. His use of the word "dominance" does not refer to economic dominance, political dominance, or even the kind of intellectual or cultural dominance to which Americans once aspired. It refers explicitly and exclusively to military power. As Robert Bartley, his neocon comrade, later admitted, "on the Right, the notion of decline faded as Ronald Reagan filled the military spare parts bins, frankly labeled the Soviet

Union an 'evil empire,' invaded Grenada, bombed Libya and revived the option of missile defense." Now that "an American-led attack [had] decimated" Iraq, "the world's new military balance was clear." America, Bartley insisted, "has not declined, it has prevailed." It was military power and military power alone in which the United States remained the world's premier nation. . . .

"Every other nation on earth would like to be in our position," insisted Charles Krauthammer who, in the wake of the war, had come closest to fulfilling Lippmann's mantle as the most influential intellectual voice in elite political culture. "Why not enjoy it?" Both the statement and the question that follow are an invitation to complacency. If we are the envy of the world, then why worry about our computer industry, our banking industry, our auto industry, our third-rate educational system, our health-care crisis, our manufacturing base, our unsafe cities, our drug epidemic, our collapsing infrastructure, and our degraded environment? In this fashion, America's "victory" in the Gulf, as interpreted by the punditocracy, will all but ensure the acceleration of America's decline as a secure and prosperous nation. The unlimited opportunities opened up by the collapse of the Cold War will go unexploited. Although the enemy had self-destructed and his stand-in had proven to be a fraud, the system was predicated upon eternal enemies, and the system worked—sort of.

In March 1992, the Pentagon leaked a draft "Defense Policy Guidance" report calling for the investment of yet another $1.2 trillion over the next five years to ensure, virtually unilaterally, that the United States be able to defeat not existing adversaries, but "potential competitors," lest they "aspire to a larger regional or global role." Bartley, George Will, Krauthammer, and company had a right to be proud. The Pentagon document represented, as the *Times* noted, "the only effort so far to put together a coherent blueprint for the post–Cold War era" more than a year after the Gulf War had ended. Fewer than thirty days later, the Senate passed a budget resolution calling for $291 billion in military spending for fiscal year 1993. Despite all the earth-shattering transformations the planet had undergone during the previous decade, there would be no new thinking in Washington so long as the punditocracy reigned.

8. THE ELECTORAL CYCLE AND THE CONDUCT OF AMERICAN FOREIGN POLICY

William B. Quandt

*T*wo hundred years ago, when the Constitution was taking shape, the conduct of the new nation's foreign affairs was not central to the concerns of the Founders. Once independence was achieved, it was widely believed, the United States would be able to remain comparatively uninvolved with the rest of the world. A wide ocean separated it from the messy politics of Europe and permitted the first president to imagine the United States could remain unentangled in the affairs of the rest of the world.

The Founders did, of course, make passing reference to the division of powers between the executive and the legislature in such matters as negotiating and ratifying treaties with foreign powers and with raising an army and a navy and directing them in time of war. As elsewhere in the Constitution, on these matters one sees the determination to prevent too much power from being concentrated in any one part of the federal government.[1] Divided responsibility was the key to avoiding abuses of power, and in the domestic arena the wisdom of this philosophical bent has been widely applauded. In the conduct of foreign policy, however, it is much more difficult to argue that the virtues of divided responsibility enhance the common defense or promote the general welfare.

Still, even the most ardent proponent of strong presidential leadership in foreign policy would have a difficult time arguing that the specific provisions of the Constitution regarding foreign policy are at the root of our contemporary problems in world affairs. . . .

The Constitution does not cripple the president in the conduct of foreign policy, at least not because of the definition of powers. These are defined sufficiently broadly and ambiguously so that a strong and popular president can provide effective leadership, while a relatively weak and unpopular one

Note: Some notes have been deleted or renumbered.

will have a difficult time. That is pretty close to what one imagines the intent of the Founders must have been.

THE PROBLEM OF THE ELECTORAL CYCLE

But there is still a constitutionally rooted problem that seriously affects the conduct of foreign policy. It derives from the structure of the electoral cycle. Here there is no ambiguity at all in the Constitution. Presidential elections take place every four years; congressional elections every two years; and since the passage of the twenty-second amendment, a president can only be elected twice. In practice, this often means that presidents have little time during their incumbency when they have both the experience and the power needed for sensible and effective conduct of foreign policy. The price we pay is a foreign policy excessively geared to short-term calculations, in which narrow domestic political considerations often outweigh sound strategic thinking, and where turnover in high positions is so frequent that consistency and coherence are lost. . . .

The electoral arrangements for the presidency and Congress have rarely been justified by the contribution they make to sound foreign policy. The rationale is almost entirely domestic. Representatives are supposed to remain closely tied to the wishes of their constituents; hence the two-year term. Senators are expected to take a broader view and thus are given six-year terms. The Senate is supposed to embody a degree of continuity, and, therefore, only one-third of its membership is up for election at any given moment. Presidents fall in between, having to renew their mandate after four years and being obliged to retire at the end of a second term. A pervasive distrust of presidential power can be detected in these arrangements, a distrust that is historically understandable, but which also can have debilitating effects on foreign policy.

In domestic policy it is probably wise to structure the federal system so that presidential authority is limited. After all, the country has so many diverse interests that it is hard to imagine the system working well unless there are strong incentives for compromise and moderation. A certain amount of inconsistency, of vacillation, of changing the calculus of winners and losers is needed to keep this heterogeneous country together. The federal structure and the electoral cycle are all part of the system that allows domestic political issues to be resolved with a minimum of conflict and violence.

Foreign policy is different. Washington speaks for the country as a whole in foreign policy. The president is supposed to be the commander-in-chief of the armed forces. And in the modern world he literally holds the power of life and death, since he has the ultimate authority to decide on the use of nuclear weapons. Such decisions might have to be made in a matter of minutes, and extraordinary measures are taken to be sure that the president is always in a position to act on the basis of the best information available. In the nuclear era there might not be time to consult with Congress, to await declarations of war, or to cultivate public understanding. An enormous **responsibility** rests with the president, and presumably it is in everyone's interest that matters affecting the nation's welfare and security be handled with skill, expertise, and intelligence. The present electoral arrangements do not contribute to that goal.

THE NATURE OF THE PROBLEM

Ideally, one would like to see a president bring wisdom and experience in foreign affairs to the Oval Office. Once there, one could hope that he or she would have the time, the power, and the authority to deal with problems of national security and foreign policy in ways that promote the national interest. But to list these desirable circumstances is to be reminded of how far they are from the recent historical record.

Wisdom is something that a president either has or lacks, and the electoral cycle cannot be held responsible. But experience and power, as well as the time and inclination to deal with foreign affairs, are tied to the rhythms of the electoral cycle. Simply stated, a newly elected president may well have the authority, the power, and the inclination to address foreign policy issues, but he rarely has the experience necessary to form sound judgments. Thus, it is common for serious errors to be made in the first year of a presidential term. During the second, and part of the third year, there may be a happy coincidence of sufficient power, experience, and time to deal with the complexities of world affairs. But during the last year or more of a typical first term, a president is drawn into the politics of reelection and rarely has much time or inclination to deal with foreign policy issues unless they seem to hold out the promise of winning votes, which is rarely the case.

A reelected president in his second term faces a somewhat different problem. Experience and authority are likely to be available, but after the midterm elections the "lame-duck" problem is very likely to set in, making it difficult for a president to conduct foreign policy. Leaders abroad will begin to ask themselves why they should bother to deal with this president, when someone else will be in the Oval Office before long, perhaps bringing a change of policy with him. The opposition party has little incentive to help the outgoing president win any foreign policy victories, and within his own party the struggle for succession may weaken his normal base of support. In normal times it would be surprising to find major foreign policy successes in the last phase of a two-term president's incumbency.

This simple descriptive model should not be seen as an absolute guide for how a president will fare in the conduct of foreign policy at different moments of his term. Crises can radically change the normal political calculus, enhancing presidential power and forging a bipartisan base of support. But if a crisis turns into a prolonged, indecisive, costly commitment—as in Vietnam and Lebanon—domestic political considerations are likely to come to the fore again and force a president's hand.

None of this would matter so much if presidents did not really have much to say about foreign policy. In theory, policy might be carried out by the experienced professionals in the bureaucracy on a nonpartisan basis. Or a grand bipartisan consensus might develop that would establish the broad lines of policy, leaving the president relatively free from domestic political considerations as long as he operated within that consensus. Those who used to proclaim that "politics stops at the water's edge" were expressing the hope that a nonpartisan foreign policy could be found. But certainly since the mid-1960s and the trauma of Vietnam, there has been no consensus on foreign policy that could insulate a president from the impact of domestic politics and the electoral cycle.

FIRST-TERM PRESIDENTS: THE TYPICAL PATTERN

A president's assessment of risks and opportunities is generally a product of his experience in office and where he stands with respect to the electoral cycle. For analytical purposes and at the risk of some distortion of a more complex reality, it is useful to distinguish among patterns in the first year of a presidential term, the second year, the third, and the fourth.

These categories are useful for understanding the typical evolution of policy over a four-year cycle. They alert the observer to the changing weight of domestic political considerations as a presidential term unfolds. The time when a president decides to do something is heavily influenced by this cycle, unless he is reacting to a foreign policy crisis.

If a president and his advisers are inattentive to the political cycle, they are apt to make serious mistakes. A learning process seems invariably to take place in the course of a four-year term. By the end, most presidents recognize that some of what they tried early in their term was unrealistic; they have become more familiar with the limits on their power; they aim lower and pay more attention to the timing of their major moves.

A skillful president will make use of the political cycle to enhance the chances of success in his foreign policy. A careless one will probably pay a high price for ignoring domestic realities. Events, of course, can get out of control, as they did for Jimmy Carter with the Iranian hostage crisis in 1979. It was particularly bad luck for him that this happened just as an election year was beginning. By contrast, Ronald Reagan managed to terminate the controversial American military presence in Lebanon just before his reelection campaign began in 1984, and the issue seemed to do him no political harm at the polls. Luck and skill go hand in hand in successful political careers.

Looking back on their time in office, presidents and their advisers usually decry the intrusion of domestic politics so heavily into the foreign policy arena. Former Secretary of State Cyrus Vance has argued that the only solution to the problem is to elect a president for one term of six years.

> From experience in the making of foreign policy in several administrations, I have concluded that a four-year presidential term has serious drawbacks, especially when it comes to foreign affairs. It takes each new president from six to nine months to learn his job and to feel comfortable in the formulation and execution of

foreign policy. For the next eighteen months the president can operate with assurance. But during the last year or so, he is running for reelection and is forced to divert much of his attention to campaigning. As a result, many issues are ignored and important decisions are deferred. Sometimes bad decisions are made under the pressures of months of primary elections. And at home and overseas, we are frequently seen as inconsistent and unstable.[2]

Others have tried to address the problem by pleading for bipartisanship, the removal of foreign policy from the domestic political agenda. Zbigniew Brzezinski, President Carter's national security adviser, has written:

> Every Administration goes through a period of an ecstatic emancipation from the past, then a discovery of continuity, and finally a growing preoccupation with Presidential reelection. As a result, the learning curve in the area of foreign policy tends to be highly compressed. Each Administration tends to expend an enormous amount of energy coping with the unintended, untoward consequences of its initial, sometimes excessive, impulses to innovate, to redeem promises, and to harbor illusions. In time, preconceptions give way to reality, disjointedness to intellectual coherence, and vision to pragmatism. But by the time this happens, the Presidential cycle is usually coming to an end. That the four-year election process has a pernicious influence on foreign policy is evident, but it is also clear that this structural handicap is not likely to be undone.[3]

The Pattern of the First Year

A president and his advisers often begin their term with relatively little background in foreign policy issues. This lack of background is especially important if the president has been a Washington outsider and if there has been a change of the party in control of the White House. But even in the case of a Washington insider, such as a senator with experience on the Foreign Relations Committee or a vice president moving up to the presidency, there is little reason to expect more than the faintest familiarity with most foreign policy issues.

Presidents are not allowed the luxury of taking no position on issues until they have learned enough to make sensible judgments. Instead, on issues that evoke strong public interest, such as the Middle East or arms control, candidates for the presidency will be expected to have a position and may even devote a major speech to the topic.

These first definitions of a president's position, often taken in the midst of the campaign, are typically of considerable importance in setting the administration's initial course. They are likely to reflect general foreign policy predispositions . . . and will generally imply that the previous administration was on the wrong track and that things will soon be put straight. (This, of course, assumes that the presidency is passing from one party to the other.) In addition to defining a course of action by contrasting it with one's predecessor in office, a newly elected president will have to decide what priority to attach to the main foreign policy issues on the agenda. Not all issues can be dealt with at once, and a signal of presidential interest or disinterest may be more important in setting the administration's policy than the substantive position papers that inevitably begin to flow to the White House from the bureaucracy.

If an issue is treated as important, and if presidential predispositions are reflected in the charting of the initial course, the early months of the new term are likely to be marked by activism. Having just won a national election, the president will probably be optimistic about his ability to use the office to achieve great results in foreign and domestic policy. If initiatives are decided upon, they tend to be ambitious. It takes time to recognize what will work and what will not.

It also takes time for a president and his advisers to develop a comfortable working style. A high degree of confusion is not unusual in the early days. Public statements may have to be retracted, and it will take time to know who really speaks for the president among the many claimants to the role. In addition, it will take time for the president and the new secretary of state to develop contacts with various foreign leaders. These encounters will eventually add to their education, but at the outset there is usually only a faint understanding of the foreign players, their agendas, and their strengths and weaknesses.

What all of this adds up to is a first year that is often somewhat experimental, where policy objectives are set in ambitious terms, where predispositions and campaign rhetoric still count for something, and where international realities are only dimly appreciated. Typically, toward the end of the first year it becomes clear that the policy agreed upon in January or February has lost momentum or is on the wrong track. Reassessments are then likely, but not until considerable time and energy have been invested in pursuing false leads and indulging in wishful thinking.

The Pattern of the Second Year

Despite the frequent disappointments of dealing with foreign policy issues in the first year, presidents rarely decide to turn their attention away from the international arena in their second year. If recent experience is a guide, year two is likely to be marked with considerably greater success, either in promoting international agreement through negotiations or in the skillful management of a crisis.

The difference between the first and the second year shows that experience can be a good teacher. Policies in the second year are often more in tune with reality. There is less of an ideological overlay in policy deliberations. At the same time, goals are likely to be less ambitious. Plans for comprehensive solutions may be replaced by attempts at more modest partial agreements.

By the second year, some of the intrabureaucratic feuding and backbiting is likely to have subsided, or at least a president has had the chance to put it to an end if he so chooses. The gap between the political appointees and the foreign service professionals has also narrowed, and more regional expertise is typically being taken into account during policy discussions. If a senior bureaucrat has survived into the second year, he is no longer seen as the enemy and has often been judged a team player. In any case, the failures of year one tend to make the president's men less contemptuous of the knowledge of the professionals.

During the second year, presidents also begin to realize that mishandling of foreign policy issues, especially in the Middle East or concerning U.S.–[Russian] relations, can be costly. Congressional elections are scheduled for November, and in most cases the party in power has to expect some losses. Such losses make it more difficult for the president to govern, and thus he has a strong interest in minimizing them. This is no time for controversial initiatives. If initiatives are to be taken, there is a high premium on the appearance of success. The mood in the White House is much less experimental than in the first year. Practical criteria come to the fore. Success may require compromises with principle. This is the year in which presidents realize that the slogan of politics being "the art of the possible" is applicable to foreign as well as domestic policy.

The Pattern of the Third Year

During the third year of a typical presidential term, foreign policy issues are likely to be assessed at the White House in terms of whether or not they can help advance the incumbent's reelection bid. The tendency, therefore, is to try for an apparent success if an initiative is underway, even if the result leaves something to be desired. The administration will even be prepared on occasions to pay heavily with concessions or with promises of aid and arms to get an agreement.

If the prospects for an agreement do not look good during the third year, the tendency is to cut one's losses and to disengage the president from the diplomatic effort. Above all, the president does not want to be seen as responsible for a foreign policy failure as the election year approaches. And certainly by the end of the third year, if not considerably earlier, the preelection season is likely to be underway.

The rush for success, along with the tendency to abandon controversial and costly policies, means that mistakes are often made in the third year. Opportunities may be lost through carelessness. The price of agreement may become very high as the parties to negotiations realize how badly Washington wants a success. Political considerations tend to override the requirements of steady, purposeful diplomacy. Nonetheless, this is sometimes a year in which genuine achievements are possible, especially if the groundwork in the second year has been good.

The Pattern of the Fourth Year

Most presidents go to great lengths to deny that electoral considerations are allowed to influence their conduct of foreign policy. But as political realists, they all know that they must take politics into account. If nothing else, the extraordinary demands on a presidential candidate mean that little time is left for consideration of complex foreign policy problems, for meeting with visiting heads of state, or for fighting great battles with Congress over aid or arms sales. Added to this is the desire not to lose the support of constituencies that have particularly strong feelings about specific foreign policy issues. This can be important in terms of votes as well as in terms of financial contributions to the party and to congressional candidates.

The guidelines for the fourth year with respect to potentially controversial foreign policy issues are thus fairly simple. Try to avoid taking a position. Steer clear of new initiatives. Stick with safe themes and patriotic rhetoric. Attack your opponent as inexperienced, ill-informed, possibly reckless. If crises are forced upon you, they must of course be dealt with, and even in election years presidents have considerable authority in emergencies.

In brief, most presidents recognize that they can hope to achieve little in foreign policy in the midst of an election campaign. Even if a president were prepared to take some bold initiative, foreign leaders would be reluctant to respond positively out of a concern that the president might not be in office the following January. Statesmen are likely to want to know who will be in the White House for the next four years before they take major decisions. This weakens the influence of the president in his fourth year even when he is not up for reelection.

THE PATTERN OF THE SECOND TERM

For a president in his second term, the four-year pattern changes significantly. The first year and half may be the best time for taking foreign policy initiatives. The president knows as much about substance as he ever will. The reelection has provided the proof he may feel he needed that the public is behind him.

Late in the second year, however, domestic considerations begin to intrude on foreign policy concerns. Midterm elections are likely to be of special importance, for they will determine to a large extent how much power the president has in his last two years. If he loses control over one or both houses of Congress, his legislative agenda will be in jeopardy. Any significant loss for his party may speed up the succession struggle and can embolden his opponents in Congress. The idea that a president who does not have to face reelection will be free to act in a statesmanlike manner in his last two years misses the point. He may be free, but he is unlikely to be taken very seriously as he reaches the end of his term. At some point in the third or fourth year, the "lame duck" phenomenon is bound to affect the president.

SOME ILLUSTRATIVE EXAMPLES

In the post–World War II era, only two men, Dwight Eisenhower and Richard Nixon, assumed the office of president with some measure of expertise in world affairs. [This article was written before the election of George Bush, who had considerable foreign policy experience before becoming president— ed.] Even for these two, however, there were vast gaps in their knowledge, and a period of on-the-job training was essential. All other presidents—Harry Truman, John Kennedy, Lyndon Johnson, Gerald Ford, Jimmy Carter, and Ronald Reagan—had relatively little experience with world affairs by the time they assumed office.

If we leave aside the cases of Truman, who became president in the midst of a war, and of Eisenhower, who had to deal with the Korean War in his first year, we can look for typical errors of inexperience especially in 1961, 1977, and 1981. These are the purest examples of a relatively inexperienced man coming to the Oval Office after having campaigned against the previous incumbent.

Whatever one may think of the brief Kennedy presidency, its first year was not its finest hour. In the spring of 1961 Kennedy stumbled into the Bay of Pigs fiasco. In addition, having campaigned on the basis of a nonexistent missile gap, he had to reverse course and adapt to new realities, but not before he had set in motion a new phase of the arms race.

For Carter, his first year was marked by excessive ambition and awkwardness. He tried to move abruptly away from the arms control guidelines that Gerald Ford and Leonid Brezhnev had laid out at Vladivostok, calling instead for deep cuts in strategic weaponry. The Soviets rejected this new proposal, and precious time was lost before arms negotiations could get back on track. In the Middle East, Carter launched an ambitious peace initiative, but compromised its success by some of his clumsy public diplomacy and by mishandling the surrounding dialogue with the Soviet Union. By fall 1977, he felt that he was paying a heavy domestic political price for his Middle East efforts and told Egypt's President Anwar Sadat that there was little more that he could do. At that point Sadat, perceiving Carter's weakness, set off on his own to deal with Israel directly.

Reagan's first-year errors were in part a product of inexperience. In the Middle East, for example, he lent his weight to a policy of building strategic consensus against the Soviet Union. From this perspective, regional problems such as the crisis in Lebanon and the Arab–Israeli conflict were relatively unimportant. Countries such as Israel, Egypt, and Saudi Arabia, all strongly anti-Soviet, would be encouraged to drop their local quarrels and cooperate in pursuit of anti-Soviet policies. Needless to say, strategic consensus was illusory, and neglecting the problems of Lebanon and the Palestinians set the stage for the explosion that came the following year.

Presidents in the second year have presumably learned something of value from their on-the-job experience. This is a time to look for initiatives that are rooted in realism and crisis management marked by some skill and self-confidence. For Kennedy, the Cuban missile crisis came in the second year and his handling of it won him high marks as a tough but flexible statesman. Nixon's deft management of the Jordan crisis, particularly the mobilization of Israeli power to help deter the Syrians, came in his second year. Carter's Camp David success was similarly timed. Finally, Reagan's well-conceived but poorly executed Middle East peace initiative also came late in his second year.

Third years are difficult to characterize. On the one hand, presidents have the power and the experience to do well, but they may feel the need to rush for success or to drop controversial issues before the election year is upon them.

Particularly in recent years the reelection campaign seems to begin about midway through the third year. Eisenhower may have been somewhat affected by these considerations in the way he handled the Soviet Union in 1955. Here was a mixture of conciliation—the spirit of Geneva—and confusion—the response to the Soviet arms deal with Egypt. On this latter point, Eisenhower wavered between trying to win Egypt's President Gamal Abdel Nasser away from the Soviets with offers of economic aid for the Aswan High Dam and punishing him for refusing to make peace with Israel and for flirting with the Soviets. Not surprisingly, as the election year arrived, the decision was to punish Nasser. The Aswan offer was abruptly withdrawn; Nasser responded by nationalizing the Suez Canal; and before long Eisenhower faced a full-scale international crisis on the eve of elections.

Kennedy's third year is difficult to judge. He seems to have been on the way toward dealing effectively with the Soviets on arms control. Where he was heading with his policy toward Southeast Asia is difficult to determine.

Carter's third year was a mixed one in foreign policy. It began with the collapse of the Shah's regime in Iran, which caused great confusion in Washington. About the same time, however, Carter threw himself into the final negotiations for [an] Egyptian–Israeli peace treaty and was successful. He also pushed SALT II through to signature. But he dropped the Middle East issue when the Palestinian autonomy negotiations were getting underway, thus insuring their failure, and he was unable to win Senate ratification for SALT II.

Election years rarely witness great success in foreign policy. Carter struggled in frustration with the Iranian hostage crisis. Reagan withdrew ignominiously from Lebanon after more than 250 Marines had died. The great exception to this pattern, of course, was Nixon in 1972. Nixon was an unusual president in many ways. He had served as vice president under Eisenhower for eight years, and thus came to the Oval Office with much more knowledge of world affairs than other presidents. He also had a shrewd sense for timing in politics and seemed to realize that his reelection prospects would be helped if he could demonstrate his skill in foreign policy in the election year. Most other presidents have shied away from foreign policy initiatives as the election drew close. Nixon, however, prepared his biggest moves in near secrecy over the previous years. Then in 1972 he brought the American involvement in Vietnam to an end, he traveled to China, and he signed the SALT I agreement in Moscow. All this took place in the space of several months and in an election year. His Democratic challenger, who had been painting Nixon as a reckless warmonger, never had a chance. Many voters, who felt little personal regard for Nixon, nonetheless had to admit that he was a master at the game of nations. His electoral victory was complete.

CONCLUSION

The American political system was not designed with the conduct of foreign policy in mind. Checks and balances, frequent elections, and the concept of popular sovereignty were all meant to limit abuses of power, not to make it easy for a president to govern. In foreign policy the constraints are often less than in the domestic arena. But in modern times even foreign policy has become highly controversial, and thus subject to all the political forces that limit the power of a president.

To understand how American foreign policy is made, one needs to look carefully at the views of key decision makers, especially the president and his top advisers. The individuals do matter. But they operate within a political context that has some very regular features. Therefore, if they are to leave their imprint on policy, they will have to understand what the broader constitutional system allows. And they will have to learn much about the world as well.

Presidents do have great power at their disposal. It is often most usable in the midst of crises, when the normal restraints of political life are suspended, at least for a little while. Presidents can also usually count on a fairly wide latitude in the conduct of foreign policy in their first two years. But in time the need to appeal to the electorate, to have congressional support, and to prepare for reelection appears to dominate thinking at the White House, regardless of who is the incumbent.

This means that the United States is structurally at a disadvantage in trying to develop and sustain policies that require a mastery of complex issues and call for consistency and a long-term vision to enhance the prospects of success. It is hard for presidents to look beyond the next few months. Consistency is often sacrificed for political expediency. Turnover of personnel in top positions erodes the prospects for continuity.

At the same time, the United States, for these very reasons, rarely pursues a strongly ideological foreign policy for long. There are pressures to pursue a course that has broad popular support, eschewing extremes of left or right. Pragmatic criteria are a common part of policy debates. Thus, if one course of action has clearly failed, another can be tried. This may be hard on the nerves of other world leaders, but sometimes this experimental approach is needed if a viable policy is to be found. . . .

Realizing the full potential of the office of the presidency is probably the best practical solution to the problems posed for the conduct of foreign policy by the constitutionally designed electoral cycle. But that requires that the American people elect statesmen as presidents, and that cannot be expected in the television era. Thus, we will probably have to live with a system that weakens the ability to conduct an effective foreign policy. Understanding that reality may be small consolation, but it may serve to temper the grandiose notion that the United States, as a great power, can reshape the world in its image. Neither the realities of the world nor those of our own political system will allow that.

NOTES

1. See James MacGregor Burns, *The Deadlock of Democracy: Four-Party Politics in America* (Englewood Cliffs, N.J.: Prentice Hall, 1963), pp. 8–23, on Madison's concept of checks and balances.

2. See Cyrus Vance, *Hard Choices: Critical Years in America's Foreign Policy* (New York: Simon & Schuster, 1983), p. 13.

3. See Zbigniew Brzezinski, *Power and Principle: Memoirs of the National Security Adviser, 1977–1981* (New York: Farrar, Straus, Giroux, 1983), p. 544.

Part II: THE INSTITUTIONAL SETTING

*F*oreign policy is a product of the actions officials take on behalf of the nation. Because of this, the way the government is structured for policymaking also arguably affects the conduct and content of foreign affairs. Thus we can hypothesize that a relationship exists between the substance of policy and the institutional setting from which it derives. The proposition is particularly compelling if attention is directed not to the foreign policy *goals* the nation's leaders select but instead to the *means* they choose to satisfy particular objectives.

A salient feature of the American institutional setting is that the president and the institutionalized presidency—the latter consisting of the president's personal staff and the Executive Office of the President—are preeminent in the foreign policymaking process. This derives in part from the authority granted the president in the Constitution and in part from the combination of judicial interpretation, legislative acquiescence, personal assertiveness, and custom and tradition that have transformed the presidency into the most powerful office in the world. The crisis-ridden atmosphere that characterized the Cold War era also contributed to the enhancement of presidential authority by encouraging the president to act energetically and decisively when dealing with global challenges. The widely shared consensus among American leaders and the mass of the American people that the international environment demanded an active American world role also contributed to the felt need for strong presidential leadership. Although some (notably in Congress) questioned this viewpoint in the immediate aftermath of Vietnam, the perceived need for strong presidential leadership was widely accepted throughout the Cold War.

Because of the president's key role in foreign policymaking, it is useful to consider the institutional arrangements that govern the process as a series of concentric circles that effectively alter the standard government organization chart so as to draw attention to the core or most immediate source of the

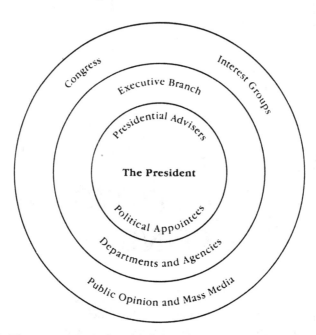

Figure II.1. The concentric circles of policy making. [Source: Adapted from Roger Hilsman, *To Move a Nation* (New York: Doubleday, 1967), pp. 541–544.]

action (see Figure II.1). Thus the innermost circle in the policymaking process consists of the president, his immediate personal advisers, and such important political appointees as the secretaries of state and defense, the director of central intelligence, and various under and assistant secretaries who bear responsibility for carrying out policy decisions. Here, in principle, is where the most important decisions involving the fate of the nation are made.

The second concentric circle contains the various departments and agencies of the executive branch. If we exclude from that circle the politically appointed heads of agencies and their immediate subordinates who are more properly placed in the innermost circle, we can think of the individuals within the second circle as career bureaucrats who provide continuity in the implementation of policy from one administration to the next. Their primary tasks—in theory—are to provide top-level policymakers with the information necessary for sound decision making and to carry out the decisions policymakers reach.

As noted in the introduction to this book, the involvement of the United States in a complex webwork of interdependent ties with other nations in the world has led to the involvement in foreign affairs of many organizations whose primary tasks are oriented toward the domestic environment. The Agriculture, Commerce, and Treasury departments are examples. Still, the State and Defense departments and the Central Intelligence Agency (CIA) command center stage among the dozens of executive-branch departments and agencies now involved in foreign affairs. The State Department's role derives from being the only department charged (in theory at least) with responsibility for the whole of America's relations with other nations. The Defense Department and the CIA, on the other hand, derived their importance from the threatening and often crisis-ridden atmosphere of the Cold War years, in which they often had ready alternatives from which top-level policymakers could choose when the more passive means of diplomacy and negotiation seemed destined to fail. Each may play a diminished role in the post–Cold War world, but both will remain principal actors in the foreign affairs government well into the future.

Moving beyond the departments and agencies of the executive branch, the third concentric circle consists of Congress and those elements of American Society (discussed in the previous part) that often seek to influence it. Although technically a single institutional entity, Congress often appears to embrace many different centers of power and authority—ranging from the House and Senate leadership to the various coalitions operative in the legislative branch, and from the various committees and subcommittees in which Congress does its real work to the individual senators and representatives who often vie with one another for publicity as well as power. Of all the institutions involved in foreign policymaking, Congress is least involved in the day-to-day conduct of the nation's foreign relations, reflected in its placement in the outermost circle.

THE INSTITUTIONAL SETTING AS AN INFLUENCE ON AMERICAN FOREIGN POLICY

Roger Hilsman suggested the conceptualization described above some years ago in *To Move a Nation,* an account of the politics of policymaking in the Kennedy administration, of which he was a part. Interestingly, Hilsman argues that while the institutional setting may affect the form and flow of policy, the politicking inherent in the process by no means conforms to the neatly compartmentalized paths his institutional framework suggests. What the nation chooses to do abroad is thus the product of an often intense political struggle among the prominent players in the policymaking process as they seek to cope with external challenges. Furthermore, it is affected not only by institutional structures but also by the policymaking positions occupied by the key decision makers and the characteristics of the individuals who act out the roles embodied in their decision-making positions.

Stephen E. Ambrose begins our examination of the institutional setting with "The Presidency and Foreign Policy," a broad historical review of the foreign policy successes and failures of the ten men who occupied the Oval Office from World War II until the Persian Gulf War. "The great successes in U.S. foreign policy tend to come in those areas in which there is a consensus and thus a continuity of policy," Ambrose observes. "Failures tend to come in those areas in which there is not a consensus and thus confusion and inconsistency in policy."

Among the causes of failure are "the swings in the location of control of foreign policy from the White House to Congress," which is a function of the separation of powers written into the Constitution. As noted, however, the president typically prevails in these struggles. In part, Ambrose argues, this is because "one of the president's assets in the struggle over control of foreign policy is his ability to act, to shoot first and answer questions later. This power was greatly strengthened during the Cold War as the United States built and maintained permanent standing armed forces." Nonetheless, the changing configuration of world power, the growing disutility of military force, and the shift in the U.S. position in the world political economy increasingly constrained post–World War II presidents, thus limiting the successes of those who occupied the most powerful position in the world. Inconsistencies in the pursuit of stated policy goals also diminished their records.

The National Security Council (NSC) system and its staff, headed by the president's assistant for national security affairs, have become principal White House mechanisms used by presidents to ensure presidential control of policymaking and to enhance prospects for policy coherence and consistency. Often the visibility and power of the national security assistant is a cause for conflict with other key participants in the process, notably the secretary of state, as was especially apparent during the Nixon and Carter presidencies. During the Reagan presidency, the NSC staff became infamous for its abuse of power when Lt. Colonel Oliver L. North undertook covert operational activities designed to divert profits from the sale of arms to Iran to the contras fighting the Sandinista regime in Nicaragua—in apparent contravention of congressional prohibitions.[1] Steps were later taken to ensure that the NSC staff would no longer engage in operational activities, and both the Bush and early Clinton presidencies were marked by the absence of public squabbles between their respective secretaries of state (James A. Baker and Warren Christopher) and national security advisers (Brent Scowcroft and Anthony Lake). It is clear nonetheless that both Scowcroft and Lake were powerful players in the policy process.

Geoffrey Kemp, himself a former member of the NSC staff, gives a brief history of the NSC system and then explains why the White House dominates foreign and national security policy decision making. As noted in the introduction to this book, personality factors help to explain how presidents choose to manage the conduct of foreign affairs. Kemp acknowledges the importance of presidential style and idiosyncracies, but he argues that "institutional factors and the policymaking process play a key role in foreign policy decision making, no matter who sits in the Oval Office. This stems from the unique role the United States plays in world politics and the unique system of government in Washington, a system that is very different from those of most other established democracies." These and other institutional realities make "a strong NSC staff . . . necessary."

Having made the case for a strong NSC staff, Kemp turns his attention to the importance of the president's schedule and explains "how the pressure of 'the schedule' influences . . . day-to-day operations, the decision-making process, career incentives, and the lack of coherent long-term planning." He also explains why "managing the media has become one of the most important tasks of the White House staff" and concludes with an assessment of the possibility of orchestrating a foreign policy that looks beyond the short term, "which is frequently measured in hours rather than in days or months."

The 1990 crisis over Kuwait and later the Persian Gulf War were heralded, respectively, as the first post–Cold War crisis and a "defining moment" in the new post–Cold War order. Kemp notes that President Bush "received high marks" for the way he handled the Persian Gulf crisis, in part "because he was seen as being in control of his own teams and insisted on loyalty from those who served him." Others, however, worry about the decision process that led to war. As Mike Moore writes in "How George Bush Won His Spurs: The President and the Power to Make War," "the Gulf crisis illuminated yet another president who was ready, willing, and enthusiastically able to ride roughshod over the war-making powers specified in the Constitution. And it defined with equal clarity another Congress willing to say in effect, 'Thank you so very much, Mr. President, for making our decision for us.'"

Moore traces the history behind the constitutional distinction between Congress's war-making power and the president's power as commander-in-chief. In practice, as Moore notes, presidents have repeatedly relied on the latter provision to justify the use of force, often without congressional sanction, as Bush apparently was also willing to do in the Persian Gulf. In 1973, in reaction to the process that led to America's protracted involvement in Vietnam, Congress passed the War Powers Resolution in an attempt to force presidents to involve Congress in use-of-force decisions, but presidents routinely ignore the resolution, which most have regarded as unconstitutional, and Congress has not insisted on its application. What Moore finds especially troublesome about George Bush is that "the Persian Gulf War marked the first time in U.S. history that an American president systematically and openly marched the nation into a major offensive war that had no Cold War overtones, such as Korea and Vietnam—while insisting at every moment that he had the legal right to do so regardless of any action that Congress might or might not take."

Congress passed the War Powers Resolution during the height of its post-Vietnam foreign policy activism. The resolution itself is a particular instance of Congress's use of substantive legislation as a foreign policymaking tool. James M. Lindsay examines substantive legislation and other congressional instruments of foreign policy influence in "Congress and Foreign Policy: Avenues of Influence." Lindsay recognizes that "the president and his subordinates continue to lead in foreign policy" and that Congress rarely initiates (legislates) its own foreign policy, but he argues that members of Congress, even when they fail to enact substantive legislation, "frequently influence policy indirectly: by pressuring the administration to modify its policies, by changing how decisions are made in the executive branch, and by framing opinion about foreign policy." How that indirect influence manifests itself is the focus of much of his analysis.

Lindsay notes that the end of divided government that occurred when the Democrats regained the presidency in 1992 removes some of the sharp ideological differences between the White House and Capitol Hill on foreign policy matters evident in recent years, but it will not end congressional activism in foreign policy. Instead, several developments may actually encourage it: the end of the Cold War, which will increase tolerance of legislative dissent in foreign affairs and encourage members of Congress to participate in the re-definition of America's world role; global interdependence, which blurs the distinction between foreign and domestic policy; and "growing fears that the American economy is falling behind the economies of Germany and Japan."

The president and Congress are constitutionally co-equal partners in the making of American foreign policy, and the two branches of government contain those policymakers elected to positions of power by the American people. But, as noted, the "fourth branch of government"—the bureaucratic organizations of the permanent foreign affairs government depicted in the second concentric circle in Figure II.1—provides continuity from one admin-istration to the next and through the continuous presidential and congression-al electoral cycles. Here career foreign policy officials ("faceless bureau-crats"?) routinely conduct the nation's foreign relations with other countries, carrying out presidential directives and administering laws passed by Con-gress.

Although career bureaucrats run the departments and agencies of the for-eign affairs government, top-level managers are political (presidential) ap-pointees. Increasingly, however, these people, too, are characterized by "pro-fessionalism" in that they follow a particular educational and career path that leads to positions of foreign policy responsibility. This is Nelson W. Polsby's thesis in "The Foreign Policy Establishment: Toward Professionalism and Centrism." Polsby notes that the development of the "presidential branch" of government—the foreign policy component of which is the NSC system and staff described by Kemp in Chapter 10—gave impetus to the emergence of the "foreign policy establishment," and he concludes that one of the conse-quences of professionalism is "centrism" in policymaking, which restricts "the range of policies an establishment is willing to consider to those options that are generated politically and placed on the table by virtue of having reputable political sponsorship." Thus it is perhaps not surprising that conti-nuity marked so much of American foreign policy during the Cold War, as captured in the themes of globalism, anticommunism, containment, military might, and interventionism, but Polsby's thesis also raises potentially trouble-some questions about the ability of the United States to adapt innovatively to the challenges and opportunities of a post–Cold War world.

The next chapter, "The Department of State in 2000: A New Model for Managing Foreign Affairs," which is part of a management reform project in the Department of State, suggests how one of the key foreign policy agencies —the "first among equals" in the foreign affairs government—proposes to rise to the challenge of a new world order. The report candidly admits that "our foreign policy institutions, including the Department of State, are still dominated by a Cold War political–military view of world events" and sug-gests that, while "military security remains vital," the department will have to change if the U.S. government is to be able to respond vigorously and con-structively to a range of new challenges and issues, "such as economic com-petitiveness and environmental protection."

Most of the report purports to explain how this adaptation should occur organizationally. The specific recommendations are less important than the picture they convey about the range of responsibilities the State Department (and others in the foreign affairs government) must routinely discharge in a competitive and often threatening international environment, and how bureaucratic structures may enhance or impede the conduct of foreign relations. The one surprise, perhaps, is that the management report urges that the "National Security Council (NSC) be the catalyst and the point of coordination for [a] new, single foreign policy process." Given the historic competition between the White House and the Department of State for the central role in creating and implementing American foreign policy—specifically the contest between the national security adviser and the secretary of state—one might have expected the State Department's management report to urge—as so many similar reports have in the past—that the department, not the White House, play the principal role in devising an American foreign policy suited to the challenges posed by the new, post–Cold War world order. Perhaps the authors of the report recognize what is now fact: that the White House is the focal point in defining the goals and interests of the United States in world politics.

Bruce Stokes's chapter, "Organizing to Trade," provides a second perspective on how the structure of the foreign affairs government relates to the process of policymaking and, in the end, policy outcomes. International trade is an increasingly salient issue in American domestic politics as well as in its relations with other nations, notably the European Community and Japan, but, according to Stokes (and many others), the U.S. government is poorly organized to deal with the challenges posed by other nations who, allegedly, routinely engage in unfair trade practices or otherwise pursue policies toward industry that give them a competitive edge in the global marketplace.

Stokes first catalogs the trade challenges the Clinton administration faces and then urges that "the burgeoning complexity of trade-related concerns can best be managed by restructuring the bureaucracies . . . that formulate U.S. trade policy." As with the State Department's management reform proposals, Stokes's particular recommendations are less important than the insight his analysis provides into how the present organizational situation operates and how it impedes the realization of more effective policy. As Stokes himself concludes, "With the emergence of a global economy and its growing importance to the domestic economic well-being of the United States, an anemic USTR [U.S. Trade Representative, located in the White House] and a Congress that works at cross-purposes with the administration sabotage America's self-interest. . . . Without a better means of coordinating and implementing America's international economic and commercial policy Washington is likely to be more of a hindrance than a help."

Much has changed at home and abroad in recent years, as the previous selections attest. John Canham-Clyne worries that too little has changed. His concern is with "Business as Usual: Iran–contra and the National Security State."

Following revelations that NSC staffer Ollie North had seemingly contravened congressional mandates when he engineered a diversion of profits to the Nicaraguan contras from an arms-for-hostages deal with Iran, Lawrence

Walsh was appointed independent prosecutor and charged with determining whether those involved in the covert operation had engaged in criminal activity. Walsh's often controversial investigation extended over several years and into the highest levels of government. Eventually—and on the very eve of the Bush–Clinton presidential contest—Walsh revealed evidence that President Bush, who was vice president when the Reagan administration hatched the Iranian arms-for-hostages operation—may himself have been culpable. What impact this revelation had on Bush's sagging reelection bid is difficult to determine precisely, but it clearly did the president no good. Nonetheless, shortly after Clinton's election, Bush pardoned Caspar Weinberger, defense secretary under Reagan whose hand-written notes implicated Bush in the scandal, thus freeing him from criminal prosecution. Others who had already gone through the criminal justice system were also pardoned.

"Beyond questions of criminal culpability," Canham-Clyne writes, "the Iran and contra affairs pose fundamental questions about the nature of American society and government. They challenge the notion that covert operations and institutional secrecy can be squared with a commitment to democratic accountability." Yet secrecy remains a seeming national security imperative, even in the post–Cold War world, with the implication that covert activities undertaken by the Central Intelligence Agency and other intelligence organizations may continue. Canham-Clyne explains how the institutions of government, executive and legislative alike, facilitated—and may still facilitate—what many regard as the greatest challenge to a democratic foreign policy, namely, the need to balance the requirement for information on which democracies thrive against the secrecy that national security sometimes demands.

NOTE

1. The whole bizarre episode conjured up reminiscences òf the Vietnam debacle, which had led the distinguished historian Arthur J. Schlesinger, Jr., to write of the "Imperial Presidency"—a label implying an abuse of presidential power that perhaps threatened the very system of checks and balances the Founding Fathers had intended when they framed the Constitution two centuries ago. See Arthur M. Schlesinger, Jr., *The Imperial Presidency* (Boston: Houghton Mifflin, 1973); and Arthur M. Schlesinger, Jr., "The Presidency and the Imperial Temptation," in Charles W. Kegley, Jr., and Eugene R. Wittkopf, eds., *The Domestic Sources of American Foreign Policy: Insights and Evidence* (New York: St. Martin's, 1988), pp. 127–141.

9. THE PRESIDENCY AND FOREIGN POLICY

Stephen E. Ambrose

*I*n the half-century between 1941 and 1991 the ten men who have served as president of the United States have scored some stupendous successes in their role as unquestioned world leader, but they have also suffered some spectacular failures. The greatest successes—the turning back of Nazism, fascism, and communism in Europe and of Japanese militarism in Asia—are of such an order of magnitude that they must be described as America's unique gift to the world. That the presidents and their nation did not achieve these triumphs for freedom on their own is obvious, but it is equally obvious that the triumphs could not have been achieved without their leadership and determination. The presidents' contribution to the end of another "ism"—colonialism—has been of lesser importance, though still a positive one, as also their contribution to the advent of peaceful relations between Egypt and Israel, not to mention the continuing existence of Israel.

The failures, however, have been spectacular. They include the unwillingness or inability to prevent communist takeovers in China, Southeast Asia, or Cuba, or to create peaceful conditions, much less prosperity, in the Middle East, Africa, and Central America. Although some progress has been made in the past few years, American presidents have failed to realize the hopes of the founders of the United Nations for a genuine collective security or an end to the arms race. And they have been unable or unwilling to slow, much less stop, the international arms trade.

The two giants among the presidents since 1941 came at the beginning of that period. Franklin D. Roosevelt committed a reluctant United States to the leading international role and, more specifically, to unalterable opposition to Nazism, fascism, and Japanese militarism. Harry S Truman committed a reluctant United States to the reconstruction of Europe, to the building of democracy in Germany and Japan, to support for Israel, to NATO, and to the containment of communism. Four decades later, the commitments made by Roosevelt and Truman in the 1940s remain the bedrock of American foreign policy. Their successors have been successful as implementors of established policy, not as creators of new policy.

PRESIDENTIAL DOCTRINES

Almost all the presidents since 1952 have attempted to create their own doctrine, using the Truman Doctrine as a model, but without much success. The doctrines articulated by Roosevelt and Truman established the precedent for future presidents. Although not an easy task, both presidents managed to convince a permanent majority of the American people that the democracy in, and close ties with, Western Europe were in the national interest; Truman, in the immediate postwar period, would include Japan. It has been difficult, however, for successive presidents to persuade a permanent majority that America's national security is at stake in other areas, except the middle East.

The Eisenhower Doctrine dealt specifically with the Middle East. In 1957 Congress granted President Dwight D. Eisenhower authority to use American armed forces in the Middle East "if the president determines the necessity . . . to assist any nation . . . requesting assistance against armed aggression from any country controlled by international communism." He implemented it in 1958 in Lebanon in a minor but precedent-setting military intervention. In its broadest sense the Eisenhower Doctrine was used by President Ronald Reagan in 1983, also in Lebanon, and by President George Bush in the recent Gulf War. But neither Reagan nor Bush cited it when they acted, in sharp contrast to Eisenhower in 1958 when he cited the Truman Doctrine as a precedent for invoking his own doctrine.

Unlike the Eisenhower Doctrine, which was based on a joint congressional resolution, President Richard M. Nixon announced his own doctrine more or less casually during an informal news conference in 1969. Nixon said that "the United States is going to encourage, and has a right to expect, that this problem [communist aggression] will be increasingly handled by, and the responsibility for it taken by, the Asian nations themselves." The Nixon Doctrine, which specifically concerned Southeast Asia, was little more than a clarification of the president's policy of Vietnamization (turning the ground war over to the South Vietnamese) and had no lasting impact.

The Carter Doctrine addressed the Persian Gulf. In 1980 President Jimmy Carter declared, without congressional authorization, that the United States would repel a Soviet assault in the Gulf "by any means necessary—including military force." The doctrine is now out-of-date, and it was not cited by Presidents Reagan or Bush when they sent U.S. armed forces to the region.

The Reagan Doctrine (circa 1983) had no specific wording and no authorization. It was more a summary of President Reagan's policies in the Third World than a doctrine. In practice it meant covert U.S. military and economic support for anticommunist forces in Nicaragua and Afghanistan. In Nicaragua democracy triumphed, contrary to predictions from the Reagan administration, which argued that the Sandinistas would never abide by the results of a fair and free election. Whether the Reagan policy of support for the contras accelerated the process and forced the Sandinistas to accept the election re-sults is a debatable point. In Afghanistan the Reagan Doctrine certainly helped the Afghanistan rebels to force a Red Army retreat, but it has not led to the demise of the communist government there.

The post-Truman doctrines for the Middle East have not had much suc-cess. It was President Anwar al-Sadat of Egypt who expelled the Soviets from the Middle East, not the Eisenhower Doctrine. Reagan's intervention in Lebanon in 1982 was a disaster. And if there were ever any danger of the Red Army moving into the Persian Gulf, it no longer exists—not because of the Carter Doctrine but because of the fall of the Soviet Union.

An obvious reason for these relative failures was American overreach. The United States either could not or would not support armed forces in every part of the world. American influence, and thus presidential doctrines, have been limited to those areas where the nation was willing to maintain large armed forces on a permanent basis. The United States has done so in Western Europe and Japan, where its influence today is great, but it has not done so in Southeast Asia, where its influence is small, nor in the Middle East, where Presidents Eisenhower, Reagan, and Bush pulled troops and ships out shortly after sending them in.

For whatever reasons—perhaps because the doctrines announced by some of his predecessors turned out to be empty canons—President Bush did not articulate what could be called a doctrine of his own. He did establish a precedent of unalterable opposition to naked aggression by one Arab nation against another. As this was based on sound principle and economic necessity, it will have more staying power than some of the earlier doctrines—if the United States is willing to maintain large armed forces in the area.

PRESIDENTIAL POWER

The great successes in U.S. foreign policy tend to come in those areas in which there is a consensus and thus a continuity in policy. (This is not an iron-clad rule; consensus on isolationism, neutrality, and disarmament in the 1920s and 1930s was surely wrong.) Failures tend to come in those areas in which there is not a consensus and thus confusion and inconsistency in policy. The most obvious example of a U.S. policy failure is Southeast Asia. In 1954 Eisenhower refused to intervene in Vietnam to stop communism; in 1964 President Lyndon B. Johnson entered a major war in Vietnam to stop commu-nism, eventually sending 550,000 troops there; in 1973 President Nixon pulled the last American troops out of Vietnam, and two years later the Vietnamese communists won a total victory. By 1976 Vietnam, described by presidents through the 1960s as vital to U.S. national interest, was inconse-quential to American policymakers and forgotten as a policy priority by the American people.

Beyond the absence of consensus about the importance of countries other than those of Western Europe and Japan to U.S. national interest, there are additional important causes for the rapid shifts in American foreign policy.

An obvious one has been the absence of continuity in the top leadership positions. In the past fifty years there have been ten presidents, five of them Democrats, five Republicans. They were all markedly different men, in personalities, agendas, experience, and political support. Only two (Eisenhower and Reagan) served more than five years; all, including Roosevelt and Truman, had major internal inconsistencies in their policies; each tried to set his own course and put his own stamp on policy; small wonder that the United States lurched first this way, then that (except in Western Europe and Japan).

The swings in the location of control of foreign policy from the White House to Congress contributed to the inconsistencies. The structural cause of these swings is constitutional. The president's most important asset in asserting control of foreign policy is Section 2, Article II, of the Constitution: "The president shall be commander in chief of the army and navy of the United States." The Constitution, however, also gives Congress power to shape foreign policy: Section 8, Article I, "The congress shall have power to . . . declare war . . . raise and support armies . . . and maintain a navy"; Section 9, Article I, "No money shall be drawn from the treasury, but in consequence of appropriations made by law"; and Section 2, Article II, which gives the president the power to "make treaties," but only "provided two-thirds of the senators present concur." These simple declarative sentences invite a constant struggle between the executive and the legislative branches for control of foreign policy.

On the eve of Pearl Harbor Congress was in charge of foreign policy, as it had been since the Senate rejected the Versailles Treaty in 1919. President Roosevelt had a clear policy—to get the United States involved in the European war as a major participant on the side of Britain and the Soviet Union and to block further Japanese expansion in Asia—but Congress would not appropriate the monies necessary to raise and maintain armed forces capable of carrying it out, or declare war on the Axis powers.

War came anyway. After Pearl Harbor Roosevelt took command and controlled foreign policy as commander in chief almost without reference to Congress. His two most important policies, the demand for unconditional surrender by the Axis and the Yalta accords with the Soviets, were his decisions alone.

Truman operated differently, though for obvious reasons. The war was over, and thus the power of the president was necessarily diminished. He did not have the political mandate Roosevelt enjoyed, and the Republicans controlled Congress in the critical years 1947–1949. Truman needed congressional approval for his great innovations, including creating America's first peacetime alliance—NATO—and an aid package to Europe, the Marshall Plan. Whereas there had been no significant national discussion about unconditional surrender or the Yalta accords, Truman led a lengthy debate over NATO and the Marshall Plan. He eventually managed to create a consensus for the policies. His third great innovation, the Truman Doctrine, was announced during a speech to Congress on March 12, 1947. The Truman Doctrine committed the United States to contain communism anywhere in the world by aiding countries that requested help against Soviet expansionism. His speech persuaded a majority in Congress to support military aid to Greece and Turkey, but that support came only after a prolonged national debate brilliantly conducted by his administration.

Truman, however, implemented his doctrine in Korea without consulting Congress. This decision turned out to be a mistake. Because of the way Truman entered the Korean War and because of the way he conducted it— twice changing U.S. policy 180 degrees, from stopping aggression to liberating North Korea and then back to stopping aggression, in each case without involving Congress in any way—he lost both popular and congressional support. Two years after he intervened in Korea, Truman's approval rating in the Gallup Poll dropped to 23 percent, the lowest in the history of the poll (Johnson slipped to 28 percent in the fall of 1968, Nixon to 25 percent in the summer of 1974).

Eisenhower brought back presidential primacy in foreign policy. The threat posed by the Soviet Union, the development of nuclear weapons and long-range bombers to carry them (and by the late 1950s intercontinental missiles), combined with the Pearl Harbor legacy of fear of surprise attack, made Congress content—even eager—to leave foreign policy decisions to the president. Eisenhower informed, rather than consulted with, congressional leaders about his major decisions: to accept a ceasefire in Korea without liberating North Korea, to stay out of Vietnam in 1954, to use the CIA to support coups in Iran in 1953 and in Guatemala in 1954, not to go to war with China over the off-shore islands (Quemoy and Matsu), not to support the Hungarian rebels in 1956 or the British/French/Israeli cabal in Suez in 1956, to force Israel to pull out of the Sinai Peninsula in 1957, to extend aid to Tito in Yugoslavia, and to hold down the cost of defense. In every case, except Vietnam in 1954, a majority of Republicans and perhaps of Congress as a whole wanted Eisenhower to adopt different policies. But thanks to his immense prestige and congressional fears he got his way.

In his less than three years in office President John F. Kennedy ran foreign policy almost without reference to Congress, most notably in the Bay of Pigs fiasco in 1961 and the Cuban missile crisis in 1962, but also in dealing with the problems of Berlin and Vietnam. Kennedy did not have Eisenhower's prestige or his political mandate, but he was the nation's leader at a time when Congress was most willing to support the president in foreign policy because the Cold War was at its hottest and American hubris at its highest.

In 1964, in the Gulf of Tonkin resolution, Congress gave President Johnson even broader powers in Southeast Asia than it had given Eisenhower in the Middle East, another reflection of the congressional attitude that "the president knows best." But although Johnson managed to get a near-unanimous vote for the resolution, he did so in the middle of a presidential election campaign and rushed it through Congress without any meaningful debate. Many congressmen later claimed they had been tricked into voting for the measure because Johnson painted the incident in the Gulf of Tonkin almost as if it were Pearl Harbor revisited. In other words the sense of permanent crisis that prevailed in the worst years of the Cold War allowed Truman, Eisenhower, Kennedy, and Johnson to act almost as unilaterally as Roosevelt had during World War II by drawing on their constitutionally given strength as commander in chief.

The agony of Vietnam caused the pendulum to swing back. Congress used its power of the purse to limit President Nixon's ability to carry out policies he thought necessary and eventually forced him to agree to a ceasefire that left the United States far short of the goals he had set. It blocked his détente initiative by refusing most-favored-nation status to the Soviets. In the 1973 War Powers Resolution Congress attempted to take control of foreign policy out of the president's hands by limiting his military option through legislation —unthinkable in previous administrations—and it rejected President Ford's pleas to support South Vietnam in its final crisis.

Perhaps exhausted by its major effort in the Nixon/Ford years, certainly relieved that the Vietnam War was over, Congress retreated from its active role during the Carter presidency. It was not involved in Carter's major triumph, the Camp David accords, except to provide the money that made the agreement possible, and it played virtually no part in the major crises of 1980— Nicaragua and the Sandinistas, Iran and the hostages, Afghanistan and the Soviet invasion.

Nor did Congress play as active a role in the eight years of Reagan's presidency as it had in the Nixon/Ford years, certainly not in his interventions in Grenada (1983) and Lebanon (1983–1984), his air strike against Libya (1986), or his attempt to swap arms for hostages in Iran. Reagan simply ignored the one attempt by Congress to control policy—the Boland amendment forbidding aid to the contras in Nicaragua (although in that case Congress was able to use its power of the purse to limit somewhat his intervention). In general Congress followed the shifting winds of Reagan's policies. When Reagan was hostile to the Soviet Union, Congress appropriated massive funds to support his military buildup (in large part because of the Soviet buildup of the 1970s). When Reagan turned to détente, Congress went along.

President Bush was able to set and carry out his own foreign policy, although like Truman before the Korean "police action" he [was] careful to involve Congress in the debate over the use of force. In the Gulf crisis of 1990–1991 he persuaded Congress to vote for the functional equivalent of a declaration of war.

One of the president's assets in the struggle over control of foreign policy is his ability to act, to shoot first and answer questions later. This power was greatly strengthened during the Cold War as the United States built and maintained permanent standing armed forces. The congressional attempt to diminish this asset through the War Powers Resolution has had at best minimal effect.

PRESIDENTIAL SUCCESSES

Since Roosevelt the only presidents to leave office with high approval ratings have been Eisenhower and Reagan. Truman, Johnson, and Nixon had less than a 30 percent approval rate at the end of their terms; Carter and Ford could not win reelection even as incumbents; Kennedy's approval rate was at about 50 percent when he was assassinated. There were many reasons, mostly domestic, for these relative failures, but certainly not least was the inability of the presidents to achieve their own stated foreign policy goals in "the American century." Their commitment to the Truman Doctrine played a role. The policy of containment was inherently frustrating and especially so to a nation that had totally defeated the Nazis and the Japanese in an all-out offensive but had to go over to the defensive in dealing with Stalin and his successors.

Roosevelt was successful in achieving the unconditional surrender of America's enemies, and in the Yalta accords he got the postwar settlement he wanted (whether he would have been better able than his successors to enforce the accords cannot be known but must be doubted). Truman successfully contained the communists in Greece and South Korea, established NATO and the Marshall Plan.

Their successors hoped for, and the public expected, such spectacular victories in other areas of the world, but these have been beyond America's grasp or willingness to pay. Even so it cannot be said too often that they have all held firm to the commitment to NATO and Japan. Bush was fortunate enough to be in office when the Truman Doctrine won its great victory, the retreat of communism from central and eastern Europe. Credit for this triumph goes to all the presidents since 1945.

PRESIDENTIAL FAILURES

One obvious cause of the relative failures in foreign policy has been the shift in the world economy and America's position in it. When Roosevelt, Truman, and Eisenhower led the United States, it was an exporter of oil, steel, automobiles, and other commodities. America was the world's creditor and enjoyed a highly favorable balance of trade.

By 1965 this situation was rapidly changing; by 1975 the United States was a major importer of oil; by 1985 the country had an unfavorable balance of trade and had become a debtor nation. Europe had recovered and then some; Japan was booming beyond the wildest expectations; the remainder of noncommunist Asia was not far behind. America was richer than ever, but its relative position in the world economy had been sharply reduced. This hampered the presidents in their attempts to be the world leader. For example, in 1956 Eisenhower was able to force the British and French out of Suez and Israel out of Sinai by threatening an oil boycott and other economic sanctions. But in 1973 Nixon could not persuade the Europeans to help him implement his policy of rearming Israel during the Yom Kippur War, and in 1981 Reagan was unable to persuade the Europeans to join in an economic boycott of Poland and Russia when the Soviet Union forced the Polish government to impose martial law in order to crush the Solidarity movement.

The military balance also shifted dramatically between 1941 and 1991. In 1941 the United States had a minuscule armed force, which was the major reason Roosevelt had so little influence on world events from the Munich crisis of 1938 through the German invasion of the Soviet Union in mid-1941. By 1945 the American armed forces were vastly superior to those of the rest of the world combined. After World War II the United States made possible the rearming of Western Europe, stopped communist aggression in Korea, and had a virtual monopoly on nuclear weapons. In 1962 Kennedy used America's overwhelming superiority to force Nikita Khrushchev to back down in the Cuban missile crisis.

But the Cuban experience, plus the continuing expansion of the American arsenal instituted by Kennedy, caused Khrushchev to start his own crash program of building nuclear weapons and missiles. Kennedy had aimed to stockpile enough weapons and missiles to give the United States clear-cut nuclear superiority, but in 1968 Secretary of Defense Robert McNamara announced that the Soviets had caught up with the United States in terms of nuclear weapons. McNamara argued, however, that this was not undesirable, since the behavior of both states was now constrained by mutual assured destruction (MAD).

In conventional forces, meanwhile, the United States cut back its number of ships, planes, and tanks, while the Soviets expanded theirs. The number of men and women in the U.S. armed services also decreased after Nixon introduced the all-volunteer force. The U.S. military, which had boasted in 1960 it could fight two-and-a-half major wars at once, by 1980 had become a pitiful helpless giant, capable of destroying the world in a nuclear spasm but incapable of fighting even one-half a war with much hope of success.

The power to destroy is not the power to control. Power is the man on the spot with the gun in his hand, and increasingly the United States was incapable of putting him there. This, too, hampered American presidents in their attempts to exert world leadership and led to inconsistencies in their policies. Simultaneously two ideas came to dominate presidential thinking and behavior. First, the world was bipolar and contained two superpowers—the United States and the Soviet Union. Excluding the superpowers, no other nation mattered very much (the British attended the first two summit meetings, at Yalta and Potsdam, as equal partners; Eisenhower took care to involve the British and French at the Geneva and Paris summits; but since 1960 summits have been limited to the United States and the Soviet Union).

Second, American hubris and the astonishing growth of the White House staff combined to reinforce the so-called Imperial Presidency, so that just as the relative importance of the president was decreasing, the presidents' views of themselves and what they could accomplish was increasing. The public agreed, which led to great expectations with each new president after Eisenhower, only to be followed by disillusion as the presidents failed to achieve their goals.

In 1960 Kennedy had set out to create a first-strike capability. By 1968 Soviet nuclear weapons deployment and advances in weaponry led to the concept of MAD. In 1970 Nixon said that he would be satisfied with strategic sufficiency, which apparently meant nuclear parity with the Soviets. In 1972 Nixon signed the Strategic Arms Limitation Treaty (SALT), an agreement with the Soviets that conceded superiority in some categories of missiles.

These fundamental policy shifts after 1960 were matched by shifts in each president's posture. Kennedy came into office full of bellicose rhetoric. He wanted to go on the offensive worldwide, ready to "pay any price, bear any burden," to ensure the triumph of freedom everywhere. He sponsored an invasion of Cuba—and then backed down at the critical moment. He took a strong stance on Berlin—and then backed down when Khrushchev built the Wall. He escalated the war in Vietnam—and then allowed the CIA to participate in a plot to overthrow the South Vietnamese president, Ngo Dinh Diem. He faced down Khrushchev in the Cuban missile crisis—and then entered into an agreement in which he promised that the United States would never invade Cuba, a promise he had no authority to make and that, had he presented it to the Senate in the form of a treaty, would never have been ratified.

FURTHER PRESIDENTIAL FAILURES

The gap between Johnson's rhetoric and promises on the one hand and his performance on the other was even greater. Johnson said he would not send American boys to Asia to do the fighting that Asian boys ought to be doing themselves, but he then ended up sending 550,000 American soldiers. Johnson said he sought no wider war, even as he widened the war. He said he would never play politics with peace and then called a bombing halt one week before the 1968 election. He said he would see to it that there was no reward for aggression and then offered to negotiate the removal of American troops while the communists held large portions of South Vietnamese territory.

Nixon extracted the United States from Vietnam, opened the door to China, promoted détente with the Soviet Union, and negotiated the first Cold War arms control agreement. In each case what he did represented a retreat, for America and for Nixon, who had stridently advocated opposite policies for two decades. When he withdrew U.S. troops from Vietnam, Nixon claimed to have achieved peace with honor. From the perspective of the South Vietnamese, what he had achieved was surrender with humiliation. What he had accomplished was to get America out of Vietnam without setting off a right-wing revolt within the United States and to give the Saigon government a chance to stand on its own two feet—not much of a chance, to be sure, but still a chance. That was an accomplishment Nixon could have pointed to with pride but, Nixon being Nixon, he had to grossly exaggerate and claim peace with honor. Saigon fell because of the incompetence and corruption of its own government. It was not Nixon's fault, but he must shoulder some of the blame for failing to make that government reform itself.

If Nixon was the man most responsible for opening the door to China in 1972, he was also one of the key men who had been most responsible for keeping it closed for the preceding 23 years. When he changed his mind, he sprang his new policy on the nation as a surprise. There had been no national debate on the subject, and thus no constituency had emerged behind it. The door, therefore, did not open very wide. Nixon was not able to solve the problem of Taiwan or establish diplomatic relations or trade agreements with China, much less enter into an alliance with that country.

Détente with the Soviets, for all its promise, was also substantially flawed by Nixon's penchant for secrecy. He negotiated in secret, especially using back-channels to cut out the State Department. Rather than consult with the Senate, he tried to go over its head or around it. He thus left his policy vulnerable to ambitious senators, led by Henry Jackson (D-Wash.), who used their power to scuttle such critical aspects of détente as most-favored-nation status for the Soviets. Détente had no staying power—recall that President Ford banned the use of the word détente in the White House—and at least part of the reason was Nixon's love of surprise and secrecy.

Carter also was unable to set a course and hold to it. In sharp contrast to the realpolitik of the Nixon/Ford administrations, the chief characteristic of the Carter administration was its idealism. In his inaugural address in 1976 Carter said he wanted to eliminate nuclear weapons and to stop arms sales abroad. He made a firm commitment to human rights, calling them "the soul of our foreign policy." But the nuclear arsenal grew during the Carter years at the same pace as in the Nixon/Ford years. Arms sales abroad actually increased. Carter's emphasis on human rights badly damaged America's relationship with many of its oldest allies. It caused resentment in the Soviet Union and contributed to Carter's failure to reach arms control agreements and to the downfall of America's most important ally in the Middle East, the shah of Iran.

Human rights had been good politics for Carter as a candidate. The issue pleased both right-wingers, who could and did use it to criticize the Soviet Union, and left-wingers, who could and did use it to criticize Chile, Brazil, South Africa, and others for their human rights abuses. But the issue made for terrible policy. It was directed against America's allies, who were vulnerable to Carter's pressures, rather than its enemies, who were basically immune. It made little sense to weaken such allies as South Korea, Argentina, South Africa, Brazil, Taiwan, Nicaragua, Iran, and others because of objections to their human rights record while continuing to advance credits, sell grain, and ship advanced technology to the Soviet Union, which had one of the worst human rights records in the world and was clearly no friend of the United States.

The Carter human rights policy represented American hubris at its most extreme, willfully ignoring the reality of America's power and ability to dictate developments abroad. It makes no sense to commit to a policy that one has no power to enforce. This applies to Roosevelt's policy toward Poland as enunciated in the Yalta accords of 1945, to the Republican promise of liberation for Eastern Europe as enunciated by Secretary of State John Foster Dulles in 1952, to the policy of paying any price to ensure the survival of freedom around the world as enunciated by Kennedy in 1961, and to Carter's human rights policy.

Further, Carter's preaching to the Soviet Union on its human rights obligations contradicted U.S. attempts to improve relations with the Kremlin. The president tried to assure the Soviet leaders that a new day had dawned in

Washington, but as he pulled back from America's advanced positions around the world, for example, by ordering the removal of nuclear weapons from Korea without demanding some balancing arms reduction by the Soviets, the Soviets responded by moving forward. They continued their arms buildup and became involved both in the Horn of Africa and Angola.

The climax came in December 1979 when the Soviets invaded Afghanistan. Carter's reaction was extreme, as was the triggering Soviet action. He placed an embargo on grain sales to the Soviets and on high-technology goods. He withdrew SALT II, drawn up by Nixon and endorsed by Ford, from the Senate ratification process. He sharply increased defense spending and announced that restrictions on CIA activities would be lifted. These were serious steps that reversed long-standing policies, not to mention his own stated goals. When Carter left office, relations with the Soviet Union were much worse than they had been when he was inaugurated. Each side had more bombs and missiles, less trade and trust. Carter in 1980 was the antithesis of Carter in 1977. By 1980 the word most often used to describe his foreign policy was "waffle." It was a stinging indictment.

Nonetheless Carter did manage some solid foreign policy successes. Most notably, the president was instrumental in negotiating the Camp David accords in 1979, the first peace treaty between Israel and an Arab state, Egypt. Another notable success was the Panama Canal treaty in 1978, returning full sovereignty over the canal zone to Panama. The treaty had been denounced by presidential candidate Reagan, endorsed by Ford and former Secretary of State Henry Kissinger. Carter put the full weight of the presidency into the debate; the treaty narrowly passed. He also established full diplomatic relations with China. But he failed completely to achieve his stated goals of ending the Cold War, improving human rights, stopping the arms race, or eliminating nuclear weapons.

With regard to the event that led to Carter's defeat in the 1980 election, the Iranian Revolution and the taking of American hostages by the revolutionaries, he moved from blunder to blunder. He praised the shah far beyond any justified level (on the eve of the revolution he called Iran an island of stability in a turbulent sea). He failed to support the shah when the revolution began. He failed to open lines of communication with the revolutionaries. He recognized a government in Iran that could not govern. He decided to allow the shah into the United States despite clear warnings about the repercussions. He had a highly emotional and grossly exaggerated response to the taking of the hostages, insisting absurdly that he was spending every waking moment on the hostage problem. He delayed and then botched the use of a military rescue option.

Reagan was also inconsistent. He came into office as the most belligerent president since Kennedy, denouncing the "evil empire," and ended up as Mikhail Gorbachev's friend and virtual ally. He entered office aiming for a first-strike capability and ended up signing the first arms reduction agreement of the Cold War. He promised never to pay ransom for hostages, then secretly sold weapons to the Iranian government in return for the release of hostages (a policy that never resulted in the release of hostages and completely undermined the U.S. boycott of arms sales to Tehran). Reagan did preside over a major increase in America's armed forces, but more often than not he was frustrated in his attempt to use the military option, as in Nicaragua. In Lebanon he was hamstrung by contradictions in his policies. He sent the marines to Beirut with no clear mission, putting them in a provocative position with orders not to shoot. In Richard Neustadt's telling judgment, he succeeded in "combining ignorance with insistence."

Still, Reagan had some impressive firsts. His administration coincided with a number of arms reduction agreements, and it managed eight years without a major war (but with a popular invasion of Grenada and an even more popular military strike against Libya). According to his admirers, Reagan's arms buildup was responsible for the retreat of communism from central and eastern Europe. They argue that the Soviet effort to keep up with the Americans bankrupted the communists. This may be true, although critics argue that communism collapsed because it is a rotten system and that it lasted as long as it did only because of the perceived threat against the Warsaw Pact nations by the Reagan buildup. Back in 1953 Eisenhower had said that the proper policy for the West was to keep up its defenses, not to threaten, and to wait for communism to self-destruct. That was a restatement of the Truman Doctrine, and it worked, thanks to its support by all of Truman's successors.

In any case, with regard to Reagan's policies, it was the contradictions that stood out. He launched the most expensive weapons development program in history, the Strategic Defense Initiative, even as he sought arms reduction. In 1986 at the conclusion of the Reykjavik Summit with Gorbachev, Secretary of State George Shultz reported that the two leaders had agreed on the elimination of all nuclear weapons and the missile systems to deliver them, and that this process of disarmament was to be completed in ten years. It seemed too good to be true, and it was. Shultz went on to say that these agreements in principle had been abandoned because Reagan refused to accept Gorbachev's demand that the United States stop its SDI program. In the Iran–contra affair, the administration violated the law and tried to cover it up, to the point that Reagan might have been impeached had the Democrats not felt that one threatened impeachment a century is enough. His administration survived, but revelations in the Iran–contra hearings seriously crippled his ability to conduct foreign policy. When he left office, Reagan was popular with the public as a person, but his politics were in danger of becoming an object of ridicule.

President Bush's policies, except toward China, were popular and successful. America's relative power position in the world continued to decline, and congressional attempts to cut back on the powers of the Imperial Presidency through investigations and revelations from Watergate through Iran–contra proved embarrassing for the White House. Yet in his first major crisis Bush was able to mobilize public opinion within his country and around the world, leading a serious debate, fully involving Congress and consulting constantly with other leaders. In the process he demonstrated beyond all doubt that the American president is still the most important person in the world. No other world leader could have put together the coalition that fought the Gulf War.

Bush also demonstrated that no other nation could project so much power so far from home as the United States. A year later, in August 1991, Bush's condemnation of the coup leaders in the Soviet Union as criminals, his support for Gorbachev and Boris Yeltsin, brought him praise and thanks from Soviet leaders, who said that his policy was of fundamental importance to the democratic elements in Moscow.

Bush's response to the 1992 crisis in Bosnia, however, was hesitant and ineffective. Thus he provided no real policy for the "new world order" to serve as a guidepost to his successor Bill Clinton, who won the 1992 election in a campaign that hardly mentioned foreign policy.

10. PRESIDENTIAL MANAGEMENT OF THE EXECUTIVE BUREAUCRACY

Geoffrey Kemp

INTRODUCTION

It is an accepted maxim that the role of the president in making foreign policy and his relationship with the National Security Council (NSC) system and its staff will vary according to his background, temperament, and management style. Jimmy Carter was a "hands-on" president; he became involved in decisions concerning tennis court allocations and the nature of beverages served to White House guests (no hard liquor). Ronald Reagan was very much a "hands-off" president, perhaps unique in recent history. On the other hand, his successor, George Bush, [was] even more activist than Carter. He has been called his "own desk officer." His personal diplomacy during the 1990–1991 Persian Gulf crisis and the attempted Soviet coup in August 1991 confirmed this reputation.

Most recent presidents have been "hands-on," especially in the conduct of foreign policy. Franklin D. Roosevelt, Harry S Truman, and Dwight Eisenhower knew how to use the powers of their office to bypass bureaucracy when necessary. Although they had very different styles, none was as passive as Reagan on matters pertaining to daily management. John F. Kennedy, Lyndon B. Johnson, and Richard M. Nixon likewise controlled foreign policy from the White House and made extensive use of the NSC staff to pursue their particular initiatives. It was under Kennedy that the NSC staff first began to be "noticed" as important players in their own right. Nixon and his national security adviser, Henry Kissinger, made White House control of foreign policy one of the most singular characteristics of the administration. Only during Gerald Ford's short tenure did some semblance of balance emerge in the distribution of foreign policy decision making. This was due, in large part, to

Note: Some notes have been deleted or renumbered.

Kissinger's presence at the State Department. Ford certainly had more day-to-day control of the White House than Reagan. It was Ford alone who decided to fire his secretary of defense, James Schlesinger, an action Reagan would never have taken on his own.

Ronald Reagan's tenure can be regarded as something of an aberration concerning the "hands-on–hands-off" debate. Yet the irony is that it was Reagan's meddling in one particular foreign policy issue (that of the Middle East hostages) and his lack of attention to detail that contributed to a major scandal—Iran–contra—and a major review of the presidential management of national security. The Iran–contra affair generated wide publicity about the role of the NSC staff in the management of foreign policy. There were frequent references to "rogue elephant" operations conducted by Oliver North from the White House basement and the Old Executive Office Building. In televised congressional hearings Secretaries of State and Defense George Shultz and Caspar Weinberger described how they were duped by the White House and cut out of the decision-making process. As a result of this crisis, the Tower Commission was established to review the affair. It recommended new guidelines for the NSC staff to ensure closer control on day-to-day operations with an enhanced role for the NSC counsel.[1]

How did it come about that the NSC staff had such power? Could such an operation happen again? What should be the correct relationship between the president, the NSC staff, and other key players in the national security bureaucracy? And to what extent does the entire national security decision-making system need overhaul in view of the new sets of problems facing the United States in both the international and domestic arenas? To answer these questions, I offer a brief history of the NSC system; this is followed by an analysis of why the White House has become, and must remain, the focus of national security decision making; and I then show why it is difficult, although not impossible, for presidents to engage in long-range thinking about foreign policy.

ORIGINS OF THE NATIONAL SECURITY COUNCIL AND ITS STAFF

During World War II, the Departments of Army, Navy, and State had to cooperate to manage a grand strategy that embraced the entire resources of the nation and the most complicated and politically difficult alliance ever assembled to fight a total war. The United States found itself faced with new global responsibilities at the end of the war. To those in Washington responsible for the new world order, it became clear that institutional changes were necessary to better manage traditionally competitive bureaucracies.

The National Security Council (NSC) was established by the National Security Act, which was signed into law by President Truman on July 26, 1947. This law also created the position of secretary of defense, to be in charge of a united Department of Defense; the director of Central Intelligence, who was to coordinate all interagency intelligence as well as run the newly created Central Intelligence Agency (CIA); and the Department of the Air Force. It reduced the individual service secretaries to subcabinet rank.

The NSC was to be an advisory body to the president. Truman determined at the time that the body would have no formal policymaking role except in the field of intelligence, for which it was legally responsible under the 1947 act. Early membership of the Council was large and included the president, the secretaries of state and defense, the three service secretaries, the chairman of the National Security Resources Board (NSRB), other cabinet officers, and other advisers and observers. Such a large gathering inevitably diminished the power and authority of the organization, especially that of the secretary of defense, James Forrestal. At Forrestal's insistence, and with Truman's blessing, an amendment to the 1947 act was passed in 1949 and coupled with a new executive order on reforms. The NSC was to be located within the Executive Office of the President. The three service secretaries and the chairman of the NSRB were stripped of membership, but the vice president was added. The chairman of the Joint Chiefs of Staff (JCS) and the Director of Central Intelligence were to be statutory members. The four permanent members have remained so ever since: the president, the vice president, and the secretaries of state and defense. A small staff was created to serve as a secretariat for the NSC. The staff was located in the Executive Office Building, and aside from the executive secretary and his assistant, all other staffers were consultants or detailees from the armed services and the State Department.

The NSC system was used extensively during the Korean War, but its output was of mixed quality, and it could hardly be described as a powerful organization. When Eisenhower became president, he enhanced the power of the NSC and appointed Robert Cutler to be a special assistant to the president for national security affairs, thus institutionalizing a position that had previously been held by personal advisers to the president, such as Colonel Edward M. House and Harry Hopkins.

However, despite these changes, the dominant figures in national security decision making during the Eisenhower administration were the president himself (he chaired more than 90 percent of the meetings) and his secretary of state, John Foster Dulles. Although there was a modest increase in staff, the primary function of the NSC staff was coordination rather than policy formulation.

Under Kennedy, the NSC dramatically changed its function. Kennedy and his special assistant for national security affairs, McGeorge Bundy, rarely used the NSC but instead created a much more personalized system whereby the NSC staff was appointed to serve the president rather than the NSC. The NSC staff was now seen as an independent organization, working directly for the president, and became advocates, rather than brokers, of national security policy. This new approach to managing national security was continued by Johnson and his special assistant, Walt Rostow, and was carried to new heights and much increased staff under Richard Nixon's and Gerald Ford's tenures, with Henry Kissinger playing the key role in managing the growth.

This dominance was continued during the Carter presidency, when Zbigniew Brzezinski was national security adviser.

One common characteristic of the NSC system from Kennedy to Reagan was the diminution of the role of the secretary of state as the principal architect of foreign policy. Dean Rusk, William Rogers, and Cyrus Vance were all overshadowed and frequently outmaneuvered by the White House. Both of Reagan's secretaries of state, Alexander Haig and George Shultz, complained bitterly of the undermining of their roles by the White House and other agencies.

During the first year of the Reagan administration, a well-intentioned but totally impractical effort was made to limit the power of the NSC staff in the hope of avoiding the infamous turf battles between the White House and State Department that had been front-page stories during the tenures of NSC advisers Kissinger and Brzezinski. The power of the NSC staff depends largely on the NSC adviser's access to the president and on his relations with the other cabinet officers who deal with foreign policy. Richard Allen, the first of six national security advisers in the Reagan administration, was very well informed on foreign policy but had poor relations with Alexander Haig and the domestic White House staff. He was not permitted direct access to the Oval Office, as his predecessors and successors have been. This "downgrading" of his role reflected on the entire NSC staff. Their ability to deal with interagency counterparts and with domestic White House staff on foreign policy questions was hampered. It led to frequent press speculation that the NSC was "irrelevant" and that it had "lost power." Such reports have a negative impact on staff morale and result in limited access to interagency meetings and diminished effectiveness as senior members of the administration.

Allen was replaced in January 1982 by William Clark. Clark had been appointed deputy secretary of state at the beginning of the Reagan administration to provide some White House "oversight" of Alexander Haig. Clark knew little about foreign policy but had excellent relations with Ronald Reagan, having been his chief of staff when he was governor of California. With Clark's arrival at the White House, things changed for the NSC staff overnight. Clark took the job on condition that he have direct access to the president. This rise in stature had an immediate and positive effect on the NSC senior staff. They not only now had better access to interagency meetings but also were frequently taken into the Oval Office to brief the president and his immediate entourage, including the chief of staff and the vice president.

The Reagan administration's early effort to limit the NSC staff's power failed because a strong managerial structure in the White House is essential to manage the day-to-day conduct of foreign affairs, irrespective of who is president. If the NSC and its staff were abolished by fiat tomorrow, a new institution with very similar authority would have to be put in its place. At the height of the Iran–contra crisis, there were rumblings about making the appointment of the national security adviser subject to congressional approval. No president could accept such constraints on his own staff, and the idea was quickly buried.

WHY THE WHITE HOUSE DOMINATES NATIONAL SECURITY DECISION MAKING

Although in no way downgrading the importance of presidential style and idiosyncracies in the management of national security, institutional factors and the policymaking process play a key role in foreign policy decision making, no matter who sits in the Oval Office. This stems from the unique role the United States plays in world politics and the unique system of open government in Washington, a system that is very different from those of most other established democracies, including those of our close allies.

Three additional institutional issues help explain why process is so important and why, as a result, White House institutions have great power. First, the U.S. executive branch has an increasingly diversified bureaucracy, cutting across many regions and functional interests. Second, the foreign policy agenda is always full. There is never enough time to cover all bases and meet all needs and demands. As a result, presidential time is the most valuable commodity in Washington. Determining how the president allocates his time, including who has access to him and how that access is used, is one of the most important attributes of power. Third, the domestic political and public aspects of foreign policy, including managing the media and relations with Congress, have become dominant, and therefore time-consuming, concerns of the modern White House. This has increased the importance of public diplomacy. There is little time in this day and age of instant communications and hour-by-hour decision making for long-term thinking or . . . "vision."

Because of these institutional realities, a strong NSC staff is necessary. Consider the first reality: the increase in the size and complexity of the bureaucracy and the changing nature of American foreign policy. It used to be that a strong secretary of state, like John Foster Dulles, and a strong president, like Franklin D. Roosevelt or Eisenhower, could determine the basic tenets and guidelines for policy without much reference to other cabinet members (unless defense and financial matters were involved, in which case the secretaries of defense and of the treasury would be consulted). However, as American dominance in world affairs has become more circumspect and as the global economy and environmental issues have become more important components of American foreign policy, more bureaucratic players now have to be consulted on decisions that require the commitment of resources, public policy initiatives, and, occasionally, new legislation. For example, when, for instance, the Japanese prime minister visits the Oval Office to discuss U.S.–Japanese relations, talking points for the president will be pulled together from position papers solicited from many different agencies. There will usually be strong differences of opinion among the Departments of Commerce, Treasury, State, Defense, and Agriculture and the Special Trade Representative on how to handle the meeting and what points to make.

As more and more bureaucratic players enter the foreign policy field, the primacy of the State Department on day-to-day issues is diminished, and the power of the White House as arbitrator of last resort is enhanced. A certain level of diversity and competition among the executive bureaucracies is healthy, provided there is a workable process to iron out the differences and present the president with alternatives. Depending on the style of the president, an individual NSC adviser—if he or she has stature—may have great leeway to determine which of various opposing cabinet views the president signs off on. For instance, it was very rare for Ronald Reagan to go against the advice of a strong NSC adviser, a fact that two strong secretaries of state, Alexander Haig and George Shultz, both had to face, particularly during William Clark's tenure in the job. There is also the additional factor that the NSC staff's mandate covers all matters relating to national security and intelligence, including issues that frequently fall outside the purview of the State Department.

A second reason why the NSC staff has become more important in recent years has to do with modern communications and crisis management. Because of the intensity of media coverage and the expectation of "instant" news and action, crises have to be managed in "real time"; the president has to respond immediately to a hostage taking, a coup, or a major accident. The White House can find itself actually *following* the crisis agenda of the networks and has to respond to questions about U.S. policy without the luxury of carefully structured analysis, NSC meetings, and interagency intelligence reports. In the nuclear age there is the added necessity of having twenty-four-hour vigilance as part of the national command authority. Crisis decision making is made immediately, usually at White House meetings called at a moment's notice. There is no time for contemplation and careful preparation. Those who have strong visions and express them well at such meetings often carry the day on policy decisions.

The secretary of state and the secretary of defense are the two cabinet members on the National Security Council who have the most day-to-day involvement with foreign and national security policy. However, the nature of their jobs requires that they frequently be out of the country or out of Washington. It is therefore essential that the president have an entourage skilled and knowledgeable about international affairs at his immediate beck and call. A crisis can come and go while the secretary of state is traveling on the other side of the world. Although he has instant communication with Washington, his power to influence crisis decision making is frequently a function of his physical proximity to the president. . . .

A third reason for the importance of the NSC staff concerns the domestic component of American foreign policy, which frequently reflects the diversity of its ethnic population. U.S. policy toward Cuba, South Africa, Israel, or Eastern Europe has to take into account the important domestic constituencies with special interests in these areas. The power of the pro-Israel lobby is well known; in the early 1990s the Eastern European lobbies, especially those for the Baltic countries, have resurfaced as a result of the collapse of Soviet communism; no presidential candidate—especially a Republican—can avoid going to Miami in an election year to denounce Fidel Castro in an appeal for the Cuban-American vote. As different ethnic groups achieve new prominence in the United States, the diversity of foreign policy concerns will increase, and so too will the overlap between foreign policy and domestic issues. Ethnic issues are now paralleled by the growing influence of environmental groups that have important domestic constituents.

In this context, the role of lobbying in U.S. domestic politics is well established, and there are strong supporters as to its effectiveness and impact on the political system. Supporters of the system, including the political action committees (PACs), believe that this is an expression of the democratic process and that the best-organized lobbies are usually the most motivated. The fact that they deliver votes on specific issues reflects their skills, which others, rather than condemning, should try to duplicate. Critics say that the role of the PACs has reached the point now where they have a disproportionate influence on policy. Members of Congress have become highly dependent on the financial support the PACs provide; this is because of new campaign laws that forbid individual donors contributing large sums of money but do permit small amounts of money from individuals being collected by PACs and presented as a package to a candidate.

The most important role the NSC plays in dealing with these lobbies is to ensure that the foreign policy elements of their activities are taken into account. Each lobby uses different techniques, but some—the American Israel Public Affairs Committee (AIPAC), for instance—have the power to influence major policy decisions, especially regarding appropriations, on Capitol Hill.

Although it is easy to become irate about the power of certain lobbies, they can play a role that the White House can exploit. Lobbies are often the repository of intelligence; some of it is scurrilous, some wildly fanciful, but occasionally a useful nugget will turn up. Such information frequently comes in the form of memos, letters, circulars, books, articles, indeed all the paraphernalia of the modern propaganda machine. There is never time to plow through all the material, but it is useful in keeping track of personalities and in anticipating trouble.

For these reasons, the president must have around him people who are sensitive to the linkage between domestic and foreign policy issues and who can deal with the lobbyists. This means that the NSC staff and the White House domestic staff must establish good working relations and should, by and large, be of equal rank. . . .

THE IMPORTANCE OF THE PRESIDENT'S SCHEDULE

Irrespective of the occupant of the Oval Office or the distribution of power within the White House and between the NSC staff and other government agencies, perhaps the least understood but intrinsically most important feature of the modern White House concerns the pressures on the president's time and how the pressure of "the schedule" influences the day-to-day operations, the decision-making process, career incentives, and the lack of coherent long-term policy planning.

Daily priorities are usually determined by morning senior staff members. Invariably, the key issues will relate to overnight crises or politically sensitive items in the morning's papers, especially the Washington papers and the *New*

York Times. This sets the agenda for questions that will come up throughout the day when the president and his senior staff have their encounters with the White House press corps. There will also be a focused discussion on the meetings scheduled *for that day.* Questions or issues about a meeting—say, with a foreign minister the following week—will get scant attention. And if anyone on the staff raises long-term issues—for example, those of ozone depletion or of the future of the space station, and how the president should be thinking about these problems with respect to his State of the Union message—that individual will receive little hearing, unless it is a *very* quiet day.

When a president assumes office, there are dates already marked in his calendar—for example, that of the annual economic summit with the Western partners. However, most of the president's calendar is, in theory, clear when he first takes up residence in the White House. One of the primary tasks of the chief of staff is to set the calendar. This requires balancing the president's own personal wishes with the needs of domestic politics and foreign affairs.

Within the foreign policy community, the competition is fierce because nearly all foreign leaders want to come to Washington, preferably with all the trappings and ceremony of a state visit. Determining which countries should receive priority is a fairly straightforward if somewhat contentious process. The top candidates are, quite naturally, the close allies: Britain, France, Germany, Italy, Japan, Canada. Mexico and Russia also rank at the top. Increasingly the middle-rank Western European powers are considered important—Spain, for instance. From 1989 onward, the new Eastern European leaders have found favor. Problems can arise in the case of Middle Eastern countries. Israel is always near the top of the list, but once Israel is invited, Egypt must follow, or even precede. And if Egypt is invited, Jordan and Saudi Arabia have to be close behind. Invite India, and Pakistan must follow; China also ranks high, as do South Korea and the Philippines. So it is not difficult to set aside all the slots for available state visits for the first two years of an administration without even considering the second-rank countries one wishes to woo or return favors to.

The solution is found in the "working visit," which has all the substance of a state visit but less of the glitz—no White House lawn with the guns and parade, no White House dinner, and therefore less television coverage. For many of the leaders who visit Washington, the coverage back home is extremely important. For the smaller but friendly countries that have no pressing claims on U.S. largesse (like access to military bases) but that are steady, reliable partners, the lack of an invitation to Washington can become an all-consuming issue. Often the primary task of the foreign nation's ambassador is to secure the invitation; his or her future can depend on the whims of the schedule and goodheartedness of a White House staffer. . . .

This is not to say that getting in to see the president is the be-all and end-all of diplomacy in Washington. However, for most visitors the lure and appeal of the White House is obviously a prime concern. It does not matter whether formal policy decisions taken on a particular country are made over on the sixth floor of the State Department by career bureaucrats. Most world leaders want it to be known that they have some personal rapport with the president of the United States. To his credit, Ronald Reagan understood this instinctively in a way that Richard Nixon and Jimmy Carter did not. Reagan was especially generous with the Oval Office photography sessions, the cozy chats, the private lunch and, in the case of the king of Morocco, horseback rides through the national parks. Style and protocol are particularly important when dealing with leaders whose egos and power depend on the perception back home that they are well regarded in Washington. Helping a friendly foreign leader with his or her domestic problems is a natural role for the White House. But it can be very time-consuming.

When the reverse occurs and a U.S. president visits a foreign country, the script of the visit can itself become an extremely important, and at times sensitive, adjunct to the policymaking process. Reagan's much-ballyhooed trip to Germany in May 1985—including the visit to the Bitburg cemetery, which contained the graves of Waffen S.S. troops—absorbed much energy and generated much angst. At the time, the Bitburg controversy dominated the visit. What was planned as a small gesture to support Chancellor Helmut Kohl became the focus of the entire trip.

Trips such as this are planned and controlled by the White House. The advance team that goes out early to set up the logistics relies heavily on the services of the State Department and the local country's protocol offices, but the final decisions are all made by the president's staff, including the Secret Service, which has the final say on security matters. It will also have the last call on who gets to ride in which helicopter, the seating arrangements on Air Force One, and attendance at the state dinners. If handled badly or with malice, these issues can create difficulties, even bad blood, within the overall delegation. It was fighting over such seeming trivia on Reagan's trip to the Versailles summit in June 1982 that convinced William Clark and James Baker that the time had come to replace Alexander Haig as Secretary of State. Bad chemistry can be as detrimental to policy as bad position papers.

DEALING WITH UNSCHEDULED EVENTS: QUARREL AND CRISIS MANAGEMENT

Unscheduled events, by definition, cannot be anticipated, so when they come along, they will disrupt a carefully orchestrated calendar. Unscheduled events usually fall into two categories: major crises that cause the president to drop what he is doing and focus on the immediate issues, and daily Washington quarrels. Crises are the ultimate test of an administration's ability to function effectively. Over the past three decades, one key lesson has emerged. If there is consensus within the executive branch on how to handle a crisis, it will be much easier to manage. The reason is simple: Consensus reduces the prospects for leaks, and leaks to the press and Congress can stymie the ability of the White House to retain control over events. The contrast between the handling of the Lebanon crisis during Reagan's first term and the Gulf crisis was vivid. In the case of Lebanon, there was bitter disagreement among all the key players over what U.S. policy should be, whereas with regard to the Gulf crisis of 1987, operations were carried out with no dissent. The more recent Gulf crisis in the summer, fall, and winter of 1990–1991 was remarkable because of the central role played by President Bush and because of the absence of major leaks to the press concerning disunity over policy.

Three types of Washington quarrels are important: those with the press, which are part of an ongoing, usually healthy, but often antagonistic relationship; those with Congress over legislation; and interagency disputes that may have to be resolved by the president himself.

It is difficult to predict on a day-to-day basis just how many quarrels will have to be dealt with at a particular time. It is on these issues that the skills of the president's staff are put to some of their toughest tests. The press secretary and the assistant for congressional liaison are among the people who can make or break the president's day. Career advancement in the White House and in other agencies frequently comes from being recognized as a good crisis or quarrel manager. Usually, promotions are given to such individuals rather than to the deep strategic thinkers who may have brilliant ideas but who do not help the president get through the next twenty-four hours.

One reason why quarrel management is so important is that, unless handled skillfully, such quarrels escalate into crises and absorb more and more of the president's time. In dealing with the major disputes with Congress, for instance, the president is probably the best quarrel manager, because he can use his authority and stature to broker deals that would not otherwise be possible. However, in doing so, he often has to offer something in exchange for the favor. He also has to take the time to woo on the phone, or meet on a one-on-one basis, those who are opposing him on a particular issue. During the Reagan administration, one of the most time-consuming and bitter quarrels with Congress had to do with the sale of AWACS airplanes to Saudi Arabia. The administration eventually won the fight by focusing great efforts on persuading four senators not to vote against the sale of the plane. From the point of view of the domestic side of the White House, the AWACS fight was a time-consuming burden that far outweighed its foreign policy importance and detracted from more important domestic legislation.

Crisis- and quarrel-management skills seem to come most naturally to men or women of action rather than philosophers or more academic types frequently found in government for short periods of time. John Poindexter and Oliver North received great kudos for their management of the *Achille Lauro* crisis in 1985, when the ship was seized by terrorists, thereby giving Ronald Reagan his first victory over terrorists. During this crisis, North and Poindexter were adroit at getting around the red tape and bureaucratic confusion that normally hamper such operations. *Achille Lauro* did a great deal to propel John Poindexter to the job of national security adviser when Robert McFarlane resigned in December 1985. It was, of course, precisely the talent for bypassing the bureaucracy that got both men into so much trouble with the Iran–contra affair. More [recently], President Bush received high marks for his handling of the Persian Gulf and Soviet crises, in part because he was seen as being in control of his own teams and insisted on loyalty from those who served him.

However, one down side to the "action-oriented" players is that long-term planning and careful deliberation of policy issues have taken a back seat. Since much policy revolves around short-term issues, the strategic thinker, for want of a better word, tends to get cut out of the action. Periodic attempts to reinvigorate the policy planning staff in the State Department and come up with long-term concepts have rarely worked because the policy planning staff finds itself being drawn more and more into crises and day-to-day events, writing speeches, delivering congressional testimony, and getting through the next summit meeting. Furthermore, it must be acknowledged that because "action" is invariably more exciting than concept planning, there is a natural tendency for even those predisposed to strategic thinking to become embroiled in short-term issues. . . .

USING THE SCHEDULE TO INFLUENCE POLICY

There are occasions when setting the schedule can become an effective bureaucratic device for focusing, and indeed changing, policy. The example of U.S. policy toward India during the Reagan administration makes the point.

At the beginning of the administration, the priority of the White House was to focus on domestic rather than foreign policy. Within the foreign policy agenda, there was a full list of problems to be tackled in the Caribbean, Europe, and East Asia. For those who believed that the time was right for a reassessment of U.S. policy toward India, which has been largely neglected by the U.S., getting the attention of the president and his topic adviser proved difficult. India was a factor during the major reassessment of policy toward Pakistan in early 1981 but was still peripheral. It was Afghanistan that was the primary concern. Such negligence was not due to ill will. There was agreement, *in principle,* that better relations with India were a good idea. But the United States has global interests, and, as has been pointed out, the agenda is always overflowing with important issues. Therefore, in the absence of some pressing need to bring an item to the top of the president's "in" box, issues that are not at the top of the political agenda become secondary and tend to be ignored. To bring noncrisis issues onto the agenda, it is necessary to have a motivating event. In the case of India, the opportunity arose when it was decided that President Reagan would meet for ten to fifteen minutes with Prime Minister Indira Gandhi at the Economic North–South Summit at Cancun, Mexico, on October 21, 1981.

Once it was agreed—for reasons of protocol as much as for anything else—that the Cancun meeting with Gandhi would take place, it became an official appointment on the president's calendar. It was now possible to send out instructions through the NSC and the State Department to all the agencies saying that "the President will meet with Mrs. Gandhi on October 21st. At that time he will review U.S. policy towards India. We need to prepare talking points for that meeting and, in the process, review where we stand on current relations." As a result of this, the bureaucracy moved into action, interagency meetings were held, papers were written, disagreements were ironed out, discussion points were proposed, briefing books were assembled, and talking points were prepared—and by the time the meeting went ahead, a new alertness to U.S.–Indian relations was under way. Ultimately, this led to much-improved economic ties and increased technical cooperation, including better relations between the Pentagon and the Indian Ministry of Defence.

Short of a crisis, the best way to get the bureaucracy to focus on an issue is to have an event on the calendar. This is why presidential meetings in the White House, or elsewhere, are so important, however brief they may be. Words uttered in the Oval Office, even with the help of prompt cards, take on an importance beyond their apparent face value. When the president speaks or reads a statement about U.S. policy toward Jerusalem or Berlin in the Oval Office, it has an immediate and significant effect on foreign policy. What happens in the meeting itself creates a chain reaction and can set in motion new trends in policy or confirm old trends.

Consequently, the process of getting a president and prime minister together for fifteen minutes not only has a life cycle before the meeting but after the meeting as well, when embellishments and clarifications of policy can be made in background briefings. If the system is working, follow-up becomes an important part of the policy process. If, however, there is confusion and disagreement among the chief players as to what happened in the Oval Office, then more confusion can result. During the Reagan years, there were many times when the president was either ambiguous about or indifferent to follow-up concerning statements he had made in the Oval Office. This meant that those present could each take their own interpretations of events back to their own agencies, and in some cases to the press, and tell different stories as to what happened. It was confusion about what happened in the Oval Office that got the Reagan administration into so much trouble on arms control, relations in the Middle East, and, most tellingly, the Iran–contra affair. President Bush, in contrast, . . . maintained much more coherence about policy, primarily because it [was] he, not his staff, who [had] the last word and who [explained] the policy in detail to the press.

THE MEDIA AND PUBLIC DIPLOMACY

Managing the media has become one of the most important tasks of the White House staff, in part because of the increased power of television and the vast amounts of raw information that come over the wire services. President Carter's ill-fated "Rose Garden" strategy, adopted at the time the U.S. hostages were first taken in Tehran in November 1979, fell apart because there was no way a president could avoid the daily glare of television and its relentless coverage of the issue. Once a story like the hostage crisis or the Iran–contra affair breaks, the White House's ability to control the news is severely limited. Bad judgment at the beginning of a public crisis can have a disastrous impact on the ensuing drama. The Reagan administration's poor handling of the early days of the Iran–contra crisis nearly toppled the presidency.

It is sometimes not appreciated how far *behind* the news the White House and other agencies of government can be during a crisis. A good example of this occurred on October 6, 1981. News was received in the White House early in the morning that President Anwar Sadat of Egypt had been shot at a national Armed Forces Day parade. There were no details of the shooting. Some reports said that Sadat had suffered minor injuries; others said that his injuries were more serious. Within half an hour a crisis-management team assembled in the White House Situation Room to monitor the events. Throughout the morning there was confusion about what was happening in Cairo. Communications between the U.S. embassy and the State Department were nonexistent, and when messages did come in, they were delayed. Telephone lines were down, and there was no direct contact between the White House and Cairo. Vice President George Bush, as the designated official in charge of crisis management, presided over a group of senior officials in the Situation Room. At one point during the morning this author was called to bring in some briefing papers. He was amazed to find the entire team of senior officials watching ABC news on the Situation Room television monitor. The reason was simple: Television was getting access to real-time intelligence far ahead of the multi-billion-dollar U.S. government network. The White House was, in fact, dependent on television for news all that morning up to the moment when it was announced that Sadat had died.[2]

DEALING WITH THE PRESIDENT'S VIEWS

Each president has strong feelings on certain subjects. Sometimes these can emerge as important factors in foreign policy management that are simply not programmable in the normal sense of the word. Controlling surprise presidential remarks is especially difficult if the president misspeaks or speaks out of line with other agency positions. Utterances from the Oval Office take on a life all of their own. The rest of the world still hangs on the news flash from the White House. Given the speed of modern communications and the need to immediately respond to untoward remarks, media management is an increasingly burdensome job; no president has learned how to master it, although some have handled it better than others.

HOW TO IMPROVE POLICY PLANNING AND COORDINATION

This chapter has stressed the impact of process on the White House management of foreign policy. It has been argued that it is difficult to orchestrate policy beyond the short term, which is frequently measured in hours rather than in days or months. But is preoccupation with the short term inevitable, and must it always be at the expense of a carefully articulated strategy?

The office of the presidency is sufficiently powerful that if a strong chief of state, preferably not one up for reelection, were determined to present a long-term agenda to the nation, he or she could probably make some headway. However, unless there was widespread support in Congress for it, the policy would not get very far. For it is not at all clear that the United States wants a president with "vision" if what is meant by this is a radical departure from the way we currently conduct business. "Visionary" figures in foreign policy conjure up images of a Lenin, a Pol Pot, a Hitler, or a Mao; a Nasser, a Begin, or a Khomeini; a Gandhi, a Sukarno, or a Nkruhmah. In this regard U.S. presidential "doctrines" seem to be more in vogue, though usually this word is applied to some statement codifying existing policy rather than to a dramatic new departure. True, the Truman Doctrine was innovative, but in 1947 the United States could, as a result of its economic strength, reshape the world with new policies. More recent "doctrines"—those of Nixon and Reagan—were less sweeping in their scope and were certainly not new in their content.

What Americans seem to want is not "visions" and "doctrines" but a better sense of how this country is going to solve some very practical and many new foreign policy problems as the year 2000 approaches. How will we reduce the trade deficit? How will we control immigration? How will we compete and cooperate with the new Europe? What to do about the importation of illegal drugs? How do we clean up the environment without collapsing the economy? How much military force do we wish to deploy overseas if the Cold War is over? What should we do about the proliferation of weapons of mass destruction? And how much foreign aid should we provide and to whom, and should it be dispensed bilaterally or multilaterally? The list goes on, and as the world becomes more complex and interactive, it will undoubtedly get longer.

Weaving all these issues together in ways that are both practical and ideologically compatible is not easy. To do this will take "vision" and, for public relations purposes, may even require the added appendage of a "doctrine." But whatever the policy is called, it must deal with the reality of the political process and the competitive pressures of the political marketplace. This cannot be done by wishing on the United States decision-making bodies that resemble the putatively rational approach of the Honda boardroom. Neither can it be done by avoiding painful questions of costs, trade-offs, and taxes. It is the type of policy statement that is tailor-made for a presidential speech—provided, of course, that the occasion is right and the substance is realistic.

The Persian Gulf crisis between August 1990 and March 1991 and the crisis in the Soviet Union in the closing days of August 1991 are vivid reminders that a new world order, democracy, and universal human rights are not yet established norms in international relations. Reliance on the use of force to change the status quo, or to restore it, remains a fact of life. Therefore, although many newly emerging problems face American foreign policy, the basic structure of the international system has not changed sufficiently to make the postwar national security system obsolete. Rather, it needs to be modified to take into account the new issues.

As more and more of these new elements in international relations become institutionalized on a global basis, the necessary bureaucratic structure to support U.S. policy on these issues will have to be created. For instance, if an annual global conference on the environment were established, similar to the annual international economic summits between the seven key industrial powers, more focused attention of environmental issues in the White House would be inevitable.

In sum, the best way to bring the new elements of national security and foreign policy into the day-to-day planning process is to ensure that formal meetings that require regular presidential participation take place. Once it is established that the president will meet every year, or whenever, with foreign leaders to focus on a specific topic, active White House involvement will be ensured. This will lead to the injection of more structured thinking on the new sets of issues that face the nation. Even though long-range policy planning analogous to that adopted by successful multinational businesses will never sit well with the American body politic, the existing policy process can be used to inject more coherent planning and, one hopes, more successful policies.

NOTES

1. For a detailed and tendentious but nevertheless useful study of the role of the White House in the Iran–contra crisis, see Theodore Draper, *A Very Thin Line: The Iran–Contra Affair* (New York: Hill & Wang, 1991).

2. Further examples of the frantic and confused life of one NSC staffer can be found in the following review article about the Reagan White House: Geoffrey Kemp, "As the World Turns," *The New Republic,* 21 November 1988.

11. HOW GEORGE BUSH WON HIS SPURS: THE PRESIDENT AND THE POWER TO MAKE WAR

Mike Moore

*I*n a televised address August 8, 1990, President George Bush said: "In the life of a nation, we're called upon to define who we are and what we believe. Sometimes these choices are not easy. But today as president, I ask for your support in a decision I've made to stand up for what's right and condemn what's wrong, all in the cause of peace."

The president got the nation's support, at least in the early weeks, for a show of force in the Persian Gulf—an enormously popular America-is-back-in-the-saddle-again move. Bush's speech also gave Americans a new cliché—"defining moment"—to run up the flagpole. Nearly everyone saluted, although it was not always clear what was being saluted. Was the Gulf crisis a defining moment? And, if so, what sort of turning point did it define?

In the months that followed, the answers to those questions have centered on classic geopolitical, philosophical, and speculative issues—whether the United Nations was well or ill used, whether the Gulf War was just or unjust, whether the prospects for peace in the Middle East were enhanced or worsened, whether the "lessons learned" could be applied elsewhere, and whether the international community was truly on the brink of inventing a "new world order" based on truth, justice, and the American Way.

Important issues, all. But a consideration of the Gulf crisis involves more than probing the substantive geopolitical and moral issues raised by the war. It also involves a close look at the *process* of going to war—and that process ought to be judged independently of whether or not the war was wise and before the sequence of events fades completely from our collective consciousness.

A generation ago, Presidents Johnson and Nixon conducted a lengthy conflict in Southeast Asia, claiming sweeping inherent war-making powers as

Note: Some notes have been deleted or renumbered.

commanders-in-chief of the nation's armed forces. Two generations ago President Truman led the nation into a bloody undeclared war in Korea based on his powers as commander-in-chief. And in the fall of 1990, another president was making war-powers claims that seemed even more sweeping.

If, as President Bush suggested, the Gulf crisis was a defining moment, it defined something more sinister than anything he envisioned. The Gulf crisis illuminated yet another president who was ready, willing, and enthusiastically able to ride roughshod over the war-making powers specified in the Constitution. And it defined with equal clarity another Congress willing to say in effect, "Thank you so very much, Mr. President, for making our decision for us."

THE FIRST GENERAL AND ADMIRAL

By the summer of 1787, the United States of America, still in its infancy, was spinning apart. It lacked a centripetal force. The principles expressed in the Articles of Confederation were incapable of holding together the former 13 colonies with their disparate interests and rebellious ways. A gravitational system would have to be devised.

By the end of the summer, delegates to the Constitutional Convention in Philadelphia had produced a Constitution establishing a system of countervailing powers in which the Constitution itself provided the gravitational field that would keep the nation together.

The extent of presidential power was a vexing issue for the delegates. Although no one wanted a president with kingly powers, the delegates reluctantly concluded that the national executive had to have the institutional wherewithal—the "energy"—to get things done. In one of the most commonly quoted passages in *The Federalist*, Alexander Hamilton said in *No. 70:* "A feeble Executive implies a feeble execution of the government. A feeble execution is but another phrase for a bad execution; and a government ill executed, whatever it may be in theory, must be, in practice, a bad government."

Hamilton also argued in *The Federalist No. 23* that the national government's power to raise and sustain military forces "ought to exist without limitation" because threats to the nation in future years were "infinite."

How could the delegates devise a system that would respond decisively to an infinite variety of threats without also giving the president unlimited power over military affairs? The answer was so self-evident that it inspired only brief debate. The president, as commander-in-chief of the nation's military forces, would have the authority to repel aggression against the United States without having to run to Congress for permission. But he would not have the power to unilaterally initiate offensive war. Only the Congress could do that, by a formal declaration of war. Hamilton wrote in *The Federalist No. 69:*

> The President is to be commander-in-chief of the army and navy of the United States. In this respect his authority would be nominally the same with that of the king of Great Britain, but in substance much inferior to it. It would amount to

nothing more than the supreme command and direction of the military and naval forces, as first general and admiral of the Confederacy: while that of the British king extends to the *declaring* of war and to the *raising* and *regulating* of fleets and armies—all of which, by the Constitution under consideration, would appertain to the legislature. [Emphasis in the original.]

A DONE DEAL

Things change. For the first three months of the Gulf crisis, while the United States shipped more than a quarter of a million men and women to the Persian Gulf, Congress played a fourth-string supporting role in determining whether the United States might actually go to war.

President Bush and his advisers took the initiative and kept it, allocating the major supporting parts to Margaret Thatcher, Mikhail Gorbachev, the U.N. Security Council, and anti-Hussein Middle Eastern states. Meanwhile, most members of Congress chose to audition for the chorus, whose basic task was to wave the flag. Few members of Congress asked tough questions about the wisdom of the Persian Gulf deployment or whether Congress ought to bring the matter to a formal vote. After all, congressional elections were coming in November; boat-rocking was not in order.

"This year," wrote R. W. Apple, Jr., of the *New York Times*, "a midterm election campaign has taken place with war threatening in the Persian Gulf, and once again the major foreign policy issue confronting the nation has generated almost no debate among the candidates about what the United States should do."

On November 8, two days after the elections, the president let the world know that he was greatly expanding the U.S. force in the Persian Gulf "to insure that the coalition has an adequate offensive military option should that be necessary to achieve our common goals." Although Congress was not consulted in advance, a handful of key congressional leaders were alerted on an FYI basis shortly before the announcement.

The possibility of offensive war finally rallied members of Congress, mostly Democrats, and congressional hearings were held in late November and early December on the advisability of waging war or giving the U.S.-imposed economic sanctions "more time to work." No vote was called.

Despite the congressional hearings, the Gulf buildup continued as an all-administration show. From the beginning of the Gulf crisis, administration spokesmen repeatedly and publicly insisted that the president—any president—had sufficient legal authority as commander-in-chief to commit the nation to war without an overt act of Congress. In early October, for instance, Walter Pincus of the *Washington Post* wrote:

> As a former House member, Bush understands it is important that Congress view any future use of force in the Persian Gulf as a "joint venture" with him, according to Defense Secretary Richard B. Cheney, himself a former House member.
>
> "If hostilities develop, it is important that Congress be on board and supportive," Cheney said in an interview.

At the same time, however, Cheney said that Bush is commander-in-chief and a decision on the use of force is "best made by him."

On October 17, Secretary of State James Baker testified before the Senate Foreign Relations Committee that the administration would "consult" with congressional leaders if military action were called for. But, Baker added, the administration did not feel "obliged" to get advance approval.

By early January, many members of Congress were insisting that Congress vote on the war-option issue. Although lawyers for the president still insisted that he could take the nation to war on his own authority, Bush yearned for a vote of confidence. But Cheney, who met with Bush and other key advisers on January 6, still argued against calling for a vote, according to Bob Woodward's kiss-and-tell book *The Commanders*. A "no" vote, said Cheney, would "undermine everything."[1]

The next day, House Speaker Tom Foley said the House would begin debate on the Gulf crisis that week. Senate Majority Leader George Mitchell said the Senate would do likewise. The president's hand had been called. Rather than remain aloof, Bush chose to throw himself fully into a lobbying effort to insure a positive vote. But a top administration lawyer told Bush that, regardless of how Congress voted, Bush still had the authority to pursue the war option. In an awkward, quasi-novelistic way, Woodward recreates Deputy Attorney General William P. Barr's assessment:

> War is in the gray zone. The war power is a shared power with Congress; the Constitution intends it to be shared. Congress has the power to declare a war, but it usually has voted after the war has started. As with any shared power, your hand is strongest when the executive branch and the Congress agree, he said. You would be in the least advantageous position if Congress does something inconsistent. [But] an inconsistent resolution would not take away your power.[2]

On January 10—on the eve of the January 15 deadline after which coalition forces were authorized by U.N. resolution to use "all necessary means" to expel Iraqi forces from Kuwait—Congress finally got around to a debate on the Gulf crisis.

The polar questions: Should Congress authorize the president to take the nation into war whenever the president deemed it advisable, pursuant to the United Nations all-necessary-means resolution? Or should the president be instructed to live with the economic-sanctions strategy a little longer? On January 12, Congress (Senate, 52–47; House, 250–183) authorized the president to go to war.

If one credits the going-to-war chronology offered in *The Commanders*—admittedly a major "if" because Woodward does not supply documentation in his books—the congressional vote was a kind of charade. Bush, writes Woodward, had been planning the "offensive option" since early October, and actually made the decision to go to war during the Christmas–New Year holidays.

Norman Schwarzkopf, the coalition's field commander, had been asked in December when he would be ready to commence war. His reply: 7 P.M., January 16, Washington time. A "warning order" confirming that day and time for the probable start of the war was faxed with "eyes only" secrecy to Schwarzkopf on December 29. On New Year's Day, says Woodward, Bush conducted another meeting with his inner-circle advisers, which—as always—did not include any members of Congress. Woodward writes:

> Cheney didn't think the decision to go to war had occurred in a definite moment or sequence of moments. There was no single discussion or meeting where it had been made. As best he could piece it together, however, by Christmas Eve it was close; by December 29, when the warning order was sent, it was solidified; and at this New Year's Day meeting it was finally ratified.[3]

PAINTING CONGRESS INTO A CORNER

Of course, Congress did act, albeit with an unseemly lack of urgency. It formally authorized war, if the president should come to believe that war was called for. (That Bush had already come to that belief, according to Woodward's chronology, was information Congress did not have.) End of argument. The constitutional requirement vis-à-vis the war-making powers had been satisfied, no matter how ineptly.

And yet, there were demurrers. Michael J. Glennon, for instance, a former legal counsel to the Senate Foreign Relations Committee, the author of *Constitutional Diplomacy*, and a professor of law at the University of California, Davis, wrote in the Spring 1991 *Foreign Affairs:*

> Starting from President Bush's unilateral commitment to defend Saudi Arabia and proceeding to Congress's jury-rigged approval, the debates episode represented a textbook example of how an audacious executive, acquiescent legislature and deferential judiciary have pushed the Constitution's system of separation of powers steadily backwards toward the monopolistic system of King George III.

The "train was set in motion" by the president, Glennon argued, and Congress simply went along for the ride.

Indeed, there was much evidence for that assessment from the congressional debates. During the three days of debate, a recurrent theme of proadministration stalwarts was that the war option must be endorsed because it was too late in the game to do otherwise. Too many troops had been sent. Too many foreign governments had joined in. Too many U.N. resolutions had been passed. The prestige of the United States—as embodied in commitments made by the commander-in-chief—was on the line. To repeat a phrase oft-used in the congressional debates, the nation "must stay the course."

Consider the words of Arlen Spector, a Republican from Pennsylvania and a supporter of the war option, responding to a point made by Sam Nunn, a Democrat from Georgia and a partisan of extended economic sanctions:

Is it not really too late, four days in advance of January 15, to pull the rug out from the expectations of our U.N. partners and the expectations of the President?

I quite agree with the distinguished Senator from Georgia that it is the congressional authority to declare war and the corollary to authorize the use of force. But should that debate not have occurred in November? And is it not so late now as to materially prejudice U.S. interests?

In short, the United States must be prepared to go to war sooner rather than later because the troops were there and it would be awkward to have them sit around much longer—and even worse to bring them home without firing a shot in battle.

Painting Congress into a corner, usually with ample help from senators and representatives, is not a new presidential strategy, of course. James K. Polk, for instance, seems to have intentionally provoked war with Mexico in 1846 to more easily acquire nearly all of the territory that we now call New Mexico, Arizona, Utah, Nevada, and California.

Polk sent General Zachary Taylor marching into a slice of disputed territory between the Nueces River and the Rio Grande, in what is now south Texas. (Texas, which had been newly admitted in the Union, claimed the land, although few Texans lived there. Mexico claimed it too, partly because it embraced several Mexican towns and settlements.) Once Mexican troops attacked the U.S. troops, which they defined as an invading force, Polk had his war. Polk told Congress that the Mexican government had "at last invaded our territory, and shed the blood of our fellow citizens on our own soil."[4] Congress had little choice but to declare war.[5]

WHERE THE BUCK STOPS

Senator Spector might also have said in his remarks during the Persian Gulf debate, "So what else is new?" Although the Constitution's framers hoped that Congress would be a useful body, there have been a few disappointments between its conception and middle age. Consider what Joseph S. Clark—like Spector, a senator from Pennsylvania—said in his 1964 book, *Congress: The Sapless Branch:*

> This is the area where democratic government is breaking down. This is where the vested-interest lobbies tend to run riot, where conflict of interest is concealed from the public, where demagoguery, sophisticated or primitive, knows few boundaries, where political lag keeps needed action often a generation behind the times, where the nineteenth century sometimes reigns supreme in committees, where ignorance can be at a premium and wisdom at a discount.[6]

Political scientists will recognize Clark's polemic as but one example in a long line of Congress-bashing tracts. Specific concerns and details change, but then and now critics of Congress suggest that senators and representatives are quick to duck responsibility on difficult issues. President Truman said, "the buck stops here," but that's not quite what the framers had in mind.

The Congress and the executive had been designed as co-equal branches of the national government.

George Washington, however, was quick to understand that the institutional powers of the president were not a fixed thing. The powers of a president depended, in large measure, on how the holder of the office perceived and interpreted them—and especially on how expansively or how conservatively he exercised leadership.

Washington generally acted with impeccable restraint, but presidents whom historians and political scientists now label "strong"—among them, Jefferson, Jackson, Polk, Lincoln, Teddy Roosevelt, Wilson, Franklin D. Roosevelt, Truman, Kennedy, Johnson, and Nixon—have interpreted their powers expansively. Nearly 100 years ago, for instance, the eminent British observer of the United States, Lord Bryce, described the wartime Lincoln as wielding "more authority than any single Englishman since Oliver Cromwell."

Bryce added, "The ordinary law was for some particular purposes practically suspended during the War of Secession. But it will always have to be similarly suspended in similar crises, and the suspension makes the president a sort of dictator."[7]

Lincoln believed that the Constitution's commander-in-chief clause conferred upon a president great *inherent* powers to respond to crises that threatened the nation's existence. Many presidents have argued similarly. The commander-in-chief clause is the "dark continent" of the Constitution, writes presidential scholar Sidney Hyman. While *The Federalist* papers "probed every word and comma in the Constitution," the commander-in-chief clause was "barely touched."[8]

"MODERN" PRESIDENTS

In common with the Constitution's thematic separation of powers, the power to conduct foreign affairs had been divided among the president, the Senate, and the Congress as a whole. But theory nose-dived against reality when President Washington issued the "Proclamation of Neutrality," which was crafted to keep the United States from taking sides in a war between France and England. It was not an altogether popular move; France had helped the United States during the American Revolution.

Alexander Hamilton, writing as "Pacificus," defended Washington's action, arguing that the direction of foreign policy was inherently an executive function in which the president could take the initiative. But, writes Hyman:

> Hamilton acknowledged that this [theory] might enable the President to present the Congress with *faits accomplis* in the diplomatic field which could force it to declare war. What formed the check on this risk? In the exercise of its own concurrent or co-ordinate powers, the Congress could refuse to back up the president.

James Madison responded to Hamilton under the name "Helvidus." Hyman writes,

Madison charged Hamilton with claiming for the President the royal prerogative of the British Crown to declare war and to make treaties. He argued, furthermore, that the right to determine foreign policy was not autonomous in nature. It was rooted in the antecedent power to declare war. And this power the Constitution lodged in Congress.

Because Theodore Roosevelt so often articulated the proposition that a president must define his role expansively, historians of the presidency commonly regard him as the first "modern" president. And by "modern" they do not mean that he happened to be the first president to serve in this century. They mean that Roosevelt—and all other "modern" presidents—subscribe to the theory that the office of the president and the Congress are not truly co-equal branches of government. In that sense, all "modern" presidents are, to some degree, Hamiltonians. They get things done while Congress diddles.

Teddy Roosevelt was not shy in expressing his lack of regard for Congress. In his view, when decisive action was called for, Congress was too often a nuisance or a brake. If Congress did not want to pay to send the Great White Fleet around the world, then he—the president—would send it steaming halfway around, and Congress would have to appropriate the funds to take it the rest of the way.

What is less well known is George Bush's admiration for Teddy Roosevelt. Sidney Blumenthal writes in the *New Republic:*

> Not once in his long presidential campaign did George Bush ever mention Theodore Roosevelt. Yet Bush as president set out immediately to refurbish the White House with touchstones of T.R. In the Cabinet Room he took down the portrait of Calvin Coolidge that Ronald Reagan had hung there and replaced it with a picture of the Republican Roosevelt. And in the Oval Office itself, Bush strategically placed not one but two sculptures of his new hero—as if to suggest the two roles through which Roosevelt so skillfully defined his glittering public career: the dude and the Rough Rider.[9]

TEDDY REBORN

A hallmark of a strong president is the virtual bypassing of Congress in the conduct of foreign affairs, including the making of war, overt and covert. *The Imperial Presidency,* by Arthur M. Schlesinger, Jr., particularly the expanded version issued in 1989, is the most comprehensive work on the issue. As portrayed by Schlesinger, the style of Lyndon Johnson was to cajole, bully, and bamboozle Congress in matters of war; Richard Nixon's style was to deceive it.[10]

The Imperial Presidency does not deal with George Bush. But a reading of *The Commanders* suggests that Bush's distinctive style was to politely but forthrightly ignore Congress as decisions were made that would eventually lead to war in the Persian Gulf. For Bush and most of his key advisers (with a few exceptions, notably Colin Powell, chairman of the Joint Chiefs of Staff),

Congress seems to have been irrelevant—except that it had to be coddled and humored because of its latent capacity to wreak political mischief.

Whether the United States should go to war in any particular instance involves pursuing a certain bundle of complex geopolitical and moral questions. But how the nation *makes* that decision is a less complex matter. The process was clear 200 years ago, and many constitutional scholars regard it as clear today.

In many ways the Constitution is ambiguous and anachronistic. But substantial numbers of constitutional scholars are in rough agreement regarding the meaning of the war-powers provisions as they apply to taking the nation into a major, intentional, offensive war. Congress has an active and surely co-equal role to play. . . .

Shortly after the Constitutional Convention ended, James Wilson of Pennsylvania, a key player at the convention and an ardent champion of executive power, expressed the conventional wisdom of the delegates:

> We are still an inviting object to one European power at least; and, if we cannot defend ourselves, the temptation may become too alluring to be resisted. I do not mean that, with an efficient government, we should mix with the commotions of Europe. No, sir, we are happily removed from them, and are not obliged to throw ourselves into the scale with any. This system will not hurry us into war; it is calculated to guard against it. It will not be in the power of a single man, or a single body of men, to involve us in such distress; for the important power of declaring war is vested in the legislature at large.[11]

Wilson spoke more than 200 years ago in a long-gone era. (In 1796, the War Department consisted of a secretary of war and two clerks.)[12] Today the United States is inevitably bound up in the "commotions of Europe." And Asia. And the Middle East. And Africa. And South and Central America. It is the world's preeminent military power.

But the Constitution's war-powers provisions have not been amended. The Pacificus–Helvidus debates regarding the presumed inherent powers of the president as commander-in-chief are a historical fact, not a constitutional mandate. Each president is sworn to protect and defend the Constitution, which says that Congress alone is vested with the power to declare war. Indeed, the Constitution is the document that enables presidents to authoritatively say, "This is a nation governed by laws, not by men."

George Bush was not the first president to treat Congress cavalierly in matters of war. Nor was he the first to assert that he had a legal right to conduct warlike operations without an affirmative vote of Congress. But other recent presidents who have asserted expansive war-making powers nevertheless limited their claims in some important—but perhaps specious—ways.

Harry Truman could point to a genuine Cold War emergency when he committed troops to Korea. Lyndon Johnson had the Tonkin Gulf Resolution, however dubious it may have been in authorizing a long and open-ended war in Vietnam. Richard Nixon noted, with mock ingenuousness, that he merely inherited a war that he was forced to expand—so that he could end it with honor.

But the Persian Gulf War marked the first time in U.S. history that an American president systematically and openly marched the nation into a major offensive war that had no Cold War overtones, such as Korea and Vietnam—while insisting at every moment that he had the legal right to do so regardless of any action that Congress might or might not take.

Teddy Roosevelt, the old Rough Rider, would have been impressed.

NOTES

1. Bob Woodward, *The Commanders* (New York: Simon & Schuster, 1991), p. 355.

2. Ibid., p. 357. See also David B. Rivkin, Jr., and Lee A. Casey, "War Powers," *Foreign Affairs* (Summer 1991), p. 150.

3. Woodward, *The Commanders,* pp. 352–354. See also Thomas L. Friedman and Patrick E. Tyler, "From the First, U.S. Resolved to Fight," *New York Times,* March 3, 1991, p. 1.

4. Edward D. Mansfield, *The Mexican War* (New York: A. S. Barnes & Co., 1848), p. 45.

5. Whether Polk actually provoked a war with Mexico or blundered into it is a matter of controversy among historians. Glenn W. Price, in *Origins of the War with Mexico* (Austin, Texas: University of Texas Press, 1967) builds a persuasive case that Polk was a villain. Paul H. Bergeron, in *The Presidency of James K. Polk* (Lawrence, Kans.: University Press of Kansas, 1987), offers a much more positive view of Polk.

6. Joseph S. Clark, *Congress: The Sapless Branch* (New York: Harper Colophon Books, 1965), p. 22.

7. James Bryce, *The American Commonwealth* (London: MacMillan Co., 1899) 3rd ed., vol. 1, p. 65.

8. Sidney Hyman, *The American President* (New York: Harper & Bros., 1954), p. 280.

9. Sidney Blumenthal, "Bull Moose," *New Republic* (January 7 and 14, 1991), p. 11.

10. Although the expanded Schlesinger book is definitive and scholarly, Richard J. Barnet, a senior fellow at the Institute for Policy Studies, addresses similar issues in an easier-to-read style in *The Rockets' Red Glare* (New York: Simon & Schuster, 1990).

11. Jonathan Eliot, *The Debates in the Several State Conventions on the Adoption of the Federal Constitution* (New York: Burt Franklin, 1888), vol. 2, p. 528.

12. Hyman, *The American President,* p. 283.

12. CONGRESS AND FOREIGN POLICY: AVENUES OF INFLUENCE

James M. Lindsay

*E*veryone agrees that Congress is more active in foreign policy today than at any time since the 1930s. Disagreement exists, however, over the consequences of congressional activism. At one extreme in the debate lie the Irreconcilables, so named because they are as opposed to congressional involvement in foreign policy as their Senate forebearers were to the Treaty of Versailles. Irreconcilables warn that "overreaching" by an "imperial Congress" has created a "fettered presidency."[1] They yearn for the "good old days" when the president ran the show. Not surprisingly, complaints about "foreign policy by Congress" tend to come from administration officials and their supporters.

At the other extreme in the debate lie the Skeptics. They argue that congressional activism is more show than substance. Congress, in their view, operates on the margins of foreign policy, so much so that one recent article felt compelled to explain "Why the President (Almost) Always Wins in Foreign Affairs."[2] If Irreconcilables count among their number many administration officials, Skeptics predominate in academia. Perhaps the best evidence of how the Skeptics' view prevails among academics is the scant attention the scholarly literature pays to Congress and foreign policy.

Yet neither Irreconcilables nor Skeptics accurately describe Congress's role in foreign policy. Irreconcilables grossly exaggerate the extent and effect of congressional activism. Although members of Congress challenge the White House far more than they did in the 1950s and 1960s, when the imperial presidency was at its peak, they by no means control foreign policy. The president and his subordinates continue to lead in foreign policy. Skeptics, on the other hand, err by equating the ability to influence policy with the ability to legislate. Skeptics rightly note that many efforts to legislate the substance of foreign policy die on Capitol Hill. But even when members of Congress fail to pass substantive legislation, they frequently influence policy indirectly: by pressuring the administration to modify its policies, by changing how decisions are made in the executive branch, and by framing opinion about foreign policy. The remainder of this chapter explores the direct and indirect avenues by which members of Congress shape the content of U.S. foreign policy.

SUBSTANTIVE LEGISLATION

Congress is a law-making body, so it is not surprising that when the question of congressional influence over foreign policy arises, most people look to see how successful members are at generating and passing their own substantive policy proposals. And Congress enjoys considerable authority to specify the substance of U.S. relations with other countries. After all, the Constitution gives Congress the power to declare war, to provide advice and consent for treaties, to regulate foreign commerce, and to determine how all federal funds will be spent.

Substantive Legislation in Practice

The 1980s saw several important instances in which members of Congress used substantive legislation to put a distinctly congressional imprint on foreign policy. In 1986, Congress overrode a veto by President Reagan and passed legislation imposing economic sanctions on South Africa. In 1987 and 1988, Congress wrote appropriations bills that forced the Reagan administration to comply with the terms of the (unratified) SALT II treaty. And in the late 1980s members placed so many constraints on U.S. relations with El Salvador and Nicaragua that U.S. policy in Central America was effectively being set on Capitol Hill.

Still, instances in which members of Congress initiate and legislate their own foreign policies are the exception rather than the rule. The nuclear freeze resolution, sanctions against Iraq, and the nuclear test ban are just a few of the legislative proposals that sparked a flurry of debate on Capitol Hill in the 1980s but failed to become law. Even when political circumstances seem favorable, Congress often fails to overrule the president. Despite the American public's revulsion at the Tiananmen Square massacre, Congress failed to pass any legislation punishing the Chinese government for its brutal suppression of the prodemocracy movement.

When members of Congress do succeed in legislating their own foreign policy preferences, the results often are less than what meets the eye. Members typically give the executive branch tremendous discretion in deciding how to implement substantive legislation. Such discretion is justified on the grounds that the president needs flexibility when conducting foreign affairs. But discretion gives the president the opportunity to subvert the intent of Congress. To take one of many possible examples, Congress appropriated military aid to El Salvador in the early 1980s provided that President Reagan certify every six months that the Salvadoran government was making progress in correcting its human rights abuses. Despite abundant evidence that the Salvadoran government continued to violate the human rights of its citizens, Reagan repeatedly provided the certification needed to release the military aid.

Obstacles to Substantive Legislation

Efforts to explain Congress's lack of success in passing its own substantive legislation and preventing executive branch abuse of the power of discretion usually cite three factors: the inherent advantages of the presidency, the pro-executive branch bias of the judiciary, and the nature and structure of Congress. But it is important to recognize a fourth factor as well: Many members believe that imposing congressional preferences on the executive branch will prove unwise or unworkable in practice.

THE INHERENT ADVANTAGES OF THE PRESIDENCY. Alexander Hamilton wrote in *Federalist No. 70* that in foreign policy the president enjoys the inherent advantages of "decision, activity, secrecy, and dispatch." These inherent advantages are greatest in national security affairs, and especially in crisis situations. As the invasion of Panama and Operation Desert Storm both attest, presidents can commit the United States to major foreign policy endeavors that leave members of Congress with little political choice but to follow.

Of course, on many occasions members of Congress do challenge the president on foreign policy. But the president's power to veto legislation means that it typically takes near unanimity on Capitol Hill for legislative preferences to become law against the wishes of the White House. In 1991, for example, 313 representatives and 55 senators—or 85 percent of the members of Congress—voted for a bill that would have punished China for the Tiananmen Square massacre. Yet the bill never became law; supporters lacked the votes needed to overturn President Bush's veto in the Senate.

The inherent advantages of the presidency also enable the executive branch to thwart substantive legislation it doesn't like. For instance, in the mid-1980s Congress passed the so-called Pressler Amendment, which states that "no assistance shall be furnished to Pakistan and no military equipment or technology shall be sold or transferred to Pakistan" if it develops the capability to build nuclear weapons. The law turned out to mean less in practice than its sponsors thought. In 1992 the Bush administration approved commercial military sales to Pakistan, even though Pakistani officials admitted their country had the ability to make nuclear weapons. The State Department defended the arms sales on the grounds that the Pressler Amendment was attached to the foreign aid bill and did not specifically ban commercial sales. The Bush administration's decision left supporters of the Pressler Amendment with no choice but to begin the arduous task of convincing their colleagues to pass new legislation explicitly banning private commercial sales.

THE PRO-EXECUTIVE BRANCH BIAS OF THE JUDICIARY. The inherent advantages of the presidency have been reinforced by the pro-executive branch bias of the federal judiciary. The courts are reluctant to hear legal challenges to presidential acts in foreign policy, dismissing the cases either because they are not ripe for judicial review or because they raise political and not judicial questions. During Operation Desert Shield, for example, the courts denied a request by some members of Congress that President Bush be barred from ordering U.S. troops into combat without congressional authorization, even though the Constitution explicitly assigns the power to declare war to Congress and not the president. Whether intended to or not, such judicial reticence strengthens the power of the executive branch in its struggles with Congress over the direction of foreign policy.

THE NATURE AND STRUCTURE OF CONGRESS.   The difficulty members of Congress have in legislating their own preferences on foreign policy cannot be laid entirely at the feet of the other two branches of government. It also owes to factors specific to the House and Senate. Partisan and institutional divisions mean that without consensus—and today consensus is often lacking on foreign policy—Congress will not act. Further exacerbating the tendency toward legislative failure is the sheer press of business on Capitol Hill. The legislative docket in Congress is overloaded. Foreign policy issues must vie with domestic policy issues for attention. Many bills get lost in the shuffle.

Beyond the problems inherent in institutional design and partisan division, the ability of Congress to pass substantive legislation is complicated by the willingness of many members to defer to presidential leadership. Congressional deference owes partly to electoral calculations. Members want to avoid taking stands that might leave them open to blame and, thus, to punishment at the polls. Because much of the public believes in the need for strong presidential leadership, many members find that following the president's lead is the politically safest course to take. But to attribute congressional deference only to electoral calculations shortchanges members. Deference also stems from the belief, widely held on Capitol Hill, that the president should be allowed to lead on foreign policy. Contrary to the complaints of Irreconcilables and Skeptics alike, legislators recognize that they are ill-equipped to manage foreign policy.

THE DISADVANTAGES OF SUBSTANTIVE LEGISLATION.   The inherent advantages of the presidency, the pro-executive branch bias of the judiciary, and the nature and structure of Congress take us a long way in explaining why members of Congress seldom overrule the president on foreign policy. These factors do not, however, tell the entire story. An essential lesson of life on Capitol Hill is that members often have sound *policy* reasons for not wanting to defeat the president. The reasons for this are many. Congressional debate is public, and the rejection of presidential requests may undermine the negotiating posture of the president or jeopardize U.S. relations with other countries. Legislation almost by necessity is rigid, but diplomacy frequently requires flexibility. Congress acts slowly, but issues can change rapidly. In some cases resorting to legislation may mean taking a sledgehammer to a problem that requires a scalpel. Legislation may even create perverse incentives: Presidents may drag their feet implementing congressional directives because they believe any policy failure will be blamed on Congress. In short, members often do not want to win because they believe that legislated solutions will prove unwise or unworkable in practice.

The disadvantages of substantive legislation are well illustrated by the battle over the MX missile. Many moderate Democrats doubted the need for yet another multiple-warhead missile. But they also worried that killing the program would be counterproductive; it would damage their party's reputation and harm the chances for arms control. As then-Representative Les Aspin (D-Wis.) explained the dilemma: "It was clear that most Democrats would vote against [the MX]. But if enough voted for it, and Reagan got it, the headline would say 'Reagan Gets MX.' If not, the headline would be 'Democrats Block MX.' Reagan could have used that as an excuse" for failing to produce an arms control agreement with the Soviet Union.[3] In the end, Aspin and many other moderates concluded that they could best achieve their policy objectives by voting for the missile and pressuring the administration to negotiate an arms control treaty.

The desire many members of Congress have to change policy without passing legislation begins to highlight the problem with measuring congressional influence solely in terms of how successful members are at generating and passing their own substantive policy proposals. Executive–legislative relations on foreign policy are far more complicated than can be captured simply by examining which bills pass. Congress often influences policy indirectly. The next three sections discuss those indirect means of influence in greater depth.

SUBSTANTIVE LEGISLATION AS LEVERAGE

Members of Congress know firsthand that substantive legislation is a flawed policymaking tool. Even assuming they can overcome partisan and institutional divisions and actually pass legislation, there is no guarantee that the administration will observe the letter, let alone the spirit, of the law. But rather than abandoning efforts to legislate their policy preferences into law, policy-oriented members view debate over substantive legislation as a lever with which to shape policy. Administration critics often can extract major policy concessions from the White House if there is strong opposition to executive branch policy on Capitol Hill.

In using substantive legislation as a lever, members count on the power of anticipated reactions. Here members calculate that the presidents will prefer to concede on some policy issues rather than risk a legislative defeat. Presidents are especially likely to anticipate the mood in Congress on foreign policy because public defeats threaten to weaken their credibility on the world scene. As Secretary of State James Baker explained President Bush's reluctance to ask Congress to authorize Operation Desert Storm: "The President has not wanted to ask for such a resolution unless the leadership of the Congress could assure him that such a resolution would be forthcoming, because your hand would be weakened if it were not forthcoming."

Examples of Successful Legislative Leverage

Examples abound of administrations changing the substance of their policy proposals to head off legislative defeats. Take, for example, arms sales. In the mid-1970s, Congress passed legislation giving itself the power to veto major arms sales proposals. Although Congress has never vetoed an arms sale, the threat of a veto appears to have shaped many presidential proposals. On several occasions the Ford and Carter administrations modified their proposed arms packages to defuse congressional opposition. Three times between 1983 and 1985 the Reagan administration proposed selling arms to Jordan, and each time it withdrew the proposal because of opposition on Capitol Hill. Following the Iraqi invasion of Kuwait the Bush administration postponed its plans to ask Congress to approve the sale of $13 billion in weapons to Saudi Arabia. Officials calculated that Israel's many supporters in Congress would have voted no had the proposal gone forward.

The threat of legislation also shapes U.S. trade policy. When members become dissatisfied with the administration's handling of trade issues, they turn quickly to protectionist legislation. A flurry of trade bills usually prompts proponents of free trade to cry that the protectionist wolf is at the door.

> As the debate proceeds, and restrictive pressures become more threatening, several new developments occur. . . . The Executive shows, in various ways, that it is listening to the Congress. . . . In short, the signals from Congress are received, and upon recognizing this, the congressional frustration quotient drops, and a liberal trade law is passed, or at the least, a restrictive bill fails.[4]

The threat of legislation may even influence the behavior of other countries. Foreign governments often try to defuse efforts to pass punitive legislation with conciliatory gestures. For example, when China was threatened with punitive legislation in 1990 it released hundreds of prodemocracy activists from prison. When Congress resurrected the legislation in 1991, China agreed to sign the Nuclear Non-Proliferation Treaty, and, for the first time in its history, it allowed a human rights delegation to visit China.

Limits to Legislative Leverage

The threat to legislate is not a foolproof instrument for influencing foreign policy. Its effectiveness depends first of all on the ability of opponents to mount a credible challenge to executive branch policy. No administration will compromise if legislative defeat is unlikely. The Reagan administration, for example, dismissed many of the legislative challenges it faced during its first six years because Republicans controlled the Senate until 1987. At the same time, presidents may be able to sustain their veto of legislation by making only minor concessions. In the case of the Tiananmen Square massacre, President Bush blocked efforts to punish the Chinese government by making cosmetic changes to his China policy.

The effectiveness of a threat to legislate also depends on the intensity of administration preferences. On some issues the executive branch may see defeat as no better, or even worse, than compromise. And the willingness to compromise on a particular issue may change from president to president. Ronald Reagan bitterly resisted congressional attempts to rewrite U.S. policy toward Central America, so much so that his subordinates broke the law in the Iran–contra affair. In contrast, George Bush made negotiation of an executive–legislative détente over Central America one of the first priorities of his administration.

The Irony of Legislative Leverage

Congressional efforts to use substantive legislation as a lever with which to pressure the White House carry with them considerable irony. The traditional standard for judging whether Congress matters on foreign policy is its ability to pass legislation. Yet as Stanley Heginbotham observes, when members use substantive legislation as leverage "congressional victory is achieved when restrictive legislation loses, but Congress extracts some policy compromises reflecting congressional concerns."[5] As a result, executive–legislation relations on foreign policy are far more complicated than can be captured simply by examining which bills pass.

PROCEDURAL LEGISLATION

A second reason why a focus on substantive legislation underestimates Congress's influence over foreign policy is that it assumes that members of Congress only try to legislate the substance of policy. Yet members are far more savvy than this assumption suggests. They know all too well that efforts to change policy directly face considerable obstacles. That's why members often resort to procedural legislation: bills that seek to change the procedures or structures that govern decision making in the executive branch. Underlying procedural legislation is the belief that changing *how* decisions are made will in turn affect *which* decisions are made.

The Appeal of Procedural Legislation

Procedural legislation has three advantages from the vantage point of Capitol Hill. First, because structural and procedural changes do not directly target the substance of policy they are often seen as politically neutral. As a result, members usually find it easier to convince their colleagues to support procedural legislation than substantive legislation.

Second, procedural legislation can save members time and effort. Structural and procedural changes that succeed in incorporating congressional preferences into executive branch policy from the start relieve members of the need to push for substantive legislation later on. At the same time, many structural and procedural changes are designed to shift the burden of monitoring agency behavior onto the executive branch (e.g., offices of the inspector general) or onto interested private groups (e.g., private sector advisory groups). And when procedural legislation targets a class of issues—say, for example, the rules used for allocating foreign aid—they save members from having to fight the executive branch each time the issue arises.

The third advantage to procedural legislation is that it can create opportunities for political profit. Many times Congress changes the decision-making process to enable affected groups to seek remedies from the agency, the courts, or even Congress itself. These structural and procedural changes in turn create what political scientists have come to call a system of fire alarms that alert members to issues that concern their constituents.[6] The procedural fire alarms enable members to allocate their oversight activities in a much more electorally efficient manner than would be the case if they themselves had to ferret out instances in which their constituents were hurt by executive branch actions.

Types of Structural and Procedural Change

The structural and procedural changes Congress can make to the decision-making process in foreign policy fall into five major categories: new agencies and positions in the executive branch, new participants in policymaking, legislative vetoes, new procedural requirements, and reporting requirements.

NEW AGENCIES AND POSITIONS.   One way Congress can influence the policies that emerge from the bureaucracy is to create new agencies and positions inside the executive branch that will (hopefully) be more responsive to congressional concerns. Over the past several decades Congress has created several institutional structures inside the executive branch in an effort to influence foreign policy. In 1961, it created the Arms Control and Disarmament Agency (ACDA) to counter what many members saw as the foreign policy bureaucracy's disregard for arms control issues. Congress established the Office of the Special Trade Representative in 1974 because members believed that the State Department—which until then had been the lead federal agency on trade issues—was insensitive to the needs of domestic economic interests. And in 1986, Congress created the post of undersecretary of defense for acquisition in the hope of reducing waste, fraud, and abuse in the Defense Department. All of these efforts proceeded from a simple assumption about bureaucratic life: If you want a policy to succeed, make sure some agency in the bureaucracy will champion it.

NEW DECISION-MAKING PARTICIPANTS.   Efforts to create new agencies and positions require major changes in the structure of government. A less drastic tool members of Congress use to shape executive branch policies is to change the participants in policymaking. Underlying this procedural change is the belief that changing who participates in decision making will produce policy proposals more in accord with congressional preferences.

Sometimes the new decision-making participants are existing agencies that share the preferences of Congress. In 1988, for example, Congress required the Defense Department to consult with the Commerce Department when negotiating agreements with foreign governments on the production of defense equipment. Members believed that Commerce would oppose agreements that hurt American commercial interests. At other times Congress incorporates nongovernmental groups into decision making. The Trade Act of 1974 requires the administration to solicit advice from an array of labor, industry, agricultural, and consumer groups during trade negotiations. Members even legislate themselves into the process. The Trade Act of 1974, for instance, stipulates that members of Congress must be appointed as official advisers to all trade negotiations. At a recent meeting of the Uruguay Round of trade talks, a dozen members of Congress and many more congressional aides participated.

THE LEGISLATIVE VETO.   A third type of procedural change Congress uses to influence foreign policy is the legislative veto. With this procedure Congress gives the president authority to act but reserves for itself the right to overturn the president's decision. The War Powers Resolution contains one of the best-known legislative vetoes. Under the terms of the resolution, Congress can order the president to terminate the use of U.S. armed forces abroad at any time.

Until 1983, Congress could veto a presidential decision by passing a simple (one-house) or concurrent (two-house) resolution. The great advantage to simple and concurrent resolutions is that neither is subject to a presidential veto. But in *I.N.S.* v. *Chadha,* the Supreme Court ruled that under most conditions simple and concurrent vetoes violate the constitutional principle that bills be passed by both houses and presented to the president for signing. Now Congress can veto presidential actions only by passing a joint resolution. Of course, the president benefitted from the *Chadha* ruling because joint resolutions are subject to a presidential veto.

The *Chadha* ruling, however, did not entirely forbid the use of simple and concurrent resolutions as legislative vetoes. So long as they affect congressional procedure rather than policy, one-house and two-house vetoes remain constitutional. Thus, the Omnibus Trade and Competitiveness Act of 1988 allows the president to extend the fast-track procedure under which Congress considers proposed trade agreements unless both the House and Senate adopt a resolution of disapproval within 60 days of the request for an extension. (Fast-track procedures bar members of Congress from trying to amend a bill, thereby speeding up the legislative process by forcing members to vote either for or against the president's proposal.) President Bush invoked the procedure in March 1991 when he asked Congress to extend for two years the fast-track procedure for considering any agreement that emerged from the Uruguay Round of negotiations on the General Agreement on Tariffs and Trade.

NEW PROCEDURAL REQUIREMENTS.   Members of Congress also shape foreign policy by writing the procedures that govern executive branch decision making. The premise here is that new procedures will produce decisions more to Congress's liking. The Super 301 provision in the 1988 Omnibus Trade bill, for example, required the president to impose sanctions on countries with "a consistent pattern of import barriers and market-distorting practices." The Omnibus Trade bill also broadened the definition of unfair trade practices and terminated the International Trade Commission's discretion to investigate claims of dumping. Both changes were designed to make it easier for injured groups to claim relief.

In writing new procedural requirements members of Congress often make use of conditional authorizations. Here the law allows the executive branch officials to proceed as they see fit so long as certain conditions are met. Section 502B of the Foreign Assistance Act, for example, stipulates that "no security assistance may be provided to any country the government of which engages in a consistent pattern of gross violations of internationally recognized human rights." The rationale for and the appeal of conditional authorizations lie in providing presidents with the discretion they need to manage foreign policy on a day-to-day basis while placing clear limits on what they can do. Of course, the restrictiveness of the limits varies greatly. In some cases, presidents enjoy tremendous discretion in deciding whether a condition has been met, while in other cases the president's discretion is quite limited.

REPORTING REQUIREMENTS.   Members of Congress can attempt to influence policy by imposing reporting requirements on the foreign policy bureaucracy. Many reporting requirements merely require the executive to inform Congress of agency decisions. Since the mid-1970s, for example, the Central Intelligence Agency (CIA) has been required to report each covert operation to the appropriate congressional committees. Other reporting requirements are designed to force the executive to assess the implications of its policies. For instance, Congress requires the Defense Department to submit an arms control impact statement for every major weapons program. Besides recurring reporting requirements, Congress also directs agencies to undertake studies of specific issues. The use of such one-time reports has been especially popular in defense policy where requests for reports rose from roughly 30 per year in the 1960s to over 500 per year in the 1980s.[7]

To be sure, not all reporting requirements are designed to influence policy. As then-Representative Aspin once observed, "There are requests where Congress orders up a report, not to aid congressional deliberations but as a substitute for deliberations." Many reports are intended to give members something to show constituents on matters of local concern. Others are a sop to members who cannot muster the votes needed to pass substantive legislation. In 1991, for instance, Senator Dale Bumpers (D-Ark.) settled for an amendment requiring the Pentagon to report on the security outlook for the Korea peninsula because he lacked the votes needed to cut the number of U.S. troops in South Korea.

But many reporting requirements are intended to influence policy. They do so in a variety of ways. Some requirements are designed to deter unpopular executive branch decisions by raising the prospect of early congressional involvement. A major impetus for the notification requirements regarding covert operations, for instance, was the belief that the need to notify Congress would discourage CIA officials from pursuing imprudent operations. Other reporting requirements are designed to give members of Congress the information they need to oversee foreign policy. Still other reporting requirements are designed to put an issue or a proposal on the agenda in the executive branch or to stimulate the exchange of information among executive agencies. In the 1980s, for example, Congress required several studies on the environmental aspects of foreign aid in order to force senior foreign policy officials to address the issue.

Success of Procedural Legislation

How successful are structural and procedural changes in shaping policy? Some procedural legislation clearly fails. By almost any measure the War Powers Resolution is a dead letter. Despite hopes that ACDA would integrate arms control concerns with military objectives, it operates largely on the margins of the weapons acquisition process. The post of undersecretary of defense for acquisition went through three appointees in its first four years, with none of the three making much of an impact on the procurement process.

These examples notwithstanding, many structural and procedural changes do affect policy. Take the case of the Omnibus Trade Bill of 1988. The Bush administration responded to the passage of the bill by initiating the Structural Impediments Initiative with Japan in an effort to avoid invoking the retaliatory provisions of the bill. The talks produced several Japanese trade concessions. The Omnibus Trade bill also altered the behavior of several of America's trading partners. South Korea, for example, apparently worked to increase its import of American-made goods in an effort to avoid becoming the target of the retaliatory provisions of the bill.

The success of procedural change in trade policy might not seem remarkable given the strong constituency interest in trade policy. But procedural changes appear to work in areas where constituency interests are less prominent. In 1986, Congress passed the Goldwater-Nichols Act, which sought to curtail the problem of interservice squabbling over combat missions in wartime by streamlining the chain of command. Many observers credit the act with helping to dampen interservice disagreements during the Gulf War. Secretary of Defense Dick Cheney, normally a passionate critic of congressional activism on defense policy, went so far as to describe Goldwater-Nichols as "the most far-reaching piece of legislation affecting the [Defense] Department since the original National Security Act of 1947. . . . Clearly, it made a major contribution to our recent military successes."

The CIA provides another example where a procedural change has had great success. As a result of the reforms implemented in the 1970s, virtually all CIA assessments go to the Intelligence Committees. The Appropriations, Armed Services, Foreign Affairs, and Foreign Relations committees also receive CIA reports, and many individual members receive CIA briefings. These reforms have made the CIA more attentive to the views of Congress. To quote Robert M. Gates, then deputy director of Central Intelligence:

The result of these realities is that the CIA today finds itself in a remarkable position, involuntarily poised equidistant between the executive and legislative branches. The administration knows that the CIA is in no position to withhold much information from Congress and is extremely sensitive to congressional demands; the Congress has enormous influence and information yet remains suspicious and mistrustful.[8]

Even the Iran–contra affair supports Gates's conclusion about Congress's influence over the CIA. William Casey tried to create an off-the-shelf covert operations team precisely because he wanted to circumvent congressional oversight of covert operations.

FRAMING OPINION

A fourth way members of Congress influence foreign policy is by changing the climate of opinion surrounding that policy. As the Bush administration's about-face on the issue of aid to Iraqi Kurds attests, what the public and the pundits think about U.S. foreign policy influences the choices the president makes. Members use many techniques to influence opinion, including committee hearings, committee reports, speeches, and appearances on radio and television news shows. As diverse as these activities may be, they share a common goal: to define the terms of debate on an issue in a way that will increase support for some policy options and decrease support for others.

Framing Opinion and Political Self-Interest

That framing constitutes a strategy for influencing policy may come as a surprise. Because framing an issue usually involves efforts to attract media coverage, critics often dismiss it as mere political grandstanding. To be sure, members sometimes run to the media thinking more of their own electoral interest than of the national interest. When the Carter administration was trying to win Senate approval of the SALT II treaty, Senator Frank Church (D-Idaho), chair of the Senate Foreign Relations Committee, revealed to the public that Soviet troops were based in Cuba. By most accounts, Church sounded the tocsin on the Soviet "brigade" in Cuba less to influence President Carter than in a bid to revive his flagging electoral prospects.

Still, complaints about political framing miss three important points. First, even when members of Congress seize on an issue for purely cynical reasons, their actions influence, for well or ill, the shape of foreign policy. Senator Church's actions played a major role in derailing the SALT II treaty. Thus, even if one disapproves of the method, the reality of congressional influence remains.

Second, complaints that framing amounts to no more than self-aggrandizement by members rest on the erroneous assumption that legislative work should be an "eat-your-peas-and-spinach" endeavor. Many observers of Congress seem comfortable only with members who shun the media spotlight and labor over the details of legislation in obscurity. But for members seeking to change policy, playing to the galleries is an essential tool for leveling the playing field with the White House. Legislators understand far better than their critics that publicity frequently can change policy. The glare of the public spotlight is often the best weapon legislators have to dislodge a bill from a hostile committee, to force the administration to reverse its course of action, or to build public support for new policy initiatives.

Third, the fact that a legislator usually stands to benefit politically from political framing does not make these efforts any less useful for influencing policy. The American political system rests on the assumption that self-interest will motivate legislators to address pressing policy issues. As James Madison wrote in *Federalist No. 51,* the best way to promote the public good is to create a system in which "the private interest of every individual may be a sentinel over the public rights." Framing also is no less useful because it typically invokes simple, if not simplistic, arguments. Not only do presidents themselves indulge in simple and dramatic appeals—recall President Reagan's Star Wars speech—such appeals are essential to winning public support. When issues are put in terms that anyone can understand, the burden of proof then rests with one's opponents.

How Framing Opinion Works

At the most general level, members of Congress try to frame issues in order to change public opinion. Writing thirty years ago, Warner Schilling argued that legislators who want to influence defense policy should "change their policy target from the budget to the climate of opinion that shaped it."[9] In the mid-1980s, Senator Charles Grassley (R-Iowa) showed the wisdom of Schilling's advice. Rather than attacking individual defense programs, Grassley released information that the Air Force had paid nearly $1,000 to purchase a small plastic cap for the leg of a navigator's stool. The story captured national headlines, and soon other legislators were scrambling to reveal stories of waste, fraud, and abuse in the Pentagon. As the *Almanac of American Politics* described Grassley's efforts: "He has shown the capacity to change the terms of the debate, and future historians may date the end of the Reagan Administration's huge increases in defense spending to Grassley's initiative."[10]

Members of Congress also try to frame issues in ways that directly pressure the administration to change its policies. In February 1986, for example, Ronald Reagan disputed reports that supporters of Ferdinand Marcos had committed massive fraud in the Philippine presidential elections. Senator Richard Lugar (R-Ind.), the chair of the Senate Foreign Relations Committee and the head of the U.S. delegation that had witnessed the voting fraud, responded to Reagan's comments by launching a two-week-long media blitz that culminated in appearances on all three Sunday morning network television interview shows. In each appearance Lugar urged Reagan to ask Marcos to resign. Lugar's efforts—complemented by those of other members of Congress—worked; Reagan withdrew his support for Marcos.

The third possible target of political grandstanding is another country.

Sometimes administrations encourage legislative framing in order to strengthen their own hand in foreign negotiations. For instance, during the Nixon administration, Secretary of Commerce Maurice Stans asked Wilbur Mills, the chairman of the Ways and Means Committee, to introduce a bill on textile quotas. Stans apparently hoped to create a "good cop/bad cop" scenario that would force the government of Japan to make additional concessions in trade negotiations.[11]

More often, however, the executive and legislative branches are not colluding. Take the case where a subsidiary of Toshiba sold sensitive technology to the Soviet Union. The government of Japan initially ignored the matter. Then the issue reached Capitol Hill. On June 20, 1987, five members of Congress took sledgehammers to a Toshiba radio on the grounds of the Capitol.

> The video clip was replayed again and again on Japanese television. One day later, the chairman and president of Toshiba Corporation announced their resignations. On July 20, the Toshiba Corporation ran a full-page ad in dozens of American newspapers apologizing for the actions of its subsidiary. By the end of July, a memorandum between MITI and the Japanese Foreign Ministry provided for ministerial review of sensitive exports, thus raising export control to a higher government level. On July 31, the Japanese government sent a tougher export control law to the Diet; the bill passed in early September. In a series of talks over the summer and fall, the Japanese agreed to become partners with the US in a new program to develop anti-submarine warfare technology. Japanese companies, led by Toshiba Corp., began formulating their own COCOM [Coordinating Committee for Multilateral Export Controls] compliance regulations.[12]

Or take Operation Desert Shield. Germany and Japan initially balked at providing aid. In September 1990, a House debate on the defense appropriations bill produced bitter complaints about German and Japanese reluctance to help support the multinational force. Within two days of the debate, Germany agreed to contribute to the Gulf effort, and Japan quadrupled its aid offer.

Limits to Framing Efforts

Framing offers members of Congress a powerful tool for shaping policy. Yet it does not always produce substantive changes in policy. Presidents may respond to congressional pressure by changing the style and not the substance of policy. President Nixon reacted to opposition to Vietnam in part by taking the war underground. President Bush responded to criticism in late 1991 that he was devoting too much attention to foreign policy by holding several highly publicized meetings with bankers, business executives, and economic advisers. The meetings were "meant more for public consumption near the start of the election campaign than as a genuine effort to bring about political changes."[13] And foreign countries can and do dismiss the symbolic actions of Congress.

Even when presidents and foreign countries change their substantive behavior it is difficult to establish that Congress's efforts are responsible. Public support for high levels of defense spending may have fallen without the efforts of Senator Grassley and his imitators. The Reagan administration might have dropped its support for Ferdinand Marcos even without being prodded by Senator Lugar and others. And Germany and Japan might have increased their financial support for Operation Desert Shield even in the absence of bitter congressional debate. Still, it is hard to deny the conclusion that members of Congress often focus the glare of the public spotlight on foreign policy issues and that sometimes the results matter. Far from injecting politics into an otherwise technocratic decision-making process, framing enables members to at least partially counter the president's inherent advantages on foreign policy.

THE FUTURE OF CONGRESSIONAL ACTIVISM

Congress plays an important, though frequently misunderstood, role in the making of foreign policy. To be sure, Skeptics are right to claim that Congress sustains the policies of the president far more frequently than it overturns them. But focusing on substantive legislation overlooks the dynamics of influence. The bulk of Congress's influence over foreign policy rests in indirect means: legislative leverage, procedural legislation, and framing opinion. Indeed, the very factors that frustrate congressional attempts to legislate the substance of foreign policy encourage members to use indirect means of influence.

What of the future of congressional activism in foreign policy? The election of Bill Clinton as president removes one of the most potent forces behind congressional activism on foreign policy, namely, deep ideological differences between Capitol Hill and the White House. Clinton's election marks the first time in over a decade that both ends of Pennsylvania Avenue are controlled by the same political party. Clinton's centrist leanings make it likely that he will be in step with a majority of Congress most of the time.

Nonetheless, several ongoing developments at home and abroad suggest that the Clinton presidency will not end congressional activism on foreign policy. The first is the end of the Cold War. With the United States now the world's sole remaining superpower, American political elites are rethinking the premises of U.S. foreign policy for the first time in fifty years. Members of Congress will play a key role in redefining America's interests and strategies. No doubt many members will attempt to squeeze defense and foreign policy programs for the money needed to rejuvenate a sluggish domestic economy and to tame the massive federal budget deficit.

Moreover as perceptions of external threat have receded, the American public is now more likely to tolerate legislative dissent on foreign affairs. Faced with fewer electoral costs in opposing the president, members of Congress are more likely to deal the president public rebuffs. After twelve years of Democratic criticism of Presidents Reagan and Bush, many Republicans no doubt will delight in attacking any shortcomings they see in President Clinton's foreign policy. And the Clinton White House cannot expect to receive a free ride from Democrats on Capitol Hill. Jimmy Carter discovered that his severest foreign policy critics were members of his own party.

A second reason why Congress is likely to become more influential is that growing global interdependence is blurring the line that once separated domestic policy from foreign policy. The disagreement between the United States and the European Community over acceptable levels of farm subsidies provides an example of such an "intermestic" issue. How much aid governments give to farmers affects not only America's relations with its major trading partners, but also the economic well-being of many Americans. Acid rain, drugs, energy policy, global warming, and immigration are other salient issues that lie astride the domestic and international spheres. Intermestic issues encourage congressional influence because they involve decisions traditionally considered part of domestic policy. Members of Congress, who can be counted on to protect their institutional prerogatives and their constituents, will feel comfortable rewriting presidential proposals on intermestic issues, regardless of the foreign policy implications.

The last development that offers to enhance Congress's power stems from growing fears that the American economy is falling behind the economies of Germany and Japan. In the words of then-Representative Aspin, today we are seeing "the emergence of an entirely new concept of national security. It embraces economics and competitive, commercial relations."[14] Former U.S. trade negotiator Clyde Prestowitz put the same point more bluntly: "Trade *is* defense. We must recognize the nature of the game."[15] If the argument that economic vitality is national security continues to gain ground, Congress will become more involved in national security policy for the same reasons it is more influential on intermestic issues. If issues are defined in domestic economic terms, Congress becomes less likely to defer to the wishes of the president.

NOTES

1. Among others, see Dick Cheney, "Congressional Overreaching in Foreign Policy," in *Foreign Policy and the Constitution,* Robert A. Goldwin and Robert A. Licht, eds. (Washington, D.C.: American Enterprise Institute, 1990); L. Gordon Crovitz and Jeremy A. Rabkin, eds., *The Fettered Presidency: Legal Constraints on the Executive Branch* (Washington, D.C.: American Enterprise Institute, 1989); and Peter W. Rodman, "The Imperial Congress," *National Interest* 1 (Fall 1985): 26–35.

2. Harold Hongju Koh, "Why the President (Almost) Always Wins in Foreign Affairs: Lessons of the Iran-Contra Affair," *Yale Law Journal* 97 (June 1988): 1255–1342.

3. Quoted in Elizabeth Drew, "A Political Journal," *New Yorker,* June 20, 1983, p. 75.

4. Robert A. Pastor, *Congress and the Politics of U.S. Foreign Economic Policy, 1929–1976* (Berkeley and Los Angeles: University of California Press, 1980), p. 193.

5. Stanley J. Heginbotham, "Dateline Washington: The Rules of the Game," *Foreign Policy* 53 (Winter 1983–1984): 170.

6. Mathew McCubbins and Thomas Schwartz, "Congressional Oversight Overlooked: Police Patrol Versus Fire Alarms," *American Journal of Political Science* 28 (February 1984): 165–179.

7. James M. Lindsay, "Congress and the Defense Budget," *Washington Quarterly* 11 (Winter 1988): 61.

8. Robert M. Gates, "The CIA and Foreign Policy," *Foreign Affairs* 66 (Winter 1987/88): 224–225.

9. Warner R. Schilling, "The Politics of National Defense: Fiscal 1950," in *Strategy, Politics, and Defense Budgets,* Warner Schilling, Paul Y. Hammond, and Glenn H. Snyder, eds. (New York: Columbia University Press, 1962), p. 248.

10. Michael Barone and Grant Ujifusa, *The Almanac of American Politics 1988* (Washington, D.C.: National Journal, 1987), p. 424.

11. Pastor, *Congress and the Politics of U.S. Foreign Economic Policy,* p. 193.

12. Anna M. Warrock and Howard Husock, "Taking Toshiba Public," Case C15-88-858.0, Harvard University, John F. Kennedy School of Government, 1988, pp. 11–12.

13. David E. Rosenbaum, "Talk About Tax Breaks Is . . . Just Talk," *New York Times,* 22 October 1991.

14. Quoted in John Greenwald, "Friend or Foe?" *Time,* April 24, 1989, p. 44.

15. Quoted in Greenwald, "Friend or Foe?" p. 45.

13. THE FOREIGN POLICY ESTABLISHMENT: TOWARD PROFESSIONALISM AND CENTRISM

Nelson W. Polsby

*E*ver since Richard Rovere published his devastating send-up of C. Wright Mills's *The Power Elite*, it has been difficult to discuss the idea of an American policymaking establishment with an altogether straight face.[1] There is, nevertheless, an intelligible core idea that seems worth pursuing. A finite, describable population exists consisting of specialists who in any generation make careers out of performing various official tasks relating to the foreign policy of the United States.

This population almost certainly is not a general all-purpose group of decision makers who dominate all domains of policy. What they actually do as individuals may vary quite a lot, and the extent of their influence as individuals will undoubtedly ebb and flow with, among other things, the influence of elected officials with whom they are allied. At any rate it does seem to make sense to speak of a foreign policy establishment in the same way that scholars have referred to "whirlpools or centers of activity focussing on particular problems"[2] or to "policy subsystems"[3] or "subgovernments"[4] or "issue networks."[5]

What is being described are policy establishments. It is important to emphasize the plurality of the phenomena in question. Rather than an all-purpose power elite, each policy establishment that operates at the national level specializes in a given subject matter. Recent, painstaking empirical work strongly suggests that lobbyists and others who look after the interests of interest groups in Washington specialize according to the specific concerns of their employers.[6] Washington law firms specialize. Congress specializes when it breaks into committees and subcommittees and thereby is organized into a highly explicit division of labor.

It seems only natural that specialization should prevail under modern circumstances in which technical information and advanced skills in obtaining and manipulating it are more or less basic requirements for participating in policymaking. Can one person know enough simultaneously about arms control and the worldwide flow of investment? Possibly, but not probably.

These, after all, are only two domains out of the very large number that generate facts and figures and theories explaining how they fit together that are in some sense required so that participants can meet minimal qualifications for thoughtful policymaking. So the notion of a specialized foreign policy establishment makes intuitive sense. It takes time and intellectual commitment to produce a population of participants capable of competent participation.

At any given time different members of a policy establishment occupy different points in the life cycle and are enjoying different political fortunes. This means that, at a minimum, a policy establishment is internally differentiated according to who is politically in and who is out; with respect to the life cycle there will be novices, prime-time players, veterans, and emeriti.[7] This characterization would in principle apply equally to policy establishments concerned with housing, constitutional law, or fiscal and monetary policy, as well as to foreign policy.

So, to begin with, let us ask: If there were a more or less professionalized foreign policy establishment, what would it look like? Presumably we would find its members clustered around the main institutions that in the United States make foreign policy. These institutions are for the most part highly visible: the presidency, for example, the State Department and the Defense Department, and Congress.

Not everyone in these institutions, to be sure, is concerned with foreign policy. A glance at a U.S. Government Organization Manual gives some helpful guidelines. Within the Executive Office of the President slightly fewer than 50 public officials hold the rank of Special Assistant to the President or above and deal with foreign affairs. These include 14 senior staff members of the National Security Council, the NSC's executive director, and two statutory advisors to the NSC (CIA director and chairman of the Joint Chiefs of Staff); three deputy assistants and above of the Office of Management and Budget under headings titled National Security and International Affairs; and 23 assistant U.S. trade representatives and above in the Office of the U.S. Trade Representative.

In the State and Defense departments a like number of senior officials are involved. Just 42 officials in the State Department hold the rank of assistant secretary or above. In the Defense Department there is an undersecretary for foreign policy and sections titled International Security Affairs (12 officials at deputy assistant secretary and above), International Security Policy (6), Special Operations (10), Security Policy (8), Trade Security, Net Assessment, Defense Policy Board (executive officer) (4).

Most of these high officials have professional staff assistance, and so from top to bottom the official foreign policy establishment might at any time number in the hundreds or possibly the low thousands and consists, more or less, of all those still living who have occupied the positions I have described.

THE PROFESSIONALIZATION
OF THE POLICY ESTABLISHMENT

Historically, the American foreign policy establishment achieved something like an institutional takeoff roughly at the turn of the twentieth century, when so many other American institutions (corporations, the professions, universities) were established in their modern form. So, too, something like an American foreign policy community emerged from the Spanish-American War and was personified in particular by Theodore Roosevelt.

New York investment bankers and Wall Street lawyers comprised the first major American anti-isolationist interest group. They founded the Council on Foreign Relations in the early 1920s and led the battle in the 1950s not only to support a bipartisan foreign policy but—in some ways more important— they waged an internal war in the Republican party to prevent the isolationist backsliding that, in the contemporary view, doomed the League of Nations and crippled international efforts to ward off World War II.

This overriding mission—the defeat of domestic isolationism—bound the foreign policy establishment together and gave a cumulative moral weight to its activities until the Vietnam War. Two trends—professionalization of the foreign policy community and the exhaustion of its historic mission—helped the Vietnam War to change the foreign policy community and give the community its present-day shape.

What do we mean by professionalization? John Foster Dulles and Dean Acheson came to their concerns about foreign affairs through their families: Acheson's father, born a Canadian, was a bishop in the American branch of the Church of England. Dulles began as secretary to his uncle, Robert Lansing, who was secretary of state in the Wilson administration. These were among the last of an old guard. Today specialists in foreign affairs have Ph.D.s or at least extensive explicit training; even Henry Kissinger, born in Germany, and Zbigniew Brzezinski, born the son of a Polish diplomat, had to do graduate work and write dissertations on their way to participation in foreign policymaking.

The careers of both were nurtured, in the first instance, at universities. Both pursued their careers through activity in foreign policy talking shops: the Council on Foreign Relations and the Trilateral Commission, respectively. The pattern of their careers is today more and more common in the foreign policy community. Foreign policy specialists are being recruited to the entourages of presidential candidates based on brains; the loyalty comes later. That's professionalization.

Professionalization also means the acquisition of advanced training as a prerequisite for competent participation. Clearly this is happening to the foreign policy community, as a simple test discloses. Approximately one-tenth of the members of the Council on Foreign Relations in 1950 was compared with approximately one-tenth of the members in 1990. Those whose names could be found in *Who's Who in America* were checked for the possession of a Ph.D. degree. Here are the results:

Members of the Council on Foreign Relations today are a lot less famous than they once were (judging from the sharp decline in their appearance in *Who's Who*) and considerably more educated, if these figures can be believed. Thus the character of the foreign policy community evolves over time.

This evolution should draw our attention to international relations Ph.D. programs in universities, to international law sections of major metropolitan law firms, to membership groups like the Council on Foreign Relations and the World Affairs Councils in the large cities, and to policy research organizations, erroneously called "think tanks," that have lately proliferated, especially in Washington.

These institutions harbor American professionals in foreign policy when they are out of office. They provide auspices for the elaboration of ideas that, with the turn of an electoral wheel, might swiftly become public policy. One famous example of this was William Quandt's blueprint for a Middle East policy that he developed at the Brookings Institution and brought with him, more or less whole, to the Carter administration's National Security Council.

IMPETUS TO THE POLICY ESTABLISHMENT: A PRESIDENTIAL BRANCH

Virtually all high officials with professional staff assistants are presidential appointees serving at the pleasure of the president. As is true of cabinet members, presidential appointees can come from any of five possible places: client groups of the agency, substantive specialists, Washington generalists, personal friends of the president, or representatives of symbolic constituencies. Members of these different groups tend to relate quite differently to the organizations they lead, to clientele, and to the president. In general, presidential appointments in foreign affairs have predominantly gone to substantive specialists, though the Bush administration secretaries of state and defense, long-time presidential friends, and both former White House chiefs of staff without specific experience in foreign affairs, pretty clearly fall into the Washington generalist category.

The experience in office of both of these leaders illustrates some of the consequences of the emergence of a new phenomenon in American government. Secretary Baker reportedly interacted with senior members of his department hardly at all. Secretary Cheney had to resort to extraordinary disciplinary measures on two highly publicized occasions in order to bring a semblance of coordination to important policies of the Defense Department. These approaches to management are the consequence of a structural problem influencing the way in which senior officials must do business if they are to maximize their own most significant governmental asset, namely access to the president—which both Baker and Cheney had. That there should be such a notable tension between participation at the presidential level and management of an executive department is an indicator of the importance of the rise of a separate and distinct presidential branch, the single most important trend in the last half century of American national government.

There are still a few observers who remember that in 1937 the President's

Committee on Administrative Management—the Brownlow Committee—could announce, with good reason, that "the President needs help." It proposed to introduce a half dozen or so specialists to the president's staff. This small corps, with its "passion for anonymity," would form an Executive Office to help the president do the nation's business. It has quite rightly been pointed out that the emergence of the presidential branch since then is in no sense a fulfillment of the Brownlow Committee's recommendations but rather a development on a far more vast and ambitious scale than the committee either anticipated or desired.

Moreover, the initial cause of the emergence of this larger development was not the adoption, in 1939, of a version of the Brownlow Committee's recommendation, but rather the burgeoning of special agencies responsible to the president as a result of the demands placed on the national government by World War II. In the realm of foreign and defense matters, the following organizational events occurred at the top of government in the immediate postwar era:

- The establishment of the National Security Council as a permanent presidential organization.
- The establishment of the Central Intelligence Agency, an agency growing out of the wartime Office of Strategic Services and responsible directly to the president on the governmental organization chart.
- The addition of a separate Air Force to the organization chart, the creation of a Joint Chiefs of Staff, and the imposition of a new layer of presidential appointees above the service secretaries through the creation of the Department of Defense.

These organizational innovations—each significantly changing the way in which national security policy was to be conducted and each shifting responsibilities massively upward and toward the president personally—were the result of a single law, the National Security Act of 1947. In turn, the rise of centralized capabilities at the presidential level interacts with professionalization lower down to produce a somewhat differently manned and qualified policymaking establishment than existed before World War II.

The emergent presidential branch, as it has developed over the past half century, is a more or less self-contained and self-sufficient organism that competes—usually quite successfully—with Congress to influence the main activities of the executive branch, that is, the bureaucratic agencies of the permanent government. The presidential branch consists, in the first place, of the Executive Office of the President, including nine agencies (White House Office, Office of Management and Budget, and National Security Council, among others), a budget of over $100 million, and a full-time staff of perhaps 1,400. It consists also of those presidential appointees to the top of the executive branch who choose—like Secretaries Baker and Cheney—in the conduct of their responsibilities to respond primarily to White House leadership rather than to the interest groups served by their agencies or the bureaucratic needs of the agencies themselves. This gives a rather porous but helpful definition of the presidential branch in calling attention to the ragged boundary between presidency and executive branch.[8]

The presidential branch is not wholly dependent on the executive branch for expert advice on program formation owing to the peculiarly American way in which our policy communities are configured, partially in, partially out of government. The presidential branch commonly holds the executive at arm's length during annual budget negotiations, during episodes of program reduction and cutback, and even during periods of programmatic innovation, especially in foreign affairs, such as President Nixon's opening to China.

THE CONSTRAINTS OF CENTRISM

Godfrey Hodgson observes that left to its own devices the foreign policy establishment is centrist in its political views. This is not wholly consistent with the notion of a professionalized establishment consisting of hired guns associated with a broad range of policy alternatives being sponsored by various elected politicians.

Three points need to be made in mitigation of the seeming differences involved:

1. Hodgson's establishment is a slightly different population from the one I am discussing. He concentrates on an older, pre-Vietnam population, on the generation of the wise men who fought World War II with Henry Stimson and built the postwar international world with Dean Acheson.[9] My establishment consists of their successors, who tend to be from the top of the class in an academic rather than a social sense, who got their basic cognitive grounding in how nations behave from reading Quincy Wright and Hans Morganthau in graduate school rather than from listening to the exhortations of Endicott Peabody (longtime headmaster at Groton) and reading the book of Common Prayer at boarding school.

2. This later establishment is in its way also centrist in that it tends to constrain the options politicians sponsor to alternatives broadly considered feasible on technical grounds. The fate of the Star Wars option in the Bush administration suggests what happens when an establishment takes custody over the medium run of a politician's favored set of impractical alternatives.

3. Centrism has its constraints, and they restrict the range of policies an establishment is willing to consider to those options that are generated politically and placed on the table by virtue of having reputable political sponsorship. It is not completely the case that the foreign policy establishment is entirely so constrained, as, for example, an examination of the rejected options that were floated about what to do with the first deliverable atomic bombs suggests.[10]

It does seem to be true that ultimately establishments tend to settle on politically centrist solutions. It is perhaps even more correct to say that professional policy establishments rarely succeed in persuading political leaders responsible for important decisions to reach for noncentrist solutions. This is at least in part because public policy in the American political system is frequently formed interactively among diverse participants (rather than hierarchically by experts feeding unitary decision makers) and requires agreement from many actors.

Over the long run the horizons of these actors can be changed, and it certainly should be counted as a major accomplishment of the American foreign policy establishment that anti-isolationist doctrines should in the postwar years have spread so widely among American politicians. But this is a long-run accomplishment, more akin to education than to policy analysis or advocacy. Professional establishments pay for the power to do this by being forever respectable over the short run. This means accepting the constraints of interactive policymaking and working over the short run within the range of the politically feasible.

I thus think it is plausible to argue that while American methods for developing a foreign and defense policy elite are by European standards messy and haphazard, they are also quite effective, and respond well to the size and decentralization of power in the American political system and to its requirements for interactive policy formation. And these methods result in a professionalized population of public servants who can manufacture, and sustain beliefs in, a suitable range of conventional wisdoms.

NOTES

1. Actually, there were two Rovere critiques of Mills, the first serious, the second farcical. Both are reprinted in Rovere's *The American Establishment and Other Reports, Opinions, and Speculations* (New York: Harcourt, Brace and World, 1962), pp. 3–21, 254–268. The work that provoked Rovere's criticisms is C. Wright Mills, *The Power Elite* (New York: Oxford, 1956).

2. Ernest S. Griffith, *Congress, Its Contemporary Role* (New York: New York University Press, 1951), pp. 37–38.

3. J. Leiper Freeman, *The Political Process: Executive Bureau-Legislative Committee Relations* (Garden City, N.Y.: Doubleday, 1955).

4. Douglass Cater, *Power in Washington* (New York: Random House, 1964), esp. pp. 26–48.

5. Hugh Heclo, "Issue Networks and the Executive Establishment" in Anthony King, ed., *The New American Political System* (Washington, D.C.: American Enterprise Institute, 1978), pp. 87–124.

6. John P. Heinz, Edward O. Laumann, Robert H. Salisbury, Robert L. Nelson, "Inner Circles or Hollow Cores? Elite Networks in National Policy Systems," *Journal of Politics* 52 (May 1990): 356–390.

7. Other bases for differentiation in the Washington community include state of origin and time of arrival in Washington. See Nelson W. Polsby, "The Washington Community 1960–1980," in Thomas E. Mann and Norman J. Ornstein, eds., *The New Congress* (Washington, D.C.: American Enterprise Institute, 1981), pp. 7–31.

8. The best recent work on this subject is by John Hart. See his *The Presidential Branch* (Elmsford, N.Y.: Pergamon, 1987) and "The President and His Staff," in Malcolm Shaw, ed., *The Modern Presidency* (New York: Harper & Row, 1987), pp. 159–205.

9. Godfrey Hodgson describes the group that surrounded Stimson in the War

Department in World War II: "Stimson, Bundy, Lovett, Harrison were all members of Skull and Bones [a Yale secret society]. Only McCloy and Patterson of the inner circle were not. Stimson, Bundy, Harrison, McCloy, and Patterson were all graduates of the Harvard Law School; only Lovett was not. Stimson, Harrison, Lovett, McCloy, and Patterson were all prominent on Wall Street; only Bundy was not, and he practiced law on State Street, the nearest thing to Wall Street in Boston. . . . The plain fact is that, during a war for democracy conducted by a Democratic president . . . the War Department was directed by a tiny clique of wealthy Republicans." *The Colonel: The Life and Wars of Henry Stimson, 1867–1950.* (New York: Knopf, 1990), p. 247. See also Walter Isaacson and Evan Thomas, *The Wise Men* (New York: Simon & Schuster, 1986); Dean G. Acheson, *Present at the Creation* (New York: Norton, 1969); and Hodgson, "The Establishment," *Foreign Policy* 10 (Spring 1973): 3–40.

10. E.g., a demonstration drop on uninhabited terrain. See Richard Rhodes, *The Making of the Atomic Bomb* (New York: Simon & Schuster, 1988).

14. THE DEPARTMENT OF STATE IN 2000: A NEW MODEL FOR MANAGING FOREIGN AFFAIRS

Management Task Force, U.S. Department of State

Since World War II, the Soviet threat has defined our national interest, driven our policy, and determined how we organized our government. The Cold War is over; the Soviet threat is gone. Today, we have other challenges:

- We must renew our economy if we are to compete in an increasingly interdependent world.
- We must support the worldwide movement toward democracy and market economies if we are to maintain and promote our own values.
- We must confront global issues, such as the environment, drugs, and AIDS if we are to protect the planet and our society.
- We must redefine our national security if we are to deal with both the legacy of the Cold War and rising threats such as the proliferation of deadly weapons of mass destruction.
- We must redirect our diplomacy if we are to capitalize on new opportunities for multilateral cooperation.

The magnitude of these challenges mandates a fundamental shift in the focus of our foreign policy and fundamental reform in how we make and implement it. We, too, must change—as a nation, a government, and a department.

First, we must integrate our foreign policy. Our foreign policy institutions, including the Department of State, are still dominated by a Cold War political–military view of world events. Military security remains vital; but so, too, are a whole range of other interests such as economic competitiveness and environmental protection. Our foreign policy agenda grows lengthier by the day and, with it, the number of actors within the U.S. government and outside it. Without a truly integrated approach, we run the risk of incoherent, even contradictory policy—a risk that we, if we are to maintain America's preeminent position in the world, can ill afford.

Second, and even more importantly, we must integrate foreign and domestic policy. We must learn, in fact, to see them as two parts of one whole. Each of the competing priorities on the nation's new foreign policy agenda, from economics and the environment to promotion of democracy and market reform, has strong links to domestic policy. Without full integration of domestic and foreign policy—without, in short, a **national** policy—we will suffer at home and abroad. . . .

The need for integration at both the foreign policy and national level has informed this Task Force's approach to reform. Above all, it has caused us to look beyond the Department of State. The department can and must play a critical role in foreign policy; but it can only do so effectively in a broader context of integrated policymaking, implementation, and resource allocation. Such integration demands change, not just at the department, but beyond it.

These, then, are the challenges that will confront us through the end of the century and beyond. To succeed, we must rethink and reorganize.

And we must begin at the top.

LEADERSHIP FROM THE TOP

The president must lead the fundamental redirection of American diplomacy. It is the president who has the capacity to merge consideration of domestic and foreign policy. It is the president who can mandate a reallocation of resources across the federal budget, maximizing the effect of scarce taxpayer dollars on new priorities. And it is the president who can unite the executive branch across agency lines, build new consensus between both ends of Pennsylvania Avenue, and marshal public support.

Single Foreign Policy Process

The end of sharp distinctions between domestic and overseas interests underscores the need for one foreign policy process, run by and responsive to the White House. There must be a single process where trade-offs can be made among domestic and foreign policy priorities, enabling a grand strategy for the post–Cold War period to emerge.

Consequently, we recommend that the National Security Council (NSC) be the catalyst and the point of coordination for this new, single foreign policy process. In practical terms, this central foreign policy role for the NSC would mean naming a different kind of assistant to the president for national security affairs and reconfiguring the staff and the agenda to reflect economic and global issues in addition to political–security concerns. Treasury, the Office of Management and Budget (OMB), Commerce, the Office of the U.S. Trade Representative (USTR), the Environmental Protection Agency (EPA), and other relevant agencies should regularly attend NSC meetings. . . .

Strategic Planning

The post–Cold War world requires the U.S. government to set clear priorities and identify major cross-cutting themes, such as economic renewal and support for democracy. To that end, the NSC should articulate clearly the president's foreign policy agenda, culminating in a presidential directive, or series of directives, to the executive branch.

In addition to substantive policy priorities, that review needs to address such major program issues as the future of U.S. foreign assistance. . . .

Policy Link to Resources

The only way that the president can achieve his/her foreign policy goals is through firm control of the budget. For the foreseeable future, resources will be constrained. The current budget process encourages duplication or, worse, programs that work at cross-purposes. The president's single policy process must therefore produce the basic guidance needed to permit the State Department to follow up and link all available resources, from inside and outside the foreign affairs (Function 150) account, to agreed priorities.

Most reallocation of resources in the federal budget is likely to go to critical domestic problems. However, the review of resources led by the NSC should try to identify where resources, especially those now spent on foreign policy programs, could be shifted. It is possible, for example, that money spent on Cold War functions by the Department of Defense (DOD) and the intelligence agencies would be more cost-effective in other accounts. It makes no sense for the Central Intelligence Agency (CIA) to assume an expanded overt reporting role on political, economic, science and technology (S&T), and global issues when the State Department already covers this function.

Working with Congress

There can be no significant or enduring consensus on new strategic priorities for U.S. policy, or for the budget decisions to implement them, if the executive and legislative branches do not work better together. An improved dialogue between the executive and the Congress should inform and underpin both the aforementioned presidential directive and the reform of the resource management and budget processes recommended in this report.

FOREIGN POLICY FORMULATION AND RESOURCE ALLOCATION

Role of the State Department

The Department of State has three core roles: policy formulation across the range of international issues, implementation or conduct of foreign relations, and coordination of major overseas programs and activities of the government. This report suggests how State can better perform these roles by refocusing its processes and its organization. Key among these major reforms is the department's role in following through on the president's basic guidance for allocating resources to foreign policy priorities.

Strategic Planning and Resource Allocation

After the NSC calls the first annual interagency meetings which thrash out grand strategy and OMB sets the consequent resource allocation guidelines, the State Department must elaborate foreign policy goals to support the strategy and relate various foreign affairs budgets to these priorities.

The secretary of state already coordinates the final presentation of the budgets in the 150 function to the president. Ambassadors are responsible for fashioning a country strategy and for coordinating all U.S. government programs in a given country. However, the current resource management/budget process does not integrate non-150 budgets into the overall strategy and does not rigorously relate all available resources to policy priorities at country, regional, and global levels.

We recommend a reformed resource management system which reaches beyond existing arrangements by giving the president a way to relate the totality of available foreign affairs resources to the nation's foreign policy agenda—including resources from the so-called domestic agencies which have overseas programs.

The Policy Process

An increasingly complex foreign policy agenda requires the Department of State, like the NSC, to strengthen its policy formulation process. All levels in the department must focus on the future and give priority to strategic considerations. In addition, there are too many layers between the bottom and the top and too many walls between and among functions and offices. The result is parochialism, a failure to bring our full resources effectively to bear on issues, and a cumbersome clearance process that impedes good policy formulation.

There should be little wonder that the top leadership in the White House and in the department have tended over the years to create separate, smaller mechanisms to deal with the key foreign policy agenda items—leaving the institution more and more marginalized.

The conduct of foreign relations, however effective personal diplomacy at high levels may be, must be underpinned by extensive preparations, reporting and analysis, and contacts on the state-to-state level. This has been the department's traditional province. In an increasingly diverse and complex global environment, this role cannot be allowed to atrophy. With effective leadership from the secretary and his/her associates, the department can be a strong and consistent player across a range of central issues. All of its parts must contribute to the nation's purpose.

We recommend the following fundamental reforms so the department can better equip itself to manage the conduct of foreign relations:

- **Streamlining.** To reduce layering and horizontal compartmentalization, we call for a series of "mergers and acquisitions" which brings the total number of bureau-level entities from 32 to 28 and the number of independent offices not attached to bureaus from 14 to 4. This is a major remodeling of the Department of State.
- **Rationalizing the Seventh Floor.** After abolishing or relocating the special offices appended to the secretary and the deputy secretary, we recommend that those bureaus and bureau-level offices which serve the secretary directly, as well as serve the department as a whole, report to a new Office of the Secretary of State. This reform, in addition to putting the undersecretaries in charge of line bureaus, should drastically cut back on Seventh Floor staffs (i.e., staffs reporting to the Department's principals) which have come to duplicate bureau functions.
- **Strategic Planning.** The Policy Planning Staff will be restructured into a new Office of Strategic Planning and Resources (SPR), made up of strategic planning and resource allocation wings. Small bureau staffs, formed from existing personnel now in regional and support offices, will work with SPR and the field to focus on strategic thinking at the bureau level and on the interagency resource management process recommended in this report.
- **Managing the Policy Process.** One of our central recommendations calls for the creation of a position resembling a chief of staff in the Office of the Secretary of State. The incumbent would be charged with managing the policy process, including State's participation in the NSC system and facilitating the interface between the secretary/deputy secretary and the institution. The executive secretary's position should be upgraded for this role.

ORGANIZING THE DEPARTMENT
FOR THE TWENTY-FIRST CENTURY

The reform of the policy process presented above is important. Alone, however, it is insufficient. We must also rationalize our organization by realigning it to meet changing priorities. There are key policy and management clusters that will define the focus of the Department through the end of the century and beyond:

- Economics and the environment
- Global issues and programs
- International security
- Regional and multilateral diplomacy
- Strategic management and program support

Such is the importance of these clusters that we believe each deserves the refocused attention of an under secretary who would have line authority over the bureaus in his/her complex. . . .

Economics and the Environment

The end of the Cold War has created a new standard for America's international performance. It is no longer military and ideological rivalry with the former Soviet Union, but, instead, economic clout and competitive muscle. Concern about America's economic renewal has moved front and center on the nation's agenda. The Department of State must reflect that change in its policies, its programs, and its personnel decisions.

No emphasis on economic growth can have enduring impact without regard to the environment. Sustainable development requires balance between environmentally sound use of resources and economically sensible use of environmental regulations. Protection of U.S. jobs and of the environment is not an either/or proposition. The U.S. can and should capitalize on what is already an estimated $300 billion annual market in green technology. Further, U.S. foreign policy increasingly reflects concern for the environment, whether in the greening of regional and global trade negotiations, in the growing environmental component in bilateral and multilateral aid, and in the interplay between energy policy and global warming.

For these reasons, we recommend that the current undersecretary for Economic and Agricultural Affairs be redesignated the undersecretary for Economic and Environmental Affairs (EE). It is important that he/she coordinate both general economic policy handled by the Bureau for Economic and Business Affairs (EBA) and issues covered by the Bureau for Oceans and International Environmental and Scientific Affairs (OES), such as the environment, science, and technology.

Outside the department, EE must bring State's unique integrative expertise to a revived NSC-based interagency process, which itself highlights economic and global issues. Inside, he/she must serve as the secretary's chief economic and environmental adviser, coordinator of the department's business promotion activities, and leader of State's new economic team approach, which includes both geographic bureaus and the two bureaus under EE's direct supervision: OES and EBA.

One of EE's top priorities must be support for U.S. business, both in the department and in the field. If competitiveness is at the heart of our economic security, State must be structured and staffed accordingly. Senior economic management in regional bureaus must be strengthened, a focal point established in EBA to work with business, and an aggressive outreach program created to promote an active partnership between State and the business community. EE should identify key trade opportunities in various countries and marshal interagency support for American success. We do not recommend integration of the Foreign Commercial Service (FCS) into State, but believe activities of the two agencies must be more closely coordinated.

For EE to operate successfully as State's primary action officer on international economic and environmental affairs, he/she will require strong staff support in the policy areas identified. . . .

Global Programs

In addition to State's traditional roles in policy formulation and coordination, we have responsibility for several major global programs which reflect the new agenda in foreign affairs—drugs, counterterrorism, refugees, and movement of peoples across national boundaries. The most recent additions to these important programs are the two task forces which coordinate U.S. government support for the transition to democratic, market-oriented systems in Eastern Europe and the former Soviet Union—i.e., what have come to be known as democracy programs.

These State-managed global programs today represent over 20 percent of the department's budget—not counting the democracy programs. Yet they have been dispersed throughout the organization, diffusing program management responsibility, and underplaying their importance to our interests.

We have not accorded these programs the sustained high-level attention required to coordinate their budget requests and present them most effectively on [Capitol] Hill. We need a senior leader at the undersecretary level who will concentrate on both the resource management dimensions of these programs and their policy coordination aspects.

We recommend the creation of an undersecretary for Global Programs (GP) who would supervise and coordinate:

- A new Bureau for Democracy, Human Rights and Labor Affairs (DRL). . . . The assistant secretary for DRL should be named as the president's worldwide coordinator for democracy programs. The ultimate goal is to disband the two task forces on Eastern Europe and on the former Soviet Union, with DRL assuming policy coordination and program direction of the elements relating to democracy programs. . . .
- A new Bureau for Narcotics, Terrorism and Crime Affairs which combines the Bureau of International Narcotics Matters, the Office of the Counter-Terrorism Coordinator, and a new unit that will coordinate policy on international criminal activities which pose an increasing challenge to the international order.
- The Bureaus of Consular and of Refugee Affairs . . . as presently constituted. GP's oversight of these two bureaus could facilitate a more coordinated and coherent policy for the increasingly important complex of issues arising from global trends in movement of people, including their implications for U.S. immigration, the asylum function, the treatment of refugees abroad, and the admission of refugees into the United States. . . .

International Security Affairs

For over forty years, our security paradigm was organized around the Soviet threat. With that threat ended, our task is to manage the transition from the Cold War alliance structure to a new international security system. Because this task is so central to our foreign policy agenda, we believe the undersecretary for International Security Affairs (IS) should shed peripheral duties and concentrate on proliferation and arms control issues and on elaborating the U.S. approach to a new collective security paradigm.

Our recommendations reflect these realities. The IS undersecretary should oversee two bureaus:

- A new bureau for Proliferation and Arms Control, to be formed from offices within the department and by integrating the Arms Control and Disarmament Agency (ACDA) into State. This streamlined bureau will significantly improve our ability to lead a diplomatic strategy to control the spread of weapons. . . .
- A Bureau of Security Policy and Operations, combining the residual functions of the Bureau for Political-Military Affairs, liaison with [the Department of Defense], and a new Office of Security Policy concentrating on new international security models, such as cooperative security.

The responsibilities of IS would not extend to a policy lead on specific regional crises or other major challenges to security. What we lack—and what IS can provide—is an integrated, strategic look at where the global security system is headed and what we want it to be. . . .

Regional and Multilateral Diplomacy

The role of the undersecretary for Political Affairs (P) as currently defined is simply overwhelming. He/she supervises the bulk of the line bureaus and operating offices both in Washington and abroad. These bureaus, themselves defined in bilateral and multilateral terms, send to P a bewildering array of issues, visitors, [congressional] testimony, NSC agendas, and most major crises. In addition, P supervises the Bureaus for Intelligence and Research, Human Rights and Humanitarian Affairs, and International Narcotic Matters.

We recommend a major shedding of responsibilities for this undersecretary, to be renamed the undersecretary for Regional and Multilateral Affairs (RM). . . . RM [should] focus on:

- Managing crises and bilateral issues.
- Bringing the Department of state fully into the increasingly important arena of multilateral diplomacy by expanding the scope of the Bureau of International Organization Affairs—transforming it into a Bureau of

Multilateral Affairs—with focus on reform of the UN system and on multilateral peacekeeping efforts.

- Mobilizing the regional bureaus and the Bureau of Multilateral Affairs, as well as the field missions, behind major foreign policy priorities.
- Supervising assistant secretaries in their new roles in the central resource allocation process recommended in this report.

This emphasis means more operational responsibilities should be given to assistant secretaries in order to free RM for more strategic thinking and managing.

As the new title implies, the undersecretary for Regional and Multilateral Affairs will lead the five regional bureaus and the Bureau of Multilateral Affairs and look for cross-cutting approaches to our key priorities.

- We must not only reduce vertical layering but also break down the horizontal barriers which impede the policy process as well as implementation of major decisions. Specifically, RM must make the geographic bureaus work together more effectively.
- Like other undersecretaries for their areas of responsibility, RM must also force the needed trade-offs among the geographic bureaus during the resource allocation process. . . .

Strategic Management

The undersecretary for Management Operations and Support (MO) must concentrate on leading a strategic management process which matches our way of doing business to the new operating environment. Budget constraints will force us to shift resources to support policy-related programs; we will also have to reallocate support funding from Washington to the field. More flexible support systems with a service orientation must be developed, and they must be based where they operate most effectively.

- The MO undersecretary should move quickly to change our support-to-operations ratio by decentralizing program support management toward the bureaus and overseas posts to the maximum degree possible. In parallel, the total proportion of our scarce resources devoted to domestic support activities must be drastically reduced. . . .
- MO should accelerate the department's transition to information age technology and methods of operations.
- MO should encourage experimentation with innovative management techniques on a pilot basis in selected departmental offices.
- MO should have a separate Management Planning Office, reporting directly to him/her, which would support the strategic planning and resource allocation process, including personnel planning, and help provide an overview of the three clusters in the MO area: human resources, financial planning and budget operations, and program support. [Management Planning Office's] chief function would be to act as an "agent for change."

- MO should develop a long-term strategy to match Foreign Service and Civil Service personnel needs to recruitment, promotion, assignment processes, and professional development, and increase the flexibility of the Civil Service system.

STARTING OVER?

If responding to dramatic change is the challenge, it is legitimate to ask if we have gone far enough in our recommendations. Some argue that we should throw out the whole current structure and start over, creating a mega-foreign ministry.

We have called for important steps in integrating policy formulation and resource allocation. While we consider other options, we believe it is time to merge ACDA into State. However, we do not believe the full integration of other foreign affairs agencies is warranted. State is primarily a policy agency. We do coordinate programs and overseas activities, but we leave the implementation, when possible, to other qualified agencies and nongovernmental organizations. In the case of AID [Agency for International Development] especially, fundamental rethinking of its role and objectives much precede any organizational decisions.

If, as a result of a major policy review, it is decided to integrate foreign assistance, or other foreign affairs functions for that matter, into the State Department, we believe the basic model we have proposed can accommodate such a proposal through back-to-back merger. The model is designed to maximize adaptability of the department to the needs and management style of the president and the secretary.

15. ORGANIZING TO TRADE

Bruce Stokes

At a time when exports often account for a substantial majority of annual U.S. economic growth and import competition threatens the survival of major sectors of the economy, like the auto industry, trade is an intrinsically political issue. Any administration, Republican or Democratic, will of necessity want to deal with trade matters at the highest political levels. The existing bureaucratic actors nominally charged with handling trade—the USTR [U.S. Trade Representative] and the Commerce Department—lack the requisite political clout. The traditional bureaucratic muscle men—the State Department, the Treasury Department, and the White House staff—inherently lack the expertise and, more important, the institutional staying power to deal with the country's increasingly complicated trade problems. The Clinton administration and the . . . Congress are likely to experience an even more acute mismatch between the country's trade policy needs and the mechanisms at hand to craft and implement that policy.

After declining for a number of years, the U.S. trade deficit is . . . on the rise and is expected to grow in the future. The global recession is curbing the world's appetite for American exports. At the same time, in 1991 Japanese industry invested—after adjusting for inflation—some $230 billion more in improving competitiveness than did U.S. manufacturers. A rising trade deficit will lead to a plethora of complaints about dumping and access to foreign markets coupled with new congressional demands for tough action against "unfair" foreigners. Those individual trade problems threaten to drive economic relations with other countries unless there is a coherent, overarching administration trade policy that addresses short-term difficulties, presents a convincing vision of how to improve the balance of trade, and provides a set of initiatives to realize that vision. A politically weak and institutionally fractured trade bureaucracy is unlikely to formulate and implement such a policy.

. . . President [Clinton] will also have to cope with the consequences of the Reagan and Bush administrations' policy of letting the dollar slide to spur exports. On a trade-weighted basis, the dollar has fallen around 40 percent since 1985, when the Reagan administration reversed its strong-dollar posture. Without a coordinated effort to use the breathing space bought by a weak dollar to prepare U.S. producers for more competitive times ahead, weakening the dollar is a quick but deceptive fix for more fundamental problems of competitiveness. Moreover, a devalued dollar complicates domestic economic policy in the long run by lowering the purchasing power of consumers who continue to buy imports, and thus increase inflationary pressures. Needed coordination of monetary, trade, and industrial policy between the Treasury Department, the USTR, and the Commerce Department has been sorely lacking in the past.

Finally, as trade becomes more central to the well-being of the economy, the Congress, which is more immediately accountable to the workers and communities affected by trade decisions, will inevitably demand a greater role in trade matters. That political impulse is likely to aggravate the growing competition between congressional committees for jurisdiction over trade-related issues and to further increase tensions along Pennsylvania Avenue. . . .

Unfortunately, the problems of crafting a coherent American trade policy are likely to worsen in the [Clinton] administration. Trade problems will be complicated by new forces: environmental concerns, conflicting regulatory regimes, and disparate tax policies. Demands that trade policy be used to help American business improve its international competitiveness will only grow.

The burgeoning complexity of trade-related concerns can best be managed by restructuring the bureaucracies—within both the executive and legislative branches—that formulate U.S. trade policy. Above all else, since trade is only one aspect of the country's international economic posture, an economic security council—modeled on the National Security Council and staffed by a small team of trade, currency, and industry experts—is vitally needed to coordinate international economic policy. In addition, to ensure that trade policy reinforces efforts to improve American competitiveness, a Department of International Trade and Industry (DITI) should be created, combining the functions of the USTR with the trade and industry activities currently housed in the Commerce Department and other agencies. Finally, to ensure greater coordination between Congress and the White House on trade matters, a Congressional Trade Office (CTO), comparable to the Congressional Budget Office, should be established. . . .

Trade reorganization is not a new idea. Piecemeal efforts have been proposed for more than a decade. Nor will redrawing the organizational charts be useful unless the president commits himself to elevating the importance accorded trade and international economic relations in administration decision making. But whatever a president's good intentions, policies, or personnel, an administration's priorities change. The purpose of bureaucratic reorganization is to improve continuity.

But restructuring is a necessary precondition for dealing with the increasingly integrated global economy. . . . The Clinton administration must bring the Uruguay Round to a conclusion and begin implementation of the North American Free Trade Agreement. Through the end of the decade the United

States will face growing competition from both Europe and Japan as well as the political problems stemming from a large trade surplus with the former and a yawning deficit with the latter. New challenges loom in structuring trade relations with Latin America, South and East Asia, and the former Soviet bloc. The [Clinton] administration and the . . . Congress lack the institutional wherewithal to meet the trade challenges of the coming years.

LEGACY OF THE EIGHTIES

The flaws in the current international economic policy apparatus have been apparent for quite some time. In the early 1980s, a strong dollar caused unprecedented trade deficits, rapid increases in the U.S. market share held by foreign auto and electronic producers, and mounting congressional pressure on the USTR to do something to stem the bleeding.

The Reagan administration passively accepted the dollar's rise because of its ideological belief that the "correct" value of the dollar was whatever the currency markets said it was. Moreover, the influx of foreign capital that kept the dollar high also helped the Treasury fund the mounting U.S. budget deficit. In any case, the USTR was too weak within the cabinet to force an effort to counter the ill effects of the strong dollar.

The trade problems engendered by the overvalued dollar built up and over time forced solutions that distorted and perverted trade policy. For example, the rising dollar was breaking the back of American steel makers, whose competitiveness problems dated back more than a decade. Facing a flood of imports, U.S. industry threatened dumping suits against European steel producers. To avoid disturbing relations with NATO partners at a delicate time, arch free-trader Ronald Reagan agreed to negotiate voluntary export restraints with major steel-producing countries. They lasted until 1992. Since the restraints were a political expediency, not part of a comprehensive vision for breathing new life into a basic industry, the adjustment process has been brutal: Several hundred thousand steelworkers have lost their jobs, and whole communities have been devastated. At present exchange rates, U.S. steel makers are now among the most cost-efficient in the world, but their competitiveness problems have not disappeared because of foreign subsidies and dumping. Now that the restraints have been lifted, dozens of dumping cases have been refiled.

Similar problems arose when the United States backed into managing trade for the beleaguered U.S. auto industry in the early 1980s. Rather than impose formal U.S. trade barriers, the Reagan administration convinced the Japanese to agree to voluntary export caps. The U.S. economy paid an enormous price. At the peak of their impact, the United States was paying $2.2 billion to Japan each year in the form of higher auto prices just for the privilege of having Japan withhold exports. Restricted in what they could ship to the United States, the Japanese shifted their product mix toward more-profitable large luxury cars and have gone on to capture a growing share of that lucrative market. Moreover, trade barriers accelerated Japanese automakers' plans to build cars in the United States. Managing auto trade in such an ad hoc fashion—letting the Japanese impose their own restraints, with no attempt to manage the composition of trade or the transfer of production—led to a U.S. automobile sector that is now more dominated by Japanese producers than was deemed possible in the early 1980s.

The pressure to manage trade in many sectors is bound to increase in the coming years. The resolution of the Uruguay Round—successful or not—is likely to open a Pandora's box of trade complaints that had been held in abeyance. Faced with an avalanche of charges of unfair foreign trade practices from U.S. manufacturers and, for the first time, from American service providers, the USTR will be tempted to do what it has always done: arrange interim market-sharing deals with foreign governments to avoid all-out trade wars.

Recent history suggests that some managed trade may be inevitable, even under the most free-market-oriented president. The challenge will be to manage trade to enhance competitiveness, not just to protect weak industries.

America's legacy of trade policy failure is complicated by the rapidly changing nature of the international economy and the many new issues that are emerging. Increasingly, trade policy is being called upon to ease the adverse consequences of trade—like pollution and income inequalities—as well as to ameliorate the adverse consequences of domestic policies—like competition policy and labor standards—that threaten to distort trade. Nowhere is the new challenge more apparent than with the politically charged issue of balancing environmental interests with the economic benefits of freer trade. Although U.S. trade officials are sensitive to the importance of the environment and can draw on the expertise of the Environmental Protection Agency, environmental concerns are still so far removed from the trade negotiators' world view that problems are inevitable.

For example, in negotiating food safety standards in the Uruguay Round, U.S. trade officials failed to assess whether any existing U.S. standards might be deemed protectionist under the American proposals. Purely by coincidence, the General Accounting Office was comparing U.S. and international food safety standards, but it did not understand the significance of its findings for the trade negotiations, and only by accident was its report brought to the USTR's attention.

Similarly, the USTR has consistently argued for a "sound science" basis for any trade barriers erected to achieve an ostensible environmental purpose, reflecting the U.S. experience with the European Community's ban on the importation of hormone-laden beef. The community had no scientific evidence to suggest that the beef was harmful to human health, and the USTR saw the ban as purely a protectionist measure designed to prop up European cattle raisers. But a "sound science" standard, which appeared reasonable to trade negotiators, could be troublesome. Fruits and vegetables with residue from the pesticide DDT have long been barred from U.S. grocery shelves, even though there is no definitive scientific evidence for their exclusion. Mexican farmers, soon to be part of a single North American market, still use DDT. Some environmentalists have worried that Mexican produce growers could successfully overturn the U.S. ban on DDT by appealing to "sound science" criteria. Undermining U.S. health and safety standards in the name of open markets would seriously weaken public support for free trade. In retrospect, the "sound science" doctrine could prove to be a serious political error made by trade officials insensitive to the broader ramifications of the issues with which they are now forced to deal.

The impact of environmental issues on trade policy is not the only new, complex issue that trade policymakers will be forced to wrestle with in the years ahead. The Commerce Department's . . . decision to impose dumping duties on imports of flat panel computer screens is an example of the costs of the current bureaucratic diffusion of trade responsibilities. The department's narrow focus has driven Apple and other U.S.-based notebook computer makers to shift their assembly operations offshore to avoid paying high duties on the screens. No one had overall responsibility for thinking through the long-term implications of the duties or for coming up with an alternative solution that might have nurtured a U.S. flat panel display industry and guaranteed U.S. computer makers access to competitively priced displays.

In 1963 the USTR was created as a lean, non-cabinet-level arm of the president; its main job beyond negotiating tariff reductions was to coordinate U.S. trade policy by acting as an honest broker between government agencies. Over the years, the USTR's role has changed as the importance of trade and international economic policy has increased. Its staff has grown to 155, the agency has achieved cabinet status, and it has become enmeshed in negotiations ranging from baseball bats to semiconductors.

The first U.S. trade representative was Christian Herter, a Republican, appointed by Democratic President John Kennedy as a symbol of the avowed bipartisan nature of U.S. trade policy. Since then the political clout of trade representatives has waxed and waned, reaching its height in the Carter administration when Robert Strauss, the former chairman of the Democratic National Committee, exercised wide influence. But recent USTRs—Clayton Yeutter and Carla Hills—have had less influence both within the executive branch and on Capitol Hill.

Rather than leading trade policy, a bureaucratically weak and directionless USTR has often been a victim of the political pressures around it. That reactive stance has often brought bad trade policy, and U.S. trade interests have suffered. The last major trade reorganization took place in 1979, after the completion of the Tokyo Round of multilateral trade talks. With that reorganization, jurisdiction over dumping and countervailing duty cases was transferred from the Treasury Department to the Commerce Department. An effort to merge the USTR and elements of the Commerce Department failed in the early 1980s, stifled by bureaucratic rivalries and turf fights.

The original mission of the USTR, coordinating disparate departmental policies, is still an important function. Implicit in that role, though, is a judgment that trade policy is a derivative of foreign policy or farm policy, not a co-equal. With the end of the Cold War, the emergence of the global market, and the growing importance of trade to the domestic economy, trade policy needs an equal advocate in the halls of government. Currently, the USTR is stretched too thin to deal with the complex of international commercial issues now facing the United States. Only five USTR officials focus on Japan full time even though Japan accounted for two-thirds of the U.S. trade deficit as of 1991. Similarly, five officials deal with international trade in services, one of the key negotiating points in the Uruguay Round. In theory, the USTR can call on the Commerce Department or other larger bureaucracies to provide staff backup on particular issues. That approach has led to endless wrangling over conflicting staffing needs. Moreover, staff sharing is only useful once a unified U.S. negotiating position on an issue has been determined. The lack of personnel has repeatedly crippled USTR in interagency disputes, where U.S. policy is first hammered out. In past trade problems with Europe and Japan where diplomatic and security concerns were involved, the State and Defense departments have often been able to outgun the USTR, burying trade officials in a blizzard of reports and tying them up in meetings until they relented.

AN EFFECTIVE TRADE OFFICE

The United States cannot have an effective trade policy separate from its agricultural policy or foreign policy. Balancing the country's various international needs and objectives, knitting them together into a coherent external economic policy, will require an Economic Security Council (ESC) within the White House. Its task will be to coordinate domestic and international economic policy much as the National Security Council (NSC) balances competing diplomatic and military concerns.

In the past, coordination has been conducted through various interagency groups that merely reflected the interests of the cabinet-level departments—including State, Treasury, Commerce, and the USTR—that they represented. There is no body comparable to the NSC—with a staff of 10–15 independent professionals—capable of doing better than the least-common-denominator policies that result from conflicting departments. An ESC would also be able to case a wide net within the executive branch, ensuring that many voices—the Environmental Protection Agency, the Federal Trade Commission, the National Aeronautics and Space Administration—are heard in the trade debate.

More important politically than the USTR, the ESC would be responsible for knocking heads among all the bureaucratic players—the State Department, the Pentagon, and others—forcing them to resolve their differences on international economic policy. The president would thus be spared from constantly refereeing interagency trade disputes, a role both Reagan and Bush increasingly had to play because of the USTR's weakness. Given that presidents usually lack a background in international economics, without an ESC they are likely to continue to make trade decisions that are politically expedient but economically flawed.

An economically minded arbiter with White House clout is now sorely missed. At the outset of the Uruguay Round, for example, the Treasury Department insisted on conducting separate negotiations on liberalizing financial services, arguing that banks and the securities industry are so important to the country's economic well-being that they should not be mere bargaining chips on the negotiating table. They won the fight not necessarily on the merits of their argument, but because of Treasury's traditional influence within the cabinet. An ESC could level the bureaucratic playing field, making sure that decisions were based on the best economic interests of the United States, not on the parochial interests of one cabinet-level department.

Beyond constituting a new ESC, the [Clinton] administration should set up a new Department of International Trade and Industry to coordinate government efforts to ensure that American industry takes every advantage of the foreign market openings negotiated by trade officials. DITI would include the USTR, the Commerce Department's International Trade Administration (with its country desk officers, product specialists, statistical analysts, and lawyers), the Export-Import Bank of the United States, the Overseas Private Investment Corporation, and the U.S. & Foreign Commercial Service, which is responsible for promoting exports. If politically feasible, the export promotion activities of the Department of Agriculture could also be included. In addition, DITI would be charged with coordinating the technology-related functions of the Commerce Department as well as the national research laboratories and a newly created advanced civilian technology agency to be the civilian equivalent of the Defense Advanced Research Projects Agency.

With that mixture of duties, DITI would be able to fashion trade policies that would complement government initiatives and improve American competitiveness. For example, if a DITI had existed in the 1980s, it could have brought the U.S. automobile industry and the unions together to design a comprehensive American auto policy. DITI could have auctioned automobile import quotas, so that the economic rents generated by the quotas accrued to the U.S. Treasury and not to the Japanese automakers. Import restraints could have been designed as a means of providing automakers with breathing room while, in close conjunction with their workers and their communities, they invested and restructured to improve their productivity and quality. DITI could have worked with the auto industry, providing some funding for research into new technologies and cutting through government red tape where necessary. DITI could also have acted as overseer, guaranteeing that environmental or antitrust laws were not trampled in the name of competitiveness. To help counter the cost of import restraints to consumers, DITI could have also required industry and labor to make sacrifices of their own, limiting wage demands, workplace rules, executive compensation, and investment options.

Of course, DITI will only prove useful if it reflects a new commitment to bring together trade- and industry-related policies. Fortunately, the old debates over industrial policy appear to have run their course. The Bush administration, through its support of precompetitive technologies, and Clinton, through his espousal of closer government–business partnerships, suggest that the country has finally gotten itself out of the ideological blind alley of laissez faire and that it is ready for Washington to take action to improve the international competitiveness of American business.

Finally, top DITI officials should be jointly appointed by Congress and the administration, much as the commissioners of the International Trade Commission have been selected during 12 years of divided government. Such an innovation would shelter the implementation of U.S. trade policy from the kind of ideological struggles waged between Democrats and Republicans in the 1980s and defuse the constitutional tug-of-war over trade between Congress and the White House.

In a different era it was deemed necessary to create the Foreign Service, an elite group of officials willing to devote their professional lives to statecraft. With the national well-being now as dependent on economic and trade matters as it is on traditional diplomacy, it is time to elevate the status of those who defend U.S. economic interests in the international marketplace. The "Trade Corps" would cut across agency lines, including all officials involved in trade work above a certain level, as long as they have a minimum, maybe two to three years, of experience dealing with trade matters. Most of the trade experts would work within DITI, creating a much-needed esprit de corps and sense of professionalism. Some of the Trade Corps should also be drawn from economics and commercial officers in the State Department, the Treasury Department, and elsewhere. Their membership would permit closer communication between departments and the development of common strategies on trade issues that transcend narrow departmental approaches.

During their careers, members of the Trade Corps would be expected to rotate through DITI (and outside it whenever feasible), spending time as industry experts before going overseas to promote exports and then returning to Washington as trade negotiators or administrators of trade law. To adequately train and maintain the skills of the trade warriors, a Trade Service Institute should be created, comparable to the Foreign Service Institute.

In recent years a growing number of trade policymaking jobs have been held by political appointees. The tenures of such officials average just more than three years, far too short a time to master the complexity of trade matters. For trade reorganization to work, [the Clinton] administration must commit itself to staff key positions with Trade Corps members. Trade Corps members will also incur obligations. In the past, a disturbing number of U.S. trade officials have left government service to work for the foreign and domestic interests that had lobbied them on trade issues. At times that trend has created a serious conflict of interest. Just as important, it has generated the impression among the public that those charged with defending the U.S. international economic well-being cannot always be trusted. In a free society, there is a limit to what controls can or should be placed on individuals' rights to sell their services. But the potential damage of a government trade negotiator crossing the table to advise the other side is so great that some restrictions are justified. For a set period, perhaps five years, Trade Corps members should be prohibited from advising any interests, domestic or foreign, on issues that directly or indirectly relate to work done during their government service.

CHANGING CONGRESS

Reorganizing the executive branch is a prerequisite for improving Washington's ability to deal with the trade issues of the coming decade. But unless the congressional approach is also radically restructured, [the Clinton] administration will be hamstrung, unable to adopt a new trade posture.

The United States is the only major industrial country where the ultimate authority over international commerce rests with a separate legislative branch, an authority Congress has exercised with increasing assertiveness in recent years. Frustrated with the Reagan and Bush administrations' inability to eliminate the trade deficit, Congress required the USTR to publish an annual report describing its efforts to reduce foreign trade barriers; Congress also mandated trade action against foreign countries under the Super 301 provision of the 1988 Trade and Competitiveness Act.

Washington pundits are quick to attribute congressional–White House tension over trade matters to partisan politics. The fact that Democrats controlled Congress while Republicans have been in the White House has obviously been a source of ongoing friction. Republican faith in market forces has often clashed with Democratic notions of government intervention. But 12 years of divided government cloud the lesson of the Carter administration, when Congress and the White House struggled mightily over such trade issues as domestic content for automobiles and the Tokyo Round of multilateral trade negotiations. Trade discord along Pennsylvania Avenue is not a partisan issue but a systemic, institutional problem.

The problem was already apparent during the crafting of the 1988 Trade Act. While the House Ways and Means Committee and the Senate Finance Committee had primary responsibility for the legislation, 23 different congressional committees were involved in the final drafting. The recent debate over renewal of fast-track trade negotiating authority—in which environmental and labor concerns dominated the discussion—only highlighted the manifold domestic economic complications attendant on America's growing integration into the global economy. A large number of senators and representatives claim those concerns as their own, meaning that future trade policy will not be the exclusive preserve of Capitol Hill's trade clique, with its close administration ties. . . .

. . . America can ill afford to continue shoe-horning trade problems into existing congressional committee jurisdictions simply to avoid bruising the egos of congressional barons. Yet, a frontal assault on the trade prerogatives of the powerful Senate Finance and House Ways and Means committees would be doomed to failure.

Moreover, separate House and Senate committees devoted solely to trade are not the answer. As in the executive branch, it makes little sense to lump together the international aspects of environmental problems, antitrust issues, and so many of the other future trade concerns in a single committee. Trade issues are increasingly tied to domestic concerns, and trying to separate the two in some arbitrary manner would only make for bad policy.

Increased coordination of trade-related legislation by the House and Senate leadership is the only way to overcome the Balkanization of trade policy created by existing congressional fiefdoms, while maximizing the expertise inherent in the existing committee structure. Moreover, the congressional leadership needs to take a more active role in trade issues to counterbalance the power of the Senate Finance and House Ways and Means Committees, which have often given short shrift to emerging trade-related issues. . . .

A Congressional Trade Office modeled on the Congressional Budget Office would help committees on Capitol Hill better assess administration actions on trade. An office of two dozen or so economists and both regional and product-specific experts could act as Congress's trade think tank, providing comprehensive analyses of everything from the effectiveness of U.S. negotiators in the Structural Impediments Initiative talks with Japan to rule-of-origin standards for autos and computers receiving duty-free treatment in the North American Free Trade Agreement. Most important, CTO representatives, as surrogates not just for one committee but for the congressional leadership, could sit in on trade negotiations, providing Congress with up-to-date progress reports. Involved in back-room discussions with U.S. trade negotiators when compromises must be made, they could advise the administration against concessions that Congress would not swallow, while implicitly committing Congress to deals deemed acceptable. . . .

The United States cannot pursue a coherent trade policy totally separate from its foreign policy, its monetary policy, its farm policy, or its environmental policy. But for too many years that reasoning has been used as an excuse by the State Department, the Treasury Department, and others to keep the trade policymaking apparatus weak.

. . . With the emergence of a global economy and its growing importance to the domestic economic well-being of the United States, an anemic USTR and a Congress that works at cross-purposes with the administration sabotage America's self-interest. Over the next few years, decisions on the regulation of imports, the promotion of exports, and the type of cooperation permitted among industries will help shape the future American economy and determine the types of jobs and incomes available to Americans.

Reorganizing trade—by constituting an economic security council, a department of international trade and industry, and a congressional trade office—will not ensure that those decisions will be the correct ones. But without a better means of coordinating and implementing America's international economic and commercial policy, Washington is likely to be more of a hindrance than a help.

16. BUSINESS AS USUAL: IRAN–CONTRA AND THE NATIONAL SECURITY STATE

John Canham-Clyne

Nearly six years after a Nicaraguan surface to air missile and a Lebanese newspaper began to unravel the covert operations known collectively as the Iran–contra affair, the official coverup [came] undone. Independent counsel Lawrence Walsh . . . believes that the highest levels of the Reagan administration were fully informed of virtually all aspects of the Iran arms sales and the illegal contra resupply operation, and that they conspired to cover them up when exposed. . . .

Beyond questions of criminal culpability, the Iran and contra affairs pose fundamental questions about the nature of American society and government. They challenge the notion that covert operations and institutional secrecy can be squared with a commitment to democratic accountability. The secret military relationships and relentless deceit that characterized the Iran and contra operations have become the norm of U.S. policy. But can a democracy abandon moral restraints on the means of foreign policy, even when in pursuit of moral ends, without mutilating its essence? Can a system of secrecy that obscures even the ends of policy from public scrutiny be reconciled with any but the most facile definition of democracy?

Covert operations and institutionalized secrecy provide a dense screen behind which senior officials create foreign policy. The numerous layers of deniability and officially sanctioned lying often make it difficult for U.S. citizens to apprehend even the barest outline of policies created in their names. This is certainly the case in the Persian Gulf.

Six years of investigations, millions of pages of documents, and two substantial wars later, the history of U.S. policy in the Persian Gulf during the past decade is barely known. Asked on the witness stand if he could characterize U.S policy toward Iran during the 1980s, Thomas Twetten, . . . then deputy chief of the Near East division, replied, "No, I don't think I could."

Note: All notes have been deleted.

The Iran–contra documentary record, when read with new reporting and the revelations of U.S. complicity in the Iraqi military buildup, suggests that during the 1980s the United States pursued a policy in the Persian Gulf completely at odds with its publicly stated and understood intent. This is not to say that an isolated, mistaken effort to ransom hostages in Lebanon worked at cross-purposes with a policy to squelch terrorism sponsored by Iran. Rather, it appears that the arms embargo on Iran, public rhetoric in opposition to terrorism, and professed neutrality in the Iran–Iraq war were at best of such a low priority that other considerations forced the administration into substantial arms relationships with both belligerents in the Iran–Iraq war. At worst, those policies were deliberate fabrications.

In Central America, official secrecy couldn't mask the well-known policy intentions of the administration. But it could constrict public debate. Congressman Lee Hamilton (D-IN) and Senator Daniel Patrick Moynihan (D-NY) both . . . revealed that they had information confirming that the Sandinistas complied with an agreement to cut off arms shipments to the rebels in El Salvador in the mid-1980s. The congressmen were prevented from decisively refuting administration claims to the contrary, however, because the information was classified.

[Former Secretary of Defense] Caspar Weinberger's personal notes, rescued from their haven at the Library of Congress, . . . offer strong evidence that a series of cabinet-level meetings were held as the scandal unfolded in November 1986 to coordinate an official story, not to pool fragmentary information. That official story included denial of U.S. participation in a November 1985 shipment of HAWK antiaircraft missiles to Iran. The administration knew this shipment was illegal and feared congressional reaction. Weinberger's notes show former Attorney General Edwin Meese saying in a November 24, 1986, meeting that Reagan had no prior knowledge of the shipment, when several of the men in the room knew that to be false.

In addition to incriminating their author, Weinberger's notes also completely undermine the official story of the scandal. Even now, most people understand the affair as the work of a few zealots who, under the nose of an inattentive president, usurped foreign policy from the normal, and presumably wiser and more law-abiding, national security policymakers. Senator George Mitchell (D) and Senator William Cohen (R) of Maine collaborated on a book whose title, *Men of Zeal,* succinctly summarizes the bipartisan story told to the nation by the 1987 congressional inquiry.

Even so astute an observer as Theodore Draper missed the story. In his 1991 book, *A Very Thin Line: The Iran-Contra Affairs,* Draper wrote:

> The questions that arise most forcefully from a study of the Iran and contra affairs are: How could a handful of little known officials take virtually complete control of policy in areas of major concern? How could they operate in total disregard of Congress, outside the purview of the two departments most concerned, State and Defense, and indeed of almost the entire structure of government?

The answer is simple—they didn't. The Weinberger notes and diaries are only the latest confirmation. The evidence of broad institutional participation on both sides of the hyphen has been there all along. Congress and the mainstream press helped perpetuate the cover story by focusing obsessively on the diversion of Iran arms sales profits to the contras. The press failed to grasp the story largely because they used the wrong metaphor. Substitute Poe's purloined letter for Watergate's smoking gun and much of the mystery surrounding Iran–contra evaporates. Members of Congress and reporters who hoped for a single document that proved Reagan's knowledge of the diversion missed the thousands of pages of documents that, when assembled, paint a picture of routine lawlessness and contempt for democracy that permeated the national security bureaucracy from the Oval Office down.

The contra war was not conceived by staff officers. It was developed by the members of the National Security Council (Reagan, Bush, Meese, Weinberger, Secretary of State George Shultz, CIA Director William Casey, and White House Chief of Staff Donald Regan), coordinated through the entire foreign policy bureaucracy, and systematically hidden from the American people. When Congress attempted to limit the executive's ability to prosecute the war, the administration simply began treating the legislature as an adjunct of the enemy.

The impetus for the Iran arms sales does appear to have come from the national security adviser and his staff, with a big boost from the Israelis. State, Defense, and CIA, however, were never bypassed. Shultz and Weinberger were informed each step of the way. And once their policy objections were overruled, their departments offered invaluable assistance to the arms sales, including an apparently illegal replenishment of HAWK missiles to Israel. The CIA provided most of the logistics for the arms shipments, including the illegal 1985 shipments, a fact about which nearly a dozen CIA officers lied to Congress.

Far from aberrations or renegade operations, these are case studies of the functioning of a national security system that has displaced the constitutional republic. They expose the two profound crises facing American government and society as it heads into the twenty-first century. First, institutionalized secrecy has eviscerated checks on executive power in foreign affairs and has helped remake the nation's foreign policy in the mold of empires past, from Rome to the Soviet Union. Second, these operations reveal a fundamental moral corruption in Washington's bureaucratic culture. Throughout the Iran arms sales and the contra war, dozens of national security officials followed orders, eagerly weaseled their way around the law, and lied when caught. Perhaps their actions reflect a public willingness to allow a patriotism defined in rigid military terms to supersede all other values, perhaps they conscientiously shared Fawn Hall's belief that civil servants can serve a "higher cause" than fealty to the constitution, but whatever the cause, the spirit of Nuremberg appears to be draining from Washington.

QUID PRO QUO AS POLICY

At former National Security Council (NSC) staff member Oliver L. North's 1989 trial, attorney Brendan Sullivan defended his client by entering into evidence a series of documents showing that North was acting at the direction of his superiors. Included among them were the so-called quid pro quo documents. As part of the illegal efforts to muster third-country support for the contras, the Reagan administration conspired to offer Central American governments extra, and sometimes expedited, foreign aid in return for continued assistance to the contras. Such exchanges were explicitly barred under U.S. law, but that didn't stop the Reagan gang. The quid pro quo document trail paints a vivid portrait of an administration that routinely considered the Congress and the American people the targets of covert action and a national security bureaucracy willing to carry out unquestioningly illegal orders behind a shield of secrecy.

The quid pro quo plan for Honduras originated on February 7, 1985, in the Crisis Pre-Planning Group (CPPG), an assistant-secretary-level interagency coordinating committee. The United States claimed it had intelligence showing that the Nicaraguan army was massing for a cross-border attack against contra camps in Honduras (even years after the fact, it is difficult to separate real "intelligence" from exaggeration and disinformation when it comes to Nicaragua). On February 6, North proposed that Reagan cable a message to Honduran President Roberto Suazo Cordova reaffirming administration support for the contras because Suazo was threatening to expel the contras from their camps.

On the 7th, the CPPG decided to sweeten the pot for Suazo. In addition to the message of support, CPPG members recommended to their bosses that they speed up delivery of $80 million in Economic Support Fund (ESF) assistance to Honduras. This despite the fact that ESF aid to Honduras had been placed on hold pending economic reforms required under U.S. law. They also agreed to speed up delivery of $23.5 million in military aid and provide an additional $4.5 million worth of CIA support to Honduran intelligence. Ambassador John Negroponte would inform President Suazo of the U.S. plan.

Each bureaucracy had a role: Defense would expedite weapons deliveries; State would deliver the message to Suazo and free up the ESF funds; CIA would give the Hondurans intelligence; and the White House would coordinate among the agencies and, perhaps, send a "discreet emissary" to Suazo to reinforce Ambassador Negroponte's original message.

The documents trace the decision-making process back up from the CPPG to the senior officials in charge of U.S. foreign policy. Assistant Secretary of Defense for International Security Affairs Richard Armitage dutifully reported to Weinberger, who signed off on the plan. Langhorne "Tony" Motley, then assistant secretary of state for Inter-American Affairs, reported the deal to his boss, Secretary of State Shultz, who also signed off on it. North brought it back to the White House and National Security Adviser Robert C. McFarlane. President Ronald Reagan topped it off, affixing his "RR" to a February 19, 1985, memo from McFarlane recommending the operation.

The initiative was delayed briefly by a bureaucratic spat that illuminates the etiquette of secret policymaking. Secretary of State Shultz, praised for his integrity during the 1987 congressional Iran–contra hearings, found himself in a tough bureaucratic position. Ambassador Negroponte had been nominated for an assistant secretary of state post and would shortly face Senate confirmation hearings. Shultz wanted Negroponte to be able to answer truthfully that no quid pro quo offers were ever made to the Hondurans. At the same time, the secretary of state worried that sending a discreet NSC emissary would diminish the ambassador's prestige in the eyes of the Honduran government. State made the argument that there was no need to ever make the "conditionality" of the enhanced aid explicit. The Hondurans, State reasoned, would get the message. Shultz seems to have been a little wiser than his colleagues about the dangers of talking about violating the law, but was no less eager to do it.

When the story of the quid pro quo broke in early 1989, most press attention focused on the question of whether Bush, during a March 1985 stopover in Honduras, acted as the "discreet emissary." At the North trial, the government admitted that Bush told Suazo that Reagan had ordered the extra military aid and expedited economic assistance. Never one to stop at a small lie, Bush declared categorically, "There was no quid pro quo."

The furor over Bush's alleged role and subsequent lie obscured the larger picture. The quid pro quo was integral to the successful circumvention of Boland Amendment restrictions on aid to the contras. Indeed, the February 6 memo from North to McFarlane describes in detail how shipments of arms were moving through Guatemala, El Salvador, and Honduras. The careful coordination of the operation suggests that senior policymakers certainly did know about the network of supposedly private individuals who supported the contras with funding from U.S. allies.

Similarly, it is now clear that all the relevant cabinet officials were aware of the Iran arms sales, including the illegal 1985 HAWK shipment, and that several lied about it to Congress. Weinberger, for example, not only knew about the November 24 HAWK shipment in advance, but checked on the prices and availability of Department of Defense (DOD) missiles to replenish Israeli stocks and reported his findings to National Security Adviser McFarlane on November 20. Yet, he denied prior knowledge of the shipment in testimony before the congressional Iran–contra committees. Virtually everything originally presumed to be scandalous about the affair appears in retrospect to be secret government business as usual. The active role of the NSC staff, the use of private citizens as surrogates for the U.S. government, and the "withholding" of information from Congress proved to be attractive red herrings for the press and convenient distractions for Congress. But little in either the Iran arms sales, the contra resupply operation, or even the diversion appears to be new.

THE NSC GOES OPERATIONAL

Within Washington, much horror was expressed that the NSC staff had "gone operational." The Tower Commission recommendations focused on returning the NSC staff to its "traditional" policy-coordinating role and leaving the skulduggery to the experts. Sprinkled liberally throughout the Iran–contra committees' depositions of CIA officers are sneering references to the amateurishness of Oliver North and his band of privateers. The CIA consistently referred to the arms deals as the "NSC Iran Initiative," so as to distance the agency from the fiasco. . . .

The NSC staff's operational role in the contra war and the Iran initiative was not a shocking exception to the normal functioning of national security policy. Rather, it was the logical result of the hostility of covert operations to democratic accountability. In *The National Security Constitution: Sharing Power After the Iran–Contra Affair,* Yale law professor Harold Hongju Koh observes that the executive branch naturally moves into "statutory lacunae" to avoid checks on its conduct of foreign affairs. Professor Koh's phrase captures perfectly the executive's penchant for creating secret institutions to hide policy. Indeed, the authority for the conduct of covert operations is the "mother" of all statutory lacunae, a vague reference in the National Security Act of 1947 to the agency's right to perform "such other functions and duties related to intelligence as the National Security Council may from time to time direct."

The history of covert operations is fraught with examples of small mysterious institutions being created, particularly within the Pentagon. DOD and State provide cover to CIA officers as a matter of course, but as Steven Emerson details in *Secret Warriors,* the Pentagon refuses to leave secret operations to Langley. During the 1980s, a host of more or less secret units within the military carried out covert operations around the globe. Delta Force and other quick reaction teams were created during the 1980s with a great deal of public fanfare. Others, like the Yellow Fruit Program and the Intelligence Support Activity, were bred in the dark and operated with virtually no accountability whatsoever.

When Congress sought to constrain support to the contras, it focused attention on the CIA and the Pentagon. So the administration naturally shifted the operations to people and institutions nominally outside the scope of the oversight committees, but not very far outside.

An operational role, complained the congressional Iran–contra report, "was a dangerous misuse of the NSC staff." Yet, the NSC staff itself has a history of usurping the operational functions of other departments. Draper quotes former National Security Adviser McGeorge Bundy to the effect that the Kennedy administration "deliberately rubbed out the distinction between planning and operation," and as a result, the NSC staff "went operational." A decade later, in a clear usurpation of the State Department's operational role, Henry Kissinger, then national security adviser, conducted the secret Vietnam peace negotiations out of the White House, complete with routine clandestine weekend trips from Washington to Paris by NSC staff members. He also planned and executed the secret opening to China without the knowledge of Secretary of State William Rogers. . . .

PRIVATE CITIZENS AND THE COMPANY

The Iran and contra operations were characterized by heavy dependence on private contractors and companies under the secret control of the U.S. government. In the wake of the scandal, the congressional intelligence committees targeted the privatization of foreign policy for reform, however tepid. In the vetoed 1990 Intelligence Authorization Act, Congress attempted to require the president to include any "anticipated" use of private citizens and third parties in covert action findings.

The meek response reflects the hypocrisy of congressional outrage. Every member of the investigating committees knew that the use of private citizens and companies in covert operations has a long, proud, secret history. The CIA and the Department of Defense have for decades maintained a web of "private" companies to run operations around the world. "Proprietaries" appear to be normal firms, accepting business through the front door and CIA instructions through the back. "Notionals" are paper front companies that do no real business, but provide cover for moving funds and people around the world. In addition, many large legitimate firms also conduct business with U.S. intelligence on a normal, albeit secret, contract basis.

The system operates with no accountability. In order to preserve secrecy, intelligence contracts are let out on a noncompetitive basis. The CIA, National Security Agency, and Defense Intelligence Agency are exempt from the requirement to publish requests for proposals and notice of successful bids in the *Commerce Business Daily.*

Even the diversion of profits from the arms sales to the contras appears now to be more common tradecraft than originally presumed. One of the key claims of [former CIA Deputy Director for Operations, who was tried for lying and obstruction] Clair George's defense was that Alan Fiers, who headed the Central American Task Force under George, cut him out of the loop on Central America. Fiers, George claimed, had regular access to Casey, and the two cooked up all sorts of wild schemes. Under questioning by George's attorney, Fiers admitted to his own little diversion. Attorney Richard Hibey asked Fiers about "a nonlethal covert action program against the Sandinista regime in Nicaragua, having nothing to do with the *contras.*" It has been widely reported that under this program, the CIA had been giving money to the Roman Catholic Church in Nicaragua, headed by Cardinal Miguel Obando y Bravo. The House Appropriations Committee explicitly ordered the funding cut off in the fiscal year 1986 intelligence appropriations bill. Fiers admitted that he and Casey decided to defy the ban. Fiers instructed an agency contractor to overcharge for its services and slip the excess to Cardinal Obando y Bravo.

Apparently this is a routine exercise. When Hibey said Fiers "created" the funding mechanism, the former spy pointedly corrected him: "I did not create a mechanism. There was a mechanism." Journalist David Corn recounts in *The Nation* on August 31/September 7, 1992, that

> several years ago David Duncan, a Miami arms dealer, told me that it was not uncommon for the CIA and other intelligence services to ask weapons traders to overcharge and then direct kickbacks to some favored cause. Because black market arms prices fluctuate widely—who's to say what a cache of captured Soviet rifles should go for?—auditors have a hard time catching the impropriety.

North's wasn't even the only Iran-related diversion in the 1985–1986 period. In the *Sunday Times* of India and the *Far Eastern Economic Review,* Lawrence Lifschultz described how Israel and the United States used Pakistan as a back door for arms shipments to Iran from 1984 to 1986. One Pakistani intelligence officer said he was aware that "crores [tens of millions] of dollars worth of weapons were shipped to Iran from [Pakistan]" between 1984 and 1986, under cover of the massive flow of arms through Pakistan to the Afghan mujaheddin. These same sources claim that Israeli intelligence officers assisted the CIA in training the mujaheddin and diverting weapons to Iran.

This information was confirmed for Lifschultz by a former Israeli intelligence officer named Ari Ben-Menashe. Ben-Menashe claimed personal knowledge of a one-time diversion to Iran of $300 million worth of CIA material intended for the mujaheddin.

Ben-Menashe's allegations of the magnitude of the diversion square with complaints from mujaheddin supporters that only a small fraction of the weapons intended for the rebels actually reached their destination. Andrew Eiva, chairman of the Federation for American Afghan Action (FAAA), calculated that only 30 percent of appropriated assistance was reaching the rebels in 1986. When former congressman William Gray (D-PA) asked the General Accounting Office to perform an independent audit, the CIA stonewalled. Whether Ben-Menashe's claims about the size of a diversion are true or not, it is clear that a substantial amount of weapons flowed through Pakistan to Iran in the mid-1980s. . . .

INSTITUTIONAL SECRECY AND CONGRESSIONAL COMPLICITY

U.S. policymakers are free to tell the public one thing and do another because they can rely on a massive secret bureaucracy to do their bidding. In the area of foreign affairs, the national security state has for the most part replaced constitutional checks and balances and public accountability. Loyalty to the system of classification and secret policy pervades all levels of the U.S. government. Although the executive often considers Congress an enemy and uses its considerable resources to evade congressional restrictions on policy, the legislature is no enemy of the national security state. On occasion, substantial congressional opposition will make it more difficult to carry out a specific policy, as in the contra war. For the most part, however, Congress has been coopted by the doctrine of bipartisanship and the glamour of being privy to the world's most sophisticated secrets. . . .

Until the demise of the Soviet Union, U.S. policymakers and bureaucrats could justify a system based on secrecy, denial, and deceit by a presumed immediate threat. That rationale, barely plausible then, now no longer exists, but the habits of empire endure. The urgent sense of special mission that attended the end of World War II and the establishment of the Cold War has evolved, naturally, into a spirit of entitlement and the arrogant assumption of superior knowledge. This spirit has bred among national security bureaucrats a sense that loyalty to institutions and policies goes beyond fealty to constitutional restraint. This attitude, in combination with billions of dollars, official permission to use any method in pursuit of policy, and a culture demanding unquestioning obedience to orders and compartmentalized secrecy, poses a fundamental threat to liberty and limited government. . . .

Former Director of Central Intelligence Richard Helms has been quoted as saying that citizens must understand the agency's need for secrecy and that "the nation must take it to a degree of faith that we too are honorable men devoted to her service." This is a profound and dangerous inversion of constitutional principle. No nation can rely on the goodwill of its bureaucrats as the primary bulwark against military and intelligence incursions on liberty. Bureaucracies will coopt even decent people, especially when the institutions operate through military discipline.

Any nation, even a democracy, will have military secrets it must protect. However, by mistaking ends and means, and sanctioning secret global war, Americans are in danger of losing political liberty. We are perilously close to throwing away the principles of open government and democratic accountability upon which the republic was founded. The end of the Soviet empire will not by itself cause the monster we have unleashed to retreat to its cage.

Already, the system is in search of new missions. Calls for continued increases in military participation in the war on drugs, stepped-up efforts to combat "international terrorism," and aggressive pursuit of "economic intelligence" can be heard from every point on the political spectrum. Several of these received early expression in the Iran and contra operations. With a little faith, the Iran operation can be viewed as a counterterror operation, albeit one whose appeasement strategy differed radically from the tough public talk of the administration. North came to it by way of his responsibilities for counterterrorism at the NSC, as did Charles Allen, the CIA analyst who became Iranian-born arms dealer Manuchehr Ghorbanifar's de facto case officer. By the same token, Reagan administration propagandists labored hard to tar Sandinista Nicaragua as a sponsor of international terrorism and drug trafficking.

It will take decades, if it is possible at all, to change the attitudes bred over years of heightened U.S. militarism. Politicians of both parties seem to lack even the language for genuine change. . . .

[Early in 1991], the Twentieth Century Fund, a liberal nonprofit research foundation, gathered more than a dozen former foreign and intelligence policymakers, most of them Democrats, to examine the prospects for covert action in the future. The committee majority concluded that "the world remains a dangerous place" and cited "terrorism, narcotics, nuclear proliferation, regional hostilities and persistent violations of human rights" as threats requiring future covert action. Former State Department spokesman Hodding Carter III noted that his fellow task force members almost "instinctively" reverted to the cliched defense of covert action.

Carter filed a blistering dissent to the report:

Given the inherent contradiction—not "tension"—between the nation's political principles and covert action, the majority report is an impressive achievement. It almost manages the alchemist's legendary accomplishment of turning lead into gold. Ultimately, however, the report's persuasive skills serve primarily to gild the immutable, leaden fact that covert action, as practiced in the past and envisioned for the future, cannot be squared with our precepts or justified by our needs.

The task force attempted to draw up a balance sheet for the efficacy of U.S. covert operations over the last 40 years. Among the successes, they counted operations that can only be described as virulently hostile to international law and the spirit of democracy, including the deposing of democratically elected President Jacobo Arbenz in Guatemala in 1954. Even granting the successes as such, the rationale for covert operations presented by the task force amounts to imperial privilege: "Covert action may be the appropriate choice when the American people do not want a foreign policy setback (such as the establishment of communist rule in Mozambique, Angola, or Afghanistan) but neither do they want another Vietnam."

A democracy, if truly threatened, should not be ashamed to declare its intention to shed the blood of its enemies openly. The resort to deadly force is the most sacred responsibility of legitimate statecraft, the most audacious presumption of tyranny. The war power of the state ought to be the most jealously guarded authority granted by the governed to the governing. Yet, the unchecked expansion of the secret intelligence system has made informed debate and public consent impossible in precisely the area of political life where it is most necessary. Covert action, by eviscerating the constitutional grant of war-making authority to the Congress, has permitted the United States to plunge smaller nations into war and deny all responsibility.

Covert action is incompatible with democracy and should be outlawed. Failing that, it should be restricted. . . .

Congress should pass legislation dramatically circumscribing the executive's ability to classify information. The legislation should adopt a high threshold for secrecy. The government should dispense with the various layers of classification and restrict authority for classifying information to the cabinet level. . . .

In addition, the nation's secret organizations should be exposed to more sunlight. The current secret appropriations process is flagrantly unconstitutional, and publishing a single top of the line figure will hardly remedy the situation. The Pentagon's recent decision to reveal the name of the National Reconnaissance Office (NRO) is an encouraging, if very timid, first step. The NRO manages satellites for the intelligence community and, at $5 to 6 billion a year, reportedly has the largest budget of any single intelligence agency. Typically, however, DOD managed to "reveal" the NRO's existence without using the word "satellite." There is no reason that the technical collection agencies cannot all be named, publish their budgets, describe and defend their programs in an open appropriations process, and still have necessary secrets kept. Article 1, Section 9 of the Constitution commands it. Iran–contra was no mere aberration, no failure of character. The violence at the heart of policy and the tyranny implicit in its deceitful means are typical of the national security state. That state will continue to bump into the principles of democratic accountability, open debate, and self-government, and that collision will continue to produce periodic, apparently ineffable, scandal.

Americans should not be fooled by the notion that the Iran–contra affair was the result of excessive zeal on the part of a few ideologically driven officers. The true lessons of U.S. policy toward Iran and Nicaragua during the 1980s have to do with ancient political wisdom. Nearly a half-century of obsession with communism and well-armed patriotism have led us to forget that regardless of the decency of the individuals in uniform, tyranny lurks in the dark corners of military secrecy, and that power unchecked will corrupt. Once forgotten, these lessons are learned anew only at excruciating cost.

Part III: DECISION MAKERS AND THEIR POLICYMAKING POSITIONS

*F*oreign policy choices are often made by a remarkably small number of individuals, most conspicuous of whom is the president. As Harry S Truman exclaimed, "I make American foreign policy."

Because of the president's power and preeminence, it is tempting to think of foreign policy as determined exclusively by presidential preferences and to personalize government by identifying a policy with its proponents. "There is properly no history, only biography" is how Ralph Waldo Emerson dramatized the view that individual leaders are the makers and movers of history. This *hero-in-history* model finds expression in the practice of attaching the names of presidents to the policies they promulgate (for example, the Truman Doctrine, the Kennedy Round, Clintonomics), as if the men were synonymous with the nation itself, and of routinely attributing foreign policy successes and failures to the administration in which they occur.

The conviction that the individual who holds office makes a difference is one of the major premises underlying the electoral process. Each new administration seeks to distinguish itself from its predecessor and to highlight policy departures as it seeks to convey the impression that it has engineered a new (and better) order. Hence leadership and policy are portrayed as synonymous, and changes in policy and policy direction are often perceived as the result of the predispositions of the leadership.

Clearly leaders' individual attributes exert a potentially powerful influence on American foreign policy, and no account of its sources would be complete without a discussion of them. It would be misleading and simplistic, however, to ascribe too much influence to the individuals responsible for the conduct of American foreign policy or to assume that influence is the same for all leaders in all circumstances. That individuals make a different is unassailable, but it is more useful to ask (1) under what circumstances will the idiosyncratic qualities of leaders exert their greatest impact; (2) what types of institutional structures and management strategies are different leaders likely to follow; and (3) what policy variations are most likely to result from different types of leaders. These questions force us to examine how individual characteristics find expression in foreign policy outcomes and how policymaking roles leaders occupy may circumscribe their individual influence.

When we consider the mediating impact of policymakers' roles, we draw attention to the fact that many different people, widely dispersed throughout the government, contribute to the making of American foreign policy. In Part II we examined some of the departments and agencies of government involved in the process. Here, in Part III, the concern is with decision makers and how the roles embedded in the foreign affairs government influence the behavior of the policymakers occupying them and, ultimately, American foreign policy itself. As a rival hypothesis to the hero-in-history image of political leadership, *role theory* posits that the positions and the processes, rather than the characteristics of the people who decide, shape the behavior and choices of those responsible for making and executing the nation's foreign policy. Furthermore, changes in policy presumably result from changes in role conceptions, rather than from changes in the individuals who occupy these roles.

Role theory and related perspectives help to answer a fundamental question: How do policymakers make foreign policy choices? The conventional view maintains that policymakers—notably the president and his principal advisers—devise strategies and implement plans to realize goals "rationally," that is, in terms of calculations about national interests defined by the relative costs and benefits associated with alternative goals and means. Many scholars have questioned the accuracy of this popular model, however. Much of the evidence drawn from case studies points in another direction: toward pressures toward conformity around policy alternatives that may be less than optimal and bargaining among competing actors within the foreign affairs government dictated by organizational preferences rather than national interests. In particular, the "bureaucratic-politics model" of decision making stresses the importance of the roles individuals occupy in large-scale organizations and the struggles that occur among their constituent units. Proponents of the model claim it captures the essence of the highly politicized foreign policy decision-making process more accurately than does the model of rational behavior, which assumes that the government operates as a single, unitary actor.

Graham Allison's book *Essence of Decision,* a study of the 1962 Cuban missile crisis, is the best-known effort to articulate and apply the bureaucratic politics model. There are two elements to the perspective. One, which Allison calls *organizational process,* reflects the constraints that organizations place on decision-makers' choices. The other, which he calls *governmental politics,* draws attention to the "pulling and hauling" that occurs among the key participants in the decision process.[1]

How, from the perspective of organizational processes, do large-scale bureaucracies affect policymaking? One way is by devising *standard operation procedures* (SOPs) for coping with policy problems when they arise. For example, Operation Desert Shield, initiated by President Bush in August 1990 to protect Saudi Arabia from Iraqi aggression, was a product of Pentagon plans devised earlier to deal with a possible Soviet or Iranian encroachment in the Middle East. Curiously, routines or SOPs for coping with emergent problems effectively limit the range of viable policy choices from which policymakers might select options. That is, rather than expanding the number of policy alternatives in a manner consistent with the logic of rational decision making, what organizations can and cannot do shapes what is possible and what is not.

Governmental politics, the second element in the bureaucratic politics model as articulated by Allison, draws attention to the way individuals act in organizational settings. Not surprisingly, and as role theory predicts, the many participants in the deliberations that lead to foreign policy choices often define issues and favor policy alternatives that reflect their organizational affiliations. "Where you stand depends on where you sit" is a favorite aphorism reflecting these bureaucratic (role) imperatives. Furthermore, because the players in the game of governmental politics are responsible for protecting the nation's security, they are "obliged to fight for what they are convinced is right."[2] The consequence is that "different groups pulling in different directions produce a result, or better a resultant—a mixture of conflicting preferences and unequal power of various individuals—distinct from what any person or group intended."[3] Thus, one explanation of why nations make the choices they do lies not in their behavior vis-à-vis one another but within their own governments. And rather than presupposing the existence of a unitary actor, "it is necessary to identify the games and players, to display the coalitions, bargains, and compromises, and to convey some feel for the confusion."[4]

DECISION MAKERS AND POLICYMAKER ROLES AS INFLUENCES ON AMERICAN FOREIGN POLICY

In virtually every situation in which the United States has contemplated the use of force over the past decade or more—in Grenada, Lebanon, Nicaragua, Panama, the Persian Gulf, Somalia, and Bosnia—policymakers and critics alike have worried about the specter of Vietnam and the "lessons" it provides. In part this is because the protracted series of decisions that took the United States into Vietnam and, eventually, after years of fighting and the loss of tens of thousands of lives, out of it on unsatisfactory terms, is fertile ground for probing how American foreign policy is made and implemented.

Part III of *The Domestic Sources of American Foreign Policy* begins with an account informed by role theory and bureaucratic politics of how the United States became involved in and conducted the prolonged war in Vietnam. "How Could Vietnam Happen?" asks James C. Thomson, Jr., almost rhetorically. The failure of Vietnam, Thomson contends, was the failure of America's policymaking process, not of its leadership. Vietnam shows that some of the most catastrophic of America's foreign policy initiatives are the result not of evil or stupid people, but of misdirected behaviors encouraged by the nature of the policymaking system and the roles and bureaucratic processes embedded in the way the government organizes itself for the making of foreign policy. Thomson's argument, however disturbing, provides insight into the milieu of decision making and identifies many syndromes crucial to understanding how the roles created by the decision-making setting influence the kinds of decisions that leaders make and that bureaucracies implement.

Mark M. Lowenthal shows that many of the determinants of behavior characteristic of Vietnam decision making are still very much alive. He examines the relationship between leaders and "careerists" as it relates to the production and consumption of intelligence, that is, the information presumed to be necessary for rational decision making. Noting that "there has been much soul-searching in the executive and Congress concerning the organization and role of the intelligence community" in the post–Cold War world, Lowenthal worries that too little attention has been given to fundamental questions about the relationship between the producers and consumers of intelligence. "A major problem is that the consumer–producer relationship resembles that of two closely related tribes that believe, mistakenly, that they speak the same language and work in the same manner for agreed outcomes. Reality . . . suggests something wholly different. Indeed, one is often reminded of George Bernard Shaw's quip about Britons and Americans being divided by a common language."

Lowenthal's insights about the intelligence process illustrate well the notion that the reasons for the choices nations make often lie not in their behavior vis-à-vis one another but within their own governments. He explains why the assumptions of intelligence consumers (policymakers) and producers (bureaucrats) often differ, why political leaders sometimes (often?) ignore the intelligence they receive, how (and why) intelligence consumers shape the information they get, and how (and why) intelligence producers shape what they give. In the end, Lowenthal concludes, "the production and use or disuse of intelligence as part of the policy process is the net result of several types of mind-sets and behavior within and between two groups that are more disparate than most observers realize."

Lowenthal's analysis is particularly useful in showing how policymaking roles shape the behavior of individuals who occupy them. Christopher M. Jones's "American Prewar Technology Sales to Iraq: A Bureaucratic Politics Explanation," which draws explicitly on Allison's earlier work, takes Lowenthal's perspective a step further and shows how bureaucratic organizations' missions and "essence" predict the policy stands they will take vis-à-vis one another on a particular issue. The case he examines is, like Vietnam, a troubling one. It deals with the sale of high-technology goods to Iraq in the period between 1984 and Iraq's invasion of Kuwait in 1990. Thus "American companies, with the consent of the federal government, played a significant role in enhancing the capability of Saddam Hussein's military machine, which the United States and its allies later had to oust from Kuwait." Furthermore, "American technology aided Iraq's unconventional weapons programs, thereby violating the long-standing U.S. goal of preventing the proliferation of weapons of mass destruction to Third World states."

How could this happen? It happened because both "the Reagan and Bush administrations established broad, conciliatory policies toward Iraq . . . [which] afforded executive agencies wide discretionary power in determining the nature and extent of American trade to Iraq." In this environment, the Commerce Department, following its mandate to promote international trade, became a vigorous proponent of technology sales to Iraq and usually prevailed in the interorganizational policy process because it was able to build a "'winning coalition' in favor of liberal export controls" with the State Department that blocked the Defense Department's objections. As Jones explains, "each agency's separate organizational mission and essence caused it to have a different perception of national security and, therefore, different reasons for supporting either trade promotion or trade control."

As noted above, "where you stand depends on where you sit" is a central proposition in the bureaucratic politics model that purports to explain why participants in the deliberations that lead to foreign policy choices often define issues and favor policy alternatives that reflect their organizational affiliations. Jones shows that the aphorism applies to organizations. Does it also apply to individuals, and especially those at the highest levels of government? Steve Smith concludes the answer is "yes" in his "Policy Preferences and Bureaucratic Position: The Case of the American Hostage Rescue Mission." As the title suggests, Smith examines the process that led the Carter administration to the fateful decision to attempt a covert, paramilitary rescue of American diplomats held hostage by Iran beginning in late 1979. As with Vietnam and high-tech sales to Iraq, this is a tale of policy shortcomings—of policy failure. How did it happen?

Smith does not attempt a complete answer to this question, but he does show that the key participants in the decision process "acted in accordance with what the bureaucratic politics approach would suggest: namely, that the national security adviser, the secretary of defense, the chairman of the Joint Chiefs of Staff, and director of the CIA would support military action . . . ; the secretary of state, and in his absence his deputy, would oppose it; those individuals who were bureaucratically tied to the president (the vice-president, the press secretary, and the political adviser) would be fundamentally concerned with what was best for the Carter presidency; and President Carter, although clearly more than just another bureaucratic actor, would act in a way that reflected bureaucratically derived as well as personal influences."

Smith's analysis is compelling not only as a study of an important episode in American foreign policy but also as an illustration of the logic of the bureaucratic politics model. It is also important because it shows the pitfalls as well as promises of the perspective and why we must examine not only policymaking roles but also policymakers themselves. Smith's conclusions are important in this respect: "Role, in and of itself, cannot explain the positions adopted by individuals. . . . Yet role occupiers do become predisposed to think in certain, bureaucratic ways, and for a variety of psychological reasons they tend to adopt mind-sets compatible with those of their closest colleagues. In addition, individuals are often chosen for a specific post *because* they have certain kinds of world views." In the final analysis, then, to understand the impact of decision makers and their policymaking positions on American foreign policy, we must understand both.

Stephen D. Krasner's "Are Bureaucracies Important?: A Reexamination of Accounts of the Cuban Missile Crisis" provides insight into why and how we might distinguish between individual and role explanations of American foreign policy. His chapter is a thoughtful critique of Allison's bureaucratic politics perspective on the 1962 Cuban missile crisis. Krasner argues that emphasizing bureaucratic roles as all-powerful determinants of policy outcomes exaggerates their importance. Indeed, Krasner's reexamination of the facts surrounding the Cuban missile crisis reveals that while bureaucracies do exert an impact on foreign policy, decision makers nonetheless have a capacity for rational choice and that the choices they make—rather than those made by bureaucratic organizations—ultimately matter most. Hence, the individuals elected by and responsible to the people they represent do matter, and how those leaders define their decision-making roles can prove decisive.

How leaders define their roles is likely to be a product of their prior experiences in combination with their personality predispositions. James David Barber argues in his well-known book *The Presidential Character* that presidents can be understood best by observing the energy they put into the job (active or passive) and their personal satisfaction with their presidential duties (negative or positive). The first dimension captures a president's images of the duties of the job. The second reflects a president's level of contentment with the job. Thus each president may be classified in one of four categories depending on his character: passive–negative (Calvin Coolidge, Dwight D. Eisenhower); passive–positive (Warren G. Harding, William Taft, Ronald Reagan); active–negative (Woodrow Wilson, Herbert Hoover, Lyndon B. Johnson, Richard M. Nixon); and active–positive (Franklin D. Roosevelt, Harry S Truman, John F. Kennedy, Jimmy Carter, George Bush). Bill Clinton, too, is an active–positive: "Like President Thomas Jefferson, [President] William Jefferson Clinton is politically active–positive, has strong political skills, and keeps working for what he believes is best."[5]

Barber distinguishes among the tendencies displayed by each of these presidential characters:

Active–positive Presidents want to achieve results. Active–negatives aim to get and keep power. Passive–positives are after love. Passive–negatives emphasize their civic virtue. The relation of activity to enjoyment in a President thus tends to outline a cluster of characteristics, to set apart the well adapted from the compulsive, compliant, and withdrawn types.[6]

In Chapter 22, "Presidential Character and Foreign Policy Performance," Barber shows how the character of two active–negative presidents contributed to the failure of their primary foreign policy objectives. One story is about Woodrow Wilson, a crusader and idealist whose vision of a new world order based on the principle of collective security inspired George Bush's rhetoric about the changes in world politics symbolized by the global community's response to Iraq's invasion of Kuwait. The other is about Lyndon Johnson, a president committed to creating a "great society" at home who became consumed by war in a distant land driven by the premise that he would not be the first American president to lose a war to the communists. Each story is the story of tragedy, not only for the presidents but for the nation. Wilson's failure to secure American participation in the League of Nations was a major factor contributing to the breakdown of international peace in the 1930s that culminated in World War II. Johnson's failure is more difficult to pinpoint, as the lessons of Vietnam are still being digested, but Vietnam doubtless cost Johnson his dreams for a better American society. The story also presents a useful counterpoise to Thomson's explanation of the Vietnam trauma, thus reaffirming that the sources of American foreign policy are often rooted in multiple causes.

Reflections of presidents' personality and background in their White House performance are often less dramatic than the Wilson and Johnson experiences suggest. Alexander George, for example, describes three different approaches presidents have evolved for managing the tasks of mobilizing available information, expertise, and analytical resources for effective policymaking they all face: the *formalistic, competitive,* and *collegial* models. What approach a president will choose and how it will operate in practice will be shaped by the president's personality: by his cognitive style (analogous to world view), by his sense of efficacy and competence, and by his general orientation to political conflict.[7]

Margaret G. Hermann and Thomas Preston build on these ideas in the concluding chapter of this book. Their essay, "Presidents and Their Advisers: Leadership Style, Advisory Systems, and Foreign Policymaking," shows how a president's personality, background, and training will influence what his advisers are like and how the organization he puts in place will approach foreign policy problems. Like Barber, they propose a typology of presidential types—Chief Executive Officer, Team Builder and Player, Director/Ideologue, and Analyst/Innovator—designed to capture the way characteristics of individual presidents ultimately manifest themselves in the foreign policymaking process. They apply their ideas to the advisory system President Bush devised and the one their ideas would anticipate for President Clinton. They conclude that "the president's style, his work habits, how he likes to receive information, the people he prefers around him, and the way he makes up his mind are all key to how the White House is organized."

NOTES

1. Graham T. Allison, *Essence of Decision: Explaining the Cuban Missile Crisis* (Boston: Little, Brown, 1971).

2. Allison, p. 145.

3. Allison, p. 145.

4. Allison, p. 146.

5. James David Barber, "Predicting Hope with Clinton at the Helm," *The News & Observer,* Raleigh, N.C., January 17, 1993.

6. James David Barber, *The Presidential Character: Predicting Performance in the White House,* 4th ed. (Englewood Cliffs, N.J.: Prentice Hall, 1992), p. 10.

7. Alexander L. George, *Presidential Decisionmaking in Foreign Policy: The Effective Use of Information and Advise* (Boulder, Colo.: Westview Press, 1980); and Alexander L. George, "The President and the Management of Foreign Policy: Styles and Models," in Charles W. Kegley, Jr., and Eugene R. Wittkopf, eds., *The Domestic Sources of American Foreign Policy: Insights and Evidence* (New York: St. Martin's, 1988), pp. 107–126.

17. HOW COULD VIETNAM HAPPEN? AN AUTOPSY

James C. Thomson, Jr.

As a case study in the making of foreign policy, the Vietnam War will fascinate historians and social scientists for many decades to come. One question that will certainly be asked: How did men of superior ability, sound training, and high ideals—American policymakers of the 1960s—create such a costly and divisive policy?

As one who watched the decision-making process in Washington from 1961 to 1966 under Presidents Kennedy and Johnson, I can suggest a preliminary answer. I can do so by briefly listing some of the factors that seemed to me to shape our Vietnam policy during my years as an East Asia specialist at the State Department and the White House. I shall deal largely with Washington as I saw or sensed it, and not with Saigon, where I . . . spent but a scant three days, in the entourage of the vice president, or with other decision centers, the capitals of interested parties. Nor will I deal with other important parts of the record: Vietnam's history prior to 1961, for instance, or the overall course of America's relations with Vietnam.

Yet a first and central ingredient in these years of Vietnam decisions does involve history. The ingredient was *the legacy of the 1950s*—by which I mean the so-called "loss of China," the Korean War, and the Far East policy of Secretary of State Dulles.

This legacy had an institutional by-product for the Kennedy administration: In 1961 the U.S. government's East Asian establishment was undoubtedly the most rigid and doctrinaire of Washington's regional divisions in foreign affairs. This was especially true at the Department of State, where the incoming administration found the Bureau of Far Eastern Affairs the hardest nut to crack. It was a bureau that had been purged of its best China expertise, and of far-sighted, dispassionate men, as a result of McCarthyism. Its members were generally committed to one policy line: the close containment and isolation of mainland China, the harassment of "neutralist" nations which sought to avoid alignment with either Washington or Peking, and the maintenance of a network of alliances with anticommunist client states on China's periphery.

Another aspect of the legacy was the special vulnerability and sensitivity of the new Democratic administration on Far East policy issues. The memory of the McCarthy era was still very sharp, and Kennedy's margin of victory was too thin. The 1960 Offshore Islands TV debate between Kennedy and Nixon had shown the president-elect the perils of "fresh thinking." The administration was inherently leery of moving too fast on Asia. As a result, the Far East Bureau (now the Bureau of East Asian and Pacific Affairs) was the last one to be overhauled. Not until Averell Harriman was brought in as assistant secretary in December 1961 were significant personnel changes attempted, and it took Harriman several months to make a deep imprint on the bureau because of his necessary preoccupation with the Laos settlement. Once he did so, there was virtually no effort to bring back the purged or exiled East Asia experts.

There were other important by-products of this "legacy of the fifties":

The new administration inherited and somewhat shared a *general perception of China-on-the-march*—a sense of China's vastness, its numbers, its belligerence; a revived sense, perhaps, of the Golden Horde. This was a perception fed by Chinese intervention in the Korean War (an intervention actually based on appallingly bad communications and mutual miscalculation on the part of Washington and Peking; but the careful unraveling of the tragedy, which scholars have accomplished, had not yet become part of the conventional wisdom).

The new administration inherited and briefly accepted *a monolithic conception of the communist bloc*. Despite much earlier predictions and reports by outside analysts, policymakers did not begin to accept the reality and possible finality of the Sino–Soviet split until the first weeks of 1962. The inevitably corrosive impact of competing nationalisms on communism was largely ignored.

The new administration inherited and to some extent shared *the "domino theory" about Asia*. This theory resulted from profound ignorance of Asian history and hence ignorance of the radical differences among Asian nations and societies. It resulted from a blindness to the power and resilience of Asian nationalisms. (It may also have resulted from a subconscious sense that, since "all Asians look alike," all Asian nations will act alike.) As a theory, the domino fallacy was not merely inaccurate but also insulting to Asian nations. . . .

Finally, the legacy of the fifties was apparently compounded by an uneasy sense of a worldwide communist challenge to the new administration after the Bay of Pigs fiasco. A first manifestation was the president's traumatic Vienna meeting with Khrushchev in June 1961; then came the Berlin crisis of the summer. All this created an atmosphere in which President Kennedy undoubtedly felt under special pressure to show his nation's mettle in Vietnam—if the Vietnamese, unlike the people of Laos, were willing to fight.

In general, the legacy of the fifties shaped such early moves of the new administration as the decisions to maintain a high-visibility SEATO (by sending the secretary of state himself instead of some underling to its first meeting in 1961), to back away from diplomatic recognition of Mongolia in the summer of 1961, and, most important, to expand U.S. military assistance to South Vietnam that winter on the basis of the much more tentative Eisenhower commitment. It should be added that the increased commitment to Vietnam was also fueled by a new breed of military strategists and academic social scientists (some of whom had entered the new administration) who had developed theories of counterguerrilla warfare and were eager to see them put to the test. To some, "counterinsurgency" seemed a new panacea for coping with the world's instability.

So much for the legacy and the history. Any new administration inherits both complicated problems and simplistic views of the world. But surely among the policymakers of the Kennedy and Johnson administrations there were men who would warn of the dangers of an open-ended commitment to the Vietnam quagmire?

This raises a central question, at the heart of the policy process: Where were the experts, the doubters, and the dissenters? Were they there at all, and if so, what happened to them?

The answer is complex but instructive.

In the first place, the American government was sorely *lacking in real Vietnam or Indochina expertise.* Originally treated as an adjunct of Embassy Paris, our Saigon embassy and the Vietnam Desk at State were largely staffed from 1954 onward by French-speaking Foreign Service personnel of narrowly European experience. Such diplomats were even more closely restricted than the normal embassy officer—by cast of mind as well as language—to contacts with Vietnam's French-speaking urban elites. For instance, Foreign Service linguists in Portugal are able to speak with the peasantry if they get out of Lisbon and choose to do so; not so the French speakers of Embassy Saigon.

In addition, the *shadow of the "loss of China"* distorted Vietnam reporting. Career officers in the department, and especially those in the field, had not forgotten the fate of their World War II colleagues who wrote in frankness from China and were later pilloried by Senate committees for critical comments on the Chinese Nationalists. Candid reporting on the strengths of the Viet Cong and the weaknesses of the Diem government was inhibited by the memory. It was also inhibited by some higher officials, notably Ambassador Nolting in Saigon, who refused to sign off on such cables.

In due course, to be sure, some Vietnam talent was discovered or developed. But a recurrent and increasingly important factor in the decision-making process was the *banishment of real expertise.* Here the underlying cause was the "closed politics" of policymaking as issues become hot: The more sensitive the issue, and the higher it rises in the bureaucracy, the more completely the experts are excluded while the harassed senior generalists take over (that is, the secretaries, undersecretaries, and presidential assistants). The frantic skimming of briefing papers in the back seats of limousines is no substitute for the presence of specialists; furthermore, in times of crisis such papers are deemed "too sensitive" even for review by the specialists. Another underlying cause of this banishment, as Vietnam became more critical, was the replacement of the experts, who were generally and increasingly pessimistic, by men described as "can-do guys," loyal and energetic fixers unsoured by expertise. In early 1965, when I confided my growing policy doubts to an older colleague on the NSC staff, he assured me that the smartest thing both of us could do was to "steer clear of the whole Vietnam mess"; the gentleman in question had the misfortune to be a "can-do guy," however, and [was subsequently] highly placed in Vietnam, under orders to solve the mess.

Despite the banishment of the experts, internal doubters and dissenters did indeed appear and persist. Yet as I watched the process, such men were effectively neutralized by a subtle dynamic: *the domestication of dissenters.* Such "domestication" arose out of a twofold clubbish need: on the one hand, the dissenter's desire to stay aboard; and on the other hand, the nondissenter's conscience. Simply stated, dissent, when recognized, was made to feel at home. On the lowest possible scale of importance, I must confess my own considerable sense of dignity and acceptance (both vital) when my senior White House employer would refer to me as his "favorite dove." Far more significant was the case of the former undersecretary of state, George Ball. Once Mr. Ball began to express doubts, he was warmly institutionalized: He was encouraged to become the inhouse devil's advocate on Vietnam. The upshot was inevitable: The process of escalation allowed for periodic requests to Mr. Ball to speak his piece; Ball felt good, I assume (he had fought for righteousness); the others felt good (they had given a full hearing to the dovish option); and there was minimal unpleasantness. The club remained intact; and it is of course possible that matters would have gotten worse faster if Mr. Ball had kept silent, or left before his final departure in the fall of 1966. There was also, of course, the case of the last institutionalized doubter, Bill Moyers. The president is said to have greeted his arrival at meetings with an affectionate, "Well, here comes Mr. Stop-the-Bombing. . . ." Here again the dynamics of domesticated dissent sustained the relationship for a while.

A related point—and crucial, I suppose, to government at all times—was *the "effectiveness" trap,* the trap that keeps men from speaking out, as clearly or as often as they might, within the government. And it is the trap that keeps men from resigning in protest and airing their dissent outside the government. The most important asset that a man brings to bureaucratic life is his "effectiveness," a mysterious combination of training, style, and connections. The most ominous complaint that can be whispered of a bureaucrat is "I'm afraid Charlie's beginning to lose his effectiveness." To preserve your effectiveness, you must decide where and when to fight the mainstream of policy; the opportunities range from pillow talk with your wife, to private drinks with your friends, to meetings with the secretary of state or the president. The inclination to remain silent or to acquiesce in the presence of the great men— to live to fight another day, to give on this issue so that you can be "effective" on later issues—is overwhelming. Nor is it the tendency of youth alone; some of our most senior officials, men of wealth and fame, whose place in history is secure, have remained silent lest their connection with power be terminated. As for the disinclination to resign in protest: While not necessarily a Washington or even American specialty, it seems more true of a government in which ministers have no parliamentary back-bench to which to retreat. In the absence of such a refuge, it is easy to rationalize the decision to stay aboard. By doing so, one may be able to prevent a few bad things from happening and perhaps even make a few good things happen. To exit is to lose even those marginal chances for "effectiveness."

Another factor must be noted: As the Vietnam controversy escalated at home, there developed *a preoccupation with Vietnam public relations as opposed to Vietnam policymaking.* And here, ironically, internal doubters and dissenters were heavily employed. For such men, by virtue of their own doubts, were often deemed best able to "massage" the doubting intelligentsia. My senior East Asia colleague at the White House, a brilliant and humane doubter who had dealt with Indochina since 1954, spent three-quarters of his working days on Vietnam public relations: drafting presidential responses to letters from important critics, writing conciliatory language for presidential speeches, and meeting quite interminably with delegations of outraged Quakers, clergymen, academics, and housewives. His regular callers were the late A. J. Muste and Norman Thomas; mine were members of the Women's Strike for Peace. Our orders from above: Keep them off the backs of busy policymakers (who usually happened to be nondoubters). Incidentally, my most discouraging assignment in the realm of public relations was the preparation of a White House pamphlet entitled *Why Vietnam*, in September 1965; in a gesture toward my conscience, I fought—and lost—a battle to have the title followed by a question mark.

Through a variety of procedures, both institutional and personal, doubt, dissent, and expertise were effectively neutralized in the making of policy. But what can be said of the men "in charge"? It is patently absurd to suggest that they produced such tragedy by intention and calculation. But it is neither absurd nor difficult to discern certain forces at work that caused decent and honorable men to do great harm.

Here I would stress the paramount role of *executive fatigue*. No factor seems to me more crucial and underrated in the making of foreign policy. The physical and emotional toll of executive responsibility in State, the Pentagon, the White House, and other executive agencies is enormous; that toll is of course compounded by extended service. Many . . . Vietnam policymakers [had] been on the job for from four to seven years. Complaints may be few, and physical health may remain unimpaired, though emotional health is far harder to gauge. But what is most seriously eroded in the deadening process of fatigue is freshness of thought, imagination, a sense of possibility, a sense of priorities and perspective—those rare assets of a new administration in its first year or two of office. The tired policymaker becomes a prisoner of his own narrowed view of the world and his own clichéd rhetoric. He becomes irritable and defensive—short on sleep, short on family ties, short on patience. Such men make bad policy and then compound it. They have neither the time nor the temperament for new ideas or preventive diplomacy.

Below the level of the fatigued executives in the making of Vietnam policy was a widespread phenomenon: *the curator mentality* in the Department of State. By this I mean the collective inertia produced by the bureaucrat's view of his job. At State, the average "desk officer" inherits from his predecessor our policy toward Country X; he regards it as his function to keep that policy intact—under glass, untampered with, and dusted—so that he may pass it on in two to four years to his successor. And such curatorial service generally merits promotion within the system. (Maintain the status quo, and you will stay out of trouble.) In some circumstances, the inertia bred by such an outlook can act as a brake against rash innovation. But on many issues, this inertia sustains the momentum of bad policy and unwise commitments—momentum that might otherwise have been resisted within the ranks. Clearly, Vietnam [was] such an issue.

To fatigue and inertia must be added the factor of internal confusion. Even among the "architects" of our Vietnam commitment, there [was] persistent *confusion as to what type of war we were fighting* and, as a direct consequence, *confusion as to how to end that war.* (The "credibility gap" [was], in part, a reflection of such internal confusion.) Was it, for instance, a civil war, in which case counterinsurgency might suffice? Or was it a war of international aggression? (This might invoke SEATO or UN commitment.) Who was the aggressor—and the "real enemy"? The Viet Cong? Hanoi? Peking? Moscow? International communism? Or maybe "Asian communism"? Differing enemies dictated differing strategies and tactics. And confused throughout, in like fashion, was the question of American objectives; your objectives depended on whom you were fighting and why. I shall not forget my assignment from an assistant secretary of state in March 1964: to draft a speech for Secretary McNamara which would, inter alia, once and for all dispose of the canard that the Vietnam conflict was a civil war. "But in some ways, of course," I mused, "it *is* a civil war." "Don't play word games with me!" snapped the assistant secretary.

Similar confusion beset the concept of "negotiations"—anathema to much of official Washington from 1961 to 1965. Not until April 1965 did "unconditional discussions" become respectable, via a presidential speech; even then the secretary of state stressed privately to newsmen that nothing had changed, since "discussions" were by no means the same as "negotiations." Months later that issue was resolved. But it took even longer to obtain a fragile internal agreement that negotiations might include the Viet Cong as something other than an appendage to Hanoi's delegation. Given such confusion as to the whos and whys of our Vietnam commitment, it is not surprising, as Theodore Draper has written, that policymakers [found] it so difficult to agree on how to end the war.

Of course, one force—a constant in the vortex of commitment—was that of *wishful thinking.* I partook of it myself at many times. I did so especially during Washington's struggle with Diem in the autumn of 1963 when some of us at State believed that for once, in dealing with a difficult client state, the U.S. government could use the leverage of our economic and military assistance to make good things happen, instead of being led around by the nose by [foreign dictators]. If we could prove that point, I thought, and move into a new day, with or without Diem, then Vietnam was well worth the effort. Later came the wishful thinking of the air-strike planners in the late autumn of 1964; there were those who actually thought that after six weeks of air strikes, the North Vietnamese would come crawling to us to ask for peace talks. And what, someone asked in one of the meetings of the time, if they don't? The answer was that we would bomb for another four weeks, and that would do the trick. And a few weeks later came one instance of wishful thinking that was symptomatic of good men misled: In January 1965, I encountered one of the very highest figures in the administration at a dinner, drew him aside, and told him of my worries about the air-strike option. He told me that I really shouldn't worry; it was his conviction that before any such plans could be put into effect, a neutralist government would come to power in Saigon that would politely invite us out. And finally, there was the recurrent wishful thinking that sustained many of us through the trying months of 1965–1966 after the air strikes had begun: that surely, somehow, one way or another, we would "be in a conference in six months," and the escalatory spiral would be suspended. The basis of our hope: "It simply can't go on."

As a further influence on policymakers I would cite the factor of *bureaucratic detachment*. By this I mean what at best might be termed the professional callousness of the surgeon (and indeed, medical lingo—the "surgical strike" for instance—seemed to crop up in the euphemisms of the times). In Washington the semantics of the military muted the reality of war for the civilian policymakers. In quiet, air-conditioned, thick-carpeted rooms, such terms as "systematic pressure," "armed reconnaissance," "targets of opportunity," and even "body count" seemed to breed a sort of games-theory detachment. Most memorable to me was a moment in the late 1964 target planning when the question under discussion was how heavy our bombing should be, and how extensive our strafing, at some midpoint in the projected pattern of systematic pressure. An assistant secretary of state resolved the point in the following words: "It seems to me that our orchestration should be mainly violins, but with periodic touches of brass." Perhaps the biggest shock of my return to Cambridge, Massachusetts, was the realization that the young men, the flesh and blood I taught and saw on these university streets, were potentially some of the numbers on the charts of those faraway planners. In a curious sense, Cambridge [was] closer to this war than Washington.

There is an unprovable factor that relates to bureaucratic detachment: the ingredient of *cryptoracism*. I do not mean to imply any conscious contempt for Asian loss of life on the part of Washington officials. But I do mean to imply that bureaucratic detachment may well be compounded by a traditional Western sense that there are so many Asians, after all; that Asians have a fatalism about life and a disregard for its loss; that they are cruel and barbaric to their own people; and that they are very different from us (and all look alike?). And I *do* mean to imply that the upshot of such subliminal views is a subliminal question whether Asians, and particularly Asian peasants, and most particularly Asian communists, are really people—like you and me. To put the matter another way: Would we have pursued quite such policies—and quite such military tactics—if the Vietnamese were white?

It is impossible to write of Vietnam decision making without writing about language. Throughout the conflict, words [were] of paramount importance. I refer here to the impact of *rhetorical escalation* and to the *problem of oversell*. In an important sense, Vietnam [became] of crucial significance to us *because we . . . said that it [was] of crucial significance*. (The issue obviously relates to the public relations preoccupation described earlier.)

The key here is domestic politics: the need to sell the American people, press, and Congress on support for an unpopular and costly war in which the objectives themselves [were] in flux. To sell means to persuade, and to persuade means rhetoric. As the difficulties and costs . . . mounted, so [did] the definition of the stakes. This is not to say that rhetorical escalation is an orderly process; executive prose is the product of many writers, and some concepts—North Vietnamese infiltration, America's "national honor," Red China as the chief enemy— . . . entered the rhetoric only gradually and even sporadically. But there [was] an upward spiral nonetheless. And once you have *said* that the American Experiment itself stands or falls on the Vietnam outcome, you have thereby created a national stake far beyond any earlier stakes.

Crucial throughout the process of Vietnam decision making was a conviction among many policymakers: that Vietnam posed a *fundamental test of America's national will*. Time and again I was told by men reared in the tradition of Henry L. Stimson that all we needed was the will, and we would then prevail. Implicit in such a view, it seemed to me, was a curious assumption that Asians lacked will, or at least that in a contest between Asian and Anglo-Saxon wills, the non-Asians must prevail. A corollary to the persistent belief in will was a *fascination with power* and an awe in the face of the power America possessed as no nation or civilization ever before. Those who doubted our role in Vietnam were said to shrink from the burdens of power, the obligations of power, the uses of power, the responsibility of power. By implication, such men were soft-headed and effete.

Finally, no discussion of the factors and forces at work on Vietnam policymakers can ignore the central fact of *human ego investment*. Men who have participated in a decision develop a stake in that decision. As they participate in further, related decisions, their stake increases. It might have been possible to dissuade a man of strong self-confidence at an early stage of the ladder of decision; but it is infinitely harder at later stages since a change of mind there usually involves implicit or explicit repudiation of a chain of previous decisions.

To put it bluntly: At the heart of the Vietnam calamity [was] a group of able, dedicated men who [were] regularly and repeatedly wrong—and whose standing with their contemporaries, and more important, with history, depended, as they [saw] it, on being proven right. These [were] not men who [could] be asked to extricate themselves from error.

The various ingredients I have cited in the making of Vietnam policy . . . created a variety of results, most of them fairly obvious. Here are some that seem to me most central:

Throughout the conflict, there [was] *persistent and repeated miscalculation* by virtually all the actors, in high echelons and low, whether dove, hawk, or something else. To cite one simple example among many: In late 1964 and early 1965, some peace-seeking planners at State who strongly opposed the projected bombing of the North urged that, instead, American ground forces be sent to South Vietnam; this would, they said, increase our bargaining leverage against the North—our "chips"—and would give us something to negotiate about (the withdrawal of our forces) at an early peace conference. Simultaneously, the air-strike option was urged by many in the military who were dead set against American participation in "another land war in Asia"; they were joined by other civilian peace-seekers who wanted to bomb Hanoi into early negotiations. By late 1965, we had ended up with the worst of all worlds: ineffective and costly air strikes against the North, spiraling ground forces in the South, and no negotiations in sight.

Throughout the conflict as well, there [was] *a steady give-in to pressures for a military solution* and only minimal and sporadic efforts at a diplomatic and political solution. In part this resulted from the confusion (earlier cited) among the civilians—confusion regarding objectives and strategy. And in part this resulted from the self-enlarging nature of military investment. Once air strikes and particularly ground forces were introduced, our investment itself had transformed the original stakes. More air power was needed to protect the ground forces; and then more ground forces to protect the ground forces. And needless to say, the military mind develops its own momentum in the absence of clear guidelines from the civilians. Once asked to save South Vietnam, rather than to "advise" it, the American military could not but press for escalation. In addition, sad to report, assorted military constituencies, once involved in Vietnam, . . . had a series of cases to prove: for instance, the utility not only of air power (the Air Force) but of supercarrier-based air power (the Navy). Also, Vietnam policy . . . suffered from one ironic by-product of Secretary McNamara's establishment of civilian control at the Pentagon: In the face of such control, interservice rivalry [gave] way to a united front among the military—reflected in the new but recurrent phenomenon of JCS unanimity. In conjunction with traditional congressional allies (mostly Southern senators and representatives) such a united front would pose a formidable problem for any president.

Throughout the conflict, there [were] *missed opportunities, large and small, to disengage ourselves from Vietnam on increasingly unpleasant but still acceptable terms.* Of the many moments from 1961 onward, I shall cite only one, the last and most important opportunity that was lost: In the summer of 1964 the president instructed his chief advisers to prepare for him as wide a range of Vietnam options as possible for postelection consideration and decision. He explicitly asked that all options be laid out. What happened next was, in effect, Lyndon Johnson's slow-motion Bay of Pigs. For the advisers so effectively converged on one single option—juxtaposed against two other, phony options (in effect, blowing up the world, or scuttle-and-run)—that the president was confronted with unanimity for bombing the North from all his trusted counselors. Had he been more confident in foreign affairs, had he been deeply informed on Vietnam and Southeast Asia, and had he raised some hard questions that unanimity had submerged, this president could have used the largest electoral mandate in history to deescalate in

Vietnam, in the clear expectation that at the worst a neutralist government would come to power in Saigon and politely invite us out. . . .

In the course of these years, another result of Vietnam decision making [was] *the abuse and distortion of history.* Vietnamese, Southeast Asian, and Far Eastern history [was] rewritten by our policymakers, and their spokesmen, to conform with the alleged necessity of our presence in Vietnam. Highly dubious analogies from our experience elsewhere—the "Munich" sellout and "containment" from Europe, the Malayan insurgency and the Korean War from Asia—[were] imported in order to justify our actions. And [later] events [were] fitted to the Procrustean bed of Vietnam. Most notably, the change of power in Indonesia in 1965–1966 has been ascribed to our Vietnam presence; and virtually all progress in the Pacific region—the rise of regionalism, new forms of cooperation, and mounting growth rates—has been similarly explained. The Indonesian allegation is undoubtedly false (I tried to prove it, during six months of careful investigation at the White House, and had to confess failure); the regional allegation is patently unprovable in either direction (except, of course, for the clear fact that the economies of both Japan and Korea . . . profited enormously from our Vietnam-related procurement in these countries; but that is a costly and highly dubious form of foreign aid).

There is a final result of Vietnam policy I would cite that holds potential danger for the future of American foreign policy: *the rise of a new breed of American ideologues who saw Vietnam as the ultimate test of their doctrine.* I have in mind those men in Washington who have given a new life to the missionary impulse in American foreign relations: who believe that this nation, in this era, has received a threefold endowment that can transform the world. As they see it, that endowment is composed of, first, our unsurpassed military might; second, our clear technological supremacy; and third, our allegedly invincible benevolence (our "altruism," our affluence, our lack of territorial aspirations). Together, it is argued, this threefold endowment provides us with the opportunity and the obligation to ease the nations of the earth toward modernization and stability: toward a full-fledged *Pax Americana Technocratica.* In reaching toward this goal, Vietnam [was] viewed as the last and crucial test. Once we . . . succeeded there, the road ahead [was seen to be] clear. In a sense, these men [were] our counterpart to the visionaries of communism's radical left: they are technocracy's own Maoists. . . .

Long before I went into government, I was told a story about Henry L. Stimson that seemed to me pertinent during the years that I watched the Vietnam tragedy unfold—and participated in that tragedy. It seems to me more pertinent than ever. . . .

In his waning years Stimson was asked by an anxious questioner, "Mr. Secretary, how on earth can we ever bring peace to the world?" Stimson is said to have answered: "You begin by bringing to Washington a small handful of able men who believe that the achievement of peace is possible.

"You work them to the bone until they no longer believe that it is possible.

"And they you throw them out—and bring in a new bunch who believe that it is possible."

18. TRIBAL TONGUES: INTELLIGENCE CONSUMERS, INTELLIGENCE PRODUCERS

Mark M. Lowenthal

*I*n the aftermath of the Cold War and the Gulf War there has been much soul-searching in the executive and Congress concerning the organization and role of the intelligence community: How should it be organized? Which issues should it be covering? What are the emerging issues that should be addressed now? These are of course important questions. But they tend to bypass more fundamental issues within the intelligence community that are of a more permanent—and thus, perhaps—more important nature because they deal with how the community functions and fulfills its role on a daily basis. One of these is the relationship between the intelligence consumers and the intelligence producers.

Most analyses of the U.S. intelligence process pay lip service to the consumer–producer relationship. Although occasional serious forays on the subject exist, such as Thomas Hughes's *The Fate of Facts in the World of Men,*[1] most either ignore or downplay the importance of this relationship as a significant shaper of intelligence *throughout* the so-called intelligence process, starting with collection and ending with its final consumption.

A major problem is that the consumer–producer relationship resembles that of two closely related tribes that believe, mistakenly, that they speak the same language and work in the same manner for agreed outcomes. Reality, when viewed from either perspective, suggests something wholly different. Indeed, one is often reminded of George Bernard Shaw's quip about Britons and Americans being divided by a common tongue.

WE ALL WANT THE SAME THING

Most policymakers (i.e., consumers) work on the assumption of basic support throughout the government for their various policy initiatives, including sup-

Note: Some notes have been deleted or renumbered.

port by the intelligence community. The first problem lies in the very word *support*. For policymakers, this means a shared and active interest and, if necessary, advocacy. This runs counter, however, to the intelligence community's long-standing position not to advocate any policy. Rather, the intelligence community tends to see itself, correctly or not, as a value-free service agency, although at its upper levels the line begins to blur.

Second, the intelligence community, like all other parts of the permanent government bureaucracy, has a "we/they" view of its political masters. The intelligence community is part of the *permanent* government; those making policy are politically driven *transients,* even when nominated from within the professional ranks of agencies. Indeed, with the exception of the uniformed military, nowhere else in the entire foreign policy and defense apparatus can there be found as many career officials at such senior levels as in the intelligence community. They can sometimes be found at the level equivalent to deputy secretary and clearly predominate at and below the level equivalent to assistant secretary.

Compounding this professional versus political, "we/they" conflict is the fact that consumers can and do advocate policy initiatives that run athwart intelligence community preferences. For example, the political demands for visibly intrusive arms-control monitoring methods, regardless of their minimal contribution to verification, pose real dangers for counterintelligence. The need to go public with information in order to justify policy initiatives or to brief foreign officials in order to build international support for policies often poses dangers to intelligence sources and methods. Such confrontations must often be resolved at the cabinet level and, although there will be some cutting and pasting to accommodate intelligence concerns, the overall policy will generally prevail. This is as it should be within the U.S. system of government. At the same time, it deepens the "we/they" syndrome.

Finally, the two groups have very different interests at stake. A successful policy is what the consumers were hired to create and execute. The intelligence community's reputation, however, rests less on the success of any policy than on its ability to assist in the formation of that policy and to predict potential outcomes—both good and bad. The producers are only vulnerable if the policy is perceived as failing because the intelligence support was in some way lacking. Ironically, the intelligence community is rarely given credit if the policy succeeds. In part, this is a self-fulfilling outcome given the distance the producers cultivate from the process; in part, it is the natural bureaucratic phenomenon of scrambling for honors.

THE VALUE OF A FREE COMMODITY: PRICELESS OR WORTHLESS?

Intelligence products arrive in the consumers' limousines, pouches, and in-boxes every morning and evening. They are part of the established routine. These products are, for their readers, basically cost-free subscriptions that were never ordered and never have to be paid for, perks of the job. High-level policy consumers have no real sense of either budgetary or mission/manpower cost to their departments or agencies for the very existence of these products, even if some of the products come from entities that they control. Thus, the secretary of defense will rarely be faced with a significant trade-off between required intelligence programs for the Defense Intelligence Agency and the National Security Agency versus next year's weapons procurement, nor will the secretary of state have to juggle the Bureau of Intelligence and Research's budget against prospective embassy closings.

Intelligence production, for the consumers, exists somewhere beyond their ken, as if unseen gnomes labor to produce the papers that magically arrive. If the analyses are good, all the better; if they are not, consumers are unlikely to advocate redirecting some of their resources to improving them.

Moreover, the very regularity with which these products appear has a lulling effect. The standard items—*the National Intelligence Daily,* the *Secretary's Morning Summary*—are essentially newspapers. Anyone who has read yesterday's edition or watched last night's 11:00 P.M. news can predict what is likely to be covered in this morning's edition. Indeed, while these publications are all lumped together as part of the "current intelligence" emphasis of the intelligence community, in reality they represent items that can safely be given to customers the next day. They are not urgent warnings or long-awaited breakthroughs, items that scream "read me now." Rather, they are part of the daily routine.

To break through this lulling effect, intelligence has to be able to prove to its consumers that it brings "value added" to the steady drone of information, analysis, and opinion that comes from both within and beyond the intelligence community. But one bureau or agency's memo looks much like another's, unless you bother to read them and assess them. How do you assure that, if only one will be read, it's yours? In reality, the unstated value added that intelligence producers bring is their sources. But, for very good reasons, raw intelligence is rarely presented to consumers. The intelligence is given context and comment, analysis that again makes it look like everyone else's.

How does the producer break out of this trap? One way is simply packaging, designing products that *do* scream for attention when there is a truly important piece of intelligence or a fast-breaking event about which the producers know first. The second is establishing a track record, although this still depends on whether the consumer reads intelligence analyses and remembers who was right and who was wrong.

In the end, consumers incur no real and regular penalty for ignoring this daily flow of information. In managing their day, high-level consumers establish methods to cut down on reading extraneous material. At the very highest levels, a large portion of daily intelligence products probably falls into this category. These consumers assume that their subordinates will read what they must within their areas of responsibility and that truly urgent items will come to their attention.

CONSUMER BEHAVIORS THAT MATTER

In reality, the intelligence consumer does more than just consume. He or she is not some eager, expectant eye and mind waiting at the end of the intelligence process. The consumer helps set the agenda, from intelligence priorities, to collection, to format.

Agenda

Consumers have their own sets of priorities and preferences, issues in which they are deeply interested, those in which they must take an interest by their nature, and those they would just as soon ignore. If they bother to communicate these preferences to the intelligence producers (a rare enough occurrence), and the producers respond accordingly, then the entire intelligence process has already been influenced. Although producers will not cease to try to cover all the issues that *they* believe are important, only those intelligence officers with a taste for abuse and a desire to be ignored will try to force these on an unwilling consumer. This can put producers in an awkward position, especially if the subject in question is one they feel quite strongly deserves attention. It can also run athwart the intelligence community's "warning function," namely, the requirement that it look ahead for issues—especially sleepers—that have the potential to become grave concerns.

Collection

The most senior consumer, the president, can also determine what gets collected and what does not for reasons of policy beyond the preferences of the intelligence producers. The U.S. policy in the shah's Iran of having no contact with the mullahs,[2] or President Jimmy Carter's termination of U-2 flights over Cuba, both come to mind.

"What Don't I Know?"

To the producer, the ideal consumer is one who knows what he doesn't know. Unfortunately, this quality can be hard to come by. It is understandable that senior officials dislike admitting areas of ignorance within their fields of responsibility. Those who do, however, have a clear advantage, especially if they are willing to take steps, among them requested analyses and briefings, to remedy the situation. Similarly, it is important for the consumers to distinguish between what they must know, what they'd like to know, and what is simply enjoyable but unnecessary. Failure to do this well, and continually, can lead to one of two traps—either consuming too much time on some subjects or too little on others. Given the primacy of time management, this should be a crucial skill for the harried consumer. Once this skill is acquired, and its results communicated to the producers, it again establishes priorities and agendas.

Dealing with Uncertainty

Neither producers nor consumers like intelligence gaps. At best they are annoying; at worst they can be both crucial and frightening. They do exist, however, and are often responsible for uncertainties in estimates and analyses. As strange as it may seem, such uncertainties appear to be very difficult to convey, at least in English. "If/then" constructions can become long laundry lists covering all the possibilities, without regard to likelihood; "on the one hand/on the other hand" often creates octopuses of sentences—too many hands spoil the analyses. The absence of an easily used subjunctive really hurts.

Unfortunately, consumers often interpret these very real problems of limited sources and uncertain outcomes as pusillanimity on the part of producers. "They have a best guess," consumers suppose, "they're just hedging so they won't be wrong." The inability on the part of producers to convey adequately the cause and nature of uncertainty and ambiguity tends to alienate a largely dubious audience.

"Shooting the Messenger"

This consumer behavior is as old as recorded history—if the messenger brings bad news, kill him. Unfortunately, it still happens. The messenger is not killed; he is first berated and then, on subsequent occasions, ignored. In part this consumer behavior stems from the darker side of the "we-all-want-the-same-thing" syndrome. Once consumers have figured out that they and their intelligence people do *not* all necessarily want the same thing, they become suspicious of the producers. Do they have their own agenda for their own dark reasons? If they are not actively supporting me, are they working against me? Unfortunately, the delivery of "bad news," usually some piece of intelligence or an analysis that questions preferred or ongoing policies, fits this more paranoid view all too well.[3]

What, however, is the producer's alternative? Suppress the intelligence and risk having the consumer blind-sided or even badly embarrassed, a sure blow to credibility? Better to err on the side of caution and risk opprobrium, knowing full well that this, too, can harm credibility. Either way, the outcome largely rests on the intelligence's reception by the consumers, on their maturity, experience, and willingness to be challenged by people who are not a threat to their policies.

The Consumer as Analyst

Consumers are, by and large, a self-confident group. They have achieved fairly exalted and responsible positions through either the trial by fire of long professional careers or through the hurly-burly of private enterprise or partisan politics. No matter the route, they assume that it is not just connections and luck that have brought them to their current positions. This self-assurance is all to the good, although it can lead to some aberrant behavior.

The first such behavior has to do with issues of long standing regarding which the consumer believes that he or she knows as much, if not more, than the intelligence analysts. Certainly, assistant secretaries of state for Europe, the Near East, and so on, are likely to have spent a large portion of their professional careers on these issues, and they probably know some of the key players in the region on a personal basis. Interestingly, the same perception eventually takes hold of senior officials dealing with Soviet issues, regardless of their previous experience. At least two factors are at work here. First, the long-standing nature of the U.S. rivalry with the Soviets lends an air of familiarity, whether deserved or not. Second, after about two years in office, the average secretary of state has met with his Soviet counterpart more than half a dozen times and probably feels he has greater insight into Soviet thinking than do "ivory tower" analysts who have only seen the Soviet Union from 150 miles up.[4] The recent upheaval in the Soviet Union and Eastern Europe may have tempered the first attitude, now that the familiar signposts of relations have gone. This probably results, however, in increased emphasis on the second attitude, the value of high-level, face-to-face contacts over analysis by those more remote from events.

For this type of reaction the "value-added" question becomes paramount. What can the producer bring to the issue that is new, insightful, and useful? Here, the natural inclination, if not necessity, to hedge analyses works against the producer and only serves to reinforce the prejudice of the consumer.

The second "consumer-as-analyst" behavior manifests itself during those periods of intense activity usually misnamed crises. Suddenly, the premium for current intelligence rises dramatically; consumers will often cry out for the "raw intelligence." There is the sudden assumption that at moments like these, trained intelligence analysts will somehow get in the way, that they will, perhaps inadvertently, distort the incoming information. Ideally, the intelligence officers should resist, offering to come back in several minutes with some sort of analysis or context along with the raw intelligence. Quite simply, consumers are probably less well suited at these moments to serve as their own analysts. Their ability to assess objectively and dispassionately what is happening is usually inverse to the importance of the issue, its intensity, and the amount of time they have been dealing with it. This is not to say that consumers have nothing of analytical value to bring to the process, including during crises. They should not, however, act to cut off the contributions of professional expertise. At worst, they will get an alternative point of view that they are always free to reject.

The Assumption of Omniscience

For the United States as a global power, it is difficult to find many issues or regions that are not of at least some minimal interest. For the consumer this translates into the erroneous assumption that somewhere in the labyrinths of the intelligence community there is at least one analyst capable of covering each issue that comes along.

The source of this assumption is most likely a conceit derived from the expectation that U.S. interests must be matched by U.S. capabilities, that intelligence managers must know that *all* bases should be covered. Interestingly, this runs counter to the often-heard criticism (and accepted folk wisdom) that the intelligence community has traditionally spent too much time and effort on the Soviet target, to the disadvantage of less sexy albeit no less important issues.

Unfortunately, there is no safe way for the producers to correct the assumption of omniscience. The intelligence community is loath to admit that it is not true and is fearful of the criticism that will ensue if this is discovered. Yet, in a world of unlimited issues and limited intelligence resources gaps are unavoidable. How resources are allotted either to close or to allow gaps remains a murky process based on past experience and known or—more likely—perceived consumer interest. Too often this process degenerates into a debate over the size of the intelligence budget, raising the suspicion among consumers (and congressional overseers) that cries of insufficient coverage are in reality pleas for more resources that will be redirected to areas that the intelligence community sees fit. Were the producers, however, to address the issue forthrightly and ask consumers, say down to the assistant secretary level, for a list of issues that had to be covered and those that could be given shorter shrift, it is unlikely that they would get consensus. Here again the "free commodity" issue is at work, only now consumers would be asked to give up something that they had always received, even if they had never had any great use for it.

Inevitably, one of the issues that has long been considered below the threshold will suddenly require attention. With a little luck there may be an analyst somewhere who has at least passing familiarity with it. This is the moment when the producers hope to shine, to prove the "value added" they bring to the process. If they succeed, however, they also reinforce the omniscience assumption, which sooner or later will be found, painfully, to be false.

The Absence of Feedback

Intelligence consumers have neither the time nor the inclination to offer much feedback on what they are getting or not getting. This stems from several sources. First, the throwing of bouquets is not a habit in government nor should it be expected.[5] Second, there is rarely enough time. As soon as one problem is solved or crisis ended, it is time to move on to the next. But the absence of feedback enforces the producers' image of top consumers as "black holes," into which intelligence is drawn without any sense of the reception or effect. The result is to deny the producers any guidance as to how they are doing.

At the same time, it must be admitted that, despite calls on their part for feedback, many in the intelligence community are quite content with the status quo. They do not favor "report cards"; they fear that they will only hear the negative and not receive any praise; they are concerned lest feedback becomes a means by which consumers would try to affect the content of intelligence to elicit greater support for policies. None of this needs to happen if the feedback process is honest and regularized.

There also would be genuine benefits. The intelligence community is made up of analysts who largely enjoy their work and who believe, as individuals, that the issues they cover are worthy of attention. At the working level, however, they exist in relative isolation, without any reference point as to how well their work fulfills its purported purposes among the consumers. Analysts will continue to work on what they believe to be relevant and important unless or until consumers offer guidance as to preferences, needs, and style. In short, producers need to be told how best to shape their products and focus for the consumers, but the initiative for doing so remains with the consumers.[6]

Feedback is also an area where Congress, in its oversight role, can be helpful. Congress has, in the past, reviewed important policy issues for which intelligence was a major factor and has offered objective assessments of the quality of intelligence and the uses to which it was put by consumers. The Senate Select Committee on Intelligence, for example, offered a critique of the famous Team A–Team B competitive Soviet analysis and called the exercise worthwhile but flawed in its execution. This same committee also found that President Jimmy Carter's release of Central Intelligence Agency analysis of Soviet oil prospects was largely driven by his own political needs. Similarly, the House Permanent Select Committee on Intelligence offered a scathing review of intelligence on Iran prior to the fall of the shah. The same committee's review of intelligence prior to the Mariel exodus from Cuba concluded that U.S. surprise on that occasion was not due to lack of intelligence warnings.

Such a service is quite useful and can be done by Congress objectively and without partisan rancor. However, the two Select Committees on Intelligence also have limits on their time and cannot provide this sort of review regularly. Congress is an intelligence consumer as well, although it is not privy to the full extent of the analyses that flow to policymakers in the executive. Thus, Congress can supplement feedback from consumers but cannot fully substitute for it.

PRODUCER BEHAVIORS THAT MATTER

Just as the consumer does more than consume, the producers do more than simply collect, analyze, and produce. Their behavior also affects the product and the perceptions held by the consumers.

Current versus Long-Term Intelligence

All intelligence agencies, managers, and analysts are constantly tugged between the need for current intelligence and the desire to write long-term intelligence. Thomas Hughes portrayed the struggle as one of "intelligence butchers" (current intelligence, done in short, sharp chops of material) versus "intelligence bakers" (long-term intelligence, done in prolonged melding and blending). As cute as Hughes's model is, it gives the mistaken impression that the choice of which type of intelligence to emphasize lies with the producers. This tends not to be so. Rather, it is the very nature of how foreign and defense policy is handled by consumers that drives the choice. Intelligence producers claim not to be bothered by this consumer preference for current intelligence, but this too is not entirely correct.

Current intelligence (i.e., tonight, tomorrow, this week) will always dominate. That is the very nature of the U.S. policy process. It is very "now" oriented, creating a series of difficult choices among issues all crying for attention. Indeed, there is very little sense of completion, because each issue laid to rest has too many successors waiting for attention as well. The drive of current events even tends to distort the notion of "long-term" analysis, which becomes the next ministerial meeting, the next arms-control round, the next summit, next year's budget process at best.

Much lip service is given by both producers and consumers to the need for long-term intelligence. Yet nothing in their daily lives indicates what use they would make of such intelligence if it existed. For consumers it would represent luxury items, things to be read when or if the press of current business allowed. For producers it would mean just a chance to be more wrong at a greater distance from the events—a constant concern.

Some will argue that the intelligence community already produces long-term analyses in the form of the National Intelligence Estimates (NIEs). But what is the function of the NIEs? In theory they represent the best judgment of the entire intelligence community on major issues, as conveyed by the director of central intelligence to the president. Some NIEs are done at the request of consumers, most often a fast-track or Special NIE (SNIE, pronounced "snee"). Other NIEs are done at the suggestion of an intelligence organization or are initiated by national intelligence officers, who perceive a need among consumers.

But beyond their impressive name and theoretical status, do NIEs really influence long-term policies? Or are they, in the scathing words of the House Permanent Select Committee on Intelligence, "not worth fighting for"? It is difficult to find many NIEs that have substantially influenced ongoing policy debates. Various intelligence agencies participate earnestly in the NIE game largely to keep track of their brethren and to preserve their own points of view. NIEs are important simply because they exist and not because of any great value that they regularly add to the process. More often they serve either as databases for budget justifications (in the case of the annual NIE on Soviet programs) or as the source of self-serving and often misleading quotations for use by consumers during policy debates.

Although both producers and consumers constantly cry out for more long-term and less current intelligence, it remains unclear that the outcry has any substance beyond a general and unsubstantiated belief that, if it were produced, long-term intelligence would give greater coherence to policy.

Portraying Uncertainty

One of the most difficult problems that producers face on a daily basis is the need to portray uncertainty. Every issue that is analyzed has gaps, unknown areas, competing plausible outcomes. As much as producers would like to be able to predict with finality, they both know that it is rarely possible and tend to write so as to cover, at least minimally, less likely outcomes so as not to be entirely wrong.

Portraying this in writing can be difficult. In the absence of a widely used subjunctive tense, producers use other techniques: "perhaps, although, however, on the one hand/on the other hand, maybe." There is nothing intrinsically wrong with any of these, although their net effect can be harmful for several reasons.

First, their use becomes habitual, creating written safety nets that allow the producers to keep all their bets covered. Second, and perhaps more important, they strike the consumer, especially with repetition, as "weasel words," efforts by the producers to avoid coming down on one side or another of any issue.

Producers do not spend enough time or effort explaining why these uncertainties remain. Consumers, being thus uninformed, tend to revert to their omniscience syndrome and see pusillanimity instead.

The Perceived Penalty for Changing Estimates

Producers do not like to be wrong, but they realize they are fallible. They also, however, do not like having to make changes in estimates, fearful of the cost to their credibility with the consumers. Wide swings are especially anathema; better to adjust one's estimates gradually, to bring the consumers along slowly to the new view. Thus, if for years the estimate has said "T is most likely," and producers now believe that "Z is most likely," few will want to jump directly from T to Z. Instead, they would rather move slowly through $U, V, W, X,$ and Y, preparing the consumer for the idea that Z is now correct.

In this case, the perception may be worse than the reality. Most consumers, if properly prepared as to why there is a change (new data, new sources, new models, and so on), are likely to accept it unless changes become so regular a phenomenon as to raise serious questions.[7] Again, it is largely an issue of communications, of adequately explaining the uncertainties inherent in any estimate and the factors that have led to the change. Unfortunately, the outcome is so dreaded that the process rarely takes place.

Miracles versus Saints

One of the necessary premiums put on all intelligence writing (with the exception of some NIEs) is brevity. Less is more when dealing with overly busy readers. Unfortunately, this runs counter to the desire burning within nearly every analyst to tell as much of the story as possible, to give the reader background, context and, in part, to show off. (For example: "You can't really understand the FMLN insurgency in El Salvador unless you go back to the Spanish land grants of the sixteenth century." A plausible point, but not an analysis that any busy reader is likely to read.)

Analysts tend not to err on the side of brevity. It becomes, therefore, the task of the intelligence production managers to edit material down to a suitable length. Analysts must be admonished to "just tell the miracles, and not the lives of all the saints involved in making them happen."

The miracles versus saints problem, however, also poses a difficult managerial decision. Analysts cannot write about the miracles with any facility until they have mastered the lives of the saints. Managers therefore have to be flexible enough to allow their analysts the time to study and even to write about the saints, if only for use in background papers sent to other analysts. But this time must not be allowed to conflict with ongoing demands for written products, including those about the very miracles in question. It's a tough call, but one that has a payoff later on.

Jaded versus Naive

Given a choice between appearing jaded or naive on a given subject, the average intelligence professional will choose to appear jaded at least nine times out of ten. No one wants to appear to be the new kid on the block. Instead, analysts act as though they have seen it all and done it all before. This is especially troublesome in group meetings with peers, where appearances matter.

What this means, in terms of analysis, is that few situations are treated as being truly new, regardless of their nature. But some situations *are* new or different and do require analysis that has not been done before. A nuclear power plant blows up catastrophically; the Chinese sell intermediate-range ballistic missiles; or the Soviet Union allows its Eastern European satellites to remove their communist governments. By taking the jaded approach analysts force themselves, first of all, to play catch-up to situations that are ongoing, having initially wasted time playing them down. Moreover, they allow themselves to appear less than perspicacious before their consumers and now must spend time explaining away their previous stance, for which there may be little justification beyond mind-set.

The fix here is apparently simple—approach issues with a more open mind. But how can this be implemented? It cannot be institutionalized or even easily taught. It largely depends on production managers who continually ask skeptical questions, forcing their analysts to rethink. It is not easy, but it is achievable.

"Covering the World"

This is the producers' version of the agenda issue. At most times there will be more issues crying out for attention than resources available to cover them all adequately. Producers, however, do not want to let any one of these issues slip, in part out of concern that they will choose the wrong ones and not be ready if they become more important or if consumer interest is suddenly piqued. Interestingly, this behavior on the part of producers only reinforces the consumers' belief in the intelligence community's omniscience. Feedback from consumers is an essential ingredient in making choices. If this is absent, however, then the intelligence producers must decide, knowing they cannot cover everything. They must also be able to distinguish, which they sometimes do not, between issues genuinely requiring serious attention and those that do not. They may also find, as noted earlier, that there are important issues that consumers do not want to address. Here, the producers are torn, their professional responsibilities and best judgment at odds with the political realities. Overall, producers tend to side with covering more than less.

Reporting "No Change"

Although the intelligence community cannot cover everything, it does keep track of more issues than most of its consumers can or want to deal with. Because of the limits on space in written products and the consumers' time, much goes unreported. But a second filtering process also takes place. On issues that are not "front burner" but are still of some interest, analysts will choose not to report developments or, more significantly, the lack of developments. The absence of activity is taken to mean the absence of any need to report.

There is value, however, to reporting periodically (admittedly at long intervals) on these issues and nondevelopments. If the analysts or managers know that the Ruritanian nuclear program is of interest but that nothing new has happened in the last six months, there is nothing wrong with reporting that to consumers. What is the effect of such a report? First, it shows the consumer that the producers are alert, that they are tracking areas of interest beyond the self-evident. Second, it allows consumers to check off that issue on their mental lists. They can assume, probably correctly, that the producers will alert them to any change. For the moment, they need not worry about it. There is, however, a cost to such reporting, in that it tends to reinforce the consumers' omniscience assumption. Still, the net effect remains a positive one, albeit infrequent.

The Absence of Self-Analysis

This is the flip side of the absence of consumer feedback. Like everyone else in the government, intelligence analysts and officials are busy people. As soon as one crisis ends they move on to the next with very little reflection on what worked and what did not. Nor do they spend much time trying to sort out why certain analyses in certain situations work well and others do not, why warnings and indicators flag proper attention in some cases but not others, why the synergism of collection resources works for this topic or region and not for that.

Admittedly, genuine critical self-examination is difficult. The payoff for having it done more regularly, not by "outside" reviewers in the intelligence community but by the analysts and their supervisors themselves, is a much clearer insight into their institutional behaviors and processes that can greatly improve their work and their ability to serve the consumers.

CONCLUSION

The production and use or disuse of intelligence as part of the policy process is the net result of several types of mind-sets and behavior within and between two groups that are more disparate than most observers realize. Moreover, the disparity is more likely to be appreciated by one group, the intelligence producers, than it is by the intelligence consumers. As argued here, the consumers play a much greater role *throughout* the intelligence process and at all stages in that process than is customarily realized. Certain aspects of the gap between these two groups will never be bridged. Other aspects, like the issue of supporting policy, *should* never be bridged. Nonetheless, there remains much that can be done—even within current structures and processes—to improve communications between the two groups.

NOTES

1. Thomas Hughes, *The Fate of Facts in the World of Men* (New York: Foreign Policy Association, 1976).

2. See Gary Sick, *All Fall Down* (New York: Penguin Books, 1985), pp. 36, 64, 91, 104–105.

3. Needless to say, not *all* paranoia is unjustified. There have undoubtedly been instances in which intelligence analysts have tried to work against policies with which they disagreed. Most analysts, however, and certainly their senior supervisors know the severe penalty for being caught in such a compromising position and would most often prefer to avoid it, even at the risk that the policy will go forward. Most often, the cost to future credibility far outweighs the value of stopping one specific policy initiative.

4. During the first U.S.–Soviet ministerial meeting of the Bush administration, the deputy national security adviser, Robert Gates, who has spent a considerable part of his intelligence career as a Soviet analyst, was in Moscow for the first time. President Mikhail Gorbachev reportedly kidded Gates, asking him if the Soviet Union looked different from the ground than it did from satellites.

5. Feedback is so rare that, when it occurs, the effect can often be comical. When one senior official noted his pleasure over a piece of intelligence analysis, the initial reaction among those responsible was, first, elation, quickly followed by doubts. Was this memo so good, they wondered, or was it that all of the others that received no such notice were so bad?

6. The President's Foreign Intelligence Advisory Board (PFIAB), a group of outside experts that reviews both intelligence analysis and operations, provides such guidance. It was PFIAB, for example, that suggested the Team A–Team B competitive analysis. However, PFIAB meets infrequently, reportedly once a month, and remains somewhat removed from the daily needs of producers. It cannot substitute entirely for direct producer feedback.

7. There have been cases, however, in which wide swings did hurt credibility. In the mid-1970s U.S. intelligence estimates of the portion of Soviet gross national product devoted to defense went from 6 to 7 percent in the mid-1970s to 10 to 15 percent, leading some consumers to question the validity of the new estimates as well. Critics in Congress suspected that the change was created to support the Ford administration's

larger defense budget. See John W. Finney, "Soviet Arms Outlay May Be Bigger Slice of Pie Than Once Thought," *New York Times,* February 23, 1976, p. 13, and "U.S. Challenged on Arms Estimate," *New York Times,* March 8, 1976, p. 11. When the intelligence community repeated its estimate a year later, this threatened to discomfit the plans of the new Carter administration, which was in the midst of its review of Presidential Review Memorandum #10 on U.S. strategy. In drawing up PRM-10, Carter administration officials purposely excluded some of the premises that they saw driving the new estimates. See Hedrick Smith, "Carter Study Takes More Hopeful View of Strategy of U.S.," *New York Times,* July 8, 1977, p. A-1.

19. AMERICAN PREWAR TECHNOLOGY SALES TO IRAQ: A BUREAUCRATIC POLITICS EXPLANATION

Christopher M. Jones

Since the conclusion of the Persian Gulf War, countless inquiries by congressional committees and journalists have revealed troubling aspects about America's prewar relations with Iraq. No facet of the courtship is more disturbing than the government's decision to authorize advanced technology sales by American manufacturers to Iraq between 1984 and the invasion of Kuwait in August 1990. The U.S. Department of Commerce approved "without condition" nearly 800 export licenses to Iraq, allowing American companies to sell $1.5 billion in products that had both civilian and military uses (Sciolino 1992a, 8; Hedges 1991b, 36 and 39).[1] These dual-use products included high-speed computers, high-frequency synthesizers, oscillographs, forges, and sophisticated machine and measurement tools. Much of the technology was either shipped directly or diverted to Iraqi ballistic missile sites and government agencies and research centers involved in the development of biological, chemical, and nuclear weapons.[2]

The dangerous implications of this export policy are clear. First, American companies, with the consent of the federal government, played a significant role in enhancing the capability of Saddam Hussein's military machine, which the United States and its allies later had to oust from Kuwait. Second, American technology aided Iraq's unconventional weapons programs, thereby violating the long-standing U.S. goal of preventing the proliferation of weapons of mass destruction to Third World states.

The military significance of the American technology has been confirmed by U.S. government officials, United Nations weapons inspectors, and other outside experts (see Milhollin 1992 and Timmerman 1992).[3] The actions of American officials also illustrate the nature of the threat. They not only found it necessary to conduct numerous wartime bombing raids on sites suspected of being tied to Iraq's unconventional weapons program, but one industrial complex was attacked by American cruise missiles as late as January 1993.[4] Lastly, postwar United Nations inspections teams found American technology at sites confirmed to be involved in the development of Iraqi weapons of mass destruction (Hedges 1991b, 39). David Kay, who led three weapons inspection teams, confirmed this fact during congressional testimony (Kay 1992). Further, he states: "On August 2, 1990, [the Iraqis] were no more than 18 months away from the acquisition of a crude nuclear weapon" (Kay 1992).

Why such a dangerous policy was sustained for so long and in the face of Saddam Hussein's ominous behavior demands explanation. Among the existing models available to explain foreign policy behavior, Allison and Halperin's bureaucratic politics paradigm (1972) best captures the case of American prewar technology sales to Iraq. The framework views the actions of government as political resultants (see also Allison 1971). These resultants emerge from a foreign policy process, characteristic of a game, where multiple players holding differing conceptions of the national interest struggle, compete, and bargain over both the nature and conduct of policy. The policy positions taken by the decision makers are determined largely by their own organizational roles and interests. The final outcome either represents a compromise among the actors or reflects outright the policy preferences of the actors who won the political game.

Allison and Halperin's framework encourages organizations to be treated as policy actors. In these instances, an organization's mission and essence become strong predictors of its policy stand on a particular issue. Furthermore, Allison and Halperin distinguish among decision games, policy games, and action games. They identify "the activity of players leading to decision by senior players as decision games, activities leading to policy as policy games, and activities that follow from or proceed in the absence of decisions by senior players as action games" (Allison and Halperin 1972, 46). These insights are important in explaining American prewar technology sales to Iraq. In essence, the case is an instance of an action game where three organizations within the executive branch fought over the implementation of a vague and unmonitored policy.

The White House and the Congress set the stage for this action game and the bureaucratic politics that pervaded it. The Reagan and Bush administrations established broad, conciliatory policies toward Iraq. Their broad, general policies afforded executive agencies wide discretionary power in determining the nature and extent of American trade to Iraq. Congress was responsible for developing the export licensing process or the "action-channel"—"a regularized means of taking government action on a specific issue" (Allison 1971, 169)—whereby the Departments of Commerce and State, on one side, and the Department of Defense, on the other, struggled over the sale of dual-use technology to Iraq. In case after case, the Defense Department warned that export licenses for advanced, dual-use products should be denied "because of the high likelihood of military end use" (Sciolino 1992b, 10). The Pentagon's objections were challenged repeatedly by the Commerce Department, which enjoyed the support of the State Department. The three executive departments' policy positions were based unequivocally on their distinct bureaucratic roles. The organizational mission and essence of each caused it to have a different perception of the national security and, therefore, different reasons for supporting or opposing export controls on American technology sales.

This chapter shows how the White House and the Congress provided a conducive environment for both the technology sales to Iraq and the bureaucratic politics that surrounded the export licensing process. It then demonstrates how major actors' policy stands and supporting arguments were directly related to their traditional bureaucratic missions and interests. Prewar dual-use exports to Iraq are treated as a whole, as the behavior of the relevant actors was remarkably consistent over time.

THE WHITE HOUSE

With one exception, neither the Reagan nor the Bush administration intervened directly into the export licensing process as it related to dual-use items intended for Iraq. Rather, both administrations adopted broad policies toward Iraq that were conciliatory in nature, though for different reasons. Once the general policy direction was set, the White House became inattentive to the details of Iraqi policy. This context permitted bureaucratic politics to determine export licensing decisions from 1984 to August 1990.

By March 1982 the Reagan administration realized that Saddam Hussein's military forces were collapsing and that Iran was nearing victory in the Iran–Iraq War. The administration feared that Iran's Islamic fundamentalist government would soon be in control of additional Middle East territory and oil. As a result, the Reagan White House, without departing from its official position of neutrality, initiated a policy "tilt" toward Iraq. Geoffrey Kemp, then Middle East section chief on the National Security Council (NSC), explains the logic behind the decision:

> The memory of the hostages was quite fresh; the Ayatollah was still calling us the Great Satan and attempting to undermine governments throughout the Gulf states. It wasn't that we wanted Iraq to win the war, we didn't want Iraq to lose. We really weren't naive. We knew he was an S.O.B., but he was our S.O.B. (Miller and Mylroie 1990, 143).

Besides preventing an Iranian victory through aid to Iraq, the White House hoped that the American "tilt" might have a moderating effect on Saddam Hussein's postwar behavior. At the very least, the administration believed that the policy would restore the war's earlier stalemate. The Reagan administration had considered the protracted conflict favorable as it diminished the military power of both Khomeini and Hussein.

There were several manifestations of the Reagan administration's new policy "tilt." First, Iraq was removed from the State Department's list of states sponsoring terrorism. This action was taken despite evidence that Iraq still harbored terrorist groups. Second, Iraq's removal from the State Department list placed it in a position to receive U.S. government loan guarantees and paved the way for American trade. In December 1982, the Agriculture Department's Commodity Credit Corporation (CCC) granted Iraq $300 million in credits to purchase badly needed staples (Miller and Mylroie 1990, 144). By 1990, the CCC had extended Iraq $1.9 billion in loan guarantees (Seib 1992, A26). It was later reported that much of this aid was diverted to finance arms and dual-use technology purchases (Tolchin 1992, D2). Third, in March 1982, the Reagan administration launched Operation Staunch, a high-level effort to encourage European allies to sell arms to Iraq but not to Iran (Waas 1991, 88–89).

Several other American actions were related to the Reagan administration's "tilt" toward Iraq. In March 1984, four months after Iraq attacked Iran with chemical weapons, the United States weakly condemned "the first sustained use of chemical weapons since the Geneva Protocol of 1925" (Henderson 1991, 183). In 1984 and 1986, then-Vice President Bush personally lobbied the president of the U.S. Export–Import Bank to extend millions of dollars in loan guarantees to Iraq (Lacayo 1992, 42). The participation of the Export–Import Bank in the "tilt" toward Iraq is significant, as its sole purpose is to stimulate American exports, including dual-use technology. A clear path to further technology sales to Iraq in a second Reagan administration was established in November 1984, when, after a 17-year suspension, full diplomatic relations with Iraq were reestablished. Surprisingly, the policy of "tilting" toward Iraq continued after the conclusion of the Iran–Iraq War and in the face of Saddam Hussein's two chemical weapons attacks on Iraqi Kurds during 1988.

In fact, the Reagan policy toward Iraq, which did not undergo review in the final months of the administration, remained on "automatic pilot" for nine months into the Bush administration (Sciolino 1991, 172). Rapidly changing events in Europe and the failure of the new administration to name high-level foreign affairs political appointees were largely responsible for delaying a policy review. On October 2, 1989, when a clear articulation of the Bush policy was finally presented in National Security Decision Directive (NSDD) 26, the direction of American policy remained unchanged. NSDD 26 changed only the pretext on which the Iraqi policy was based. The American "tilt" toward Iraq would no longer be based on preventing an Iranian war victory, but instead on influencing and "moderating the behavior of Iraq through economic and political incentives" (ABC News 1992a, 1–2). Like its predecessor, the Bush administration encouraged trade, provided Export–Import and CCC loans, and opposed U.S. trade sanctions when Iraq's behavior worsened. Following the conclusion of the Persian Gulf War, President Bush consistently justified his prewar policy toward Iraq with the argument that "we tried to bring [Saddam Hussein] into the family of nations through commerce and failed" (Seib 1992, A26).

Unfortunately, it appears that Bush was not fully informed about the nature of U.S.–Iraqi trade in 1989 and 1990. His inattention to the details of American prewar export policy became apparent during the 1992 presidential campaign with repeated statements like the following on October 19:

> There wasn't one single iota of evidence that any U.S. weapons were on the battlefield, and that nuclear capability has been searched by the United Nations and there hasn't been one single scintilla of evidence that there's any U.S. technology involved in it. (ABC News 1992b, 2)

Bush admitted some dual-use technology may have gone to Iraq, but he dismissed its significance, arguing his policy was in place. He stated on October 28:

> We had a policy on dual use. We had a policy to screen, to be sure that key [dual-use] elements did not go to nuclear weapons or for arms. Now, if a Tandy computer or an IBM personal computer ends up somewhere in a nuclear program, too bad, but the policy was not to do that. (ABC News 1992b, 3)

NSDD 26 was indeed in place. However, declassified sections reveal its ambiguity. For instance, one portion reads: "We should pursue, and seek to facilitate, opportunities for U.S. firms to participate in the reconstruction of the Iraqi economy, particularly in the energy area, where they do not conflict with our nonproliferation and other significant objectives" (Safire 1992, A13). It appears the Bush administration wanted to encourage American trade to Iraq *and* prevent Saddam Hussein from acquiring weapons of mass destruction. Given the nature of dual-use technology, however, the goals may have been mutually exclusive. Furthermore, the Bush policy did not provide the bureaucrats responsible for issuing export licenses with guidelines for making decisions. A declassified State Department memorandum from November 1989 illustrates the disarray surrounding the implementation of NSDD 26: "The problem is not that we lack a policy on Iraq. We have a policy. However, the policy has proven very hard to implement when considering proposed exports of dual-use commodities to ostensibly non-nuclear end users, particularly state enterprises" (Sciolino 1992c, A10).

The ambiguity of NSDD 26 was further exacerbated by the paucity of senior-level concern with Iraq in general and with the details of the export licensing process in particular. First, "the National Security Council never met once to discuss Iraq from the time NSDD 26 was signed until the invasion of Kuwait" (Sciolino 1991, 173). Second, the White House only blocked one dual-use export to Iraq. The intervention occurred in July 1990 when, after considerable publicity and pressure from a group of Republican senators, the White House stopped the shipment of three industrial furnaces to Iraq (Wines 1990a, A3). In other cases, the NSC did not provide the necessary policy coordination or intervention to mitigate the intense bureaucratic rivalry that surrounded most licensing decisions. Like the Reagan White House, this neglect by the Bush administration allowed advanced American technology to go to Saddam Hussein's unconventional weapons programs.

THE ACTION CHANNEL

Congress did not pass trade sanctions or conduct a review of export control policy prior to the Gulf War. Its main contribution to the case of prewar technology sales to Iraq was legislating the rules for the export licensing process or "action game." Most dual-use industrial goods controlled for national security purposes are on the Commodity Control List (CCL) and, therefore, fall under the jurisdiction of the Commerce Department's Bureau of Export Administration (BXA). Nuclear-related, dual-use items on the Nuclear Referral List (NRL) also require export licenses from the Commerce Department. Only a small portion of dual-use goods are not controlled directly by the BXA. These products fall exclusively on the Munitions List (ML), which is under the control of the State Department's Center for Defense Trade. Some ambiguous, dual-use goods can appear on both the CCL and the ML because the two control lists do not have mutually exclusive categories. However, this overlap, which is sometimes a source of contention between the Commerce and State departments, appears not to have played a role in the Iraqi case.

The BXA can operate along two action channels. A decision on whether to approve a particular license is made either unilaterally by the Commerce Department or through an interagency review process where, after consultations, the Commerce Department has the final decision. The review process, which is activated in 70 percent or more of the dual-use licensing cases (National Academy of Sciences 1991, 80–81), brings together diverse actors and interests and is, therefore, the action channel where bureaucratic politics are most prevalent.

In terms of dual-use goods, interagency reviews are initiated when specific applications for export licenses raise policy or technical questions that exceed the expertise of the Commerce Department. Interestingly, an interagency review can only be initiated at the request of the Commerce Department (Henderson 1991, 212), which has the legal authority to oversee and administer the Commodity Control List. This fact allows the Department of Commerce to determine what other actors will become involved in the national security licensing process under its authority. Since the State Department holds a preponderance of foreign policy and country-specific expertise, it is frequently brought into the process. In cases where goods are controlled for foreign policy purposes (e.g., regional stability, terrorism, and human rights), State Department recommendations are especially valuable. In national security cases (as distinct from foreign policy cases [National Academy of Sciences 1991, 76–85]), the Pentagon's Defense Technology Security Agency (DTSA) is another actor that is also consistently involved. In practice, however, the DTSA's power is severely circumscribed by a number of factors (discussed below).

In terms of national security cases, the goal of the interagency review and licensing processes is to fulfill "the national security objective" as set forth originally by the Export Control Act of 1949 and maintained in the current Export Administration Act (EAA). Specifically, that objective is "to restrict the export of goods and technology which would make a significant contribution to the military potential of any other country or combination of countries which would prove detrimental to the national security of the United States." The objective has remained constant, but subsequent legislation, the Export Administration Acts of 1969 and 1979 and the EAA Amendments of 1981, 1985, and 1988, incorporates additional objectives. The different organizations involved in the process not only interpret the original national security objective differently, but they also become associated with particular definitions of national security based on the newer objectives specified in the act. These disparate conceptions of national security, the result of distinct organizational missions and interests, are difficult to balance and often lead to acute policy differences.

Differences between the relevant bureaucratic organizations involved in national security export controls can become so intractable that formal dispute resolution mechanisms are necessary. The Export Administration Review Board (EARB) is a three-tier structure designed to resolve interagency disputes over national security licenses to proscribed destinations. "Although the EARB's process for resolving disputed licenses has worked fairly successfully for exports to proscribed destinations, as late as 1990 there was no parallel system for exports to nonproscribed countries or for proliferation cases" (National Academy of Sciences, 1991, 99). This shortcoming is not only serious, but is directly relevant to the case under study. With regard to export controls for national security purposes, Iraq was a "nonproscribed country" prior to the Persian Gulf War. If the Commerce Department granted an export license for a dual-use item to a nonproscribed destination, then only a direct intervention from the White House could stop its delivery. Such senior-level intervention was rare. In fact, it occurred only once, when in July 1990, as noted, the White House permanently blocked the shipment of three industrial furnaces to Iraq. Its decisions to override the Commerce Department's approval of the controversial sale was based on concern that the furnaces might be used by Iraq in nuclear weapons projects (Wines 1990a, A3).

THE DEFENSE DEPARTMENT

Within the interagency review process, the Department of Defense was the most vigorous opponent of American prewar technology sales to Iraq. Its policy stand and corresponding arguments toward export controls were directly related to its organizational mission. Charged with ensuring the defense and security of the United States and its allies, the Pentagon's position on dual-use exports was motivated by a military perception of national security. It believed U.S. technology would contribute to the military capability of Iraq and, therefore, be harmful to the long-term security interests of the United States and its Middle Eastern friends. The Defense Technology Security Agency (DTSA), a small unit with expertise in militarily critical technologies, waged the Pentagon's bureaucratic battles with Commerce and State over sale of dual-use technology. Although the DTSA was successful in using its expertise to control the export of dual-use items to the Soviet Union and Eastern bloc, it failed in the case of Iraq.

DTSA's powerlessness emanates from its numerous bargaining disadvantages. First, unlike the Department of Commerce, which works on behalf of American corporations, trade associations, and foreign importers, the Defense Department has no natural constituency to assist it in its export control struggles. Second, the DTSA has no specific statutory export control authority. It is only granted a consulting role (National Academy of Sciences 1991, 80). Although it is customary for the DTSA to review dual-use exports to proscribed destinations and "to nonproscribed destinations that may pose a risk of diversion to a proscribed destination" (National Academy of Sciences 1991, 80), its right to review exports intended for direct shipment to nonproscribed destinations—as in the case of Iraq from 1984 to 1990—is not automatic. Third, the DTSA can officially enter the export licensing process only when either the Commerce or State Departments ask it to review a case. Commerce rarely seeks technical reviews from the Pentagon. Rather, it opts to go to other agencies like the Department of Energy or the intelligence community. Fourth, even if the Pentagon is invited into the review process, there is no guarantee its views will be heard. Stephen Bryen, a deputy undersecretary of defense (1981– 1988), comments: "It was routine for our recommendations to be ignored. [The Commerce Department] disregarded five years of thorough technical and intelligence evaluations by Defense and the CIA" (Waas 1991, 91). Lastly, although the DTSA can register objections to export licenses issued by the Commerce Department, it cannot veto the sale of a dual-use item. Barring White House intervention, the Commerce Department has the final say.

The DTSA employed a number of arguments in promoting and defending its position on export controls. These justifications, like its policy stand, were derived from the Pentagon's organizational mission and military perception of national security. Its most widely cited justifications for denying dual-use exports to Iraq were legal arguments relating to nonproliferation and, second, the actual military threat they posed. As Bryen stated: "We have a law called the Nuclear Nonproliferation Act, and if you have knowledge that a technology could be used to build nuclear weapons and intelligence to back it up . . . , then you don't sell it" (ABC News 1991, 5). On military grounds, the Defense Department opposed many dual-use exports with the argument that the products had clear and dangerous military applications. The DTSA supported its military use argument by referencing its own Military Critical Technologies List (MCTL). The MCTL is a classified document used to determine whether certain dual-use technologies and munitions can be exported without jeopardizing national security (Heinz 1991, 25). In the case of Iraq, the vast majority of high-technology items the Pentagon opposed fell into the MCTL's categories or were, in its view, clear precursors to weapons of mass destruction.

Two notable cases were the authorized sales of a hybrid analog computer system and an image enhancement system. In the first case, a November 1986 memorandum warned that the sale of a hybrid computer to Iraq's Saad 16 missile facility should not be approved "because of the high likelihood of military end use and the association of the involved companies in sensitive military applications." It also cautioned that "the computer could be used to monitor wind-tunnel tests for ballistic missiles" (Sciolino 1992b, A10). In the second, which occurred in 1987, the Pentagon attempted to block the export license for an image enhancement system, arguing: "We believe that the real purpose of this equipment [is] to assist the Iraqis in targeting sites far from the Iraqi borders, giving them eyes in the day and the night thousands of miles from their territory. That, to us, . . . [is] a very dangerous thing to be doing" (ABC News 1992a, 1).

Besides the nonproliferation and potential military use arguments, the Pentagon at times employed other reasons for controlling dual-use exports to Iraq. For instance, it raised the possibility of deception with regard to the products' end use. As Assistant Secretary of Defense Richard Perle wrote in 1985:

> Iraq continues to actively pursue an interest in nuclear weapons; a large number of Warsaw Pact nationals in Iraq makes diversion a real possibility; and in the past, Iraq has been somewhat less than honest in regard to the intended end use of high technology equipment. (Sciolino 1992c, A10)

An additional argument was that the Commerce Department's promotion of technology exports inhibited the U.S. ability to convince its allies to limit their own sale of advanced technology to Baghdad. Bryen reports the comments of the Germans and Italians when the Pentagon approached them regarding missile technology: "They pointed the finger right back at us and . . . said you people are exporting the same kinds of goods. . . . Why don't you stop your own companies?" (ABC News 1991, 7–8). Finally, in objecting to prewar technology sales, the Pentagon also raised such issues as upsetting the regional balance of power, the repressive nature of the Iraqi regime,[5] and the reputation of several of the exporting companies in contributing to nuclear-related projects elsewhere.[6]

When dual-use exports to Iraq from 1984 to 1990 are examined as a whole, a common pattern arises. The Pentagon embraced the original "national security objective" and consistently argued that Iraq should be denied U.S. technology. The Commerce Department, on the other hand, repeatedly overrode the DTSA's objections and approved the sales of advanced technology without condition. Indeed, the Pentagon's DTSA was interested in expanding its domain in export control policy as a means of protecting and promoting its vision of national security. However, the fact that its "rejection rate for Iraqi cases (it was allowed to see) was 40 percent, compared to 5 percent for the Soviet Union" indicates that the Defense Department was also truly concerned about the nature of technology that Iraq was purchasing (ABC News 1991, 4).

THE COMMERCE DEPARTMENT

The Commerce Department favored repeatedly the sale of a wide array of dual-use products to Iraq. Therefore, it held an export policy position diametrically opposed to the Pentagon's. The policy stand and corresponding arguments in favor of liberal export controls embraced by Commerce were directly related to its organizational role. Specifically, the department's mission is to "encourage, serve, and promote the Nation's international trade, economic growth, and technological advancement." This mission, in addition to motivating its position on export controls, was responsible for the department's *active promotion* of Iraqi–American trade, of which dual-use technology was a large part. Although Congress had attempted to separate the Commerce Department's export control and trade promotion functions between its Bureau of Export Administration (BXA) and its International Trade Administration (ITA), the two offices worked in tandem to facilitate the sale of American technology to Iraq. The ITA vigorously promoted the sale of American products to Iraq, while the BXA provided the necessary export licenses. Such interbureau cooperation leaves little doubt about the Commerce Department's organizational essence, that is, "the view held by the dominant group in the organization of what [its] missions and capabilities should be" (Halperin 1974, 28).

The International Trade Administration (ITA) viewed the prewar sale of American products (including high-technology items) to Iraq as both a fulfillment of its mission and a benefit to the country's trade balance. As a result, from before 1984 until August 2, 1990,[7] the ITA was engaged in a number of activities designed to facilitate contact between U.S. companies and Iraqi importers. It sponsored trade fairs, missions, and shows, for instance. From 1982 through 1984, the ITA supported the participation of more than twenty major U.S. companies in the annual Baghdad International Trade Fair (Roth 1982, 32–33; U.S. Department of Commerce 1986, 25). Second, from 1985 through 1989, the ITA also "sponsored its own *official* U.S. pavilion" at those same annual trade expositions (Roth 1985, 52; U.S. Department of Commerce 1990, i). Moreover, the number of participating companies increased each year. Third, the Commerce Department scheduled special events, such as 1990 Executive Aerospace Trade Mission to Iraq (Safire 1990, A19).

Besides promotional activities in Iraq, the ITA provided information and open encouragement to potential American exporters. For example, it worked actively on behalf of U.S. corporations by disseminating trade data, providing ad hoc counseling, and, in some instances, lobbying potential Iraqi importers. In ITA's official publication, *Business America*, Iraq was touted consistently as "the last major untapped market in the Near East for American goods and services" (Reiner 1985, 22).

Many of the exports ITA promoted clearly had dual uses and were of a sophisticated nature. In 1987, Thomas Sams, ITA's country desk officer for Iraq, wrote encouragingly: "Computers and software offer good export sales opportunities for the United States. Since 1980, the Iraqi government has been firmly committed to the expanded use and application of computers and related technology" (Sams 1987, 28). It is now known that this "commitment" included dangerous military "uses" and "applications." Surprisingly, the Commerce Department even dismissed direct warnings from U.S. companies that their products had both civilian and military uses. Regarding a sale of industrial furnaces to Iraq, for example, Henry M. Rowan, chairman of Inductotherm Industries Inc., writes:

> The [Commerce] Department was adamant that our doubts were unfounded—that the Iraqis did not have nuclear designs—and strongly encouraged our exports. An expert sent by the department to our office even left a brochure, *Helpful Hints to Exporters*. And when Baghdad approved our $11 million contract . . . , a State Department representative in Baghdad sent a telex saying, "Hooray for you!" (Rowan 1992, A25)

Despite the ITA's promotional role, it was the Bureau of Export Administration (BXA) that ensured that American products would ultimately reach Iraq. It successfully fought the Commerce Department's bureaucratic battles with the Pentagon over the licensing of dual-use, high-tech products to Iraq; and it issued the necessary export licenses. The BXA was aided in its confrontations with the Defense Department by a number of bargaining advantages. These included the preponderance of formal authority under the Export Administration Act (EAA), the lack of White House intervention, the State Department's support within the interagency review process (discussed below), and the presence of a business constituency to reinforce its policy stand and interests in the larger U.S. policymaking arena. The constituency embraced the U.S.–Iraq Business Forum, Iraq's American lobbyists, and corporations interested in exporting to Iraq.

In terms of the bureaucratic politics that surrounded the export licensing process, BXA's major disadvantage was its lack of technical expertise regarding militarily critical technologies and foreign policy. This limitation frequently forced the BXA into the interagency review process, where the Pentagon challenged Commerce's policy stand and its parochial interests. Nevertheless, Commerce was often able to mitigate its bargaining disadvantage by blocking the DTSA's participation in the review process. Its usual justification for not allowing the Defense Department to review a particular export license was that another agency was a more appropriate source of expertise. Former Undersecretary of Commerce Paul Freedenberg comments: "[Licenses] were made available to the intelligence community and were aired fully before the State Department. It would depend on [the nature of] the particular license if the Defense Department had an automatic right to see it" (ABC News 1991, 8). Also, the BXA was reluctant to consult the Pentagon on many dual-use exports to Iraq, fearing DTSA's well-known delays as well as its attempts to gain "turf" in export control policy.

In case after case, the BXA employed a number of consistent arguments in support of its policy stand against export controls on Iraq. These justifications, like its policy stand, were derived from its dominant organizational mission and its economic perception of national security. Two arguments were particularly popular. First, there is no international agreement or set of national regulations prohibiting the sale of dual-use technology to Iraq (Wines 1991, A13; ABC News 1991, 7–8). As former Undersecretary of Commerce

Freedenberg observed, "One of the problems you had was you didn't have an international agreement on controlling technology to Iraq the way you did in controlling technology to the Soviet Union. And that meant that if the U.S. was going to turn something down, we also had to get our allies to turn it down" (ABC News 1991, 7). Second, there is no reason to believe that the Iraqis would not use the dual-use technology for its stated purpose. In regard to the second claim, the Commerce Department could point to the need for reconstruction after the Iran–Iraq War and for economic development in general. Moreover, the BXA often cited Iraqi assurances that it would use the technology for peaceful purposes as well as "insufficient documentation" to support the Pentagon's policy stand in favor of controls (Sciolino 1991, 153–154). However, the department's position in support of liberal export controls for Iraq hinged ultimately on one, all-encompassing argument: the need to protect America's economic interests, including its jobs, market share, and trade balance. In short, if U.S. companies were not going to reap the profits available in Iraq, other foreign exporters surely would.

The Commerce Department consistently favored and promoted dual-use exports to Iraq from 1984 to 1990. Its behavior within the interagency licensing and review process was completely consistent with its organizational mission and economic perception of national security. Embracing newer national security objectives introduced by the Export Administration Acts of 1969 and 1979 (see Heinz 1991), the department believed liberal export controls on U.S. trade with Iraq would benefit the country's balances of trade and payments and, therefore, its overall national security. The separation of the department's trade promotion and trade control functions between the ITA and the BXA made little difference on the issue. The case of Iraq illustrates that Commerce Department personnel, regardless of their bureau assignment, believe the department's primary mission lies with trade promotion rather than trade control. Much to the department's embarrassment, some of its officials engaged in criminal activity while fulfilling this mission. "In 68 instances involving dual-use exports to Iraq, references to military designations were deleted from the Commerce Department's official records and from copies sent to congressional investigators" (Sciolino 1992d, A18).

THE STATE DEPARTMENT

Within the interagency licensing and review process, the State Department repeatedly joined the Department of Commerce in favoring prewar technology sales to Iraq. Like the Pentagon and Commerce Department, its policy stand and supporting arguments were directly related to its organizational mission. Specifically, the State Department is responsible for the development and conduct of American foreign policy. Its primary objective is to conduct the nation's foreign relations so as to promote its security and well-being. There is a consensus among the members of the organization that this objective should be accomplished through negotiation, representation, and reporting. Consistent with this organizational mission and essence, the State Department's policy stand regarding dual-use exports to Iraq was based on diplomatic and foreign policy interests. These concerns did not exclude economic and military considerations but encompassed them within a multidimensional conception of national security and well-being. In short, the State Department perceived the technology sales to be beneficial to U.S. interests.

Regardless of whether it was licensing or simply reviewing a particular dual-use export to Iraq, the State Department was consistently against export controls for national security purposes. First, in the few instances where dual-use goods fell on the Munitions List (ML) rather than on the Commodity Control List (CCL), the State Department did not hesitate to authorize the necessary licenses. For example, its Office of Defense Trade Controls authorized the sale of 45 Bell-214 helicopters to Iraq in 1984. It was later reported that these same helicopters, originally intended for "recreation," had been converted for military use (Waas 1991, 90–91). Second, in the vast majority of the cases where it did not have licensing authority over dual-use items, the State Department fully supported the Commerce Department's export licensing decisions. Because of its foreign policy expertise and intragovernmental clout, the State Department was a great ally to the Commerce Department during its political battles with the Pentagon. This fact was important to Commerce, since despite its preponderance of formal authority, it would have had difficulty maintaining its policy stand within the interagency review process without support from other actors.

In addition to its reluctance to advocate national security controls, the State Department, with one exception, did not recommend trade restrictions on Iraq for foreign policy purposes. According to the Export Administration Regulations (EAR), possible foreign policy and nonproliferation controls include crime control, antiterrorism, regional stability, embargoed countries, biological organisms, nuclear nonproliferation, missile technology controls, and chemical weapons. Although chemical weapons controls were placed on Saddam Hussein's regime in 1987, Iraq easily qualified for a number of other restrictions given its known association with terrorists and its development of weapons of mass destruction. Moreover, despite the fact that the State Department itself chairs the Policy Coordinating Committee on Missile Technology Proliferation, it refused to label Iraq a "country of concern" (Safire 1990, A19). Thus the State Department failed to act to protect "national security" in the most obvious cases.

Besides its behavior related to export licensing and review, the State Department's actions in the general area of U.S.–Iraqi relations facilitated the flow of advanced, dual-use technology. First, it certified to Congress that Saddam Hussein had stopped supporting terrorist groups when it removed Iraq from its list of states sponsoring terrorism in 1982. This move paved the way for American trade and loans. Second, it actively lobbied the Export–Import Bank to extend loan guarantees to Iraq (see Hedges 1991a, 37, and Lacayo 1992, 42). Third, despite Iraq's unconventional weapons programs and human rights violations, the department repeatedly and actively opposed the imposition of trade sanctions against Iraq, thereby allowing the continued purchase of American dual-use technology. Even when Saddam Hussein's behavior became particularly aggressive between March and July of 1990, the State Department failed to express its displeasure to the Commerce Department and White House in any meaningful way.

The Department of State consistently employed a number of similar arguments in support of its policy stand against export controls on Iraq. These justifications, like its policy stand, were derived from its organizational mission and multidimensional conception of national security. Its economic rationale was similar to that used by the Commerce Department. For instance, it wrote regarding the sale of 45 Bell-214 helicopters to Iraq: "We believe that increased American penetration of the extremely competitive civilian aircraft market would serve the United States' interests by improving our balance of trade and lessening unemployment in the aircraft industry" (Waas 1991, 91). Similarly, it believed if American corporations did not sell Iraq the dual-use technology it desired, then foreign companies would. The position echoed that of the Commerce Department.

Unlike Commerce, however, the State Department extended its justifications for liberal export controls beyond economics to diplomatic and foreign policy concerns. First, it argued that Iraq was important to U.S. interests in the Persian Gulf region and, therefore, should not be ignored or castigated. Marshall W. Wiley, a foreign service officer, observed that "Iraq plays an important political and geographical role in addition to being an important trading partner for us, and we can't push all these considerations to the side and shut our eyes to them because of some perceived human rights violations" (Conason 1991, 83). Second, the State Department did not want the United States to be isolated in such an important region. It saw relations with Iraq as more feasible and tolerable than ties with Iran. Third, it maintained that business ties were a means of both improving U.S.–Iraqi relations and moderating Iraq's international behavior. Richard W. Murphy, President Reagan's senior Middle East diplomat, commented after leaving office: "We didn't support sanctions when they first came up, because we thought we were getting somewhere in private channels" (Wines 1990b, A11). Fourth, the department asserted that trade with Iraq was consistent with the policy direction set by Reagan's "tilt" toward Iraq in the Iran–Iraq War and Bush's NSDD 26. Finally, the State Department supported its export policy stand by arguing that there were clear signs that Iraq's behavior was changing. As late as April 26, 1990, John Kelly, assistant secretary for the Near East, told a congressional committee "that Iraq had stopped supplying arms to General Aoun in Lebanon; that Iraq was discussing a new constitution that potentially would provide for a greater recognition of human rights; [and] that Iraq had participated in two disarmament conferences on chemical weapons" (Henderson 1991, 187).

It was not until July 25, 1990, just days before the Iraqi invasion of Kuwait, that the Department of State proposed a change in U.S. export policy toward Iraq. This belated recommendation came in the form of a memorandum from Secretary of State Baker to Secretary of Commerce Mossbacher (Sciolino 1992e, A6).[8] The department's previously consistent policy stand in favor of dual-use exports to Iraq was motivated directly by its distinct organizational role and perception of national security. Moreover, its behavior in supporting dual-use technology exports from 1984 to 1990 provides its critics with evidence that the department is too sensitive to the needs of foreign countries at the expense of U.S. interests (see Clarke 1989, 89).

CONCLUSION

The government's decision to authorize dual-use technology sales to Iraq from 1984 until August 1990 was the result of an implementation process pervaded by bureaucratic politics. The major actors within this process, the Departments of Commerce, Defense, and State, held policy positions on dual-use exports to Iraq that were based directly on their distinct bureaucratic roles. Each agency's separate organizational mission and essence caused it to have a different perception of national security and, therefore, different reasons for supporting either trade promotion or trade control. These differing stands, perceptions, and arguments largely explain the interagency conflict that surrounded prewar export control policy. These interorganizational differences were further exacerbated by the nature of the U.S. export control system: the multiplicity of actors, the lack of clear control criteria for dual-use items, the ambiguity surrounding the Pentagon's "consulting role," the Commerce Department's conflicting missions, and the absence of clear definitions for key concepts (e.g., national security, military critical, and dual-use). Moreover, this conflict and ambiguity persisted due to the absence of an adequate dispute resolution mechanism, insufficient coordination from the White House, and congressional inaction. In the end, the Pentagon never had a chance. The Departments of Commerce and State, motivated by different interests and aided by a number of bargaining advantages, built a "winning" coalition in favor of liberal export controls and, therefore, determined the final action.

NOTES

Author's Note: The author wishes to thank James P. Bennett, Patricia W. Ingraham, Eugene R. Wittkopf, and the members of the Presidency and War panel at the 1992 meeting of the Southern Political Science Association for their constructive comments.

It should be noted that information about America's prewar relationship with Iraq is still being revealed.

1. It appears that $500 million of this dual-use technology was actually delivered (Sciolino 1991, 141–142).

2. Rep. Henry Gonzalez (D-TX) told the Senate Banking Committee on October 17, 1992: "Between 1985 and the Iraqi invasion of Kuwait, the Commerce Department approved at least 220 export licenses for the Iraqi armed forces, major weapons complexes and enterprises identified by the CIA as diverting technology to weapons programs" (Gonzalez 1992).

3. On April 24, 1992, *The New York Times* published a detailed list of strategic American exports that went to Iraq's atomic weapons program. The compilation was

prepared by the Wisconsin Project on Nuclear Arms Control and identifies the specific product, the Iraqi destination, the amount of the transaction, and the name of the exporting company for each sale (see Milhollin and Edensword 1992, A35).

4. This was industrial complex at Zaafaraniya where "the International Atomic Energy Agency had found advanced computer-controlled machinery that Iraq had used in its nuclear weapons program" (Gordon 1993, A1 and A10).

5. Former Undersecretary of Defense Stephen Bryen: "You don't sell things that can be used to create a strategic option in dictatorships" (ABC News 1991, 5).

6. During the "skull" furnace controversy in 1990, the Pentagon raised the issue that Consarc Corporation, the manufacturer of the furnaces, had sold similar technology to the former Soviet Union which was used to make missile nose cones (Henderson 1991, 211).

7. The Commerce Department canceled participation in the Baghdad International Trade Fair and suspended all other promotional activities regarding Iraq as of August 2, 1990.

8. Those analysts seeking an alternative explanation for why the Departments of Commerce and State consistently prevailed over the Pentagon in prewar export control policy might point to the strong personal ties that Robert Mossbacher and James Baker each had with President Bush. Yet, a personalist explanation is weakened by the high-level inattention that characterized the Iraqi case.

REFERENCES

ABC News Nightline. 1991. "Doing Business with Saddam," February 6.

ABC News Nightline. 1992a. "World Class Leadership," June 9.

ABC News Nightline. 1992b. "Arming Saddam: Cover-Up or Witch-hunt?" October 28.

Allison, Graham T. 1971. *Essence of Decision: Explaining the Cuban Missile Crisis.* Boston: Little, Brown.

Allison, Graham T., and Morton H. Halperin. 1972. "Bureaucratic Politics: A Paradigm and Some Policy Implications." *World Politics* 24:40–80 (Spring Supplement).

Clarke, Duncan L. 1989. *American Defense and Foreign Policy Institutions: Toward a Sound Foundation.* New York: Harper & Row.

Conason, Joe. 1991. "The Iraq Lobby: Kissinger, The Business Forum & Co.," in *The Gulf War Reader,* eds. Micah L. Sifry and Christopher Cerf. New York: Times Books (Random House). 79–84.

Gordon, Michael R. 1993. "Targets in South." *The New York Times,* January 19, A1 and A10.

Gonzalez, Henry B. 1992. "U.S. Export Policy with Iraq." Statement before the U.S. Senate Banking Committee. October 27.

Halperin, Morton H. 1974. *Bureaucratic Politics and Foreign Policy.* Washington, D.C.: The Brookings Institution.

Hedges, Stephen J. 1991a. "How America Appeased Iraq." *U.S. News & World Report.* April 22, 37.

Hedges, Stephen J. 1991b. "Special Report: Saddam's Secret Bomb." *U.S. News & World Report,* November 25, 34–41.

Heinz, John. 1991. *U.S. Strategic Trade: An Export Control System for the 1990s.* Boulder, Colo.: Westview Press.

Henderson, Simon, 1991. *Instant Empire: Saddam Hussein's Ambition for Iraq.* San Francisco: Mercury House.

Kay, David. 1992. "U.S. Export Policy with Iraq." Statement before U.S. Senate Banking Committee, October 27.

Lacayo, Richard. 1992. "Did Bush Create This Monster?" *Time,* June 8, 41–42.

Milhollin, Gary. 1992. "U.S. Export Policy with Iraq." Statement before U.S. Senate Banking Committee, October 27.

Milhollin, Gary, and Diane Edensword. 1992. "Iraq's Bomb, Chip by Chip." *The New York Times.* April 24. A35.

Miller, Judith, and Laurie Mylroie. 1990. *Saddam Hussein and the Crisis in the Gulf.* New York: Times Books (Random House).

National Academy of Sciences. 1991. *Finding Common Ground.* Washington, D.C.: National Academy Press.

Reiner, Karl S. 1985. "U.S. and Iraqi Trade Officials Discuss Improvement in Commercial Relations." *Business America,* February 4, 22.

Roth, Mark. 1982. "Post-War Opportunities May Be Open To Some U.S. Firms." *Business America.* August 9, 32–33.

Roth, Mark. 1985. "Market Is Improving But Financing Is Key To Sales." *Business America,* March 4, 52.

Rowan, Henry M. 1992. "Left Holding the Bag in Iraq," *The New York Times,* October 14, A25.

Safire, William. 1990. "Country of Concern." *The New York Times,* April 9, A19.

Safire, William. 1992. "Digging Deeper in Iraqgate," *The New York Times,* July 6, A13.

Sams, Thomas A. 1987. "Trade Agreement Will Boost Sales Prospects." *Business America,* September 28, 28–29.

Sciolino, Elaine. 1991. *The Outlaw State: Saddam Hussein's Quest for Power and the Gulf Crisis.* New York: John Wiley & Sons.

Sciolino, Elaine with Michael Wines. 1992a. "Bush's Greatest Glory Fades as Questions on Iraq Persist," *The New York Times,* June 7, A1 and A8.

Sciolino, Elaine. 1992b. "Documents Warned in '85 of Iraqi Nuclear Arms," *The New York Times,* July 5. A10.

Sciolino, Elaine. 1992c. "U.S. Was Aware That the Iraqis Were Buying Technology," *The New York Times,* July 22, A10.

Sciolino, Elaine. 1992d. "Iraq Policy Still Bedevils Bush as Congress Asks: Were Crimes Committed?" *The New York Times,* August 9, A18.

Sciolino, Elaine. 1992e. "Baker Warned U.S. of Iraqi Buildup, Papers Show," *The New York Times,* September 24, A6.

Seib, Gerald F. 1992. "Attention Refocuses on U.S. Courtship of Iraq, Illustrating How an Issue Can Be Rekindled." *The Wall Street Journal,* May 12, A26.

Timmerman, Kenneth R. 1992. "U.S. Export Policy with Iraq." Statement before U.S. Senate Banking Committee, October 27.

Tolchin, Martin. 1992. "Inquiry Into U.S. Aid to Iraq Urged," *The New York Times,* May 18, D1 and D2.

U.S. Department of Commerce. 1986. "The Baghdad International Fair Is a Good Marketing Vehicle." *Business America,* July 7, 25.

U.S. Department of Commerce. 1990. "Trade Watch: Iraq." *Business America,* August 13, i.

Waas, Murray. 1991. "What Washington Gave Saddam For Christmas." In *The Gulf War Reader,* eds. Micah L. Sifry and Christopher Cerf. New York: Times Books (Random House), 85–95.

Wines, Michael. 1990a. "White House Blocks Furnace Export to Iraq," *The New York Times,* July 20, A3.

Wines, Michael. 1990b. "U.S. Aid Helped Hussein's Climb; Now Critics Say, the Bill Is Due," *The New York Times,* August 13, A1 and A11.

Wines, Michael. 1991. "U.S. Tells of Prewar Technology Sales to Iraq Worth $500 Million, *The New York Times,* March 12, A13.

20. POLICY PREFERENCES AND BUREAUCRATIC POSITION: THE CASE OF THE AMERICAN HOSTAGE RESCUE MISSION

Steve Smith

Within two days of the seizure by student revolutionaries of the American embassy in Tehran on 4 November 1979, planning began on a possible rescue mission. Initial estimates of the probability of success were "zero," given the severe logistic problems involved in getting to the embassy in Iran and back out of the country without losing a large number of the hostages as casualties. Nevertheless, as negotiations dragged on with very little promise of success, and as the 1980 American presidential election campaign approached, the decision was made to undertake a very bold rescue mission. Photographs of the charred remains of the burnt-out helicopters in the Dasht-e-Kavir desert provide the most vivid image of the failure of that mission.

The decisions about the mission were taken at three meetings on 22 March, 11 April, and 15 April 1980 by a very small group of people (on average, there were nine participants). Since 1980, the hostage rescue mission has received considerable coverage in the press and in the memoirs of the participants in that decision-making process. As such, it is an excellent case study for one of the most widely cited but rarely tested theories of foreign policy behavior: the bureaucratic politics approach.

THE THEORETICAL BACKGROUND

The dominant theories of why states act as they do derive from the basic assumption of rationality. Most theories of foreign policy are based on the premise that states act in a more or less monolithic way: Foreign policy is,

Note: Some notes have been deleted or renumbered.

accordingly, behavior that is goal-directed and intentional. Of course, many practitioners and academics quickly move away from the monolith assumption, but they can rarely command the kind of detailed information that would enable them to assess precisely what the factions are and how the balance of views lies in any decision-making group. It is, therefore, very common to talk of states as entities and to analyze "their" foreign policies according to some notion of a linkage between the means "they" choose and the ends these must be directed toward. Since practitioners and academics do not literally "know" why State X undertook Action Y, it becomes necessary to impute intentions to the behavior of states. The rationality linkage makes this task much easier; hence the popularity of the idea of the national interest, which incorporates very clear and powerful views on what the ends of governments are in international society and, therefore, on how the behavior can be linked to intentions. The most important attack on this viewpoint has been the "bureaucratic politics approach," most extensively outlined by Graham Allison in his *Essence of Decision*.[1] According to this approach, foreign policy is the result of pulling and hauling between the various components of the decision-making process. Foreign policy may, therefore, be better explained as the outcome of bureaucratic bargaining than as a conscious choice by a decision-making group. As Allison puts it, the outcome of the decision-making process is not really a result but "a resultant—a mixture of conflicting preferences and unequal power of various individuals—distinct from what any person or group intended."[2] The critical point is that these conflicting preferences are determined, above all, by bureaucratic position. Foreign policy, according to this perspective, is therefore to be explained by analyzing the bureaucratic battleground of policymaking, rather than imputing to something called the state a set of motives and interests. On the bureaucratic battleground, the preferences of the participants are governed by the aphorism . . . "where you stand depends on where you sit."[3] . . .

The decision of the United States government to attempt a rescue of the 53 American hostages held in Iran offers an excellent opportunity . . . to test . . . Allison's claims about bureaucratic position and policy preference. . . .

The planning process for the rescue mission began on 6 November 1979, just two days after the hostages were seized in Tehran. During the winter and spring the planning continued, focusing on the composition and training of the rescue force, on the precise location of the hostages and the nature and location of their captors, and on the enormously complex logistic problems involved in mounting the mission. These preparations continued in secret alongside an equally complex process of negotiation for the release of the hostages with the various elements of the Iranian government (including a secret contact in Paris). Bargaining was also under way with the United States's allies, in an attempt to persuade them to impose sanctions on Iran. As noted above, there were three key meetings at which the rescue plan was discussed (on 22 March, 11 and 15 April 1980), although the actual decision to proceed, taken on 11 April and confirmed on 15 April, was in many ways only the formal ratification of what had by then become the dominant mode of thinking among President Carter's most senior advisers. There were two schools of thought in the initial reaction to the seizure of the hostages: first, that the United States should impose economic sanctions on Iran; second, that it should make use of international public opinion and international law to force the Iranian government to release the hostages. As these measures appeared less and less likely to succeed, the U.S. government became involved in attempts to persuade its allies to join in economic sanctions—a move that succeeded just two days before the rescue mission.

President Carter's initial reaction to the seizure was to stress the importance of putting the lives of the hostages first. He declared on 7 December 1979, "I am not going to take any military action that would cause bloodshed or cause the unstable captors of our hostages to attack or punish them." Yet leaks from the White House indicated that military plans were being considered. By late March 1980, President Carter and his advisers were becoming convinced that negotiations were not going to be successful, a view confirmed by the secret source in the Iranian government. At a meeting held on 22 March at Camp David, the president agreed to a reconnaissance flight into Iran to find an initial landing site for the rescue force (Desert One). The plan called for eight RH-53 helicopters from the aircraft carrier *Nimitz* to fly nearly 600 miles, at a very low altitude and with radio blackout, from the Arabian Sea to Desert One. There, they would meet the rescue force of 97 men (code named "Delta Force") who would have arrived from Egypt via Oman on four C-130 transport aircraft. The helicopters would refuel from the C-130s and then take Delta Force to a second location (Desert Two) some 50 miles southeast of Tehran, where Central Intelligence Agency (CIA) agents would meet them and hide the rescue force at a "mountain hideout." Delta Force would remain hidden during the day before being picked up by CIA operatives early the next night and driven to a location known as "the warehouse" just inside Tehran. From there they would attack the embassy and the Foreign Ministry where three of the hostages were held, rescue the hostages, and take them to a nearby soccer stadium, where the helicopters would meet them and transfer them to a further airstrip at Monzariyeh, to be taken to Egypt by the C-130s. The planning process had meant that very definite deadlines had emerged: By 1 May there would only be 16 minutes of darkness more than required for the mission; by 10 May, the temperature would be so high that it would seriously hamper helicopter performance. 1 May appeared to be the latest feasible date for the mission, and by late March the planners were recommending 24 April for the mission (primarily because a very low level of moonlight was expected that night). But the rescue mission failed. It never got beyond Desert One. Of the eight helicopters assigned to the mission, one got lost in a duststorm and returned to the *Nimitz* and two suffered mechanical breakdowns. This left only five helicopters in working order at Desert One, whereas the plan had called for six to move on to Desert Two. The mission was subsequently aborted, and, in the process of maneuvering to vacate Desert One, one of the helicopters hit a C-130, causing the death of eight men.

It is critical, in any discussion of the applicability of the bureaucratic politics approach, to focus on the actual decisions that led to this mission and to review the positions adopted by the participants. . . . We know that the three meetings of 22 March, 11 and 15 April were the decisive ones, and we know who took part and what they said. The key meeting in terms of the actual decision was on 11 April, when the "go-ahead" was given. The meeting on 22 March was important because at it President Carter gave permission for aircraft to verify the site for Desert One. The meeting of 15 April was important because Cyrus Vance, the secretary of state, presented his reservations about the decision. As Zbigniew Brzezinski, President Carter's national security adviser, pointed out: "In a way, the decision [on 11 April] had been foreshadowed by the discussion initiated at the March 22 briefing at Camp David. From that date on, the rescue mission became the obvious option if negotiations failed—and on that point there was almost unanimous consent within the top echelons of the Administration."[4] A virtually identical set of people were present at those meetings. On 22 March, there attended President Carter, Walter Mondale (the vice president) Cyrus Vance (the secretary of state), Harold Brown (the secretary of defense), David Jones (the chairman of the Joint Chiefs of Staff), Stansfield Turner (the director of the CIA), Zbigniew Brzezinski (the national security adviser), Jody Powell (the press secretary), and David Aaron (the deputy national security adviser). On 11 April, the same participants convened, except that Warren Christopher, the deputy secretary of state, replaced Cyrus Vance, and Carter's aide Hamilton Jordan replaced Aaron. The final meeting on 15 April was attended by the same people who attended on 11 April, except that Vance replaced Christopher.

In order to outline the positions adopted by the participants in this decision-making group, the participants can be divided into four subgroups: President Carter, "hawks," "doves," and "presidential supporters." (These terms are only intended as analytical shorthand.) . . . Although there is a risk of fitting evidence to a preconception, the conclusion . . . is that these groups acted in accordance with what the bureaucratic politics approach would suggest: namely, that the national security adviser, the secretary of defense, the chairman of the Joint Chiefs of Staff, and the director of the CIA would support military action . . . ; the secretary of state, and in his absence his deputy, would oppose it; those individuals who were bureaucratically tied to the president (the vice president, the press secretary, and the political adviser) would be fundamentally concerned with what was best for the Carter presidency; and President Carter, although clearly more than just another bureaucratic actor, would act in a way that reflected bureaucratically derived as well as personal influences.

PRESIDENT CARTER

The key to understanding President Carter's position lies in the interaction between his desire to avoid the blatant use of American military power and the great pressure on him to satisfy his public and "do something." From the earliest days of the crisis, he was attacked in the press and by the Republican party for failing to act decisively. 1980 was, of course, a presidential election year, the president's public opinion rating was poor, and he was being challenged strongly for the Democratic party's nomination. His promise not to campaign for the election so long as the hostages were in Iran made his situation worse. He was advised by his campaign staff that decisive action was needed (especially after the fiasco of the morning of the Wisconsin primary, on 1 April, when the president announced that the hostages were about to be released). That inaccurate assessment was seen by many as a reflection of his lack of control over events; it was also portrayed as manipulating the issue for his own political ends.

Another factor which added to the president's frustration was the desire to make the allies go ahead with sanctions against Iran. It later turned out that the allies' belief that the U.S. administration was planning military action was their main incentive to join in the sanctions, in the hope of forestalling it. But the critical moment came when the president felt that the only alternative to military action was to wait until, possibly, the end of the year for the release of the hostages by negotiation. That was the impression he gained in the early days of April: Information coming out of Tehran indicated that the release of the hostages would be delayed for months by the parliamentary elections due to be held in Iran on 16 May. Indeed, by the time the rescue mission was undertaken, the favorite estimate of how long the new government in Iran would take to negotiate was five or six months. So, as a result of fear that the hostages might be held until the end of 1980, President Carter determined on a change in policy: "We could no longer afford to depend on diplomacy. I decided to act."[5] In fact, the president threatened military action on 12 and 17 April, unless the allies undertook economic sanctions. This action (which, he said, had not been decided on yet) would involve the interruption of trade with Iran. (This was widely interpreted as meaning a naval blockade or the mining of Iranian harbors.) Of course, this was a deliberate smokescreen: Accordingly, when on 23 April the European countries agreed to the imposition of sanctions on Iran, the White House let it be known that this would delay any military action until the summer!

Yet the desire of the president for drastic action is only part of the story. It is evident that he was also extremely concerned to limit the size of the operation, in order to avoid unnecessary loss of life. At the briefing with the mission commander, Colonel Beckwith, on 16 April, Carter said: "It will be easy and tempting for your men to become engaged in gunfire with others and to try and settle some scores for our nation. That will interfere with your objective of getting our people out safely. In the eyes of the world, it is important that the scope of this mission be seen as simply removing our people." William Safire has argued that the reason why the mission was unsuccessful was precisely because Carter wanted the rescue to be a humanitarian rather than a combat mission and stipulated only a small force with very limited backup.[6] Hence, in explaining President Carter's position on the rescue mission, two factors seem dominant: a personal concern to ensure that the mission was not to be seen as a punitive military action and a role-governed perception that American national honor was at stake. . . .

Carter's actions were, of course, a response to a number of factors. The bureaucratic politics approach draws our attention to certain of these: specifically, his desire for reelection and his perception of his responsibility as the individual charged with protecting American national honor. Clearly, Carter's personality was an important factor . . . , but the bureaucratic politics approach seems much more useful in identifying the kinds of considerations that would be important to Carter than concentrating on notions of what would be most rational for the American nation. This is not to imply that bureaucratic factors are the only important ones in explaining what Carter did; but it is to claim that a bureaucratic perspective paints a far more accurate picture of what caused Carter to act as he did than any of the rival theories of foreign policymaking.

THE HAWKS

The leading political proponents of military action throughout the crisis were Brzezinski and Brown. Drew Middleton wrote, "For months, a hard-nosed Pentagon view had held that the seizure of the hostages itself was an act of war and that the United States was, therefore, justified in adopting a military response."[7] Indeed, just two days after the hostages were taken, Brzezinski, Brown, and Jones began discussing the possibilities of a rescue mission. Their discussions led to the conclusion that an immediate mission was impossible, but Brzezinski felt that "one needed such a contingency scheme in the event . . . that some of the hostages either were put on trial and then sentenced to death or were murdered. . . . Accordingly, in such circumstances, we would have to undertake a rescue mission out of a moral as well as a political obligation, both to keep faith with our people imprisoned in Iran and to safeguard American national honor." In fact, Brzezinski felt a rescue mission was not enough: "It would [be] better if the United States were to engage in a generalized retaliatory strike, which could be publicly described as a punitive action and which would be accompanied by the rescue attempt. If the rescue succeeded, that would be all to the good; if it failed, the U.S. government could announce that it had executed a punitive mission against Iran."[8] This punitive action, he thought, could take the form of a military blockade along with airstrikes. In the earliest days of the crisis, Brzezinski, Turner, Jones, and Brown began to meet regularly in private and discuss military options; Brzezinski alone took (handwritten) notes. It was this group which directed the planning for the mission (which used military and CIA personnel) and gave the eventual plan its most detailed review. Similarly, it was Brzezinski who pressed for the reconnaissance flight into Iran, agreed on 22 March, and the same group of four who proposed the rescue plan at the 11 April meeting, led by Brown and Jones. But it is clear from the available evidence that Brzezinski was the political force behind military action.

As early as February, Brzezinski felt increasing pressure from the public and from Congress for direct action to be taken against Iran. Brzezinski thought there were three choices: to continue negotiations, to undertake a large military operation, or to mount a small rescue mission. What swung him away from his earlier first choice, a punitive military operation, was the consideration that, after the Soviet intervention in Afghanistan in December 1979, any military action might give the Soviet Union additional opportunities for influence in the Persian Gulf and Indian Ocean: "It now seemed to me more important to forge an anti-Soviet Islamic coalition. It was in this context that the rescue mission started to look more attractive to me."⁹ As negotiations failed, Brzezinski sent a memorandum to Carter on 10 April in which he argued that a choice must be made between a punitive military action or a rescue mission. Given his fears about the spread of Soviet influence, Brzezinski recommended the latter option, concluding, "We have to think beyond the fate of the 50 Americans and consider the deleterious effects of a protracted stalemate, growing public frustration, and international humiliation of the U.S."¹⁰ At both the 11 April and 15 April meetings, Brzezinski spoke forcefully in favor of the mission.

Brown and Jones were the main advocates of the actual rescue plan. . . . These two men presented the plan to the 11 April meeting and conducted the detailed private briefing with Carter on 16 April; it was Harold Brown who gave the detailed account, and defense, of the mission to the press after its failure. It was also Brown who spoke against the Christopher/Vance position at the 11 April and 15 April meetings. Finally, both Brown and Brzezinski spoke very strongly in justification of the mission after its failure, stating that it had been morally right and politically justified. Brzezinski was said to be "downright cocky about it [the mission] in private and insisting that military action might be necessary in future."¹¹ He also warned America's opponents: "Do not scoff at America's power. Do not scoff at American reach."¹²

Turner, the director of the CIA, was also very much in favor of the mission, so much so that it appears that he did not voice the very serious doubts about the mission which had been expressed in a report by a special CIA review group, prepared for him on 16 March 1980. According to this report, the rescue plan would probably result in the loss of 60 percent of the hostages during the mission: "The estimate of a loss rate of 60 percent for the AmEmbassy hostages represents the best estimate." The report also estimated that the mission was as likely to prove a complete failure as a complete success. Yet it was exactly at this time that the review of the plan was undertaken by Brzezinski's small group. To quote Brzezinski again: "A very comprehensive review of the rescue plan undertaken by Brown, Jones, and me in mid-March led me to the conclusion that the rescue mission had a reasonably good chance of success though there probably would be some casualties. *There was no certain way of estimating how large they might be* [emphasis added]."¹³ Turner was involved in the detailed briefings of the president; at the meeting of 11 April he even said, "The conditions inside and around the compound are good." The evidence does not suggest that he made his agency's doubts public at any of these meetings, either in the small group or in the group of nine.

To sum up: The positions adopted by those classified here as "hawks" could have been predicted in advance. What is striking about the evidence is the consistency with which these four men—Brown, Brzezinski, Jones, and

Turner—proposed policies that reflected their position in the bureaucratic network. . . . To the extent that the bureaucratic politics approach explains the policies adopted by these individuals, it illustrates the weaknesses of rationality-based theories of U.S. foreign policy.

PRESIDENTIAL SUPPORTERS

The next group to consider are those who do not fit into the traditional "hawks–doves" characterization of U.S. government. These are individuals whose primary loyalty is to the president and who would therefore be expected to adopt positions that promised to bolster the president's domestic standing. Unlike those groups discussed so far, the first concern of this group is not the nature of U.S. relations with other states, but, rather, the domestic position of the president. Mondale, Powell, and Jordan seem to have been neither "hawks" nor "doves" in their views of the Iranian action; rather, their policy proposals show that their concern was first and foremost with the effect of the crisis on the Carter presidency. This can be seen very clearly in Jordan's memoirs,[14] which reveal both a loyalty to Carter and an evaluation of the rescue mission in terms of how it helped Carter out of a domestic political problem. "I knew our hard-line approach would not bring the hostages home any sooner, but I hoped that maybe it would buy us a little more time and patience from the public." The rescue mission was "the best of a lousy set of options." Throughout his memoirs, at every juncture of the mission's planning, failure, and consequences, Jordan's position is consistently one in which he advocates what he believed would benefit the president. This determined his reaction to Vance's objections (Vance was failing to support the president when he needed it, thereby putting Carter in an uncomfortable position), to the failure of the mission (Congress's reaction would be to concentrate on the lack of consultation, and it might accuse Carter of violating the War Powers Resolution), and to Vance's resignation and his replacement by Ed Muskie (the former created a problem for Carter, the latter was a vote of confidence in Carter's political future).

The evidence also unambiguously supports the contention that Mondale and Powell were motivated above all by an awareness of the president's domestic standing and their perceptions of how it might be improved. Brzezinski notes that Powell, Mondale, and Jordan "were feeling increasingly frustrated and concerned about rising public pressures for more direct action against Iran."[15] All of them seemed to think that direct action was needed to stem this public pressure, *especially* after the Wisconsin primary announcement on 1 April. As Powell put it on 1 April: "We are about to have an enormous credibility problem. The combination of not campaigning and that early-morning announcement has made skeptics out of even our friends in the press." Salinger argues that Carter's "campaign for reelection registered the frustrations of the American public. While his political fortunes had risen after the taking of the hostages, he was beginning to slip in the polls and had lost a key primary in New York to Senator Kennedy. Jimmy Carter was now in the midst of a fight for his political life, and it looked as if he was losing. A military operation that freed the hostages would dramatically alter the odds."[16] The position of the "presidential supporters" was summed up in Mondale's contribution to the 11 April meeting, when he said, "The rescue offered us the best way out of a situation which was becoming intolerably humiliating." . . .

The "presidential supporters," then, proposed policies which reflected their own bureaucratic position. Mondale, Powell, and Jordan had no vast bureaucratic interests to represent, nor was their chief concern the relationship between U.S. foreign policy and other states. Each of them owed their influence to their position vis-à-vis President Carter (as, of course, did Brzezinski), and their concern was to act so as to aid his presidency, above all his domestic political fortunes. In contemporary press reports, it was these three men who voiced concern about the president's relations with Congress and his chances of reelection. This was in contrast to both the "hawks" and the "doves" who were far more concerned with Carter's relations with Iran, the Soviet Union, and U.S. allies. As in the case of the "hawks," the policy preferences of the "presidential supporters" seem to have been predominantly determined by their bureaucratic role.

THE DOVES

The evidence that bureaucratic role determines policy stance is strongest of all in the case of the "doves": Cyrus Vance, the secretary of state, and Warren Christopher, the deputy secretary of state. Not only did the two men take virtually identical stands on the subject of the rescue mission, but, as will be discussed below, Christopher did not know what Vance's position was when he attended the 11 April meeting.

From the earliest days of the crisis Vance had advised against the use of military force. At the meeting on 22 March, Vance agreed that a reconnaissance flight should go ahead in case a rescue mission should prove necessary (in the case of a threat to the hostages' lives), but argued against "the use of any military force, including a blockade or mining, as long as the hostages were unharmed and in no imminent danger. In addition to risking the lives of the hostages, I believed military action could jeopardize our interests in the Persian Gulf. . . . Our only realistic course was to keep up the pressure on Iran while we waited for Khomeini to determine that . . . the hostages were of no further value. As painful as it would be, our national interests and the need to protect the lives of our fellow Americans dictated that we continued to exercise restraint." After this meeting, Vance felt there was no indication that a decision on the use of military force was imminent, and on 10 April he left for a long weekend's rest in Florida.

But on the very next day the meeting was held that made the decision to go ahead with the rescue mission. Jody Powell explained to the press later that Cyrus Vance was on a well-earned vacation and that "Vance was not called back because it would have attracted too much attention when the operation had to remain secret." There is no evidence as to why the meeting was called in his absence, but it is clear that Vance did not know that the mission was being so seriously considered and that everyone else involved knew that Vance would disagree. Tom Wicker argues that Vance was deliberately shunted aside from the critical meeting in order to weaken his (and the State Department's) ability to prevent the mission from proceeding.[17] All the Carter, Brzezinski, and Jordan memoirs say is that Vance was on "a brief and much needed vacation" (Carter), "on vacation" (Brzezinski), and "in Florida on a long overdue vacation" (Jordan). In many ways the exclusion of Vance can be interpreted as a symptom of what Irving Janis calls "groupthink"; other symptoms can also be determined in this case study of the phenomenon, which refers to the tendency for groups to maintain amiability and cohesiveness at the cost of critical thinking about decisions.[18]

The president opened the meeting of 11 April by saying that he was seriously considering undertaking a rescue mission, and he invited Brown and Jones to brief those present on the planned mission. At this point, Jordan turned to Christopher and said: "What do you think?" "I'm not sure. Does Cy know about this?" "The contingency rescue plan? Of course." "No, no— does he realize how far along the President is in his thinking about this?" "I don't know . . . I assume they've talked about it." When the briefing finished, Christopher was first to speak. He outlined a number of alternatives to a rescue mission: a return to the U.N. for more discussions, the blacklisting of Iranian ships and aircraft, the possibility of getting European support for sanctions against Iran. Brown immediately dismissed these as "not impressive," and he was supported by Brzezinski, Jones, Turner, Powell, and Jordan, all of whom wanted to go ahead. Christopher was alone in his opposition to the plan. He declined to take up a formal position on the rescue mission since he had not been told about it in advance by Vance; he therefore felt that Vance had either accepted the plan or had felt that the State Department could not really prevent its going ahead. . . . His impression was reinforced when Carter informed the meeting that Vance "prior to leaving for his vacation in Florida, had told the President that he opposed any military action but if a choice had to be made between a rescue and a wider blockade, he preferred the rescue." Christopher knew that Vance had opposed the use of military force, but it is logical to assume that he felt all he could do was to offer nonbelligerent alternatives (they were, after all, State Department people being held hostage) to any use of military force, but remain silent on the actual mission; particularly as it had been strongly suggested that Vance had *already* agreed to it. In support of this conclusion, it is interesting to note that Christopher did not contact Vance on holiday to tell him what had happened. . . .

Vance's reaction to the news was "that he was dismayed and mortified."[19] Vance writes: "Stunned and angry that such a momentous decision had been made in my absence, I went to see the President."[20] At this meeting Vance listed his objections to the mission, and Carter offered him the opportunity to present his views to the group which had made the original decision in the meeting to be held on 15 April. Vance's statement at that meeting focused on issues almost entirely dictated by his bureaucratic position. He said, first, that to undertake the mission when the United States had been trying to get the Europeans to support sanctions on the explicit promise that this would rule out military action would look like deliberate deception; second, the hostages, who were State Department employees, were in no immediate physical danger; third, there were apparently moves in Iran to form a functioning government with which the United States could negotiate; fourth, that even if it succeeded, the mission might simply lead to the taking of more American (or allied) hostages by the Iranians; fifth, it might force the Iranians into the arms of the Soviet Union; and, finally, there would almost certainly be heavy casualties (he cited the figure of 15 out of the 53 hostages and 30 out of the rescue force as a likely death toll).

After Vance's comments, Brown turned to him and asked him when he expected the hostages to be released; Vance replied that he did not know. No one supported Vance: His objections were met by "a deafening silence." Although Vance said later that, after the meeting, a number of participants told him that he had indeed raised serious objections, no one mentioned them at the time—an example of "groupthink"? Carter noted that Vance "was alone in his opposition to the rescue mission among all my advisers, and he knew it."[21] In their memoirs, Carter and Brzezinski put Vance's subsequent resignation down to tiredness: "He looked worn out, his temper would flare up, his eyes were puffy, and he projected unhappiness. . . . Cy seemed to be burned out and determined to quit" (Brzezinski); "Vance has been extremely despondent lately . . . for the third or fourth time, he indicated that he might resign . . . but after he goes through a phase of uncertainty and disapproval, then he joins in with adequate support for me" (Carter). Even worries expressed by Vance about the details of the plan at the 16 April briefing were dismissed on the grounds that they reflected his opposition to the raid in principle. On 21 April, Vance offered his resignation to Carter; it was accepted, with the agreement that it would not be made public until after the rescue mission, whatever the outcome. Vance duly resigned on 28 April. The press reports about his resignation suggested that opposition to the mission was only the last incident in a long line and that Vance's resignation stemmed from his battle with Brzezinski over the direction of U.S. foreign policy. As a White House aide said, it had been "clear for some time that Mr. Vance was no longer part of the foreign policy mainstream in the Carter administration."

That Vance and Christopher opposed the rescue mission is not, in itself, proof of the applicability of the bureaucratic politics approach. What is critical is that their opposition was generated *not* simply from their personal views, but more as a result of their bureaucratic position (although there is a problem in weighting these). Three factors warrant this conclusion. First, Christopher, without knowing Vance's position on the rescue mission, and having been told (erroneously) that Vance supported it, still outlined alternatives. In fact, his opposition to the mission was on the same grounds as Vance's, even though he was led to believe that his superior had given the go-ahead. Second, Vance's statement at the 15 April meeting very clearly reflected State Department concerns. The response of Brown and Brzezinski did not address the problems Vance had outlined (for example, the position of the allies), but stressed issues such as national honor and security. These are role-governed ·policy prescriptions. Third, Vance was not opposed to a rescue mission as such, but only to one at a time when negotiation was still possible; his objection did not simply reflect a personal attitude toward violence. . . .

CONCLUSION

In the three key meetings that led to the decision to undertake the hostage rescue mission, the evidence presented here suggests that the participants adopted positions that reflected their location in the bureaucratic structure. The influence of bureaucratic structure makes it possible to explain the change in policy that occurred between the 22 March meeting and that of 11 April. In each case, the same group proposed a rescue mission, and the same group (Vance on 22 March, Christopher on 11 April) opposed it. The change came about because the "presidential supporters" and President Carter himself felt that the situation had altered significantly. While this alteration was due in part to external events (the breakdown of negotiations), the evidence . . . suggests that an even stronger reason was the extent of domestic criticism of Carter's inaction (especially after the Wisconsin primary fiasco). The "presidential supporters" felt it was "time to act." For similar reasons, Cyrus Vance's inability to change the rescue decision at the 15 April meeting is also explicable from a bureaucratic political standpoint. In the event, of course, his doubts were only too clearly vindicated. What this case study shows, therefore, is the limitations of an attempt to explain foreign policy decision making as if the state were monolithic and as if "it" had interests. Such an approach makes policymaking appear rational, and this is a major reason for the popularity of such a perspective; but the case of the hostage rescue mission amply demonstrates the limitations of such conceptions of rationality, in that the key decisions are more powerfully explained by the bureaucratic politics perspective.

However, this conclusion requires some qualification since it raises fundamental problems about the precise claims advanced by proponents of the bureaucratic politics approach. . . . The question that must be addressed is whether bureaucratic position alone leads to the adoption of certain policy positions. As it stands, the bureaucratic politics approach is rather mechanical and static; it commits one to the rather simplistic notion that individuals will propose policy alternatives because of their bureaucratic position. Two problems emerge when this is applied to a case study such as this one. The first is that the bureaucratic politics approach lacks a causal mechanism; it cannot simply be true that occupying a role in a bureaucratic structure leads the occupant to hold certain views. The second relates to the wider issue of belief systems, in that certain individuals are "hawkish" irrespective of their precise position in a bureaucracy. The latter problem is most clearly illustrated by the case of Brzezinski, since it is arguable that whatever position he had occupied in Carter's administration, he would have adopted roughly similar views. Together, these problems force us to focus on one issue, namely, the exact meaning of the notion of role in the context of the bureaucratic politics approach.

This issue has been dealt with . . . in the work of Alexander George and of Glenn Snyder and Paul Diesing.[22] George is concerned with the ways in which U.S. decision makers use (and abuse) information and advice in the policy process. He examines in some depth the ways in which individuals and bureaucracies will select information to assist their rather parochial goals. In other words, through his study of the use of information, George arrives at precisely the same kind of concern that this study has led to, namely, the relationship between individuals and their policy advocacy. More salient, in their comprehensive survey of crisis decision making, Snyder and Diesing discuss the psychological makeup of those groups of individuals named in their study (as in this) "hawks" and "doves." They believe that "hard and soft attitudes are more a function of personality than of governmental roles," and they offer a very useful summary of what the world views of hard- and soft-liners are. As such, the works of George and of Snyder and Diesing are the best available discussions of the impact of role on belief and of belief on information processing. . . .

While it is clear that it is simplistic to assume that bureaucratic position *per se* causes policy preference, it is equally clear that bureaucratic position has some impact. Role, in and of itself, cannot explain the positions adopted by individuals; after all, the very notion of role implies a certain latitude over how to play the role. Further, a role does not involve a single goal, and there is therefore significant room for maneuver and judgment in trading off various goals against each other. Thus, for example, it is not a sufficient explanation of Vance's position just to say that he was secretary of state. There was a complex interplay between his role, his personality, the decision under consideration, and other personal and bureaucratic goals. Yet role occupiers do become predisposed to think in certain, bureaucratic, ways, and for a variety of psychological reasons they tend to adopt mind-sets compatible with those of their closest colleagues. In addition, individuals are often chosen for a specific post *because* they have certain kinds of world views. So for reasons of selection, training, and the need to get on with colleagues, it is not surprising that individuals in certain jobs have certain world views. . . . Thus, while it is clearly the case that Brzezinski was a hawk, it is neither accurate to say that this was because he was national security adviser (since this would not in and of itself cause hawkishness), nor to say that his views were simply personal (since it is surely the case that, had he been secretary of state, he would have had to argue for courses of action other than those he did argue for—given the State Department's concern with getting the allies to agree on sanctions).

This case study therefore leaves us with some critical questions unanswered. On the one hand, the empirical findings are important in that they illustrate the weaknesses of the rational actor approach as an explanation of foreign policy behavior. States are not monoliths, and we might impute very misleading intentions to them if we assume that decisions are rational in this anthropomorphic way. The evidence indicates that the bureaucratic politics approach is very useful in explaining the decision to make an attempt to rescue the hostages. The linkage between the policy preferences of those individuals who made the decision and their bureaucratic position is a more powerful explanation of that decision than any of the alternatives. But . . . the bureaucratic politics approach overemphasizes certain factors and underemphasizes others. On the other hand, the theoretical implications of this case study force us to consider the issue of the sources of the beliefs of decision makers. The "hawks–doves" dichotomy is brought out very strongly in this case study; and yet the bureaucratic politics approach as it stands is not capable of supporting a convincing mechanism for linking position and world view. . . . What is needed is to link the concept of individual rationality with the structural influence of bureaucratic position. . . . This [chapter], therefore, points both to the utility of the bureaucratic politics approach and to its theoretical weaknesses. The very fact that bureaucratic position was so important in determining policy preference over the decision to attempt to rescue the hostages makes the clarification of the nature of bureaucratic role all the more important. . . .

NOTES

1. Graham Allison, *Essence of Decision* (Boston: Little, Brown, 1971).
2. Allison, *Essence of Decision*, p. 145.
3. See Allison, *Essence of Decision*, p. 176.
4. Zbigniew Brzezinski, *Power and Principle* (London: Weidenfeld & Nicolson, 1983), p. 493.
5. [Jimmy] Carter, *Keeping Faith* [(London: Collins, 1982)], p. 506.
6. W. Safire, *International Herald Tribune*, 29 April 1980, p. 5.
7. Drew Middleton, "Going the Military Route," *New York Times Magazine*, 17 May 1981, p. 103.
8. Brzezinski, *Power and Principle*, pp. 487–488.
9. Brzezinski, *Power and Principle*, p. 489.
10. Brzezinski, *Power and Principle*, p. 492.
11. *The Times*, 1 May 1980, p. 16.
12. *International Herald Tribune*, 28 April 1980, p. 1.
13. Brzezinski, *Power and Principle*, pp. 489–490.
14. [Hamilton Jordan, *Crisis The Last Year of the Carter Presidency* (New York: G. P. Putnam's Sons, 1982), pp. 248–289.]
15. Brzezinski, *Power and Principle*, p. 490.
16. [Pierre] Salinger, *America Held Hostage*, [(New York: Doubleday, 1981)], p. 235. See also *Newsweek*, 5 May 1980, pp. 24–26, for a discussion of the domestic context.
17. Tom Wicker, "A Tale of Two Silences," *New York Times*, 4 May 1980, p. E.23.
18. See Irving Janis, *Groupthink*, 2nd ed. (Boston: Houghton Mifflin, 1982). . . .
19. Brzezinski, *Power and Principle*, p. 493.
20. [Cyrus] Vance, *Hard Choices* [(New York: Simon & Schuster, 1983)], p. 409.
21. Carter, *Keeping Faith*, p. 513.
22. Alexander George, *Presidential Decision-Making in Foreign Policy: The Effective Use of Information and Advice* (Boulder, Colo.: Westview, 1980); and Glenn Snyder and Paul Diesing, *Conflict Among Nations* (Princeton, N.J.: Princeton University Press, 1977).

21. ARE BUREAUCRACIES IMPORTANT? A REEXAMINATION OF ACCOUNTS OF THE CUBAN MISSILE CRISIS

Stephen D. Krasner

Who and what shapes foreign policy? In recent years, analyses have increasingly emphasized not rational calculations of the national interest or the political goals of national leaders but rather bureaucratic procedures and bureaucratic politics. Starting with Richard Neustadt's *Presidential Power*, a judicious study of leadership published in 1960, this approach has come to portray the American president as trapped by a permanent government more enemy than ally. Bureaucratic theorists imply that it is exceedingly difficult if not impossible for political leaders to control the organizational web which surrounds them. Important decisions result from numerous smaller actions taken by individuals at different levels in the bureaucracy who have partially incompatible national, bureaucratic, political, and personal objectives. They are not necessarily a reflection of the aims and values of high officials. . . .

. . . Analyses of bureaucratic politics have been used to explain alliance behavior during the 1956 Suez crisis and the [1962] Skybolt incident, Truman's relations with MacArthur, American policy in Vietnam, and now most thoroughly the Cuban missile crisis in Graham Allison's *Essence of Decision: Explaining the Cuban Missile Crisis,* published in 1971 (Little, Brown & Company). Allison's volume is the elaboration of an earlier and influential article on this subject. With the publication of his book this approach to foreign policy now receives its definitive statement. The bureaucratic interpretation of foreign policy has become the conventional wisdom.

My argument here is that this vision is misleading, dangerous, and compelling: misleading because it obscures the power of the president; dangerous because it undermines the assumptions of democratic politics by relieving

311

high officials of responsibility; and compelling because it offers leaders an excuse for their failures and scholars an opportunity for innumerable reinterpretations and publications.

The contention that the chief executive is trammeled by the permanent government has disturbing implications for any effort to impute responsibility to public officials. A democratic political philosophy assumes that responsibility for the acts of governments can be attributed to elected officials. The charges of these men are embodied in legal statutes. The electorate punishes an erring official by rejecting him at the polls. Punishment is senseless unless high officials are responsible for the acts of government. Elections have some impact only if government, that most complex of modern organizations, can be controlled. If the bureaucratic machine escapes manipulation and direction even by the highest officials, then punishment is illogical. Elections are a farce not because the people suffer from false consciousness, but because public officials are impotent, enmeshed in a bureaucracy so large that the actions of government are not responsive to their will. What sense to vote a man out of office when his successor, regardless of his values, will be trapped in the same web of only incrementally mutable standard operating procedures?

THE RATIONAL ACTOR MODEL

Conventional analyses that focus on the values and objectives of foreign policy, what Allison calls the rational actor model, are perfectly coincident with the ethical assumptions of democratic politics. The state is viewed as a rational unified actor. The behavior of states is the outcome of a rational decision-making process. This process has three steps. The options for a given situation are spelled out. The consequences of each option are projected. A choice is made which maximizes the values held by decision makers. The analyst knows what the state did. His objective is to explain why by imputing to decision makers a set of values which are maximized by observed behavior. These values are his explanation of foreign policy.

The citizen, like the analyst, attributes error to either inappropriate values or lack of foresight. Ideally the electorate judges the officeholder by governmental performance which is assumed to reflect the objectives and perspicacity of political leaders. Poor policy is made by leaders who fail to foresee accurately the consequences of their decisions or attempt to maximize values not held by the electorate. Political appeals, couched in terms of aims and values, are an appropriate guide for voters. For both the analyst who adheres to the rational actor model and the citizen who decides elections, values are assumed to be the primary determinant of government behavior.

The bureaucratic politics paradigm points to quite different determinants of policy. Political leaders can only with great difficulty overcome the inertia and self-serving interests of the permanent government. What counts is managerial skill. In *Essence of Decision*, Graham Allison maintains that "the central questions of policy analysis are quite different from the kinds of questions analysts have traditionally asked. Indeed, the crucial questions seem to be matters of planning for management." Administrative feasibility, not substance, becomes the central concern.

The paradoxical conclusion—that bureaucratic analysis with its emphasis on policy guidance implies political nonresponsibility—has most clearly been brought out by discussions of American policy in Vietnam. Richard Neustadt on the concluding page of *Alliance Politics* . . . muses about a conversation he would have had with President Kennedy in the fall of 1963 had tragedy not intervened. "I considered asking whether, in the light of our machine's performance on a British problem, he conceived that it could cope with South Vietnam's. . . . [I]t was a good question, better than I knew. It haunts me still." For adherents of the bureaucratic politics paradigm, Vietnam was a failure of the "machine," a war in Arthur Schlesinger's words "which no President . . . desired or intended."[1] The machine dictated a policy which it could not successfully terminate. The machine not the Cold War ideology and hubris of Kennedy and Johnson determined American behavior in Vietnam. Vietnam could hardly be a tragedy for tragedies are made by choice and character, not fate. A knowing electorate would express sympathy, not levy blame. Machines cannot be held responsible for what they do, nor can the men caught in their workings.

The strength of the bureaucratic web has been attributed to two sources: organizational necessity and bureaucratic interest. The costs of coordination and search procedures are so high that complex organizations *must* settle for satisfactory rather than optimal solutions. Bureaucracies have interests defined in terms of budget allocation, autonomy, morale, and scope which they defend in a game of political bargaining and compromise within the executive branch.

The imperatives of organizational behavior limit flexibility. Without a division of labor and the establishment of standard operating procedures, it would be impossible for large organizations to begin to fulfill their statutory objectives, that is, to perform tasks designed to meet societal needs rather than merely to perpetuate the organization. A division of labor among and within organizations reduces the job of each particular division to manageable proportions. Once this division is made, the complexity confronting an organization or one of its parts is further reduced through the establishment of standard operating procedures. To deal with each problem as if it were *sui generis* would be impossible given limited resources and information processing capacity, and would make intraorganizational coordination extremely difficult. Bureaucracies are then unavoidably rigid; but without the rigidity imposed by division of labor and standard operating procedures, they could hardly begin to function at all.

However, this rigidity inevitably introduces distortions. All of the options to a given problem will not be presented with equal lucidity and conviction unless by some happenstance the organization has worked out its scenarios for that particular problem in advance. It is more likely that the organization will have addressed itself to something *like* the problem with which it is confronted. It has a set of options for such a hypothetical problem, and these options will be presented to deal with the actual issue at hand. Similarly, organizations cannot execute all policy suggestions with equal facility. The development of new standard operating procedures takes time. The procedures which would most faithfully execute a new policy are not likely to have been worked out. The clash between the rigidity of standard operating procedures which are absolutely necessary to achieve coordination among and within large organizations, and the flexibility needed to spell out the options and their consequences for a new problem and to execute new policies is inevitable. It cannot be avoided even with the best of intentions of bureaucratic chiefs anxious to faithfully execute the desires of their leaders.

THE COSTS OF COORDINATION

The limitations imposed by the need to simplify and coordinate indicate that the great increase in governmental power accompanying industrialization has not been achieved without some costs in terms of control. Bureaucratic organizations and the material and symbolic resources which they direct have enormously increased the ability of the American president to influence the international environment. He operates, however, within limits set by organizational procedures.

A recognition of the limits imposed by bureaucratic necessities is a useful qualification of the assumption that states always maximize their interest. This does not, however, imply that the analyst should abandon a focus on values or assumptions of rationality. Standard operating procedures are rational given the costs of search procedures and need for coordination. The behavior of states is still determined by values although foreign policy may reflect satisfactory rather than optimal outcomes.

An emphasis on the procedural limits of large organizations cannot explain nonincremental change. If government policy is an outcome of standard operating procedures, then behavior at Time T is only incrementally different from behavior at time T-1. The exceptions to this prediction leap out of [such] events . . . [as Nixon's] visit to China and [his] new economic policy. Focusing on the needs dictated by organizational complexity is adequate only during periods when policy is altered very little or not at all. To reduce policymakers to nothing more than the caretakers and minor adjustors of standard operating procedures rings hollow in an era rife with debates and changes of the most fundamental kind in America's conception of its objectives and capabilities.

Bureaucratic analysts do not, however, place the burden of their argument on standard operating procedures, but on bureaucratic politics. The objectives of officials are dictated by their bureaucratic position. Each bureau has its own interests. The interests which bureaucratic analysts emphasize are not clientalistic ties between government departments and societal groups, or special relations with congressional committees. They are, rather, needs dictated by organizational survival and growth—budget allocations, internal morale, and autonomy. Conflicting objectives advocated by different bureau chiefs are reconciled by a political process. Policy results from compromises and bargaining. It does not necessarily reflect the values of the president, let alone of lesser actors.

The clearest expression of the motivational aspects of the bureaucratic politics approach is the by now well-known aphorism—where you stand depends upon where you sit. Decision makers, however, often do not stand where they sit. Sometimes they are not sitting anywhere. This is clearly illustrated by the positions taken by members of the ExCom during the Cuban missile crisis, which Allison elucidates at some length. While the military, in Pavlovian fashion, urged the use of arms, the secretary of defense took a much more pacific position. The wise old men, such as Acheson, imported for the occasion, had no bureaucratic position to defend. Two of the most important members of the ExCom, Robert Kennedy and Theodore Sorensen, were loyal to the president, not to some bureaucratic barony. Similarly, in discussions of Vietnam in 1966 and 1967, it was the secretary of defense who advocated diplomacy and the secretary of state who defended the prerogatives of the military. During Skybolt, McNamara was attuned to the president's budgetary concerns, not those of the Air Force.

Allison, the most recent expositor of the bureaucratic politics approach, realizes the problems which these facts present. In describing motivation, he backs off from an exclusive focus on bureaucratic position, arguing instead that decision makers are motivated by national, organizational, group, and personal interests. While maintaining that the "propensities and priorities stemming from position are sufficient to allow analysts to make reliable predictions about a player's stand" (a proposition violated by his own presentation), he also notes that "these propensities are filtered through the baggage that players bring to positions." For both the missile crisis and Vietnam, it was the "baggage" of culture and values, not bureaucratic position, which determined the aims of high officials.

Bureaucratic analysis is also inadequate in its description of how policy is made. Its axiomatic assumption is that politics is a game with the preferences of players given and independent. This is not true. The president chooses most of the important players and sets the rules. He selects the men who head the large bureaucracies. These individuals must share his values. Certainly they identify with his beliefs to a greater extent than would a randomly chosen group of candidates. They also feel some personal fealty to the president who has elevated them from positions of corporate or legal to ones of historic significance. While bureau chiefs are undoubtedly torn by conflicting pressures arising either from their need to protect their own bureaucracies or from personal conviction, they must remain the president's men. At some point disagreement results in dismissal. The values which bureau chiefs assign to policy outcomes are not independent. They are related through a perspective shared with the president.

The president also structures the governmental environment in which he acts through his impact on what Allison calls "action channels." These are decision-making processes which describe the participation of actors and their influence. The most important "action channel" in the government is the president's ear. The president has a major role in determining who whispers into it. John Kennedy's reliance on his brother, whose bureaucratic position did not afford him any claim to a decision-making role in the missile crisis, is merely an extreme example. By allocating tasks, selecting the White House bureaucracy, and demonstrating special affections, the president also influences "action channels" at lower levels of the government.

The president has an important impact on bureaucratic interests. Internal morale is partially determined by presidential behavior. The obscurity in which Secretary of State Rogers languished during the China trip affected both State Department morale and recruitment prospects. Through the budget the president has a direct impact on that most vital of bureaucratic interests. While a bureau may use its societal clients and congressional allies to secure desired locations, it is surely easier with the president's support than without it. The president can delimit or redefine the scope of an organization's activities by transferring tasks or establishing new agencies. Through public statements he can affect attitudes towards members of a particular bureaucracy and their functions.

THE PRESIDENT AS "KING"

The success a bureau enjoys in furthering its interests depends on maintaining the support and affection of the president. The implicit assumption of the bureaucratic politics approach that departmental and presidential behavior are independent and comparably important is false. Allison, for instance, vacillates between describing the president as one "chief" among several and as a "king" standing above all other men. He describes in great detail the deliberations of the ExCom implying that Kennedy's decision was in large part determined by its recommendations and yet notes that during the crisis Kennedy vetoed an ExCom decision to bomb a SAM base after an American U-2 was shot down on October 27. In general, bureaucratic analysts ignore the critical effect which the president has in choosing his advisers, establishing their access to decision making, and influencing bureaucratic interests.

All of this is not to deny that bureaucratic interests may sometimes be decisive in the formulation of foreign policy. Some policy options are never presented to the president. Others he deals with only cursorily, not going beyond options presented by the bureaucracy. This will only be the case if presidential interest and attention are absent. The failure of a chief executive to specify policy does not mean that the government takes no action. Individual bureaucracies may initiate policies which suit their own needs and objectives. The actions of different organizations may work at cross-purposes. The behavior of the state, that is of some of its official organizations, in the international system appears confused or even contradictory. This is a situation which develops, however, not because of the independent power of government organizations but because of failures by decision makers to assert control.

The ability of bureaucracies to independently establish policies is a function of presidential attention. Presidential attention is a function of presidential values. The chief executive involves himself in those areas which he determines to be important. When the president does devote time and attention to an issue, he can compel the bureaucracy to present him with alternatives. He may do this as Nixon apparently [did] by establishing an organization under his Special Assistant for National Security Affairs, whose only bureaucratic interest [was] maintaining the president's confidence. The president may also rely upon several bureaucracies to secure proposals. The president may even resort to his own knowledge and sense of history to find options which his bureaucracy fails to present. Even when presidential attention is totally absent, bureaus are sensitive to his values. Policies which violate presidential objectives may bring presidential wrath.

While the president is undoubtedly constrained in the implementation of policy by existing bureaucratic procedures, he even has options in this area. As Allison points out, he can choose which agencies will perform what tasks. Programs are fungible and can be broken down into their individual standard operating procedures and recombined. Such exercises take time and effort but the expenditure of such energies by the president is ultimately a reflection of his own values and not those of the bureaucracy. Within the structure which he has partially created himself he can, if he chooses, further manipulate both the options presented to him and the organizational tools for implementing them.

Neither organizational necessity nor bureaucratic interests are the fundamental determinants of policy. The limits imposed by standard operating procedures as well as the direction of policy are a function of the values of decision makers. The president creates much of the bureaucratic environment which surrounds him through his selection of bureau chiefs, determination of "action channels," and statutory powers.

THE MISSILE CRISIS

Adherents of the bureaucratic politics framework have not relied exclusively on general argument. They have attempted to substantiate their contentions with detailed investigations of particular historical events. The most painstaking is Graham Allison's analysis of the Cuban missile crisis in his *Essence of Decision*. In a superlative heuristic exercise Allison attempts to show that critical facts and relationships are ignored by conventional analysis that assumes states are unified rational actors. Only by examining the missile crisis in terms of organizational necessity, and bureaucratic interests and politics, can the formulation and implementation of policy be understood.

The missile crisis, as Allison notes, is a situation in which conventional analysis would appear most appropriate. The president devoted large amounts of time to policy formulation and implementation. Regular bureaucratic channels were short-circuited by the creation of an executive committee which included representatives of the bipartisan foreign policy establishment, bureau chiefs, and the president's special aides. The president dealt with details which would normally be left to bureaucratic subordinates. If, under such circumstances, the president could not effectively control policy formulation and implementation, then the rational actor model is gravely suspect.

In his analysis of the missile crisis, Allison deals with three issues: the American choice of a blockade, the Soviet decision to place MRBMs and IRBMs on Cuba, and the Soviet decision to withdraw the missiles from Cuba. The American decision is given the most detailed attention. Allison notes three ways in which bureaucratic procedures and interests influenced the formulation of American policy: first, in the elimination of the nonforcible alternatives; second, through the collection of information; third, through the standard operating procedures of the Air Force.

In formulating the U.S. response, the ExCom considered six alternatives. These were:

1. Do nothing
2. Diplomatic pressure
3. A secret approach to Castro
4. Invasion
5. A surgical air strike
6. A naval blockade

The approach to Castro was abandoned because he did not have direct control of the missiles. An invasion was eliminated as a first step because it would not have been precluded by any of the other options. Bureaucratic factors were not involved.

The two nonmilitary options of doing nothing and lodging diplomatic protests were also abandoned from the outset because the president was not interested in them. In terms of both domestic and international politics this was the most important decision of the crisis. It was a decision which only the president had authority to make. Allison's case rests on proving that this decision was foreordained by bureaucratic roles. He lists several reasons for Kennedy's elimination of the nonforcible alternatives. Failure to act decisively would undermine the confidence of members of his administration, convince the permanent government that his administration lacked leadership, hurt the Democrats in the forthcoming election, destroy his reputation among members of Congress, create public distrust, encourage American allies and enemies to question American courage, invite a second Bay of Pigs, and feed his own doubts about himself. Allison quotes a statement by Kennedy that he feared impeachment and concludes that the "non-forcible paths—avoiding military measures, resorting instead to diplomacy—could not have been more irrelevant to *his* problems." Thus Allison argues that Kennedy had no choice.

Bureaucratic analysis, what Allison calls in his book the governmental politics model, implies that any man in the same position would have had no choice. The elimination of passivity and diplomacy was ordained by the office and not by the man.

Such a judgment is essential to the governmental politics model, for the resort to the "baggage" of values, culture, and psychology which the president carries with him undermines the explanatory and predictive power of the approach. To adopt, however, the view that the office determined Kennedy's action is both to underrate his power and to relieve him of responsibility. The president defines his own role. A different man could have chosen differently. Kennedy's *Profiles in Courage* had precisely dealt with men who had risked losing their political roles because of their "baggage" of values and culture.

Allison's use of the term "intragovernmental balance of power" to describe John Kennedy's elimination of diplomacy and passivity is misleading. The American government is not a balance of power system; at the very least it is a loose hierarchical one. Kennedy's judgments of the domestic, international, bureaucratic, and personal ramifications of his choice were determined by *who* he was, as well as *what* he was. The central mystery of the crisis remains why Kennedy chose to risk nuclear war over missile placements which he knew did not dramatically alter the strategic balance. The answer to this puzzle can only be found through an examination of values, the central concern of conventional analysis.

The impact of bureaucratic interests and standard operating procedures is reduced then to the choice of the blockade instead of the surgical air strike. Allison places considerable emphasis on intelligence gathering in the determination of this choice. U-2 flights were the most important source of data about Cuba; their information was supplemented by refugee reports, analyses of shipping, and other kinds of intelligence. The timing of the U-2 flights, which Allison argues was determined primarily by bureaucratic struggles, was instrumental in determining Kennedy's decision:

Had a U-2 flown over the western end of Cuba three weeks earlier, it could have discovered the missiles, giving the administration more time to consider alternatives and to act before the danger of operational missiles in Cuba became a major factor in the equation. Had the missiles not been discovered until two weeks later, the blockade would have been irrelevant, since the Soviet missile shipments would have been completed. . . . An explanation of the politics of the discovery is consequently a considerable piece of the explanation of the U.S. blockade.

The delay, however, from September 15 to October 14 when the missiles were discovered reflected presidential values more than bureaucratic politics. The October 14 flight took place 10 days after COMOR, the interdepartmental committee which directed the activity of the U-2s, had decided the flights should be made. "This 10 day delay constitutes some form of 'failure,'" Allison contends. It was the result, he argues, of a struggle between the Central Intelligence Agency and the Air Force over who would control the flights. The Air Force maintained that the flights over Cuba were sufficiently dangerous to warrant military supervision; the Central Intelligence Agency, anxious to guard its own prerogatives, maintained that its U-2s were technically superior.

However, the 10-day delay after the decision to make a flight over western Cuba was not entirely attributable to bureaucratic bickering. Allison reports an attempt to make a flight on October 9 which failed because the U-2 flamed out. Further delays resulted from bad weather. Thus the inactivity caused by bureaucratic infighting amounted to only five days (October 4 to October 9) once the general decision to make the flight was taken. The other five days' delay caused by engine failure and the weather must be attributed to some higher source than the machinations of the American bureaucracy.

However, there was also a long period of hesitation before October 4. John McCone, director of the Central Intelligence Agency, had indicated to the president on August 22 that he thought there was a strong possibility that the Soviets were preparing to put offensive missiles on Cuba. He did not have firm evidence, and his contentions were met with skepticism in the administration.

INCREASED RISKS

On September 10, COMOR had decided to restrict further U-2 flights over western Cuba. This decision was based upon factors which closely fit the rational actor model of foreign policy formulation. COMOR decided to halt the flights because the recent installation of SAMs in western Cuba coupled with the loss of a Nationalist Chinese U-2 increased the probability and costs of a U-2 loss over Cuba. International opinion might force the cancellation of the flights altogether. The absence of information from U-2s would be a national, not simply a bureaucratic, cost. The president had been forcefully attacking the critics of his Cuba policy, arguing that patience and restraint were the best course of action. The loss of a U-2 over Cuba would tend to undermine the president's position. Thus, COMOR's decision on September 10 reflected a sensitivity to the needs and policies of the president rather than the parochial concerns of the permanent government.

The decision on October 4 to allow further flights was taken only after consultation with the president. The timing was determined largely by the wishes of the president. His actions were not circumscribed by decisions made at lower levels of the bureaucracy of which he was not aware. The flights were delayed because of conflicting pressures and risks confronting Kennedy. He was forced to weigh the potential benefits of additional knowledge against the possible losses if a U-2 were shot down.

What if the missiles had not been discovered until after October 14? Allison argues that had the missiles been discovered two weeks later the blockade would have been irrelevant since the missile shipments would have been completed. This is true but only to a limited extent. The blockade was irrelevant even when it was put in place for there were missiles already on the island. As Allison points out in his rational actor cut at explaining the crisis, the blockade was both an act preventing the shipment of additional missiles and a signal of American firmness. The missiles already on Cuba were removed because of what the blockade meant and not because of what it did.

An inescapable dilemma confronted the United States. It could not retaliate until the missiles were on the island. Military threats or action required definitive proof. The United States could only justify actions with photographic evidence. It could only take photos after the missiles were on Cuba. The blockade could only be a demonstration of American firmness. Even if the missiles had not been discovered until they were operational, the United States might still have begun its response with a blockade.

Aside from the timing of the discovery of the missiles, Allison argues that the standard operating procedures of the Air Force affected the decision to blockade rather than to launch a surgical air strike. When the missiles were first discovered, the Air Force had no specific contingency plans for dealing with such a situation. They did, however, have a plan for a large-scale air strike carried out in conjunction with an invasion of Cuba. The plan called for the air bombardment of many targets. This led to some confusion during the first week of the ExCom's considerations because the Air Force was talking in terms of an air strike of some 500 sorties while there were only some 40 known missile sites on Cuba. Before this confusion was clarified, a strong coalition of advisers was backing the blockade.

As a further example of the impact of standard operating procedures, Allison notes that the Air Force had classified the missiles as mobile. Because this classification assumed that the missiles might be moved immediately before an air strike, the commander of the Air Force would not guarantee that a surgical air strike would be completely effective. By the end of the first week of the ExCom's deliberations when Kennedy made his decision for a block-ade, the surgical air strike was presented as a "null option." The examination of the strike was not reopened until the following week when civilian experts found that the missiles were not in fact mobile.

This incident suggests one caveat to Allison's assertion that the missile crisis is a case which discriminates against bureaucratic analysis. In crises when time is short the president may have to accept bureaucratic options which could be amended under more leisurely conditions.

NOT ANOTHER PEARL HARBOR

The impact of the Air Force's standard operating procedures on Kennedy's decision must, however, to some extent remain obscure. It is not likely that either McNamara, who initially called for a diplomatic response, or Robert Kennedy, who was partially concerned with the ethical implications of a surprise air strike, would have changed their recommendations even if the Air Force had estimated its capacities more optimistically. There were other rea-sons for choosing the blockade aside from the apparent infeasibility of the air strike. John Kennedy was not anxious to have the Pearl Harbor analogy applied to the United States. At one of the early meetings of the ExCom, his brother had passed a note saying, "I now know how Tojo felt when he was planning Pearl Harbor." The air strike could still be considered even if the blockade failed. A chief executive anxious to keep his options open would find a blockade a more prudent initial course of action.

Even if the Air Force had stated that a surgical air strike was feasible, this might have been discounted by the president. Kennedy had already experi-enced unrealistic military estimates. The Bay of Pigs was the most notable example. The United States did not use low-flying photographic reconnaissance until after the president had made his public announcement of the blockade. Prior to the president's speech on October 22, 20 high altitude U-2 flights were made. After the speech there were 85 low-level missions, indicating that the intelligence community was not entirely confident that U-2 flights alone would reveal all of the missile sites. The Soviets might have been camouflaging some missiles on Cuba. Thus, even if the immobility of the missiles had been correctly estimated, it would have been rash to assume that an air strike would have extirpated all of the missiles. There were several reasons, aside from the Air Force's estimate, for rejecting the surgical strike.

Thus, in terms of policy formulation, it is not clear that the examples offered by Allison concerning the timing of discovery of the missiles and the standard operating procedures of the Air Force had a decisive impact on the choice of a blockade over a surgical air strike. The ultimate decisions did rest with the president. The elimination of the nonforcible options was a reflection of Kennedy's values. An explanation of the Cuban missile crisis which fails to explain policy in terms of the values of the chief decision maker must inevitably lose sight of the forest for the trees.

The most chilling passages in *Essence of Decision* are concerned not with the formulation of policy but with its implementation. In carrying out the blockade the limitations on the president's ability to control events became painfully clear. Kennedy did keep extraordinarily close tabs on the workings of the blockade. The first Russian ship to reach the blockade was allowed to pass through without being intercepted on direct orders from the president. Kennedy felt it would be wise to allow Khrushchev more time. The president overrode the ExCom's decision to fire on a Cuban SAM base after a U-2 was shot down on October 27. A spy ship similar to the *Pueblo* was patrolling perilously close to Cuba and was ordered to move further out to sea.

Despite concerted presidential attention coupled with an awareness of the necessity of watching minute details which would normally be left to lower levels of bureaucracy, the president still had exceptional difficulty in controlling events. Kennedy personally ordered the Navy to pull in the blockade from 800 miles to 500 miles to give Khrushchev additional time in which to make his decision. Allison suggests that the ships were not drawn in. The Navy being both anxious to guard its prerogatives and confronted with the difficulty of moving large numbers of ships over millions of square miles of ocean, failed to promptly execute a presidential directive.

There were several random events which might have changed the outcome of the crisis. The Navy used the blockade to test its antisubmarine operations. It was forcing Soviet submarines to surface at a time when the president and his advisers were unaware that contact with Russian ships had been made. A U-2 accidentally strayed over Siberia on October 22. Any one of these events, and perhaps others still unknown, could have triggered escalatory actions by the Russians.

Taken together, they strongly indicate how much caution is necessary when a random event may have costly consequences. A nation, like a drunk staggering on a cliff, should stay far from the edge. The only conclusion which can be drawn from the inability of the chief executive to fully control the implementation of a policy in which he was intensely interested and to which he devoted virtually all of his time for an extended period is that the risks were even greater than the president knew. Allison is more convincing on the problems concerned with policy implementation than on questions relating to policy formulation. Neither bureaucratic interests nor organizational procedures explain the positions taken by members of the ExCom, the elimination of passivity and diplomacy, or the choice of a blockade instead of an air strike.

CONCLUSION

. . . Before the niceties of bureaucratic implementation are investigated, it is necessary to know what objectives are being sought. Objectives are ultimately a reflection of values, of beliefs concerning what man and society ought to be. The failure of the American government to take decisive action in a number of critical areas reflects not so much the inertia of a large bureaucratic machine as a confusion over values which afflicts the society in general and its leaders in particular. It is, in such circumstances, too comforting to attribute failure to organizational inertia, although nothing could be more convenient for political leaders who having either not formulated any policy or advocated bad policies can blame their failures on the governmental structure. Both psychologically and politically, leaders may find it advantageous to have others think of them as ineffectual rather than evil. But the facts are otherwise— particularly in foreign policy. There the choices—and the responsibility—rest squarely with the president.

NOTE

1. Quoted in Daniel Ellsberg, "The Quagmire Myth and the Stalemate Machine," *Public Policy* (Spring 1971): 218. [For an exemplary treatment of this thesis, see James C. Thomson's essay in this volume—ed.]

22. PRESIDENTIAL CHARACTER AND FOREIGN POLICY PERFORMANCE

James David Barber

*I*n our peculiar democracy, as Richard Neustadt clarified so effectively, political power is the power to *persuade*. Only very rarely can a president issue definitive commands and expect to see them executed. He is always about the business of persuading people to do what he wants them to do in their own interests. The contradiction of power is that the president, like most actors in the political system, is dependent on his dependents, subject to his subjects, forever in the position of supplicant for renewal of his license to rule. A president can so dissipate his real powers that he has nothing left but the shell of office. The most powerful man in the world is also the man most vulnerable to the complex mix of consent on which his power rests.

This chapter is about [two] presidents who seem to have forgotten that power means persuasion. Different as they were in other ways, Woodrow Wilson . . . and Lyndon B. Johnson came to share in their presidencies a common pattern: a process of rigidification, and a movement from political dexterity to narrow insistence on a failing course of action despite abundant evidence of the failure. Each . . . helped arrange his own defeat, and, in the course of doing that, left the nation worse off than it might have been. Not by accident, [they] . . . are prime twentieth-century examples of the active-negative type. Their political tragedies developed . . . out of inner dramas in which themes of power and themes of conscience struggled for preeminence. . . .

WILSON DEFEATS THE LEAGUE

In many respects Woodrow Wilson was one of the nation's most successful presidents; certainly he was not the machinelike psychotic some have made him out to be. . . . We are dealing with neither a patient nor a god but with a

Note: Some notes have been deleted or renumbered.

324

man who, trying hard to do the right thing, killed a dream he shared with millions throughout the world. . . .

The history of Wilson and the League [of Nations] extends far back into Wilson's own history and far out into the world he had to deal with. Perhaps the clearest place to grasp the essentials is the president's return from the Paris Peace Conference in July 1919 with the Covenant of the League of Nations, which required ratification by two-thirds of the Senate, or 64 votes. The situation he faced was as follows:

Republicans controlled the Senate by a majority of two. In the House, the Republicans had a majority of 39. In 1918, Democrat Wilson had taken the unusual step, over the protests of his key advisers and his wife, of asking the people to vote for Democrats for Congress; a Republican victory, he had said, "would certainly be interpreted on the other side of the water as a repudiation of my leadership." Only five months earlier the wartime President had declared politics "adjourned" for the duration. The election had been a massive defeat for Wilson, resulting in the Republican majorities.

The chairman of the Senate Foreign Relations Committee, Wilson's arch-enemy Henry Cabot Lodge, was responsible for initial consideration of the Treaty. Lodge had stacked the Committee with opponents of the League. Ten of the eighteen members were determined to kill it.

Senator Lodge was also majority leader of the Republican party in the Senate. Forty-nine Senators had declared themselves, shortly before Wilson's return from Paris, in favor of "reservations" (basically, amendments) to the League Treaty.

Nevertheless, there was strong support both within the Senate and in the country at large for some form of the League. In a preliminary poll by the "League to Enforce Peace," 64 Senators were prepared to vote for ratification, 20 were doubtful, and 12 opposed. And even Senator Lodge confessed that "the vocal masses of the community"—most clergy, professors, editors and so forth—were "friendly to the League."

In other words, the president faced an implacable enemy in Lodge, a very difficult proposition in the Foreign Relations Committee, a near standoff in the Senate as a whole, and a generally favorable climate of opinion in the "vocal" public. Rarely had there been a situation which called more clearly for the most adroit political leadership by the president of favorably inclined senators and the most intense efforts at developing the compromises necessary to bring around the waverers. Long before, Wilson himself had advised presidents in such circumstances to

be less stiff and offish, [to] himself act in the true spirit of the Constitution and establish intimate relations of confidence with the Senate on his own initiative, not carrying his plans to completion and then laying them in final form before the Senate to be accepted or rejected, but keeping himself in confidential communication with the leaders of the Senate while his plans are in course . . . in order that there may be veritable counsel and a real accommodation of views instead of a final challenge and contest.[1]

Like others of his character, Wilson found this lesson of life easier to expound than to live by.

Before leaving Paris, the president had sent a message to the American people, a message which began, "The treaty of peace has been signed. If it is ratified and acted upon in full and sincere execution of its terms it will furnish the charter for a new order of affairs in the world." He rested only one day after arriving in the United States, then appeared before the Senate to speak on the treaty. But before leaving the White House for the Senate chamber, he held a press conference; to a reporter who inquired whether the treaty would pass the Senate with "reservations," Wilson snapped: "I do not think hypothetical questions are concerned. The Senate is going to ratify the treaty." However, his speech that day first developed a conciliatory theme:

> My services and all the information I possess will be at your disposal and at the disposal of your Committee on Foreign Relations at any time, either informally or in session, as you may prefer; and I hope that you will not hesitate to make use of them. . . .[2]

But his tone changed as his rhetoric rose. The League was "a practical necessity," "an indispensable instrumentality." "Statesmen might see difficulties," he said,

> but the people could see none and could brook no denial. . . . The League of Nations was . . . the only hope for mankind . . . the main object of the peace . . . the only thing that could complete it or make it worthwhile . . . the hope of the world. . . . Shall we or any other free people hesitate to accept this great duty? Dare we reject it and break the heart of the world? There can be no question of our ceasing to be a world power. The only question is whether we can refuse the moral leadership that is offered us, whether we shall accept or reject the confidence of the world.

"Accept or reject"—that was the way Wilson posed the question. The Senate was challenged on moral grounds. Putting aside his notes, the president concluded with an image which made clear his view that only one course was available to the Senate:

> The stage is set, the destiny disclosed. It has come about by no plan of our conceiving, but by the hand of God who led us into this way. We cannot turn back. We can only go forward, with lifted eyes and freshened spirit, to follow the vision. It was of this that we dreamed at our birth. America shall in truth show the way. The light streams upon the path ahead, and nowhere else.[3]

Wilson's friend William Gibbs McAdoo saw the effect of this speech as "casting pearls before swine, so far as the senatorial cabal is concerned." Another senator called it "soap bubbles of oratory and soufflé of phrases," and Senator Warren G. Harding, characteristically, found the speech "utterly lacking in ringing Americanism."

Henry Cabot Lodge began his committee's deliberations on the treaty by reading aloud its entire text, 268 pages. It took him two weeks; often he read to a clerk alone, as the committee members drifted away. Lodge's strategy is evident from his correspondence at the time: He hoped to wreck the League, to prevent the Democrats from entering the 1920 election as the party of peace, not by a frontal assault on the treaty but by offering a barrage of "reservations" he thought Wilson would not accept. . . .

Lodge shared this purpose with the Senate "irreconcilables," about fifteen in number. But many other senators were undecided, somewhat confused, ready to consider possibilities and alternatives. In response, Wilson adopted a peculiar position: He would entertain the possibility of "interpretations" passed simultaneously but separately from the treaty, but would not agree to "reservations" attached to the treaty itself. This issue of the *form* by which the Senate could express its understanding of the treaty's meaning loomed large in Wilson's mind; he stuck to the stance that no word of the treaty could be changed without resubmitting it to the European powers and to the view that "reservations"—but not "interpretations"—should be rejected because they would change the treaty.

Lodge sought much information from Wilson, but Wilson, despite his generous offer in the Senate speech, refused many of these requests. Lodge pointed to the president's behavior as proof of Wilson's disrespect for the Senate. . . .

According to McAdoo, Wilson had a political reason for his adamance: He would not be averse to "mild" reservations, but was convinced "that the opponents of the treaty had not advanced them in good faith and the moment there was any indication on his part of a willingness to accept them, partisan opponents would immediately propose other and more objectionable reservations which it would be impossible to consider. They were, he said, determined to prevent ratification at whatever cost; therefore, it was impossible for him to discuss compromise."

"Subsequent events proved clearly," McAdoo continued, "the correctness of his judgment. Lodge and the opponents of the treaty were determined to defeat it, regardless of consequences."

What this line of argument totally ignores is the presence of a large and potentially decisive body of senatorial opinion held by those senators ready to vote for the league with a few minor modifications. Indeed, Senator Lodge was out to kill the League by fair means or foul, as his subsequent behavior and correspondence revealed. Wilson could not hope to compromise with Lodge. But the "mild reservationists" were another story. Wilson gave [his Senate leader Gilbert] Hitchcock a draft of four "interpretations" which were virtually identical with the four "reservations" being sponsored by the mild reservationists. But he would never drop the distinction. To partisan opposition by the Republicans he added institutional opposition: The Senate was not to "advise and consent" on this treaty except in the most passive way. For many members this was probably a critical point, though one hard to state publicly. If there was to be a dramatic new move for peace after the World War, they wanted to have a hand in it. Wilson slapped them back continually, offering only to "explain," in the style of a schoolmaster.

Wilson often argued that the Allies would not accept reservations, but the biographies do not show that he tried to find out if they would. Later it became clear that the French and British wanted America in and were not much concerned with what French premier Georges Clemenceau called "a few harmless compromises."

On September 3, 1919, President Wilson left the tangle of Washington politics to launch a nationwide speaking tour for the League of Nations, delivering 40 addresses in 22 days before he collapsed with a stroke in Colorado. Others tried to carry on the work of compromise, but eventually, on March 19, 1920, the Senate voted to reject the treaty, with Lodge's reservations, by a margin of seven votes. Wilson refused to the end even to free his Senate supporters to vote their own consciences, which would have resulted in the entry of the United States into the League of Nations.

Much later, on Armistice Day, 1923,

> a throng of well-wishers gathered in front of his "S" Street house. Wilson appeared on the balcony and, overcome by emotion, made a brief speech. "I am not one of those that have the least anxiety about the triumph of the principles I have stood for," he concluded. "I have seen fools resist Providence before and I have seen their destruction, as will come upon these again—utter destruction and contempt. That we shall prevail is as sure as that God reigns." (The main headline in the *New York Times* the day Wilson's remarks appeared read, across three columns, HITLER FORCES RALLYING NEAR MUNICH)[4]. . . .

JOHNSON ESCALATES THE WAR

The ghost of Woodrow Wilson drifts through the careers of the presidents I call active-negative. Hoover wrote a book about Wilson's ordeal; Nixon had Wilson's desk moved into the White House for his use. And Lyndon Johnson's crucial decision on the war in Vietnam was made in a conversation with another Henry Cabot Lodge. Johnson—who, Eric Goldman thinks, "re-enacted the presbyterian professor Woodrow Wilson"—had a style radically different from Wilson's,[5] yet there is a curious similarity to their histories. Each started out strong and wound up defeated. Each fastened on a particular line of policy and stubbornly pursued it to the end. It is probably not too much to say that each played a crucial role in the disillusionment of a political generation.

In November 1963, immediately after the eulogy for President Kennedy in the Great Rotunda of the Capitol, Johnson, with tears still on his face, met with Lodge. Lodge, then ambassador to Vietnam, reviewed the situation there and said of the hard decisions coming, "Unfortunately, Mr. President, you will have to make them." Johnson replied with feeling, "I am not going to lose Vietnam. I am not going to be the President who saw Southeast Asia go the way China went." Later that day he told his advisers to "increase the pressure and press on." There in the emotional backwash of the assassination began Lyndon Johnson's intense personal commitment to a line of policy that would lead him, his nation, and Indochina to disaster.

To those who attribute the Vietnam disaster to "the system," to some institutional inevitability in the American government, there is a hard question in the Johnson history. What was it in the system that made John Kennedy determined to withdraw from Vietnam after what he hoped would be his reelection in 1964? What in the same basic system led Johnson, in contrast, to increase the number of men in Vietnam by some 2,500 percent, to more than 535,000, and to pour in American money at the rate of some $30 billion per year? The men and money were the president's to command; Johnson commanded and the men and money moved. If any "system" was moving inexorably down the track toward tragedy in Vietnam, it was Johnson's own system—his character—not some structure of government or set of abstractions. . . .

Lyndon Johnson's escalation of the war in Vietnam was a complex checker game in which the meaning of each little move is hard to unravel. It is easy to get lost in the maze of verbiage, hard to stand back and see clearly what was happening at any given time. But in the end, the result was a series of tremendous losses—of life, health, national spirit, and of confidence in the presidency. Through it all, Johnson's credibility crumbled as he hewed stubbornly to an increasingly unrealistic line of policy. Three lines of development first ran parallel, and then diverged: Johnson and the public; Johnson as commander-in-chief; Johnson and the peace feelers.

With the public, Johnson repeatedly stressed his peaceable ways, his opposition to hawkish opponents, and his desire to turn his hand to the building of America. In the 1960 campaign, he had disdained Richard Nixon: "One of my friends that drinks Pepsi-Cola—a former Vice-President—went out to Vietnam and said we ought to have a little more war. Well, we won't."

As 1964 moved toward election day, "Peaceable" Lyndon thumped more and more on the contrast between himself and his opponent, Senator Barry Goldwater. . . .

. . . The week before the voting, Johnson said in Los Angeles that "the only real issue in this campaign, the only one you ought to get concerned about, is who can best keep the peace. . . . I tell you, as your Commander-in-Chief of the mightiest nation in all the world, we can keep the peace, in the words of the prophet Isaiah, by reasoning together, by responsibility, by negotiation." He won the election by a landslide. He continued, through his term of office, to present himself as the determined seeker after peace. . . .

He offered one billion dollars for development of Southeast Asia after the fighting stopped. Many times Johnson had left the impression with the public that he set no conditions whatever for negotiations, that he would meet with the Pope and Ho Chi Minh at the North Pole if necessary to make peace. . . . In his fifth State of the Union address on January 17, 1968, the president said, "Our goal is peace, and peace at the earliest possible moment." . . . The message to the public was a continual barrage of hope and promise, an apparently heartfelt desire for nothing so much as an end of the killing.

Meanwhile, in his role as commander-in-chief, Johnson made war with a vengeance. After the Kennedy funeral he had given his pledge not to lose Vietnam; increasingly he saw escalation as the only way to fulfill that pledge.

In the spring and summer of 1964, he set in motion the detailed studies of how to heat up the war, as revealed in the leaked "Pentagon Papers" of 1971. Even before that, in February, "an elaborate program of covert military operations against the state of North Vietnam" was started, including U-2 flights over Laos, commando raids, and naval bombardment of the North Vietnamese coast. The Pentagon drew up a plan calling for full-scale bombing of North Vietnam and the possible use of ground combat forces to protect the air bases. A resolution was drawn up for possible congressional approval of "wider U.S. actions in Southeast Asia." . . .

Johnson's public escalation of the war began in circumstances which seem nearly comic in retrospect. In the first days of August 1964, an American destroyer escorting South Vietnamese ships on a raid against a North Vietnamese island installation (a practice not widely known by the public or by Congress) was approached by three North Vietnamese torpedo boats. The American skipper later said he fired the first shot, then sank two of the PT boats. On August 4, the president went on television to recount an unprovoked attack on the destroyers *Maddox* and *C. Turner Joy*. Johnson warned, "These acts of violence against the armed forces of the United States must be met not only by alert defense, but with positive reply. . . . That reply is being given as I speak to you. Air action is now in execution against gunboats and certain supporting facilities of North Vietnam which have been used in these hostile operations." He also called upon Congress to pass a resolution he had been carrying around in his pocket for weeks, asserting

That the Congress approves and supports the determination of the President, as Commander-in-Chief, to take all necessary measures to repel any armed attack against the forces of the United States and to prevent further aggression.

The United States regards as vital to its national interest and to world peace the maintenance of international peace and security in Southeast Asia. [Consonant with the Constitution and treaty obligations,] the United States is, therefore, prepared, as the President determines, to take all necessary steps, including the use of armed force, to assist any member or protocol state of the Southeast Asia Collective Defense Treaty requesting assistance in defense of its freedom.

The president then had his resolution, a virtual blank check, when the measure passed the Senate 88 to 2 and the House 416 to 0 on August 7. Heading into their own elections, and accustomed to deferring to presidential judgment in foreign military affairs, Congressmen dashed to his support. . . .

Finally, on February 7, Johnson . . . began the massive escalation of the air war. The occasion was an attack on Pleiku, an American base 240 miles north of Saigon; seven were killed and 109 wounded. Strangely, "a week earlier the State Department had guessed that Pleiku would be the Viet Cong target." But the enemy infiltrators were able to get through the South Vietnamese guardline and reach the American barracks.

President Johnson received the news of the Pleiku attack at 3:00 P.M., Saturday, February 6, 1965. For months he had been studying aerial photographs of North Vietnam, speculating on targets. That evening at 7:45 he told a meeting of the National Security Council, "I've had enough of this," and explained, "The worst thing we could possibly do would be to let this go by. It would be a big mistake. It would open the door to a major misunderstanding." . . .

The story of the war's escalation from that point on is relatively familiar. At each point the public was reassured that the increase in military activity was not a departure from previous policy. Thus Johnson said in Washington that the raids carried out in response to Pleiku meant "no wider war." In January 1967, he called it "the most careful and most self-limited air war in history." But in 1965, the Air Force had flown 24,570 sorties over North Vietnam. In 1966 the Pentagon reported what looked like a decrease: 23,577 missions. Not many realized that a "sortie" was an individual plane flight and a "mission" normally consisted of *four* planes, making the actual number of sorties some 94,308 in 1966—almost four times as high.

Three days after the Pleiku raids, the president ordered regular, not just retaliatory, bombing of major installations in North Vietnam. "They woke us up in the middle of the night and we woke them up in the middle of the night. Then they did it again, and we did it again," he said. Soon the relationship between stimulus and response was lost. The purposes offered in justification varied. One was to slow down infiltration of men and supplies from the North. Yet in February 1966, McNamara testified that even the total destruction of North Vietnamese industry would have "no measurable effect" on their ability to supply the forces in the South, and as regards morale, he pointed out that massive bombing had not lowered the enemy's will to fight in Japan, in World War II, or in Korea. Another justification was to improve the stability of the South Vietnamese government—an institution that could stand some improvement. In Saigon there were eight heads of state during the Johnson presidency; in the summer of 1965 the last civilian government fell and Air Vice-Marshal Ky ("People ask me who my heroes are. I have only one—Hitler") took over. Ky closed down newspapers and on July 24 declared that "support for neutralism" would be punishable by death. That same day, 39 "recruits" to the South Vietnamese army seeking to escape from military service jumped from a boat and drowned. In 1966, desertions from the South Vietnamese army numbered 116,858. "After seventeen months of bombing, the White House had to admit that there were 100 percent more North Vietnamese troops in South Vietnam than when the bombings began."

Eventually, then, the war from the air became a turkey shoot, North and South, with villages selected as targets on the "probability" that Viet Cong might be in them and with fire directed at unseen persons in the jungle whose body heat registered on airborne instruments. Millions of people were made homeless, hundreds of thousands killed and maimed by Americans. In 1967 the American chemical industry was producing a record 50 million pounds of napalm per month. The new language of gamesmanship developed by games theorists and systems analysts helped the policymakers obscure from themselves and others the enormity of their actions.

On the ground, Vietnam was more and more crowded with American soldiers, from 15,000 at the start of 1965 to 190,000 in January 1966, to 380,000 a year later. In the first year of escalation, 1,350 Americans had been killed, 5,300 wounded. The war raged on.

Johnson had claimed another purpose for the continuous bombing of North Vietnam: "to force the North Vietnamese into negotiation." Paralleling the history of Johnson as espouser of peace and Johnson as practitioner of escalation is that of Johnson as decliner of diplomatic peace initiatives. The history is complex in the extreme, but again the broad outlines are clear enough. The same president who hewed to his line of negotiations "anytime, anywhere" and continually announced his willingness to enter "unconditional discussions" repeatedly refused to exploit diplomatic opportunities for talks. Indeed, a strong and carefully documented case has been made that the president's behavior showed a "somber, recurring pattern of political exploration cut short by [American] military escalation." In other words, Johnson repeatedly responded to pressures for and possibilities of negotiations by raising the level of killing in Vietnam. This history of these possibilities only slowly got through to the public. . . .

In February 1966, the chairman of the Senate Foreign Relations Committee J. William Fulbright began hearings on the war in Vietnam. The story from that point on is too recent to have faded from memory, though pieces of it are still not in place. The rise of Senate opposition, and particularly the increasingly bitter feud between the president and Senator Robert F. Kennedy; Johnson's break with Fulbright; the raids and civilian casualties in Hanoi; the mounting protest at home over American—and, eventually, Indochinese—casualties, all led up to the climactic moment on March 31, 1968, when Johnson announced a partial pause in the bombing of North Vietnam and his own decision not to run for reelection or accept a draft in 1968.

As late as March 16, 1968, Johnson was telling his staff:

> Let's get one thing clear! I'm telling you now I am not going to stop the bombing. Now I don't want to hear any more about it. . . . I've heard every argument. I'm not going to stop it. Now is there anybody here who doesn't understand that?[6]

Over the next two weeks he changed his mind. But, as if to undercut his credibility even at that point, Johnson let himself in for one last wave of disbelief. He claimed to have ordered air and naval forces "to make no attacks on North Vietnam, except in the area north of the demilitarized zone where the continuing enemy buildup directly threatens allied forward positions and where the movements of their troops and supplies are clearly related to that threat." On the very next day, April 1, 1968, American planes struck targets 205 miles north of the demilitarized zone, 70 miles south of Hanoi. . . .

There was much to Lyndon Johnson's presidency besides Vietnam, including the "Great Society," progress in civil rights, and a remarkable legislative record. Yet from at least 1966 onward, he and the nation were grappling primarily with a dismal war in the wrong place for the wrong cause. The president became the first clear resigner from that office; even Calvin Coolidge, despite his demurrers, had hopes for 1928. The war contributed its share to the first period in recent national history in which the average American was pessimistic about the future of his country. And Johnson's stubborn insistence, until the failure and death toll had mounted out of all proportion to his purpose, easily matched that of Woodrow Wilson . . . The "system" was roughly the same for Eisenhower, Kennedy, and Nixon as for Lyndon Johnson. But he seemed in the grip of forces a good deal older, in his experience, than the system itself. "I was born the way I am." he said. "I can't do anything about it."

RIGIDIFICATION

These [two] stories show a common pattern, the essence of which is this: The president defeated both his own purposes and the nation's purposes by adhering rigidly to a line of policy long after it had proved itself a failure. The problem was not depravity but blindness. In light of the facts, it is simply implausible that President Wilson consciously set out to prevent American entry into the League . . . or that Lyndon Johnson found conscious satisfaction in the oceans of blood he left behind him. *Each meant well.* . . . They were "wrong" in terms of logic and evidence. . . .

What needs explaining is why, in the face of the *facts* of failure, these presidents held tightly to their courses. For in each of these histories the president appears as a man unable to see what, eventually, nearly everyone else around him sees: that the line of action simply is not working—that, for whatever reason, the costs of persevering in it are far too high. . . .

WILSON'S INNER STRUGGLE

For Woodrow Wilson the League became a highly personal crusade. He fastened upon the league as *his* League, his unique contribution to history. As early as January 1917, Wilson had come to see himself as *the* leader of an afflicted humanity longing for peace. "Perhaps I am the only person in high authority amongst all the peoples of the world," he said, "who is at liberty to speak and hold nothing back. I would fain believe that I am speaking for the silent mass of mankind everywhere who have as yet had no place or opportunity to speak their real hearts out." He thought in 1918 that if necessary "I can reach the peoples of Europe over the heads of their Rulers."

Both Colonel House and Secretary of State Robert Lansing had advised Wilson not to attend the Paris Peace Conference, to maintain his position above the grubby details, to remain free to play a larger and more flexible role. Wilson would have none of it. Not only would he go, he would preside. His choice of advisers to accompany him raised a storm of protest: All except one aging and inactive Republican were entirely dependent on the president— House, his personal adviser; Lansing, his secretary of state; and Tasker H. Bliss, a general in his army. Eminences such as Elihu Root, Charles Evan

Hughes, Charles Eliot, and particularly William Howard Taft were left out, for Wilson resented the interference of "butters-in" and "wool gatherers." He failed to include any senator who could have helped him sell the treaty at home. In Paris, his fellow commissioners filled their diaries with complaints that they were being excluded. Lansing was left completely in the dark: Wilson had never even shown his secretary of state his plan for the League Covenant. When Lansing tried to help, Wilson barked that he did not intend to have lawyers drafting the treaty. Lansing, the only lawyer on the Commission (besides Wilson himself), in turn abandoned his work.

Wilson was involved in high drama. On the ship taking him to the Paris Conference he had said, in a pensive tone, "What I seem to see—with all my heart I hope I am wrong—is a tragedy of disappointment." He flabbergasted the wily European diplomats with this question and answer:

> Why has Jesus Christ so far not succeeded in inducing the world to follow His teachings in these matters? It is because He taught the ideal without devising any practical means of attaining it. That is why I am proposing a practical scheme to carry out His aims.[7]

Wilson was ill much of the time at Paris, but he continued day after day, to the point of complete exhaustion, taking only an occasional break for a game of solitaire. He got edgy and angry, calling Clemenceau and Lloyd George "madmen." "Logic! Logic! I don't give a damn for logic!" blurted this champion of reason. He attributed a blinding headache to "bottled-up wrath at Lloyd George." Finally he went to bed with a fever. During his illness he acted strangely, suspecting that the French servants were spies who spoke perfect English, that furnishings were being stolen from the house he stayed in, that the staff was using official automobiles for recreational drives. He kept all his documents in a locked safe near him, had the furniture itemized, and ordered use of the cars restricted to official missions. Back on his feet, he infuriated the Europeans by lecturing at them. "I never knew anyone to talk more like Jesus Christ and act more like Lloyd George," said Clemenceau. Again and again he insisted on going into conferences alone—no secretary, no aides, no advisers.

On Memorial Day, 1919, President Wilson gave a moving address at an American Army cemetery in France; its climax shows Wilson in the role of Martin Luther, compelled by God to do the right [thing]. . . . Over and over, Wilson denied that he personally had any self-interest in the league (some of his enemies had said he wanted to be first president of the world): "I would be glad to die that it might be consummated." "I thank God that on this occasion the whole issue has nothing to do with me." And in his last speech before his breakdown and return to Washington: "The chief pleasure of my trip has been that it has nothing to do with my personal fortunes, that it has nothing to do with my personal reputation, that it has nothing to do with anything except great principles." . . . Worn to the bone, Wilson was at last forced to stop speaking, despite his protest—"No, no, no, I must keep on."

President Wilson, then, demonstrated the most intense personal commitment to the League of Nations treaty throughout his struggle. The incredible energy he poured into the fight, his insistence that he and he alone create it and get it approved, his identification of the League with the will of God, with the will of history, and with his obligation to the dead, and his reiterated insistence that he was completely selfless in pursuing it—all contribute to a pattern of emotional investment far beyond what is ordinary in the making of public policy.

Wilson's commitment is shown from a different angle in the negative side of his fight, particularly his intense aggressiveness against his opponents (increasingly focusing on Lodge) and his rejection of allies who meant to help him (culminating in his break with Colonel House). Wilson came back from Paris spoiling for a fight. The day he landed he made a speech "throwing down the glove of defiance to all senators and others who oppose the League of Nations," as the *New York Times* saw it. Wilson denigrated "those narrow, selfish provincial purposes which seem so dear to some minds that have no sweep beyond the nearest horizon. I should welcome no sweeter challenge than that. I have fighting blood in me and it is sometimes a delight to let it have scope, but if it is challenged on this occasion it will be an indulgence."

He was up against formidable opposition in the Senate. Lodge ridiculed his scholarship: Of the League Covenant he said, "As an English production, it does not rank high. It might get by at Princeton but certainly not at Harvard." He had made a careful assessment of Wilson's "temperament, intentions, and purposes" and decided that "the key to all he did was that he thought of everything in terms of Wilson. . . . Mr. Wilson was devoured by the desire for power." . . .

Wilson detested his foes and he progressively sacrificed the friends who tried to steer him to compromise, which left him at last with no independent mind around him. Ex-President Taft was driven away fairly early; Secretary Lansing was excluded and finally fired for meeting with the cabinet when Wilson was ill. But Wilson's most intimate adviser had for long been Colonel House. House had long shown an "extraordinary capacity for enhancing the President's self-esteem." He kept always in the background, until at Paris he occupied an official position which led him into more and more independent behavior, making suggestions, meeting with the press, treating with the Allied statesmen. All House's energies were devoted to the League cause, but his independence began to irritate Wilson. "Sooner or later," House wrote in his diary, "I suppose I shall get into trouble." He did. He was progressively excluded from Wilson's deliberations after standing in for the president when he was ill. In June 1919, just before Wilson returned to the United States, House urged him to be conciliatory with the Senate. Wilson replied, "House, I have found one can never get anything in this life that is worthwhile without fighting for it." At that, they separated for good.

At last, everyone seemed to turn against him. Sick and isolated after his collapse, Wilson heard his wife say, "For my sake, won't you accept these reservations and get this awful thing settled?" . . .

There is a second level, then, on which Wilson's fight for the League can be understood. Behind all the substantive issues, all the calculations about reservations and interpretations and understandings, was Wilson's own personal struggle—to win out alone, to yield nothing, to meet his binding obligation to his individual values, to crush the enemies who scoffed at him. And perhaps one should add, to die in the attempt. . . .

JOHNSON'S INNER STRUGGLE

Even more clearly than Wilson . . . , Lyndon Johnson took his tragedy personally. His initial commitment to the war was made in personal terms: "*I am not going to lose Vietnam. I* am not going to be the President who saw Southeast Asia go the way China went." By 1965 Johnson was speaking of "my Security Council," "my State Department," "my troops." With a sigh he would excuse himself from dinner saying, "I've got to go to Da Nang." It was *his* war, his struggle; when the Viet Cong attacked, they attacked him. After Pleiku, his response was "I've had enough of this." "Just like the Alamo," he said, "somebody damn well needed to go to their aid. Well, by God, I'm going to Vietnam's aid." Returning from a whirlwind tour of Vietnam, Johnson dictated a statement mentioning himself eleven times in the first few minutes and saying, "Do you know that some of those men had just climbed out of foxholes to be with me, they had just come from battle carrying guns on their backs?" And he would say to startled visitors, "I could have bombed again last night, but I didn't," and "I don't want China to spit in my eye and I don't want to spit in China's eye." The Viet Cong, he said, "actually thought that pressure on an American President would be so great that he'd pull out of Vietnam. They don't know the President of the United States. He's not pulling out!" The one escape Lyndon Johnson rarely used was to pass the buck to someone else. It was his war and he would run it his way. There was in all aspects of his presidency an extraordinary personalism in Johnson's policymaking, but nowhere was this tendency stronger than with respect to Vietnam.

Not only did he talk that way, but he invested his energies as intensely as his words. He had always been a fantastically active politician, driving himself well beyond what those around him could do. "Lyndon acts as if there is never going to be a tomorrow," his wife said, and this was part of his code: "When you have something to do, don't just sit there. Do it, and do it fast." . . .

Mrs. Johnson remarked in 1965, "I just hope that foreign problems do not keep mounting. They do not represent Lyndon's kind of Presidency." But they did keep mounting. "Oh me," the president would wail, "I try so hard. Why do these things have to happen to me?"

He had an answer to that question: His miseries came from the "knee-jerk liberals," "crackpots," and "trouble-makers." By the spring of 1967, Johnson was calling his critics "Nervous Nellies" and "cussers and doubters" in public and using rather more colorful language in private. "McNamara has gone dovish on me"—that "military genius." The list of Nervous Nellies expanded: Fulbright, Mansfield, Pope Paul. "I can't trust anybody!" he blurted to an aide. "What are you trying to do to me? Everybody is trying to cut me down, destroy me!" He came to see the Russians behind his Senate critics, feeding them material for speeches. FBI checks were instituted for all White House guests, including the presidential scholars. Citizens who wrote to the president in support of antiwar demonstrations received answers from the Internal Security Division of the Justice Department.

But the prime villain, for Johnson, became Robert F. Kennedy, the rival he had always called "Sonny Boy." Johnson alternated between rage (Vice President Hubert Humphrey said that when Johnson and Kennedy got together "all sense flies out the window, and they become two animals tearing at each other's throats") and despair (his friend Senator George Smathers would "walk in and find him sitting there in his chair with his face all screwed up sadly and a fist against his cheek, and he greets me with a sort of cry: 'Tell me what to do about Bobby, that little blankety-blank'"). Nothing enraged him more than Robert Kennedy's suggestion that an independent commission— including Kennedy—should be formed to develop proposals for ending the war. . . .

As Johnson saw it, the cause in Vietnam was of such overriding importance that criticism itself was immoral, even unpatriotic. He had made up his mind: "Appeasement would be disaster." "If we quit in Vietnam," he said, "tomorrow we'll be fighting in Hawaii and next week we'll have to fight in San Francisco." . . .

In the course of his crusade, Johnson slowly whittled his advisers down to those ready to back his course. George Ball had opposed the war from the early days, but Johnson had managed to plug him so firmly into the role of official dissenter that his views were listened to and then easily dismissed. One by one his aides resigned: McNamara, Reedy, Valenti, Busby, Moyers, Jacobson; all departed, leaving six loyal Texans in his top staff of ten. Walt Rostow, the chief pusher of escalation, remained to follow Johnson into retirement at the University of Texas. Near the end, Johnson turned to his old friend Clark Clifford to replace McNamara. When Clifford convinced himself that the war was not working, he put his advice squarely to the president and contributed to Johnson's decision to resign.

But by then it was almost all over. In order to meet the immense manpower needs which the military told him in 1968 it would need to achieve its mission, reserves would have to be called up and wage and price controls might have to be imposed—highly unpopular steps, just at a time when the polls showed Johnson's public support rapidly leaking away and the primaries looking bad. So he stepped down, hoping that if he went away the war would go away, or at least that negotiations could begin in earnest. . . .

THE COMMON STRUGGLE

Each of these . . . stories . . . is really two stories. The first is external: The facts demonstrate, I have argued, that each of the . . . presidents persevered in a destructive line of policy long after it had shown its destructiveness. The results of the policies for society were disastrous: The United States did bow out of world politics and another World War followed, . . . and Vietnam did come to mean death and maiming for hundreds of thousands of human beings. [Neither] of these disasters appeared suddenly; the awful realities revealed themselves gradually, a piece at a time. . . . That is the factual story. . . .

Underlying that is a story of each president's highly personal involvement in the policies he supported. These are not case studies in cool calculation, not neutral histories. Wilson . . . and Johnson *cared,* deeply and sincerely, about what they were doing. They experienced intense anxiety, frustration, and near despair as they clung to their battle flags. Their personalities were engaged— not peripherally, but centrally—in fights against great odds. Their actions cannot be understood apart from the passions each poured into his task.

Even when we focus only upon feelings directly connected with the major policy lines of these . . . cases, the following themes are evident in [both] of them:

The Fight against "Giving In"

The president experiences a sense of temptation. The issue is highly moralized, a matter of principle, not prudence. Therefore to compromise, to move toward any easy "panacea," is seen not only as mistaken but evil. In moral terms the cost of compromise is simply too high for the president as a person: He would have to sacrifice his own integrity, his stance as a being responsible to his conscience. Furthermore, he sees the conflict as one between strength and weakness. He himself, he feels, must be tough—and others should also show their mettle, their fiber, their manhood. The soft way out is closed to him, for his fight against giving in is a double fight, against both sinfulness and weakness.

The Answer in Effort

The president experiences severe depression as the personal implications of his policy unfold. In an attempt to overcome his practical problems he turns to work, which he progressively transforms into grueling labor in which his effort is more and more narrowly focused. He loses himself in his task, concentrates on repetitious plunges into the most difficult labors. Throughout his working, he suffers—and reminds himself, again and again, how much pain and self-sacrifice he is experiencing.

The Lone Struggle

Increasingly as the issue develops, the president feels that the responsibility for success depends entirely on him. The policy becomes his policy, inexorably welded to his person; its defeat means his defeat. The reason he must bear the burden alone is, as he feels it, that others who might help him keep deserting him. In a way he would prefer to welcome them as followers, but bitter experience has taught him not to trust them when the chips are down. The result is a president isolated from independent voices in his own camp.

The Appeal to Faith

The president increasingly uses opportunities for persuasion as opportunities for exhortation. The policy problem is transformed from a matter of calculation of results to a matter of emotional loyalty to ideals. The president appeals for faith in himself as keeper of the nation's promises. Because the cause is so tremendously important, the president concentrates on whatever rhetorical tactics are necessary for his grand strategy; *his* view of reality must be accepted lest the cause fall apart.

The Emergent Enemy

The president experiences intense anger as he meets the frustrations imposed upon him. That anger moves gradually away from him, outward to targets in the environment. The beginnings may be mere irritation kept in the privacy of his staff, but this extends and deepens to include whole categories of weak and immoral people on the outside. As the process of rigidification moves along, the president finds among his enemies an individual who, to him, personifies the threat. That person becomes the focus for the president's aggression; the critical task becomes defined as defeating this emergent enemy at all costs. The alternative is defeat at his hands, surrender.

For the active-negative president, that is the ultimate threat. For him, surrender is suicide, an admission of guilt and weakness. Having invested all his moral capital in the cause, he will—he must—plunge on to the end.

NOTES

1. Woodrow Wilson, *Constitutional Government in the United States* (New York: Columbia University Press, 1917), pp. 139–140.

2. Alexander L. and Juliette L. George, *Woodrow Wilson and Colonel House* (New York: John Day, 1956), p. 273.

3. Ibid.

4. Ibid., p. 314.

5. Eric F. Goldman, *The Tragedy of Lyndon Johnson* (New York: Knopf, 1969), p. 518.

6. *New York Times*, March 6, 1969, p. 14.

7. George and George, *op. cit.*, p. 230.

23. PRESIDENTS AND THEIR ADVISERS: LEADERSHIP STYLE, ADVISORY SYSTEMS, AND FOREIGN POLICYMAKING

Margaret G. Hermann
Thomas Preston

As the world grows more complex, interdependent, and filled with uncertainties, presidents face an increasing dilemma in the making of foreign policy. More parts of the government have become involved in the foreign policymaking process, and increasing numbers of agencies, organizations, and people have developed some interest in what happens in the international arena. Presidents inevitably are drawn into the "whirlpool of foreign affairs" (Fallows 1981, p. 147). At issue are (1) how presidents maintain control over foreign policy while still delegating authority to other actors in the government to deal with problems and take advantage of opportunities and (2) how they shape the foreign policy agenda when situations are being defined and problems as well as opportunities are being perceived and structured by others in the political system.

These concerns have precipitated an increase in the size of the White House staff as presidents have worked to improve coordination among the various entities that define and shape foreign policy (cf. Crabb and Mulcahy 1988; Hess 1988). As a result, the presidency has become a complex organization or advisory system (cf. Burke and Greenstein 1991; Feldman 1990). In effect, as in any organization, the president's staff extends his capabilities by increasing his "available attention, knowledge, and expertise" and by coordinating the behavior of the other units involved in making and implementing foreign policy (Feldman 1990, p. 17). Because the president participates in the selection of members of this organization and sets into place the norms and rules that determine its organizational culture, what the president is like (e.g., his personality, background, training) influences what his advisers are like and how his organization tackles foreign policy issues. In effect, what the president is like helps to shape the relationships among the advisers and his relationship with them. As Greenstein (1988, p. 352) has observed: "Leadership in the modern presidency is not carried out by the president alone, but rather by presidents with their associates. It depends therefore on both the president's strengths and weaknesses and on the quality of the aides' support"—that is, on the nature of the relationship between a president and his associates.

In this chapter we examine how a president's leadership style influences the way he structures his advisory system. The framework we use builds on previous studies of how presidents have organized their relations with their advisers and how they have coordinated and structured their advisory systems. To illustrate the framework we explore how Presidents Bush and Clinton have organized and used their advisers.

CHARACTERISTICS OF PRESIDENTIAL LEADERSHIP STYLE

Research on the leadership style of American presidents highlights five characteristics that seem to influence the way presidents organize the White House: (1) degree of involvement in the policymaking process, (2) willingness to tolerate conflict, (3) motivation or reason for choosing to be president, (4) preferred strategies for managing information, and (5) preferred strategies for resolving conflict (see Hermann and Preston 1994).

Involvement in the policymaking process takes into account both the president's interest and expertise in foreign policymaking as well as his preference for personal rather than institutional decision making. In effect, a president is more likely to be involved in making foreign policy if he is interested in foreign policy, has experience in foreign policymaking, and has a desire to do business personally rather than through institutionalized routines (see, e.g., Crabb and Mulcahy 1988; George 1980; Hermann 1988). A president's sense of efficacy in the foreign policy arena is especially likely to be enhanced when he is either interested or experienced in foreign policymaking (George 1980). Generally such presidents find this part of the job both satisfying and easier, and they prefer to focus on foreign policy when they can choose what to attend to. With increased involvement comes personal engagement in the process and a desire to be a part of what is happening, to be on top of problem solving in the White House. Those who are less involved are more likely to delegate authority to others.

Willingness to tolerate conflict, a second important facet of presidential leadership style, is an orientation or set that a president brings to the presidency. It is indicative of the degree of disagreement and disharmony he will tolerate among his advisers. This leadership characteristic suggests the climate in which the president feels comfortable operating. For some presidents (e.g., Franklin Roosevelt), conflict is permitted because it facilitates the generation of new alternatives and perspectives on issues among advisers by stimulating debate and dialogue in the advisory organization. For such presidents, disagreement is perceived as enhancing the opportunities for a range of information to get into the system. For other presidents (e.g., Richard Nixon), conflict is something to be dealt with before it surfaces at the presidential level. For them, conflict decreases the likelihood of building consensus and achieving a coherent foreign policy. Moreover, it increases the time it takes to make a decision (see, e.g., George 1980; Johnson 1974).

The president's reason for leading—his motivation for wanting to become president—is a third aspect of leadership style that is suggestive of his orientation to the presidency and helps to structure the environment in which he will feel comfortable operating (see, e.g., George 1980; Hermann 1987, 1988; Johnson 1974). Motivation in this context refers to the more general, overarching goals that a president is trying to achieve. Does the president have a cause he wants to pursue or problem he wants to solve? Is he motivated by power and the need for status? Is he interested in approval, support, and popularity? Does he want to accomplish a particular task or change a specific policy? Or does he have a desire to see the country be a more moral place in which to live? Goals help to define the constituencies most important to a president and how he is likely to deal with them. Moreover, they indicate the type of advisers the president is likely to seek. Presidents interested in a particular cause surround themselves with "advocates"; those interested in power and influence look for "implementors"; those interested in support seek "team players"; and those who want to accomplish some task or change some policy enlist "experts." Advisers are sought who complement presidents' needs and facilitate presidents doing what they perceive needs to be done.

The other two characteristics of leadership style focus on the process of decision making—how presidents manage information and resolve conflicts. Problems are defined, options raised and evaluated, and outcomes considered through the management of information. Coalitions are formed, consensus is built, people become part of decision-making units, and rules of the game are designed to resolve conflicts. Each of these processes can be organized in a variety of different ways (see, e.g., Hermann 1987; Johnson 1974; Kotter and Lawrence 1974; Smith 1988). In managing information, for example, a president can be the hub of the communication wheel—the person who receives and disperses information—or he can be at the end of a hierarchy that distills the information and presents him with a set of alternatives to review and choose among. Similarly, in dealing with conflict a president can insist on his own preferences; he can invite consensus building by designing a team that works together; or he can push for a working majority. These different processes suggest different ways of structuring an advisory organization.

In describing executive and presidential organizations, scholars (e.g., Campbell 1986; Feldman 1990; Wilensky 1967) have emphasized several functions such organizations serve. The functions revolve around mastery of the task, motivation and control, and coordination and coherence. There is a need within the president's advisory system to solve problems, to motivate, to have some semblance of control, and to arrive at policies that receive support. These functions lead to specialization, hierarchy, and centralization (Wilensky 1967). In what follows we will argue that the five characteristics of leadership-style variables discussed above shape the way specialization, hierarchy, and centralization are defined in any particular president's administration. We propose that presidential involvement in the foreign policymaking process is indicative of specialization in foreign policy. Such involvement suggests that presidents will want to shape the foreign policy agenda. Preferred strategies for managing information and resolving conflict are indicative of the amount of control the president will try to assert and the ways he will seek to motivate those under him—strategies that influence how authority is structured in the White House. And a president's willingness to tolerate conflict and his motivation for leading suggest how he will go about coordinating policymaking and where he will look for support for his policies—that is, how policymaking is centralized in the White House.

IMPACT OF PRESIDENTIAL LEADERSHIP STYLE ON THE ADVISORY SYSTEM

Specialization

Degree of involvement in the foreign policymaking process is used here to denote specialization. We propose that a president's leadership style will have more impact on the advisers who are chosen and how they are organized when the president is interested and experienced in the foreign policy arena. A president involved in foreign policymaking will personally want to organize the White House staff responsible for foreign policy and to have an imprint on the nature of that staff. Moreover, such presidents are more likely to pay attention to foreign policy issues and be attuned to potential problems and opportunities in the international arena. Foreign policy issues become a central part of such presidents' agendas. As a result, who the president's foreign policy advisers are and how they are configured can influence the nature of the policy.

Focus of Centralization and Coordination

Presidents appear to differ in how they coordinate their advisers. The focus of centralization in the White House typically takes one of two forms—either a focus on building concurrence among relevant advisers or a focus on accomplishing a task. Scholarly research on group dynamics suggests that leaders play two major functions in groups—they help the group work through a task or they facilitate group interaction, participation, and satisfaction (e.g., Bass 1981; McGrath 1984; Stogdill 1974). This theme also appears in the literature on organizations, where researchers talk about the twin goals of leadership as organizational survival and policy achievement (e.g., Hargrove 1989; Meier 1989; Miller 1987). How comfortable presidents feel in an environment where there is conflict and disagreement and the presidents' motivation for leading are the characteristics of leadership style that we propose are likely to predict how a president will seek to coordinate policy.

Building concurrence and a sense of belonging among members of a group and developing a climate of cooperation and support are critical in facilitating group satisfaction and organizational survival. Conflict and disagreement are perceived as dysfunctional in such an environment, as interest is centered around promoting a sense of community. At issue is how members are helped to feel a part of the group or organization and to see their participation as valued and needed. Generally there is little tolerance for conflict, and much attention is paid to providing approval and support. Translated to the presidential advisory system, presidents with a focus on group satisfaction and organizational survival will want advisers who feel empowered, who believe that their opinions and interests count, but who function best in a climate of cooperation and trust. The advisory system becomes a community of interlocking parts with a shared interest in containing conflict and disagreement and in enhancing common values and beliefs.

When the focus of coordination in a group or organization, on the other hand, becomes accomplishing a task or policy achievement, attention turns to getting something done. It is not how members feel about the group or organization but how present problems can be solved or defining the nature of problems that becomes the major impetus for action. There is a change from seeing the group as a community to perceiving the group as a producer. The emphasis is on solving problems and taking advantage of opportunities toward some end. There often is a sense of mission and a bottom line. Leadership facilitates movement on the mission and achievement of the goal. Conflict and disagreement are generally valued with such a focus because they introduce different perspectives into the discussion and enhance the chances for innovative solutions as members wrestle with their differences of opinion. Presidential advisory systems with this focus are interested in doing a good job, in addressing issues facing the administration in an effective manner with positive results. Advisers do not have to like one another, but they need to acknowledge and admire each other's problem-solving competencies and skills. This advisory system is like a well-oiled machine with members both defining and carrying out roles and functions with the quality of the product in mind.

Scholars knowledgeable about the advisory systems of the Eisenhower and Johnson administrations (Burke and Greenstein 1991, p. 290) have differentiated between two aspects of political reality testing—"the political component of selling policies and mustering the support necessary to win approval and the substantive component of devising and analyzing policies and the means of implementing them." These two components parallel the two ways of coordinating policy proposed here. The political component is similar to the focus on concurrence and community; the substantive component is similar to the focus on accomplishing a task or policy achievement. In one the emphasis is on the process of building support; in the other, the emphasis is on solving the problem and developing good policy. Burke and Greenstein (1991) observe that Eisenhower and Johnson each felt more comfortable in dealing with one rather than both of these and, thus, tended to shape their advisory systems with that focus in mind. Eisenhower was predisposed toward tackling the problem which meant his advisory system focused on substantive and policy analysis. Johnson was predisposed toward the process, which meant his advisory system focused on building support and managing what happened politically.

Hierarchy and Control

Presidents also appear to differ in the degree of control they need over the policymaking process. Complex organizations include people with different goals and interests—differences that generally cannot be resolved through voting but can be resolved through the establishment of a hierarchy and a pattern of organizational authority (cf. Downs 1967). How much control a president wants to exert over his advisory system helps to shape the nature of the pattern of authority that develops.

Presidential interest in control is evident in the strategies a president prefers for managing information and conflict. If the president wants to make the final decision—that is, have his preferences prevail—he will seek to control what happens in the foreign policy arena. His is the ultimate authority and cannot be reversed. Similarly, such a president is likely to organize authority into a hierarchical system with himself at the apex of a formal chain of command. Information processing, problem definition, and option generation will occur at lower levels and percolate up to the president. The advisory system will be organized into a formal and rather inflexible hierarchy. In effect, there is a correct way to do things, and authority patterns are well defined.

If, on the other hand, the president is more comfortable when decisions are made through consensus or concurrence, he is less likely to use a formal hierarchical pattern of authority. Who participates in decision making and how structured the process is become determined largely by the situation and problem the president faces. There will be a looseness and informality to the pattern of authority that facilitates the president building consensus. Often leaders in loose hierarchical systems manage information in the system by putting themselves at the hub of the communications network. In this way they gain control over who gets what information and knowledge about what information others know. As a result, they have the basis on which to organize a decision-making unit that can reach consensus. In effect, the pattern of authority is more informal and is structured and restructured in relation to the particular problem at hand. The president is still on top but he has purposively chosen to involve others directly in decision making and to use more informal channels of authority.

Once more Burke and Greenstein (1991) provide evidence for this distinction in their discussion of the Eisenhower and Johnson decisions on Vietnam. They describe the formal system of authority that Eisenhower set up and nurtured as contrasted with the informal system of authority that was Johnson's style. "No formal system in the modern presidency was more explicitly and extensively articulated than Eisenhower's," they observe. In contrast, "the formal component of Johnson's advising was minimal" (Burke and

Greenstein 1991, p. 276). Eisenhower had rules, routines, and procedures by which policy choices were defined, discussed, and selected among. Those involved in the process understood and worked by these rules. The system was organized to present Eisenhower with well-thought-out problems and options for his decision. For Johnson, there were no explicit operating rules and procedures. People had access because of who they were and their position on the war.

TOWARD A TYPOLOGY OF PRESIDENTIAL PATTERNS OF AUTHORITY AND POLICY COORDINATION

The two ways of coordinating policy and the two types of authority patterns create a fourfold typology of advisory systems based on the president's leadership style. This typology is illustrated in Figure 23.1.

Each cell of the typology indicates a different pattern of authority and policy coordination. The terms in the cells give an overall impression of the way a president's leadership style shapes the advisory system for the corresponding pattern. The terms describe the role that a president with each pattern plays in the policymaking process and, in turn, the kinds of advisers he will choose and how he will organize them. Figure 23.1 also provides examples of presidents who appear to fit each type. Let us examine these types in more detail.

The Chief Executive Officer

The chief executive officer (CEO) has a leadership style that leads to a rather formal pattern of authority and a focus on process. This type of president wants his preferences to prevail and to have a formal chain of command—to sit at the top of a well-defined hierarchy. Such a president is interested in

Focus of Policy Coordination	Authority Pattern	
	FORMAL	INFORMAL
FOCUS ON POLITICAL PROCESS	The Chief Executive Officer (Truman and Nixon)	The Team Builder and Player (Johnson, Ford, and Carter)
FOCUS ON SUBSTANCE OF PROBLEM	The Director/ Ideologue (Reagan)	The Analyst/ Innovator (Franklin Roosevelt)

Figure 23.1. Typology of presidential patterns of authority and policy coordination.

working in a cooperative environment where he has status and support. As a result, he will work to set up an advisory system with him at the apex but with those surrounding him supportive of him and able to work out conflicts before they come up the chain of command. His is the task of making the important decisions in an environment that facilitates reflection and evaluation.

Scholarly literature on presidential leadership style suggests that this kind of advisory structure was characteristic of Truman and Nixon among recent presidents (see, e.g., George 1980; Hess 1988; Johnson 1974; Light 1982). These two presidents had a rather low tolerance for conflict, were more interested in having power and gaining approval than in promoting a cause, wanted their preferences to prevail, and believed in a formal chain of command for the processing of information as well as the definition of problems and the identification of options—all characteristics that are suggestive of the CEO style of leadership. And their advisory systems reflected many of these traits. They were interested in loyalty among their advisers. In fact, loyalty was a unifying theme for the Truman and Nixon administrations (Hess 1988). Moreover, they both wanted to preserve their time for the "big" decisions and were interested in evaluating rather than generating options (Johnson 1974). George (1980) has described how orderly and well-defined the rules and procedures were in these administrations.

The Director/Ideologue

The director/ideologue also wants his preferences to prevail and to have a formal chain of command. This type of president, however, has a cause he is promoting or a problem he needs to see solved that focuses his attention and energies. Advisers are selected who believe in the cause, too, and are skillful at ensuring that the president's decisions are implemented. Conflict is tolerated around discussions of possible ways of achieving the goal or solving the problem that is important to them all but not around the goal or problem itself. It is assumed by all that the goal or problem is critical. In effect, the director sits atop a tightly controlled hierarchy that is focused and finely tuned toward a particular end.

Reagan is the one modern president whose leadership style fits this type. He focused the nation's priorities around his own ideology and pushed to see that the goals he set for his administration were achieved (see Light 1982). But Reagan did so within a formal hierarchical system with gatekeepers that managed his advisory system during his first term and a dominant chief of staff who decided what he should see and consider during the second term (see Hess 1988). He was interested in aides whose opinions were similar to his own and whom he could trust to evaluate and implement specific policies for him (see Campbell 1986; Hess 1988).

The Team Builder and Player

The team builder and player is like the captain of a football or basketball team who is dependent on others to work with him to make things happen. This president is interested in arriving at decisions through consensus and sees himself at the center of the information-gathering process. Working as a team means that advisers are empowered to participate in all aspects of policymaking and to share in the accountability for what happens. There is a desire to create an environment where all members of the team feel comfortable and have a sense of loyalty to the president. Moreover, they are sensitive to and supportive of the beliefs and values of the president. Conflict is not tolerated, and team members can be dropped from the team for being disagreeable.

The three modern presidents exhibiting this pattern in their advisory systems are Johnson, Ford, and Carter (see, e.g., Burke and Greenstein 1991; Campbell 1986; Crabb and Mulcahy 1988; Hess 1988; Johnson 1974). For each of these presidents, there was an emphasis among their advisers on working within a team setting in which options were sought that minimized conflict and disagreement while fostering a sharing of accountability and a feeling of inclusion in the process. Among those writing about these presidents, Campbell (1986) and Hess (1988) have discussed Carter's dependence on his Georgian friends as advisers—people who had helped him move into politics, the governorship, and the White House. Burke and Greenstein (1991) have noted the importance of Johnson's Tuesday Lunch group for discussions and decision making on Vietnam. Members of this group were advisers with whom Johnson felt comfortable and on whom he relied for advice and support. They allowed the president to blow off steam. Hess (1988) has observed the importance to Ford of having consensus and a sense of cohesion and loyalty among his advisers.

The Analyst/Innovator

The analyst/innovator, like the team builder, wants to arrive at decisions through consensus or, at the least, a working majority. But this type of president is interested in gathering information on all aspects of the problem and in getting a diverse range of perspectives and opinions on possible solutions. Such a president is quite willing to have conflicting positions presented because debate enlightens him on what is feasible under the current circumstances. Like the scientist with a set of hypotheses, the analyst runs ideas by his advisers to see how those with different perspectives from his own will react. This type of president, like the director type, has a cause or problem that is engaging his attention. He, however, unlike the director type, searches the environment for discrepant information to insure he is making the best as well as most "doable" decision.

Franklin Roosevelt (FDR) is the president often used to exemplify this style (see, e.g., George 1980; Hess 1988; Johnson 1974). FDR had an insatiable appetite for information (see Hess 1988). He wanted to have an open, freewheeling discussion of problems and to have diverse opinions and options put on the table (see George 1980). As a result, he sought multiple channels of communication, placing himself at the center of the information network so that he knew more than anyone else. Often FDR promoted overlapping jurisdictions of authority in order to hear how persons with differing perspectives would tackle the same problem. In his view, disagreement insured that the difficulties with any options would be aired and considered before a decision was made and an action taken. Thus, the chances for success were enhanced.

Mixed Types

Figure 23-2 suggests the kinds of advisers that these four types of presidents are likely to select and the relations they are likely to develop with these advisers. We have discussed these four patterns of control and coordination as if they were mutually exclusive and pure types. An argument can be made that some presidents emphasize one or the other of the two dimensions that make

Focus of Policy Coordination	Authority Pattern	
	FORMAL	INFORMAL
FOCUS ON POLITICAL PROCESS	• Loyalty important • Advisers used as sounding board • Interested in focusing on important decisions • Interested in evaluating rather than generating options • Leader-dominated groupthink possible • Procedures well-defined and highly structured	• Advisers seen as part of team • Sharing of accountability • Group cohesion is valued • Advisers provide psychological support • Options sought that minimize conflict and disagreement
FOCUS ON SUBSTANCE OF PROBLEM	• Select advisers who share cause/concern/ ideology • Advisers seen as implementors and advocates • Advisers tailor information to fit biases • One or two advisers play gatekeeper roles for information & access • Decisions shaped by shared vision • Disagreements center on means rather than ends	• Wants experts as advisers • Advisers seen as providing information & guidance • Open to using bureaucracy to get information • Time spent on generating options & considering consequences • Seeks "doable" solution to problem • Disagreement is valued

Figure 23-2. The influence of presidential leadership style on advisory selection and organization.

up this typology—either control or coordination—and move across the other dimension depending on the situation in which they find themselves. It can also be argued that presidents change who is involved in the advisory process as the nature of the problem or topic changes. In each case our position would be that aspects of the president's leadership style have become linked with characteristics of the context. When a particular contextual variable is present, it elicits certain aspects of the president's style. An example is in order here.

Eisenhower appeared to mix both formal and informal procedures in his advisory system (see Burke and Greenstein 1991). In the language of the typology, certain aspects of his advisory system could be characterized as formal and other aspects as informal. In both cases Eisenhower was interested in devising and analyzing policies—in focusing on problems or the substance of issues. The proposition can be advanced that Eisenhower involved advisers in an informal way when he was "engaging in distilling available information, stating options, and preparing recommendations" (Burke and Greenstein, 1991, p. 288). In other words, an informal advisory system was useful when Eisenhower was searching for information on which to base a decision. He used the National Security Council Planning Board, as its name suggests, for developing plans and considering hard problems (see Burke and Greenstein 1991, p. 277). As one of Eisenhower's aides indicated, this group debated and argued a range of views on major issues in preparation for crises that might arise. A more formal system, however, was used in the decision-making and implementation phases of dealing with a problem. Eisenhower made decisions on his own and expected his aides to implement them through their various positions in the hierarchy (Burke and Greenstein 1991, pp. 287–288).

In effect, Eisenhower's focus of policy coordination was on the problem and policy development; he used formal and informal systems to deal with various phases of decision making. He emphasized one of the two variables in the typology while varying the other depending on where in the decision-making process he found himself. His leadership type was that of the analyst /innovator when the problem was being defined and the director/ideologue when it came time for making a decision. Defining the problem, specifying the options, and considering potential consequences were the prerogative of a more informal planning and search network. The choice and implementation stages were much more formalized and within a chain of command. Stage in the decision-making process was the contextual factor that was linked to leadership style for Eisenhower. He was more comfortable being the center of the information network and seeing if consensus was possible in setting forth and analyzing the problem than in actually deciding what to do. In the choice-making stage Eisenhower wanted to be in command and have his preferences prevail.

Our general proposal is that presidents have a dominant style that fits within the typology we have outlined above. But there may be certain situations or contextual factors that lead presidents to be more comfortable with another leadership style. Barber (1977) has argued that a president's first political success helps to shape the leadership style he will depend on in future political settings. If this style continues to be rewarded with success in the future, it becomes even more a part of a president's repertoire. Presidents begin to rely on this style, and it defines the way they will approach decision making and their interpersonal interactions. There may, however, be certain situations in which presidents have found their usual leadership style is not useful and have learned to adapt it in order to cope with the demands placed on them. Knowing something about presidents' personalities can help shed some light on when such changes in leadership style are likely.

In another place, one of the authors (Hermann 1993; Hermann and Hermann 1989) has shown how leaders' sensitivity to the political context and information about what is happening politically can influence when contextual factors are likely to shape how they engage in decision making. Leaders who show less sensitivity to contextual cues from their environments tend to be top-down information processors or cognitive misers. In effect, they are more ideological and principled, more reliant on heuristics to guide how they perceive any problem, less willing to deal with discrepant information, and more interested in advocating a specific option than learning about alternative possibilities. Such leaders are more likely to find a leadership style that is successful in getting them what they want and to rely on it in most situations. These leaders will probably build an advisory system that is fairly stable across time and situation and evidence only *one* of the patterns in the typology.

Leaders who are more sensitive to contextual information, on the other hand, appear to be bottom-up information processors or hypothesis testers. They use contextual information to guide what they do, being more pragmatic and opportunistic, interested in learning about discrepant information, and concerned about option generation. If they have a position, such leaders use contextual information to gain ideas about whether the time is right to do what they are interested in doing and if their actions will receive constituent support. If they do not have a position, they use information from the context to help them decide where to look for a position. Leaders who are sensitive to contextual information are likely to use different types of advisory systems for different types of problems and are likely to use information from the environment to guide whom they select to become part of the decision unit on any occasion. Cues about how such a president is likely to organize his advisory system can be gleaned from knowledge about the topics or constituents of importance to him in any particular situation. How a president reacts to those topics or constituents will help to determine the way leadership style will impact on shaping the advisory system.

THE BUSH AND CLINTON ADVISORY SYSTEMS

Building on the typology we have presented here, how would we classify the Bush and Clinton administrations' advisory systems? For the Bush administration we have a rather diverse set of materials on which to base our judgments (see, e.g., Dowd and Friedman 1990; Winter, Hermann, Weintraub, and

Walker 1991; Woodward 1991). For the Clinton administration we will ex-trapolate from a personality profile of Clinton and his leadership style (Her-mann 1992) to suggest the kind of advisory system he will have. An examina-tion of the personalities of these presidents indicates that each is sensitive to contextual information (Winter et al. 1991; Hermann 1992). Thus, we expect their administrations to evidence mixed types of advisory systems that differ with characteristics of the situation.

Bush and His Advisers

The Bush administration exhibited two types of advisory systems: (1) the team builder and player and (2) the director/ideologue. For Bush the contex-tual factor that led him to change his advisory system was the stress he was experiencing. For many of the foreign policy decisions in his administration, Bush used a team approach to decision making with consensus building and information sharing the mechanisms for control and with a low tolerance for conflict and a need for approval and support defining what was a comfortable climate in which to operate (see Winter et al. 1991). Bush wanted team players around him who would be loyal and interested in participating in "bull sessions" and building consensus (Dowd and Friedman 1990, p. 58). Advisers were seen as a source of emotional support with Bush desirous of keeping his advisers laughing and in a good mood (see Preston and Young 1992; Woodward 1991). Group cohesion and minimization of open disagree-ments were the order of the day. At issue was making decisions that would play well with Congress, the media, and public opinion—"the focus was on managing the reaction" (Woodward 1991, p. 81).

Of interest is what happened to this advisory system when Bush felt him-self backed into a corner—for example, prior to the Panamanian invasion, after the Iraqi invasion of Kuwait, on his China policy. In such circumstances, Bush appeared to shift from the type of system characterized by team building to one characterized by formal control and a problem focus—the direc-tor/ideologue type. He became a man with a mission wanting advisers who would act as advocates and implementors of *his* policy decisions; he became a director, an ideologue. Only advisers who shared in Bush's vision became part of the inner circle (see Woodward 1991). Disagreements when they appeared were tolerated on means but not ends. For example, questions raised about options other than the offensive military policy being pushed by Bush after the Iraqi invasion were never considered in meetings at which Bush was present (Woodward 1991, pp. 300–301). Motivation changed from the need for approval and support to promoting a cause, and coordination, in turn, switched from concurrence among relevant advisers to accomplishing a task. As Bush observed during the initial stages of the Gulf crisis: "Let's be clear about one thing: We are not here to talk about adapting. . . . We are not going to plan how to live with this" (Friedman and Tyler 1991, p. 18).

When Bush perceived a threat not only to the policies of his administration but to policies important to his political well-being and place in history (see Hermann 1979), he became more task focused and more driven to see something happen that would deal with the situation and save him face. At such times Bush became more certain he knew what to do and what was right. Problems were defined in moral terms and driven less by the polls and what people wanted than by the challenge to his integrity and expertise. His leadership style shifted from that of team builder and player to taking charge and dominating. A certain type of situation—a perceived threat to his sense of self-worth and political reputation—changed how Bush viewed the leadership setting and what he needed from his advisers. When the problem he faced was threatening to him or his policies, Bush organized his advisory system differently than when the problem was not threatening. He went from an advisory system with an informal authority pattern and the political process as the focus of policy coordination to a system with a formal authority pattern (and himself in command) and the problem as the focus of policy coordination.

Clinton and His Advisers

Like Bush, Clinton is sensitive to the political context. It has been noted that he will be the "networking president"; the president who continually runs for election; the president who thrives on friends (see Alter 1992). As one reporter observed, "He is exceptionally good at massaging legislators; as president he would probably be the best at that since LBJ" (Alter 1992, p. 26). Given his sensitivity to contextual information, we might expect Clinton to organize several types of advisory systems depending on the situation. And, indeed, his leadership style and choice of advisers suggest when he may have a need for different advisory structures.

When Clinton knows what he wants and has a goal in mind, he appears interested in taking charge—in playing the chief executive officer (CEO) role. But when he has little expertise or has not yet settled on an option, he seems ready to play the role of analyst, seeking a wide range of information and perspectives. A personality assessment of President Clinton (see Hermann 1992) indicates he is motivated both by a need to solve problems and a need for approval and support. He has learned to combine these two motives in his networking. By developing an elaborate set of Friends of Bill that cuts across different types of constituencies, groups, and organizations, Clinton maintains an information-gathering system that provides data on a variety of people's needs and opinions as well as support and interest in him. With these two motives Clinton has the ability to change the focus of policy coordination in his advisory system depending on his own sense of what needs doing. When he has an idea of what he wants done, his emphasis shifts to the political process and building consensus; when he is wrestling with a problem, his focus is on problem solving, and he wants all the perspectives and views he can get.

Clinton's choice of advisers reflects this distinction. He has chosen individuals with process skills for positions where he already has settled on options and is interested in having things happen. And he has selected people who are known for their innovative ideas for positions where he is uncertain what needs to be done. Thus, in the economic arena, he has put into cabinet positions advisers who are good at process and can help in working Clinton's package through Congress. In the field of defense, he has put in advisers who are idea generators and likely to explore the vast array of new ways of defining national and international security.

When he is wrestling with what a particular policy should be, Clinton is the analyst and innovator, wanting to be at the center of what is going on and wanting to have policies argued and debated in front of him. At these times he seeks out expert opinion and encourages presentation of a range of possible options. That positions may be conflicting is not as important as that a variety of perspectives are represented. When, on the other hand, Clinton becomes convinced of a particular option, he wants a chain of command that is loyal and skilled in massaging the political process. He becomes the CEO interested in having his advisers facilitate getting others on board. To the extent that Clinton has surveyed the range of opinion on a particular problem before making a decision, this two-tiered advisory system can work effectively. When, however, key constituents or players are excluded from the consensus-building process in decision making, these parties may become difficult during the selling of the policy. The initial exclusion of key congressional and defense personnel from consideration of the policy on gays in the military is a case in point. These constituencies raised all kinds of problems with the proposed policy when they learned about it.

In effect, Clinton prefers an informal setting in the shaping of policy and a more formal setting for the selling of policy. In his mind there is a difference between how a policy is put together and how it is pushed through politically. A wide-ranging brainstorming session or focus group facilitates the formation of policy, the understanding of the issues, and the shaping of options. A more ordered system is needed when a policy is being worked through the political process with people knowing their functions and limits. Clinton's campaign reflected these two types of advisory structures. In coming to some consensus on the image and positions Clinton would espouse in the campaign, a series of focus groups and free-wheeling discussions were held among experts, selected "people on the streets," and campaign staff. The day-to-day campaign was run from the Little Rock headquarters with staffers given directives and specific functions to perform (see "The Age of Clinton," 1993).

CONCLUSION

In this chapter we have focused on how the president's leadership style influences the nature of his advisory system. As one scholar has observed (Hess 1988), the president's style, his work habits, how he likes to receive information, the people he prefers around him, and the way he makes up his mind are all key to how the White House is organized. We have presented a typology indicating four ways presidents have organized their advisory systems that build from what the president is like. We also have argued that whether presidents will choose to play the role of chief executive officer, team builder and player, director/ideologue, or analyst/innovator depends on how much they need to control what happens and whether they are more attune to the political process or the substance of the problem at hand. In sum, we have proposed that what the president is like can have an effect on the way the executive branch of government works and needs to be taken into account when discussing presidential leadership and foreign policy decision making.

NOTE

This chapter was written with the support of a grant from the National Science Foundation (DIR-9113599) to the Mershon Center Research Training Group on the Role of Cognition in Collective Political Decision Making at The Ohio State University. It elaborates on Hermann and Preston (1994).

REFERENCES

Alter, Jonathan. "How He Would Govern," *Newsweek,* October 26, 1992. pp.22–26.

"The Age of Clinton," *Newsweek Commemorative Issue,* Winter/Spring, 1993.

Barber, James David. 1977. *The Presidential Character.* Englewood Cliffs, N.J.: Prentice-Hall.

Bass, Bernard M. 1981. *Stogdill's Handbook of Leadership: A Survey of Theory and Research.* New York: Free Press.

Burke, John P. and Fred I. Greenstein. 1991. *How Presidents Test Reality: Decisions on Vietnam, 1954 and 1965.* New York: Russell Sage Foundation.

Campbell, Colin. 1986. *Managing the Presidency: Carter, Reagan and the Search for Executive Harmony.* Pittsburgh: University of Pittsburgh Press.

Crabb, Cecil V., Jr., and Kevin V. Mulcahy. 1988. *Presidents and Foreign Policy Making.* Baton Rouge, LA.: Louisiana State University Press.

Dowd, Maureen, and Thomas L. Friedman. 1990. "The Fabulous Bush and Baker Boys," *New York Times Magazine,* May 6.

Downs, Anthony. 1967. *Inside Bureaucracy.* Boston: Little, Brown.

Fallows, James. 1981. *National Defense.* New York: Random House.

Feldman, Martha S. 1990. *Organization Theory and the Study of the Presidency.* Paper presented at the Institute for Policy Studies, University of Pittsburgh.

Friedman, Thomas L. and Patrick Tyler. "From the First, U.S. Resolve to Fight: The Path to War, Bush's Crucial Decisions," *The New York Times,* March 3, 1991 A1, A18–A19.

George, Alexander L. 1980. *Presidential Decisionmaking in Foreign Policy: The Effective Use of Information and Advice.* Boulder, Colo.: Westview Press.

Greenstein, Fred I. 1988. *Leadership in the Modern Presidency.* Cambridge, Mass.: Harvard University Press.

Hargrove, Erwin C. 1989. "Two Conceptions of Institutional Leadership." In Bryan D. Jones, ed., *Leadership and Politics.* Lawrence, Kans.: University of Kansas Press.

Hermann, Margaret G. 1979. "Indicators of Stress in Policy Makers during Foreign Policy Crises." *Political Psychology* 1:27–46.

Hermann, Margaret G. 1987. "Leaders' Policy Orientations and the Quality of Foreign Policy Decisions." In Stephen G. Walker, ed., *Role Theory and Foreign Policy Analysis.* Durham, N.C.: Duke University Press.

Hermann, Margaret G. 1988. "The Role of Leaders and Leadership in the Making of American Foreign Policy." In Charles W. Kegley, Jr., and Eugene Wittkopf, eds., *The Domestic Sources of American Foreign Policy.* New York: St. Martin's Press.

Hermann, Margaret G. 1992. "Profiles of Bush, Perot, and Clinton: How Their Personalities Are Likely to Influence Policy." Invited Address, Drew University, October 30.

Hermann, Margaret G. 1993. "Leaders and Foreign Policy Decision Making." In Dan Caldwell and Timothy McKeown, eds., *Diplomacy, Force, and Leadership: Essays in Honor of Alexander George.* Boulder, Colo.: Westview Press.

Hermann, Margaret G., and Charles F. Hermann. 1989. "Who Makes Foreign Policy Decisions and How: An Empirical Inquiry." *International Studies Quarterly* 33: 361–387.

Hermann, Margaret G., and Thomas Preston. 1994. "Presidents, Advisers, and Foreign Policy: The Effect of Leadership Style on Executive Arrangements." *Political Psychology,* forthcoming.

Hess, Stephen. 1988. *Organizing the Presidency.* Washington, D.C.: The Brookings Institution.

Johnson, Richard T. 1974. *Managing the White House: An Intimate Study of the Presidency.* New York: Harper & Row.

Kotter, John P., and Paul R. Lawrence. 1974. *Mayors in Action.* New York: Wiley.

Light, Paul. 1982. *The President's Agenda: Domestic Policy Choice from Kennedy to Carter.* Baltimore: Johns Hopkins University Press.

McGrath, Joseph E. 1984. *Groups: Interaction and Performance.* Englewood Cliffs, N.J.: Prentice Hall.

Meier, Kenneth J. 1989. "Bureaucratic Leadership in Public Organization." In Bryan D. Jones, ed., *Leadership and Politics.* Lawrence, Kans.: University of Kansas Press.

Miller, Gary J. 1987. "Administrative Dilemmas: The Role of Political Leadership." Political Economy Working Paper, Washington University, St. Louis, June.

Preston, Thomas, and Michael D. Young. 1992. "An Approach to Understanding Decision Making: The Bush Administration, the Gulf Crisis, Management Style, and Worldview." Paper presented at the International Studies Association meeting, Atlanta, Georgia, April 1–4.

Smith, Hedrick K. 1988. *The Power Game: How Washington Works.* New York: Ballantine Books.

Stogdill, Ralph D. 1974. *Handbook of Leadership.* New York: Free Press.

Wilensky, Harold. 1967. *Organizational Intelligence.* New York: Basic Books.

Winter, David G., Margaret G. Hermann, Walter Weintraub, and Stephen G. Walker. 1991. "The Personalities of Bush and Gorbachev Measured at a Distance: Procedures, Portraits, and Policy." *Political Psychology* 12:215–245.

Woodward, Robert. 1991. *The Commanders.* New York: Simon & Schuster.

Acknowledgments (continued from copyright page)

CONTRIBUTORS

Gordon Adams is director of the Defense Budget Project.

Eric Alterman is senior fellow of the World Policy Institute at the New School for Social Research.

Stephen E. Ambrose is Boyd Professor of History and director of the Eisenhower Center at the University of New Orleans.

James David Barber is James B. Duke Professor of Political Science at Duke University.

Mitchell Geoffrey Bard is executive director of the American–Israeli Cooperative Enterprise.

John Canham-Clyne is a correspondent for *In These Times*.

Pete Domenici is United States Senator from New Mexico.

Margaret G. Hermann is professor of political science and research associate in political psychology at the Mershon Center, The Ohio State University.

Ole R. Holsti is George V. Allen Professor of Political Science at Duke University.

Bruce W. Jentleson is special assistant to the Director of Policy Planning, U.S. Department of State, and associate professor of political science at the University of California, Davis.

Christopher M. Jones is university fellow and a doctoral candidate at the Maxwell School of Citizenship and Public Affairs, Syracuse University.

John B. Judis is a contributing editor to *The New Republic* and the Washington correspondent for *In These Times*.

Geoffrey Kemp is a senior associate at the Carnegie Endowment for International Peace.

Stephen D. Krasner is professor of political science at Stanford University.

James M. Lindsay is associate professor of political science at the University of Iowa.

Mark M. Lowenthal is the senior specialist in American foreign policy at the Congressional Research Service, Library of Congress.

Debra L. Miller is senior fellow at the Center for Strategic and International Studies and director of the CSIS Strengthening of America Commission.

Mike Moore is editor of *The Bulletin of the Atomic Scientists.*

Sam Nunn is United States Senator from Georgia.

Nelson W. Polsby is professor of political science and director of the Institute of Governmental Studies at the University of California, Berkeley.

Thomas Preston is a doctoral candidate at The Ohio State University.

William B. Quandt is a senior fellow at the Brookings Institution.

Steve Smith is professor of international politics at the University College of Wales.

Bruce Stokes is international economics correspondent for the *National Journal.*

James C. Thomson, Jr. is professor in the College of Communications at Boston University.

ABOUT THE EDITOR

Eugene R. Wittkopf is professor of political science at Louisiana State University. He has also held appointments at the University of Florida and the University of North Carolina at Chapel Hill. He received his Ph.D. from Syracuse University in 1971 and is a past president of the Florida Political Science Association and the International Studies Association/South.

Wittkopf is editor of *The Future of American Foreign Policy* (St. Martin's, 2nd ed., 1994) and author of *Faces of Internationalism: Public Opinion and American Foreign Policy* (Duke University Press, 1990) and numerous articles and chapters on foreign policy and international politics. His research on public opinion and foreign policy has been supported by grants from the National Science Foundation. He has also published (with Charles W. Kegley, Jr.) *American Foreign Policy: Pattern and Process* (St. Martin's, 4th ed., 1991), *World Politics: Trend and Transformation* (St. Martin's, 4th ed., 1993), *The Nuclear Reader: Strategy, Weapons, War* (St. Martin's, 2nd ed., 1989), and *The Global Agenda: Issues and Perspectives* (McGraw-Hill, 3rd ed., 1992).